Seaside Stranger

Volume One:
Umibe no Étranger

story & art by
Kii Kanna

CONTENTS

Seaside Stranger VOL.1 UMIBE NO ÉTRANGER

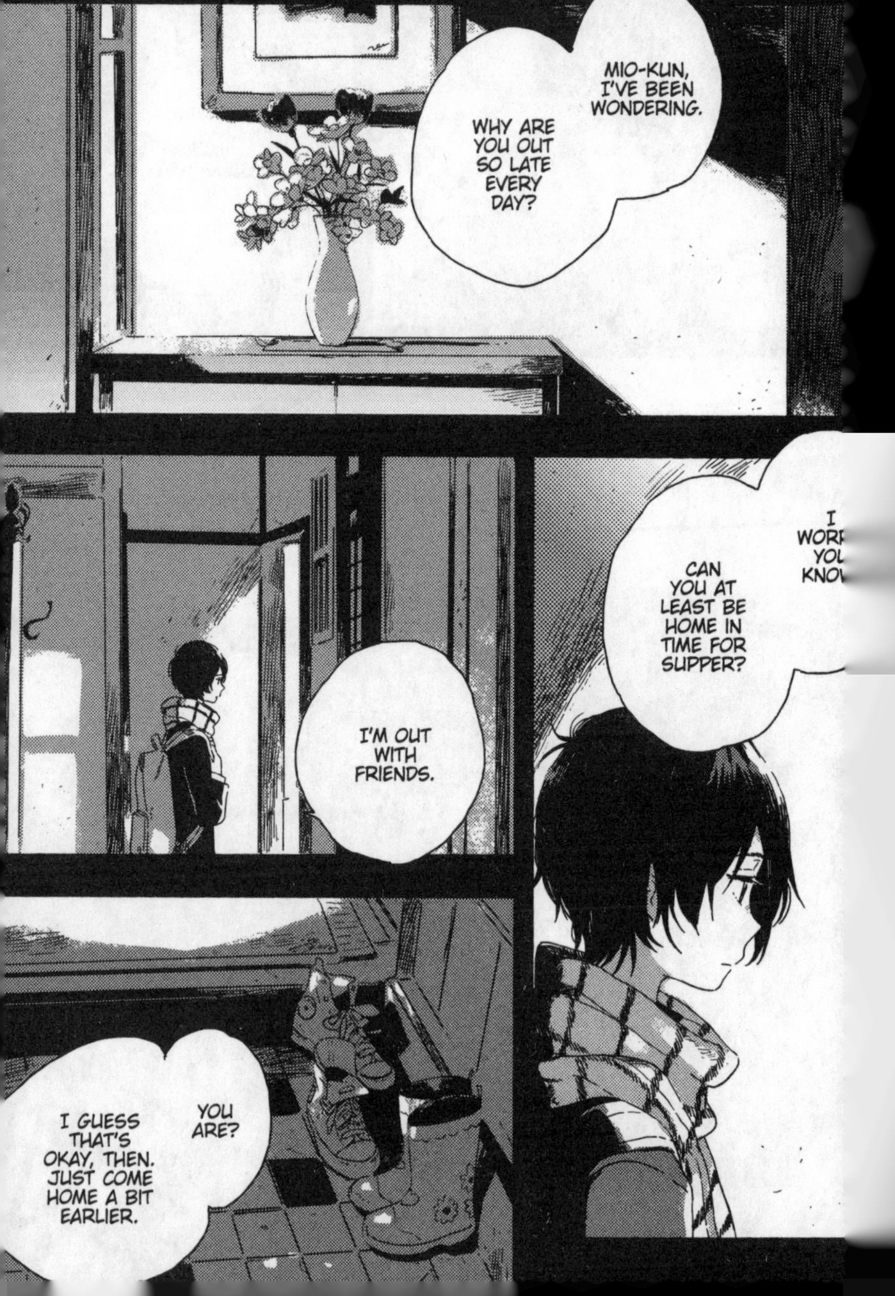
MIO-KUN, I'VE BEEN WONDERING.
WHY ARE YOU OUT SO LATE EVERY DAY?
I WORR YOU KNOW
CAN YOU AT LEAST BE HOME IN TIME FOR SUPPER?
I'M OUT WITH FRIENDS.
YOU ARE?
I GUESS THAT'S OKAY, THEN. JUST COME HOME A BIT EARLIER.

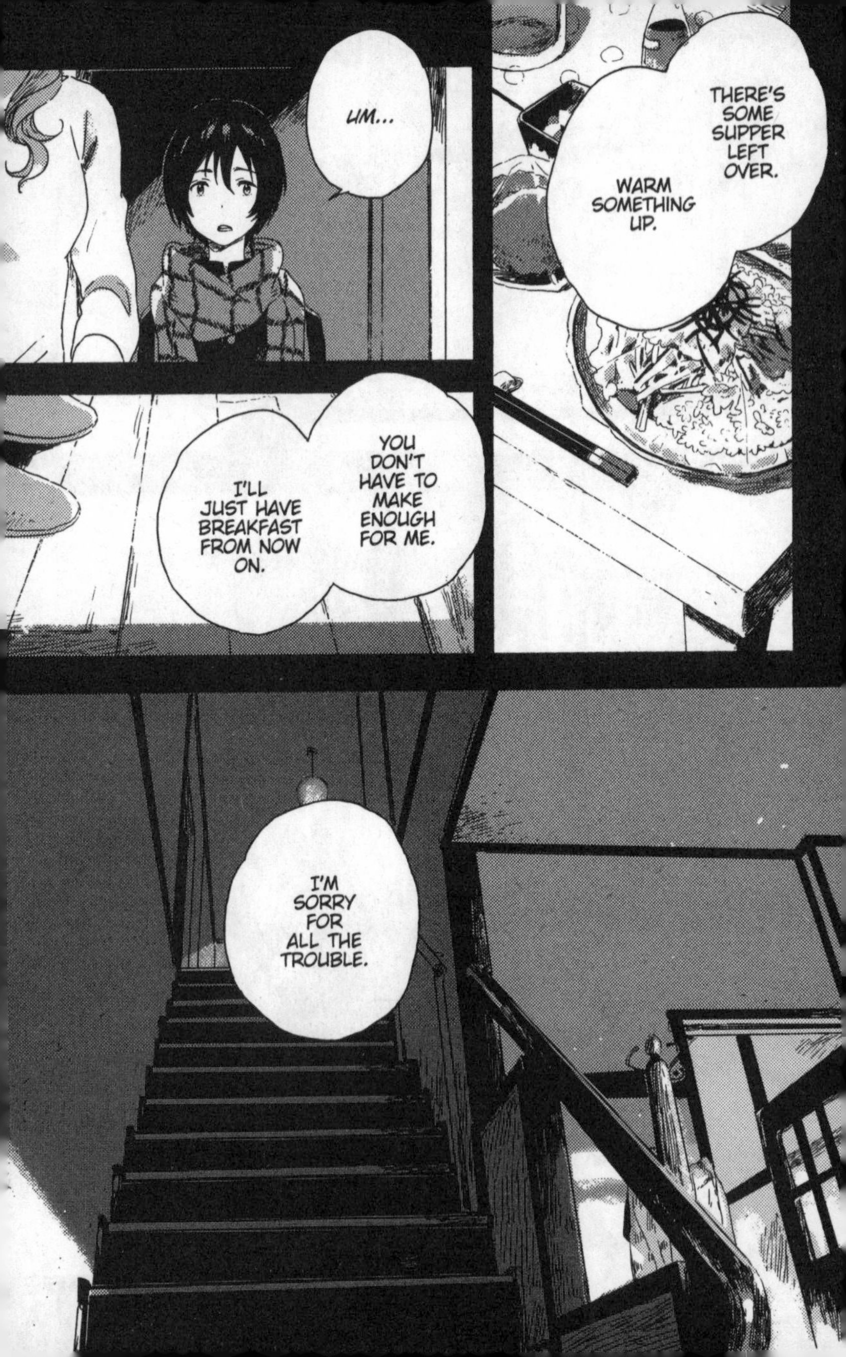
THERE'S SOME SUPPER LEFT OVER.
WARM SOMETHING UP.
UM...
YOU DON'T HAVE TO MAKE ENOUGH FOR ME.
I'LL JUST HAVE BREAKFAST FROM NOW ON.
I'M SORRY FOR ALL THE TROUBLE.

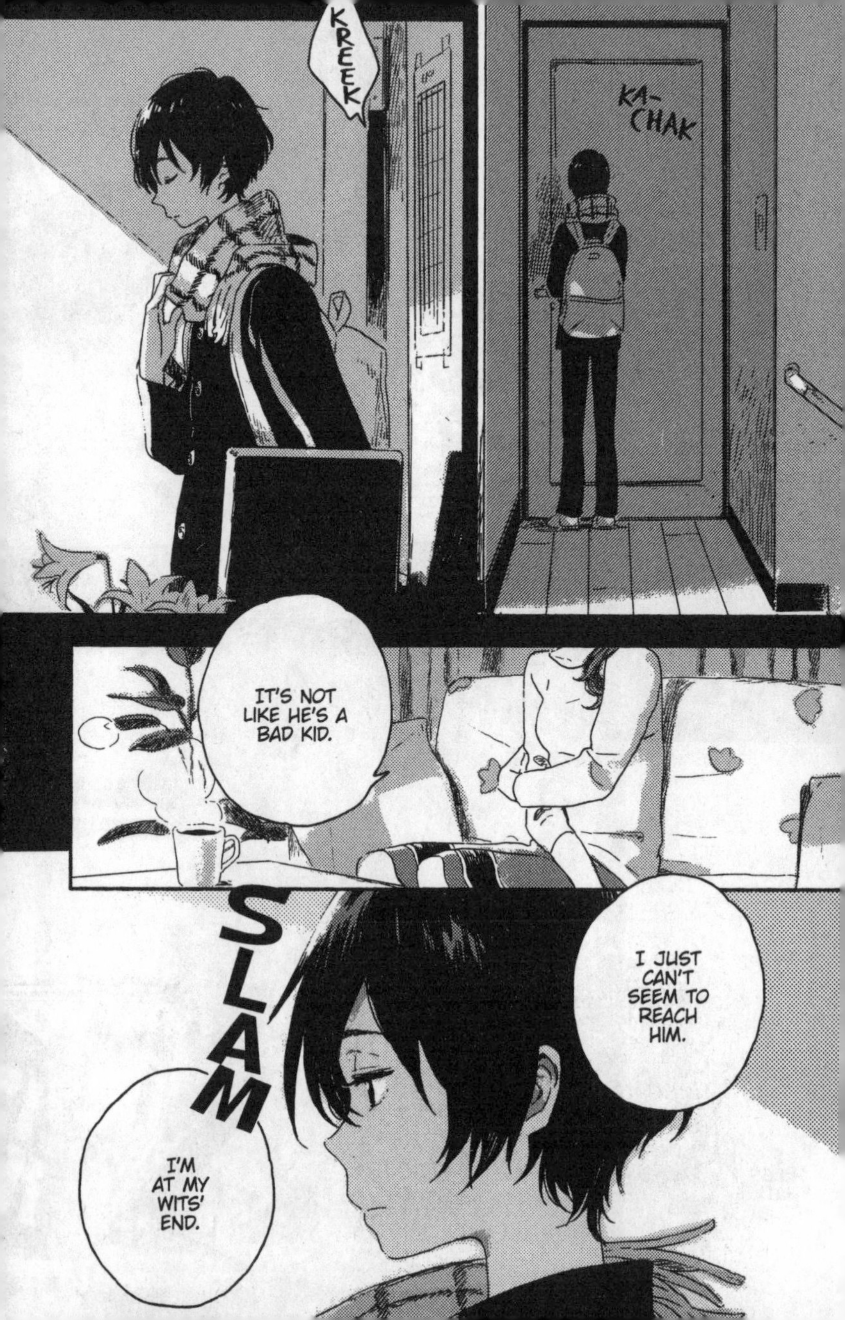
KA-CHAK
KREEK
IT'S NOT LIKE HE'S A BAD KID.
I JUST CAN'T SEEM TO REACH HIM.
SLAM
I'M AT MY WITS' END.

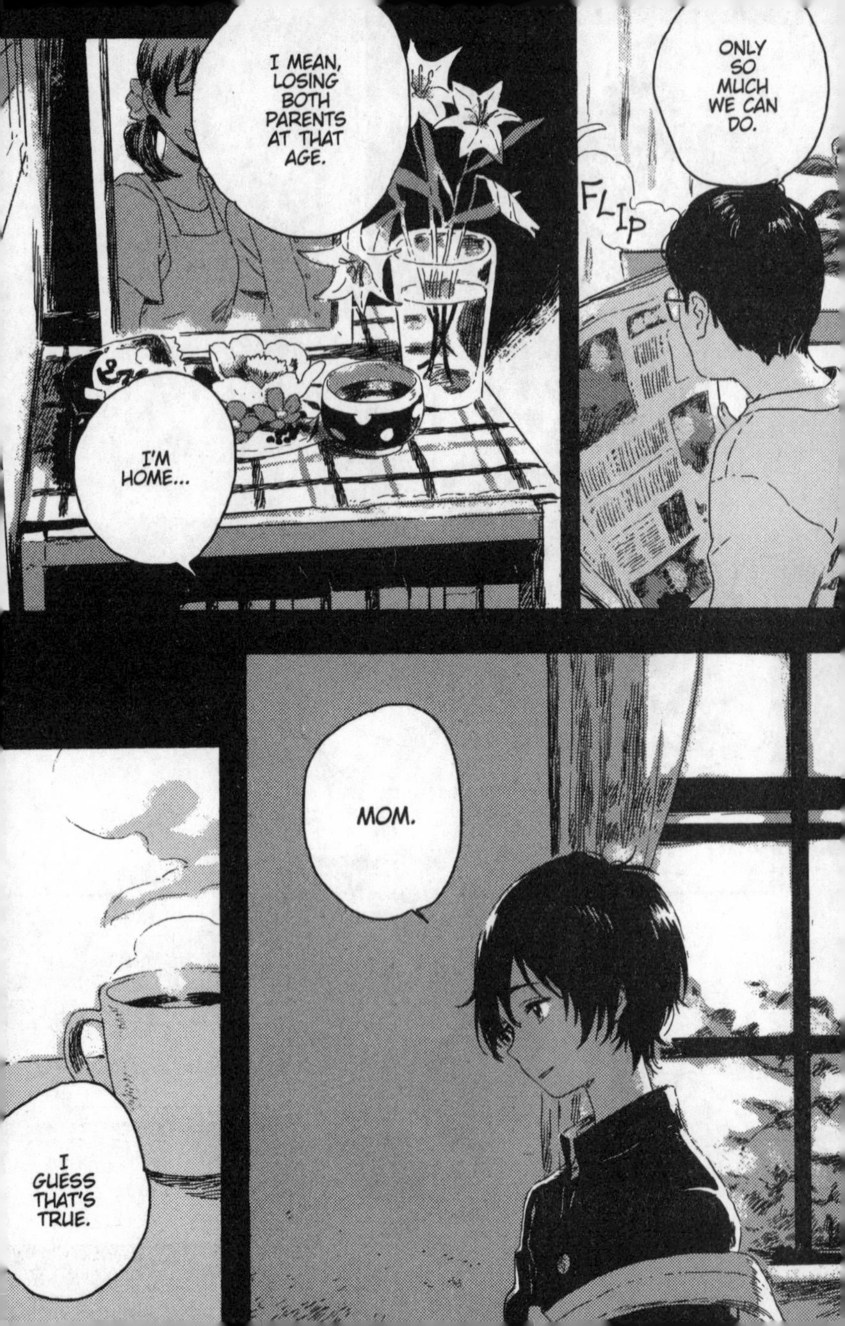
ONLY SO MUCH WE CAN DO.
FLIP
I MEAN, LOSING BOTH PARENTS AT THAT AGE.
I'M HOME...
MOM.
I GUESS THAT'S TRUE.

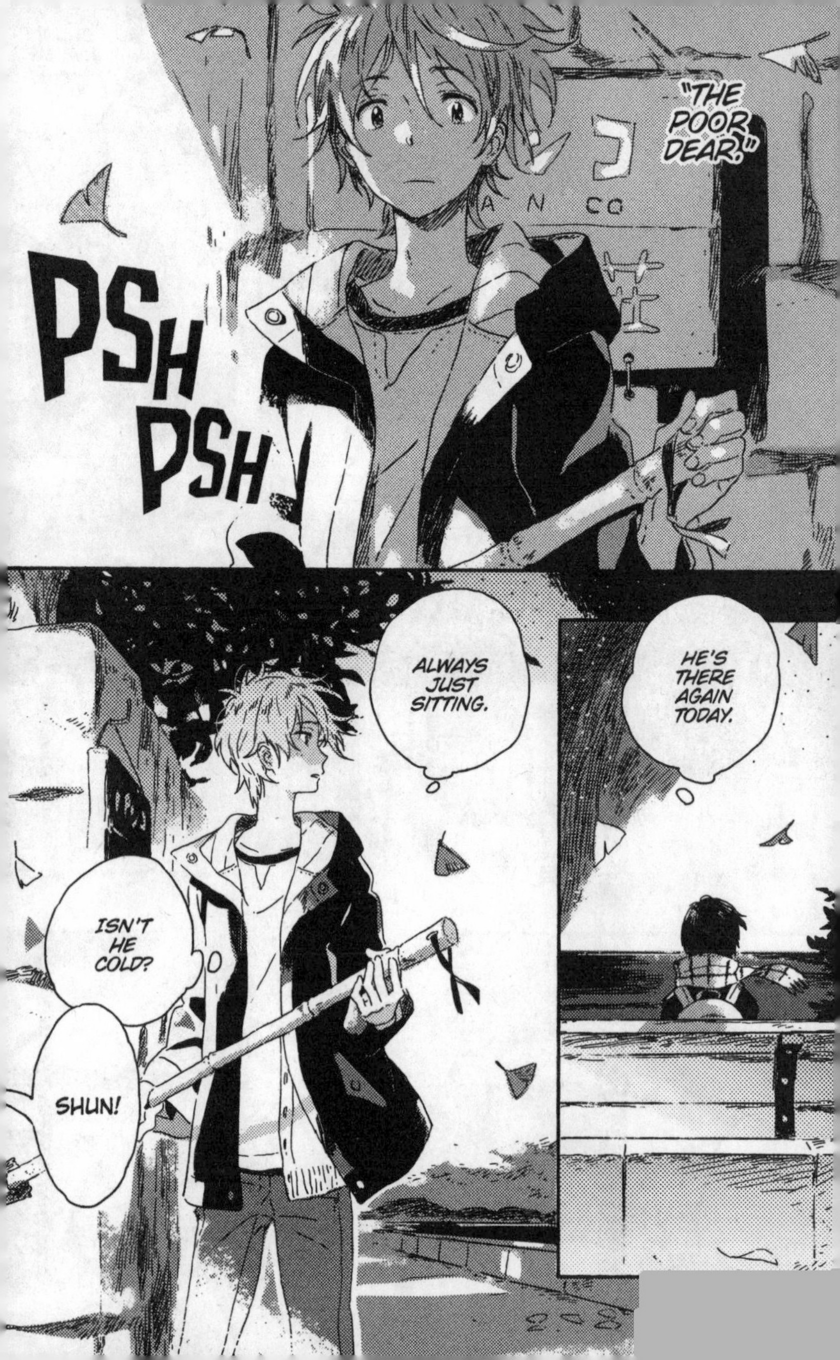
"THE POOR DEAR."
PSH PSH
HE'S THERE AGAIN TODAY.
ALWAYS JUST SITTING.
ISN'T HE COLD?
SHUN!

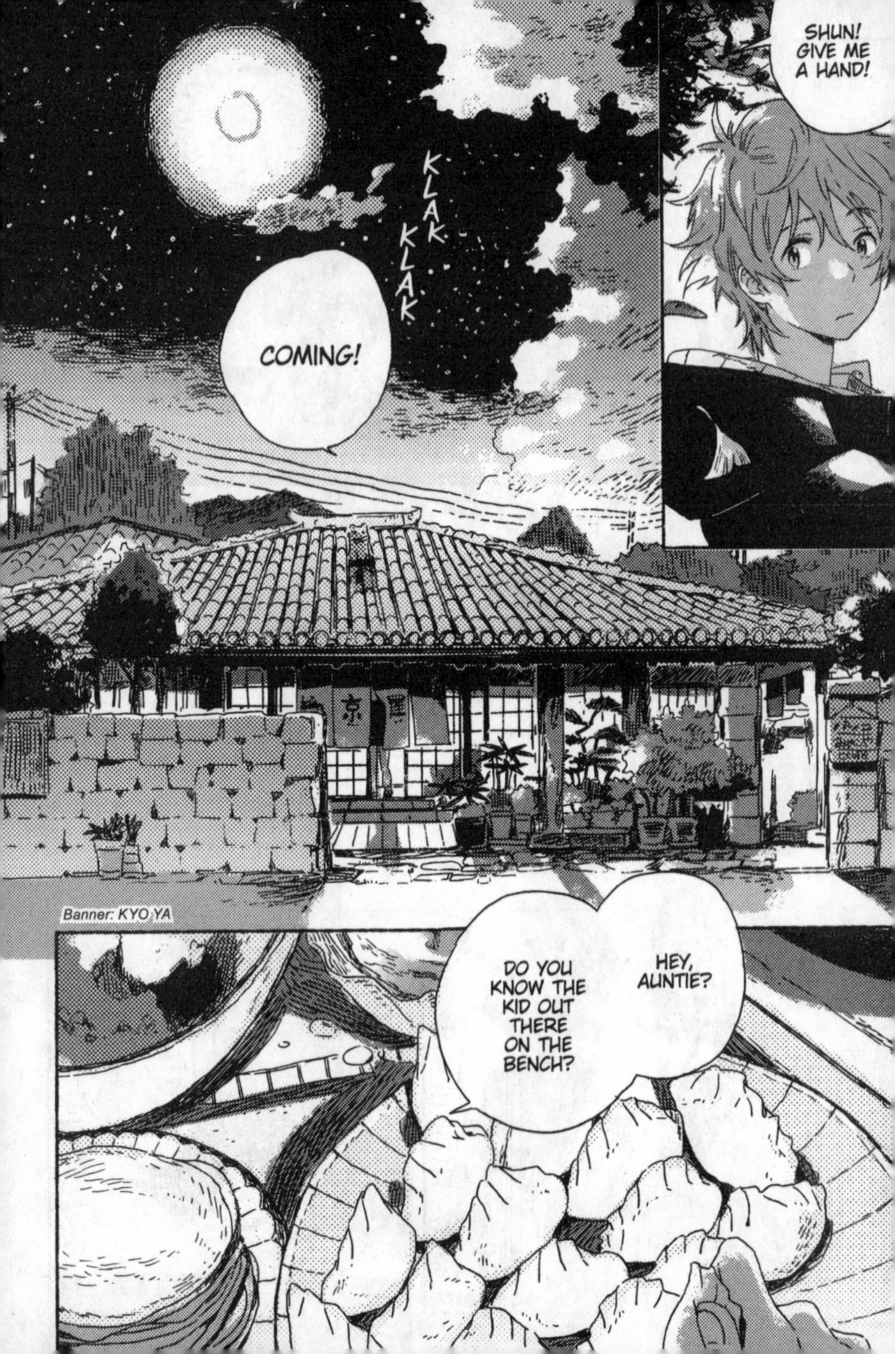
SHUN! GIVE ME A HAND!
KLAK KLAK KLAK
COMING!
Banner: KYO YA
HEY, AUNTIE?
DO YOU KNOW THE KID OUT THERE ON THE BENCH?

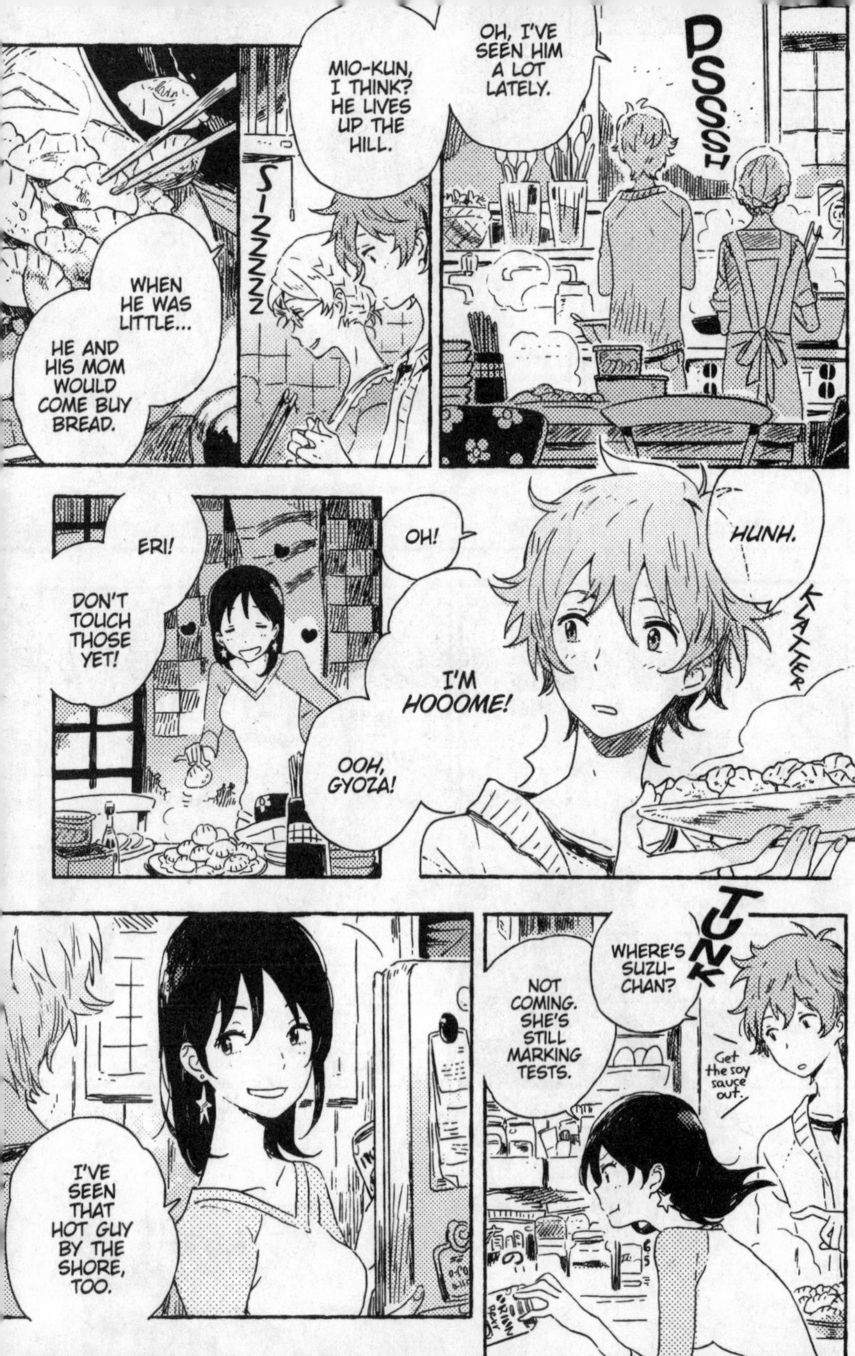
DSSSH
OH, I'VE SEEN HIM A LOT LATELY.
MIO-KUN, I THINK? HE LIVES UP THE HILL.
SIZZZZZ
WHEN HE WAS LITTLE...
HE AND HIS MOM WOULD COME BUY BREAD.
HUNH.
KLATTER
I'M HOOOME!
OOH, GYOZA!
OH!
ERI!
DON'T TOUCH THOSE YET!
TUNK
WHERE'S SUZU-CHAN?
NOT COMING. SHE'S STILL MARKING TESTS.
Get the soy sauce out.
I'VE SEEN THAT HOT GUY BY THE SHORE, TOO.

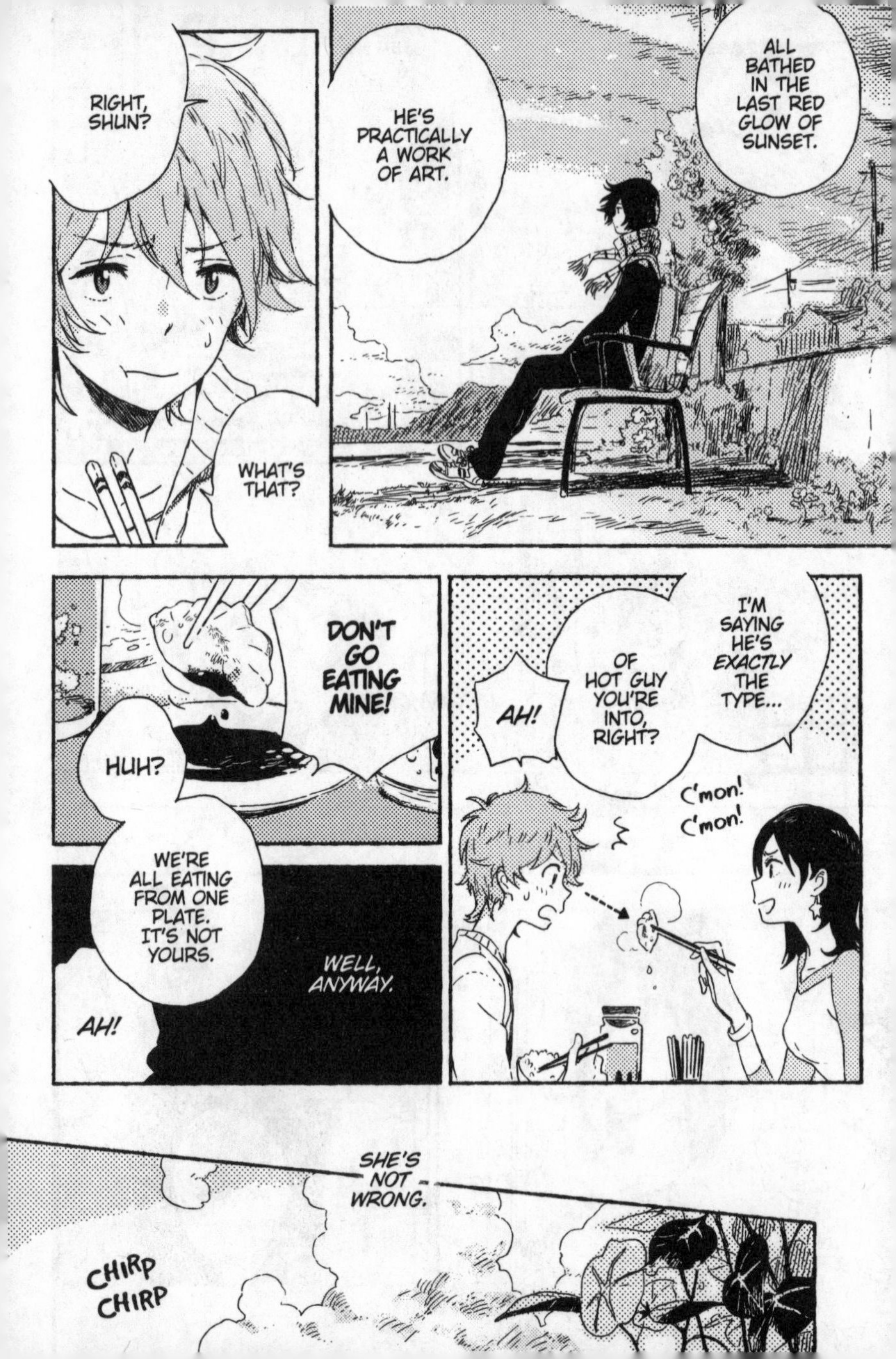
ALL BATHED IN THE LAST RED GLOW OF SUNSET.
HE'S PRACTICALLY A WORK OF ART.
RIGHT, SHUN?
WHAT'S THAT?
I'M SAYING HE'S *EXACTLY* THE TYPE...
OF HOT GUY YOU'RE INTO, RIGHT?
AH!
C'mon! C'mon!
DON'T GO EATING MINE!
HUH?
WE'RE ALL EATING FROM ONE PLATE. IT'S NOT YOURS.
WELL, ANYWAY.
AH!
SHE'S NOT WRONG.
CHIRP CHIRP

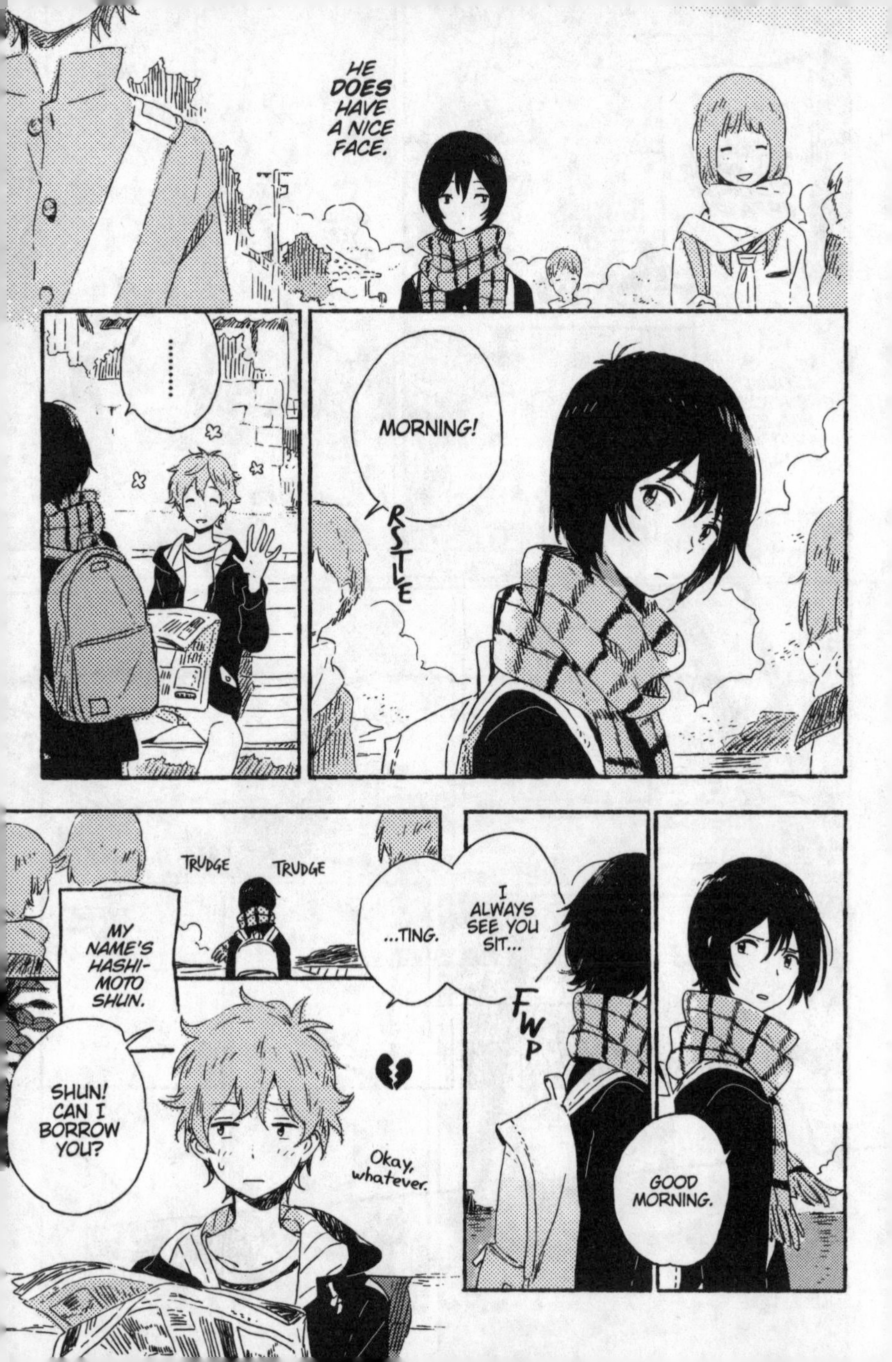
HE DOES HAVE A NICE FACE.
MORNING!
RSTLE
......
GOOD MORNING.
I ALWAYS SEE YOU SIT...
FWP
TRUDGE TRUDGE
...TING.
MY NAME'S HASHI-MOTO SHUN.
SHUN! CAN I BORROW YOU?
Okay, whatever.

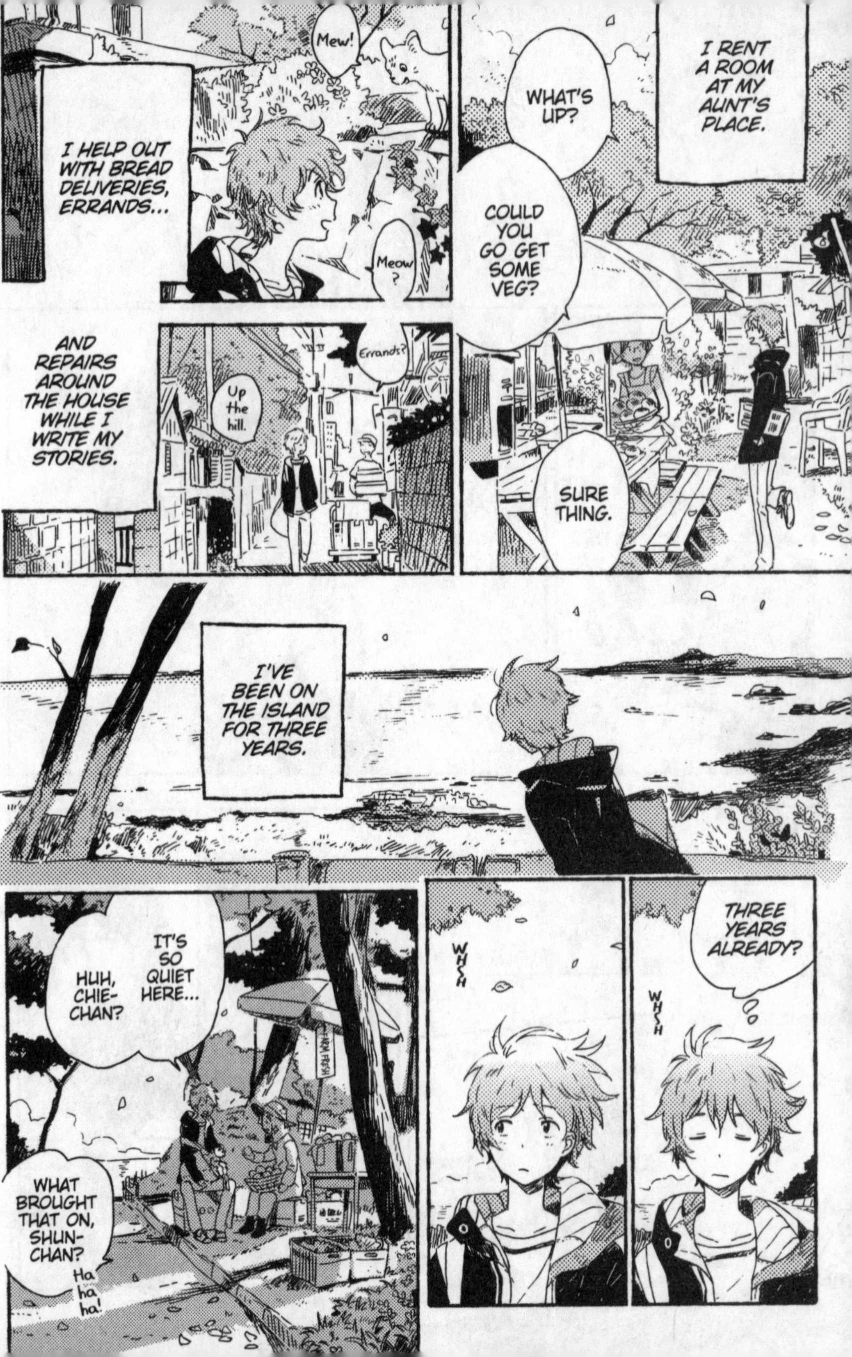
I RENT A ROOM AT MY AUNT'S PLACE.
WHAT'S UP?
COULD YOU GO GET SOME VEG?
SURE THING.
Mew!
I HELP OUT WITH BREAD DELIVERIES, ERRANDS...
Meow?
AND REPAIRS AROUND THE HOUSE WHILE I WRITE MY STORIES.
Errands?
Up the hill.
I'VE BEEN ON THE ISLAND FOR THREE YEARS.
THREE YEARS ALREADY?
WHSH
WHSH
IT'S SO QUIET HERE...
HUH, CHIE-CHAN?
WHAT BROUGHT THAT ON, SHUN-CHAN?
Ha ha ha!

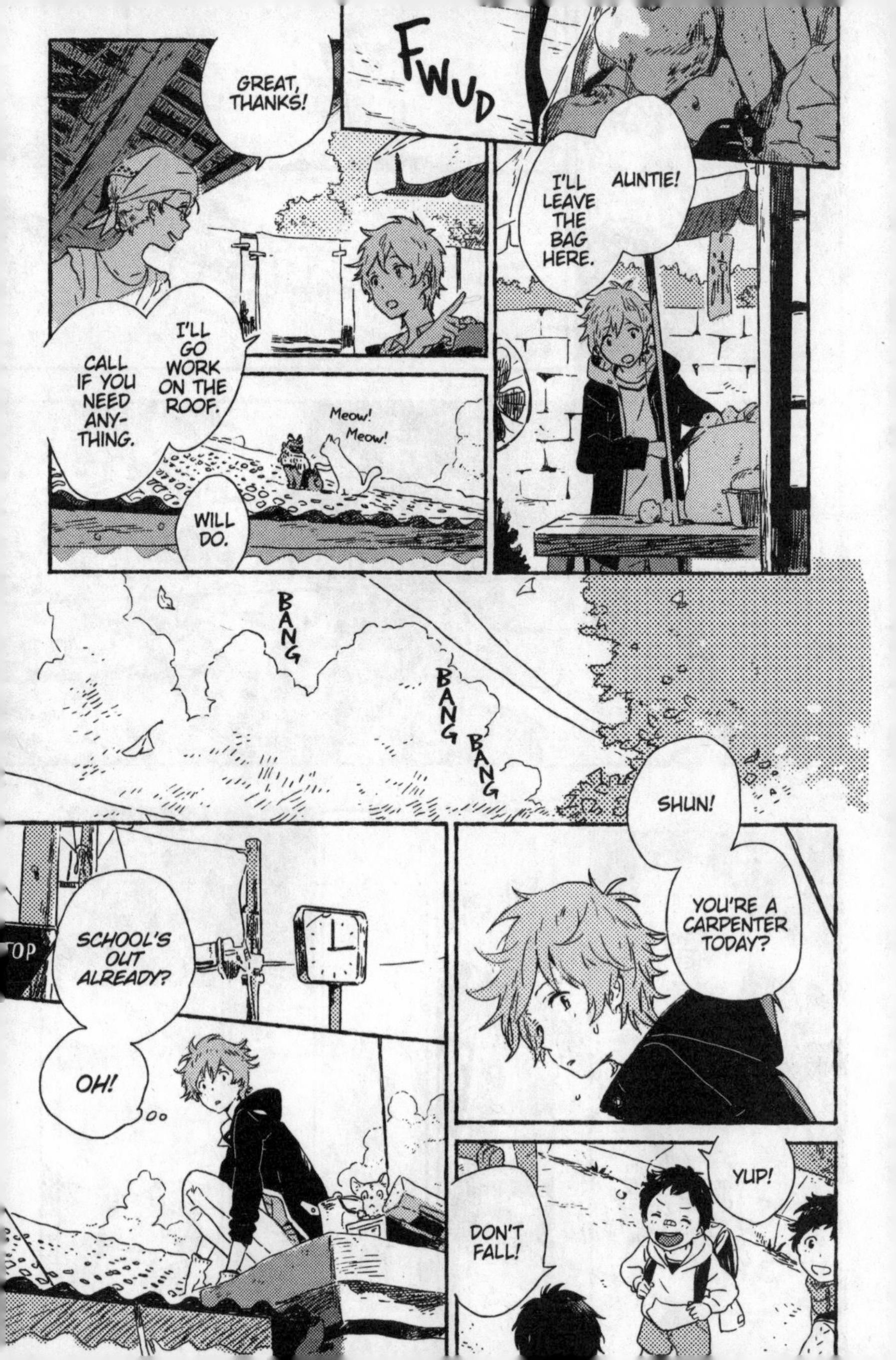
FWUD
AUNTIE!
I'LL LEAVE THE BAG HERE.
GREAT, THANKS!
I'LL GO WORK ON THE ROOF.
CALL IF YOU NEED ANY-THING.
Meow!
Meow!
WILL DO.
BANG
BANG
BANG
SHUN!
YOU'RE A CARPENTER TODAY?
YUP!
DON'T FALL!
TOP
SCHOOL'S OUT ALREADY?
OH!

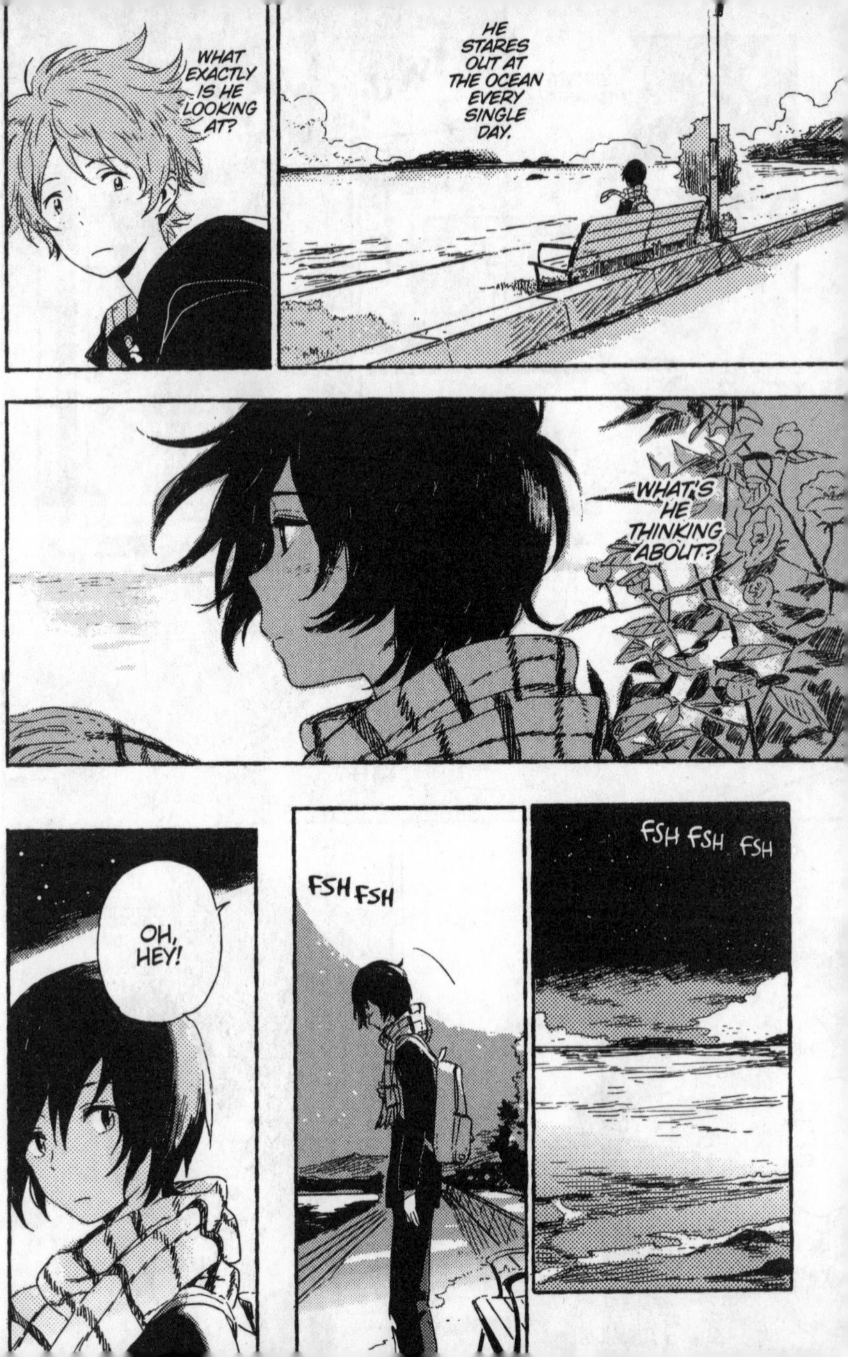
HE STARES OUT AT THE OCEAN EVERY SINGLE DAY.
WHAT EXACTLY IS HE LOOKING AT?
WHAT'S HE THINKING ABOUT?
FSH FSH FSH
FSH FSH
OH, HEY!

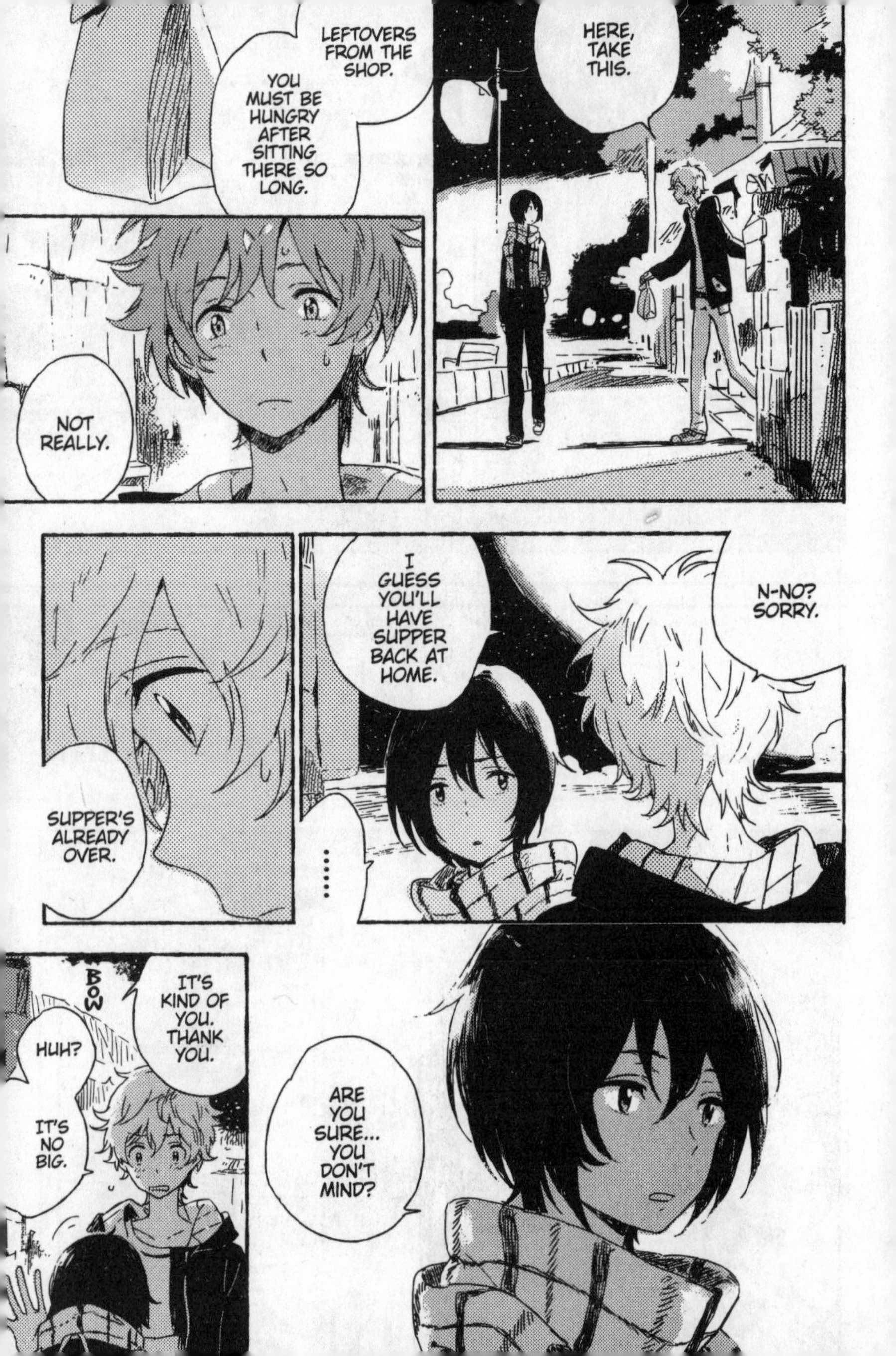
HERE, TAKE THIS.
LEFTOVERS FROM THE SHOP.
YOU MUST BE HUNGRY AFTER SITTING THERE SO LONG.
NOT REALLY.
N-NO? SORRY.
I GUESS YOU'LL HAVE SUPPER BACK AT HOME.
......
SUPPER'S ALREADY OVER.
ARE YOU SURE... YOU DON'T MIND?
IT'S KIND OF YOU. THANK YOU.
BOW
HUH?
IT'S NO BIG.

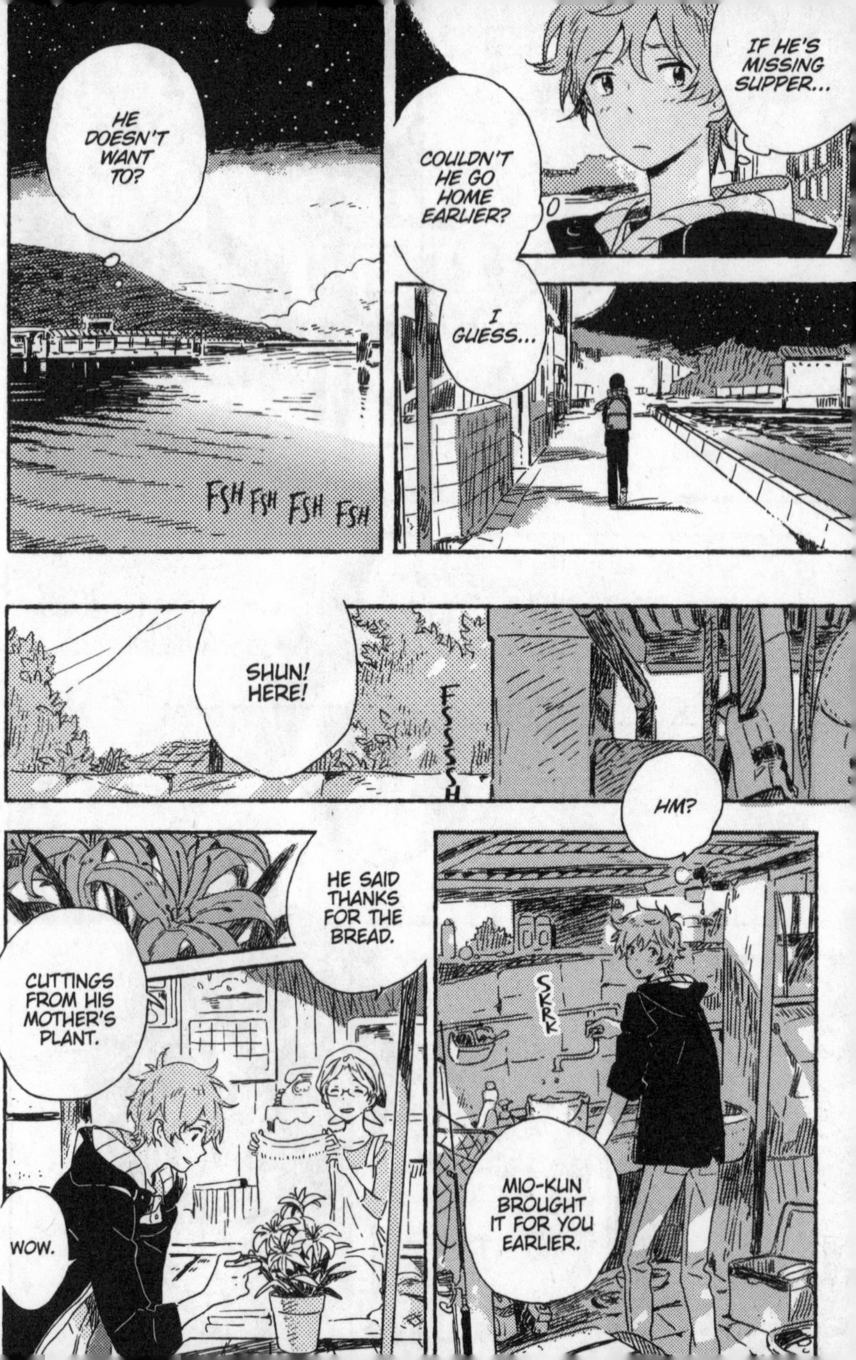
IF HE'S MISSING SUPPER...
COULDN'T HE GO HOME EARLIER?
I GUESS...
HE DOESN'T WANT TO?
FSH FSH FSH FSH
SHUN! HERE!
FSSSH
HM?
SKRK
MIO-KUN BROUGHT IT FOR YOU EARLIER.
HE SAID THANKS FOR THE BREAD.
CUTTINGS FROM HIS MOTHER'S PLANT.
WOW.

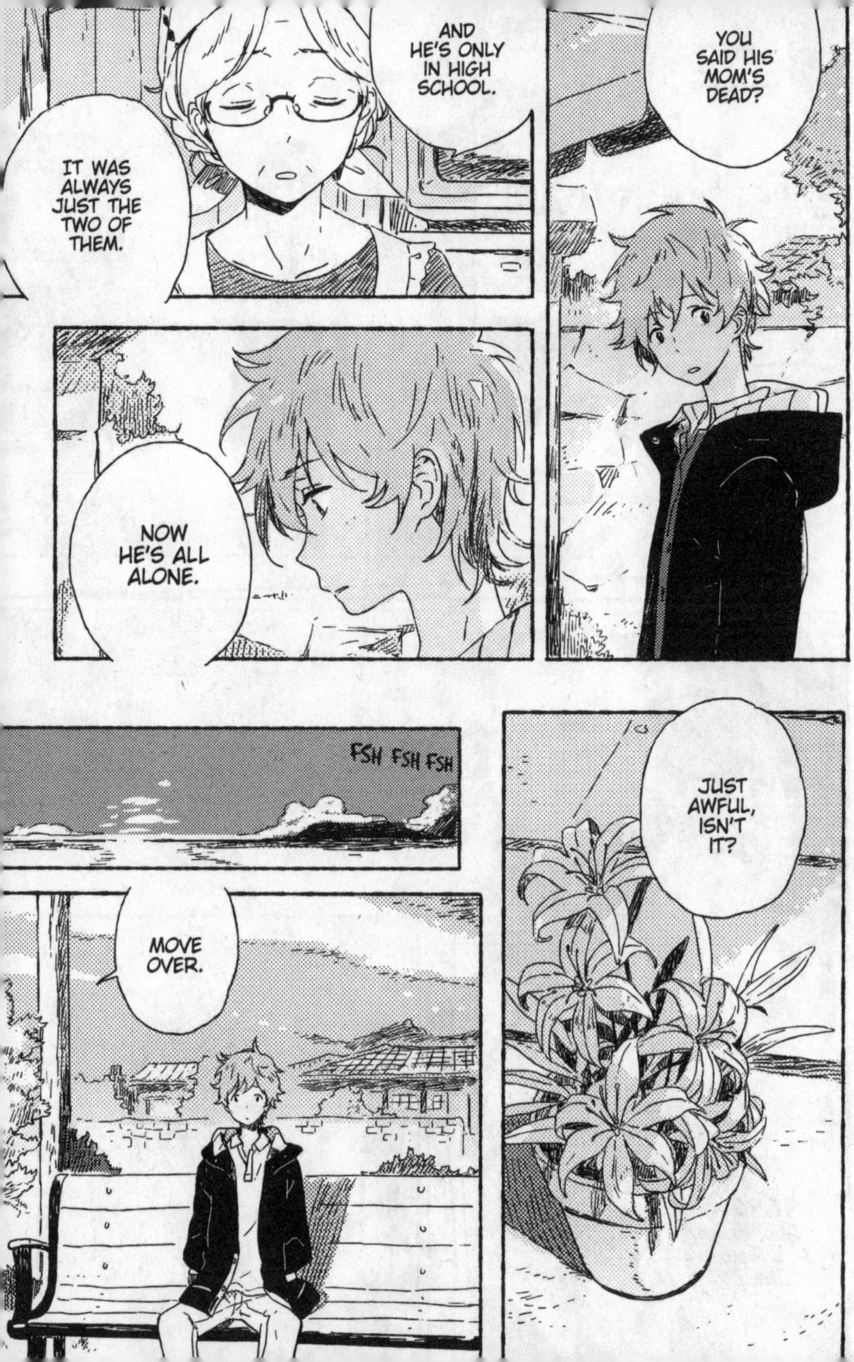
YOU SAID HIS MOM'S DEAD?
AND HE'S ONLY IN HIGH SCHOOL.
IT WAS ALWAYS JUST THE TWO OF THEM.
NOW HE'S ALL ALONE.
JUST AWFUL, ISN'T IT?
FSH FSH FSH
MOVE OVER.

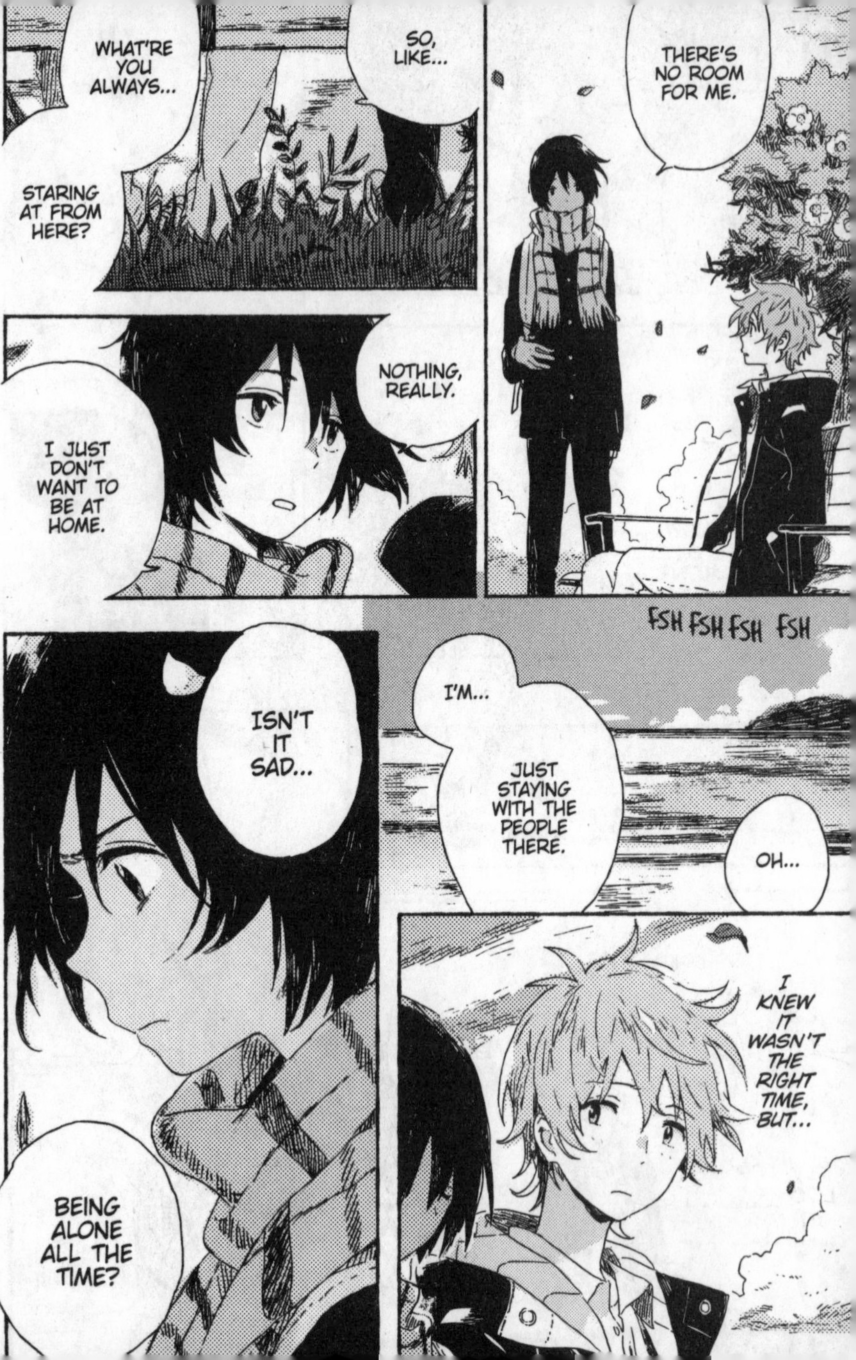
THERE'S NO ROOM FOR ME.
SO, LIKE...
WHAT'RE YOU ALWAYS...
STARING AT FROM HERE?
NOTHING, REALLY.
I JUST DON'T WANT TO BE AT HOME.
FSH FSH FSH FSH
I'M...
JUST STAYING WITH THE PEOPLE THERE.
OH...
I KNEW IT WASN'T THE RIGHT TIME, BUT...
ISN'T IT SAD...
BEING ALONE ALL THE TIME?

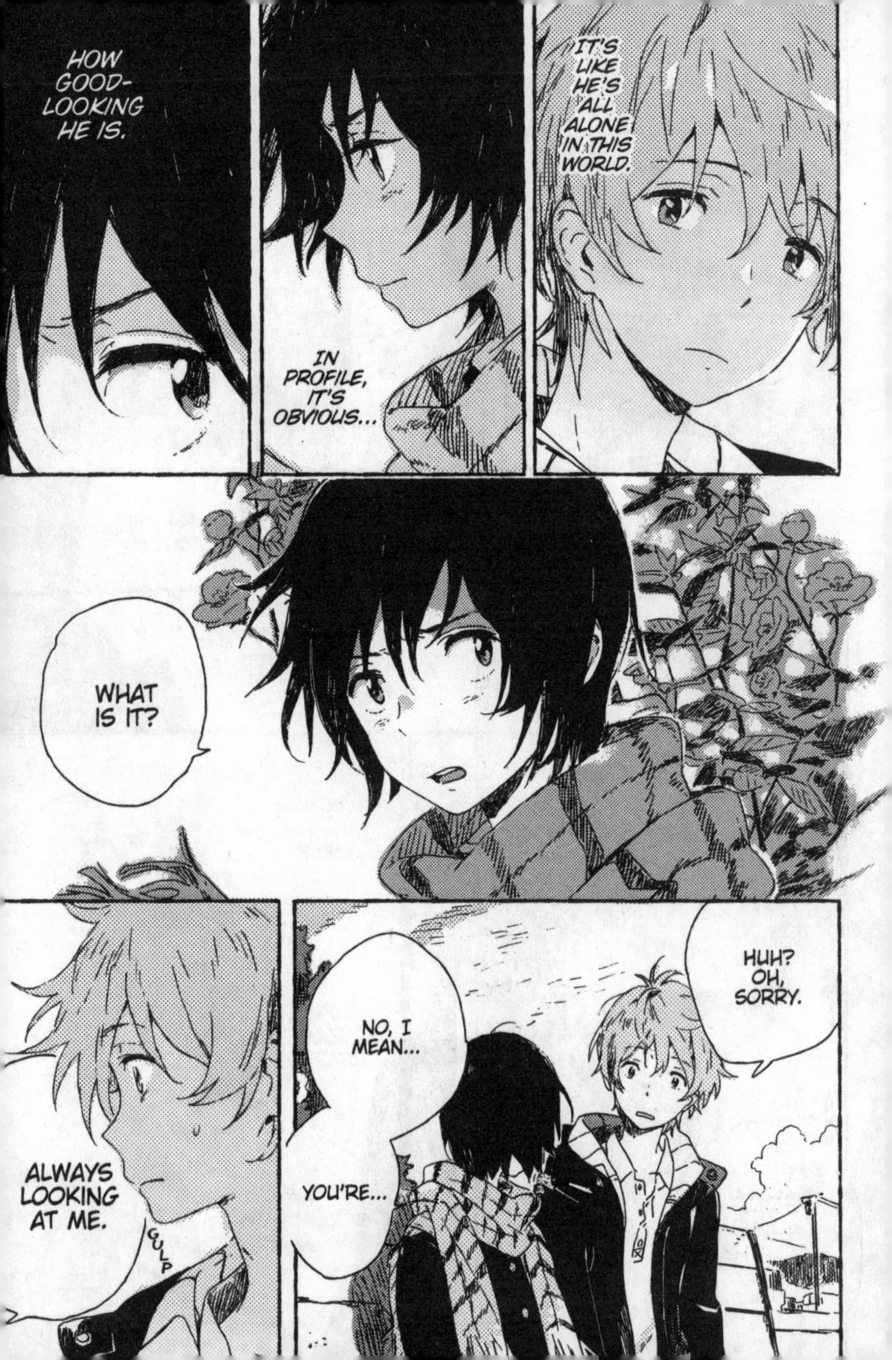
IT'S LIKE HE'S ALL ALONE IN THIS WORLD.
IN PROFILE, IT'S OBVIOUS...
HOW GOOD-LOOKING HE IS.
WHAT IS IT?
HUH? OH, SORRY.
NO, I MEAN...
YOU'RE...
ALWAYS LOOKING AT ME.
GULP

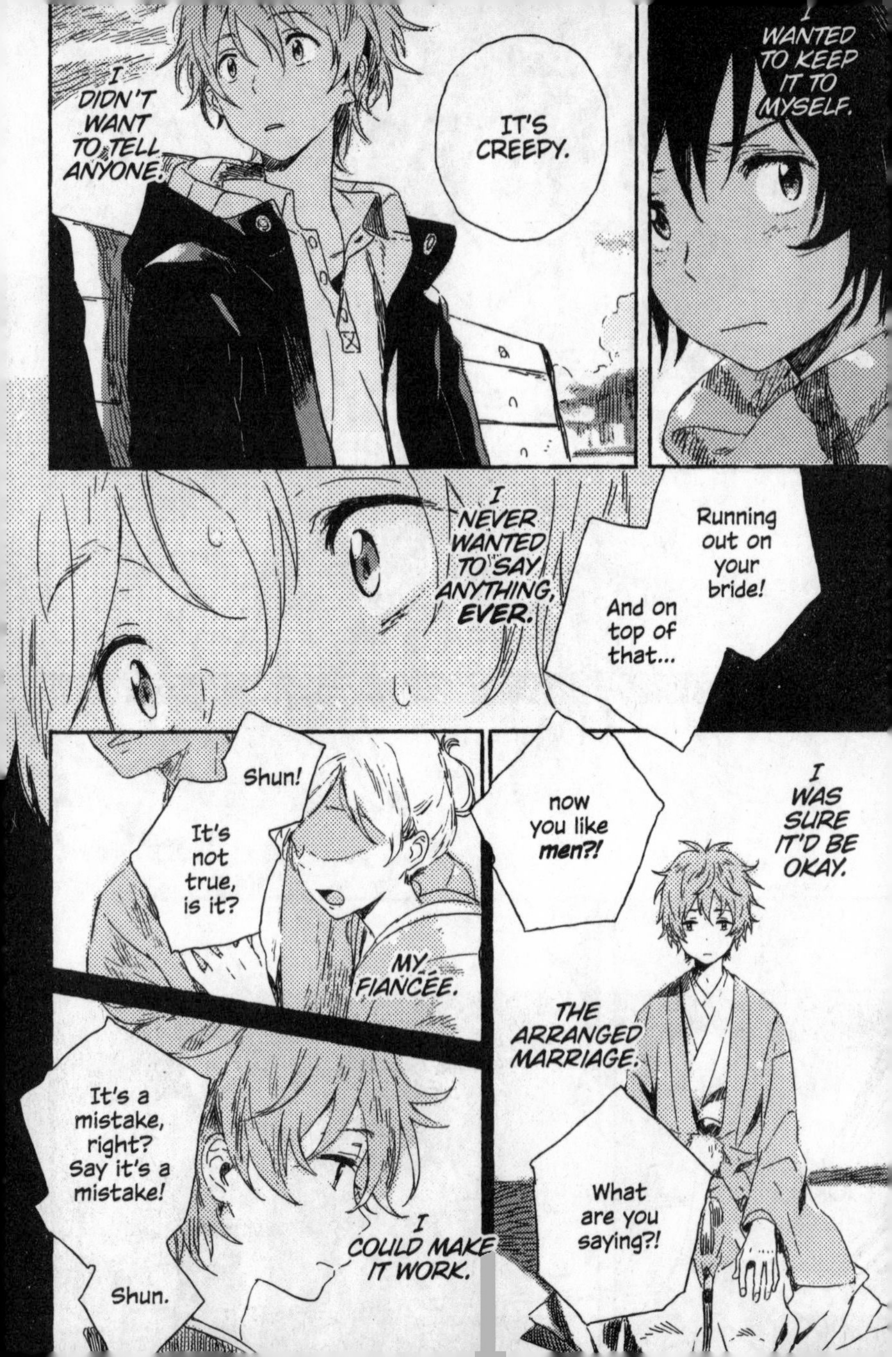
I WANTED TO KEEP IT TO MYSELF.
IT'S CREEPY.
I DIDN'T WANT TO TELL ANYONE.
Running out on your bride!
And on top of that...
I NEVER WANTED TO SAY ANYTHING, EVER.
now you like men?!
I WAS SURE IT'D BE OKAY.
THE ARRANGED MARRIAGE.
What are you saying?!
Shun!
It's not true, is it?
MY FIANCÉE.
It's a mistake, right? Say it's a mistake!
I COULD MAKE IT WORK.
Shun.

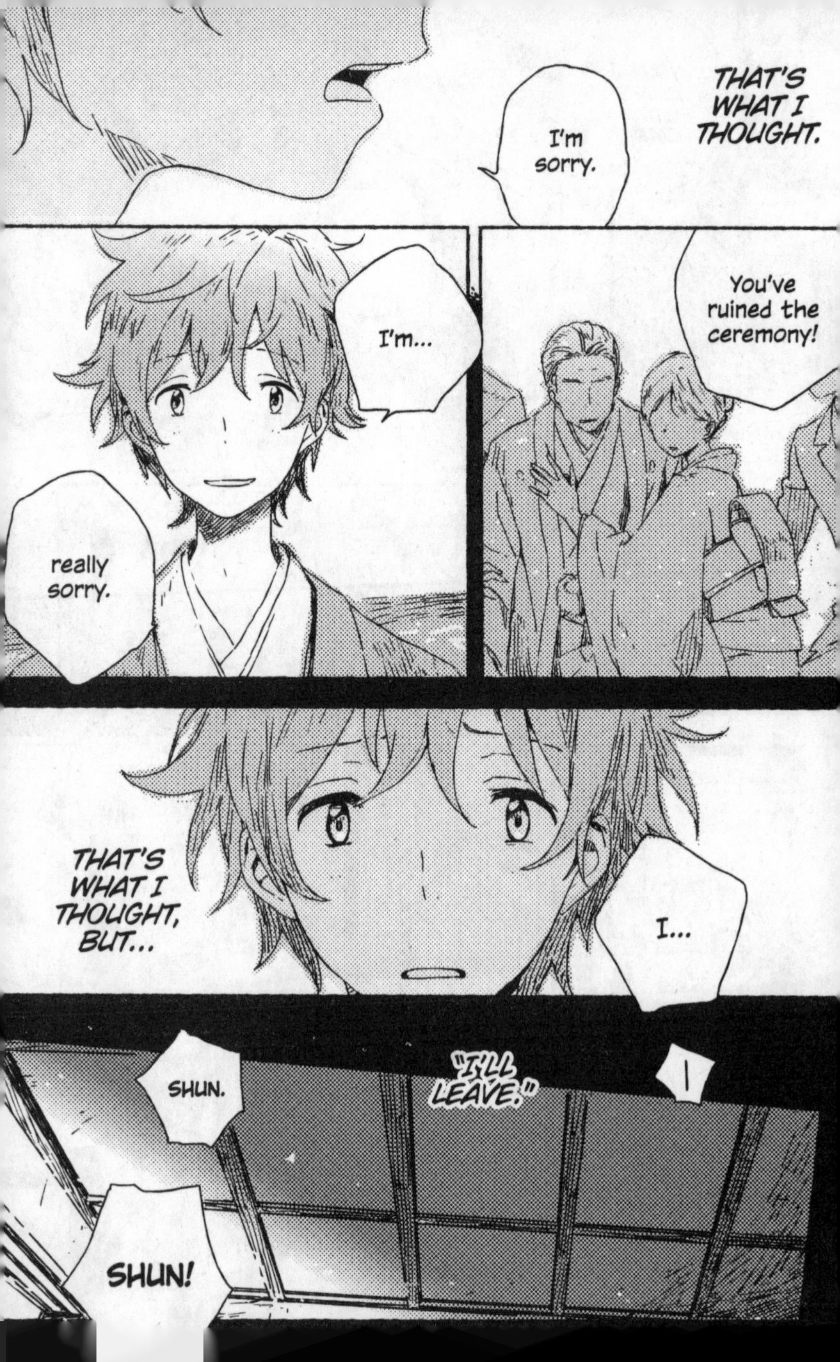
THAT'S WHAT I THOUGHT.
I'm sorry.
You've ruined the ceremony!
I'm...
really sorry.
I...
THAT'S WHAT I THOUGHT, BUT...
I
"I'LL LEAVE."
SHUN.
SHUN!

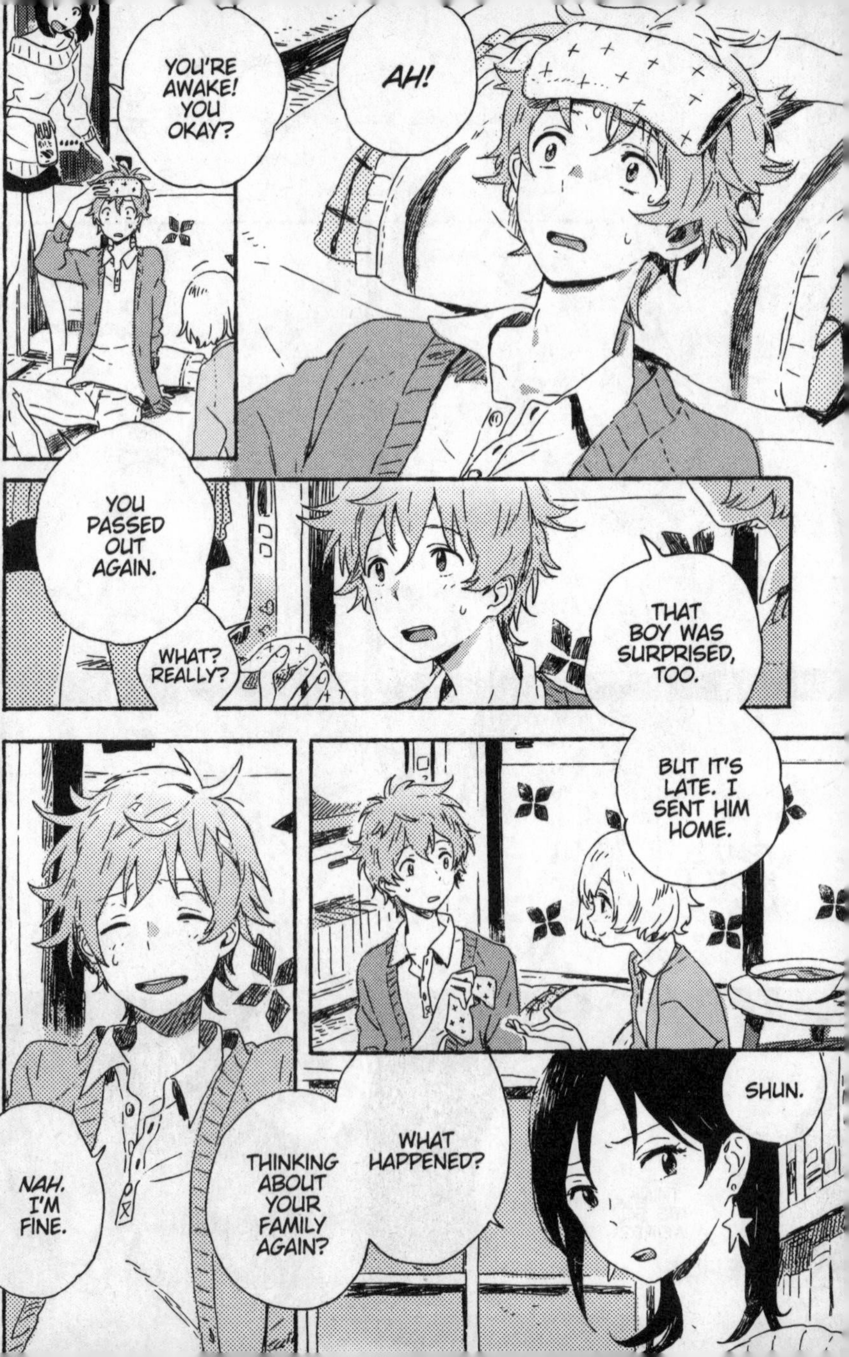
AH!
YOU'RE AWAKE! YOU OKAY?
YOU PASSED OUT AGAIN.
WHAT? REALLY?
THAT BOY WAS SURPRISED, TOO.
BUT IT'S LATE. I SENT HIM HOME.
SHUN.
WHAT HAPPENED?
THINKING ABOUT YOUR FAMILY AGAIN?
NAH. I'M FINE.

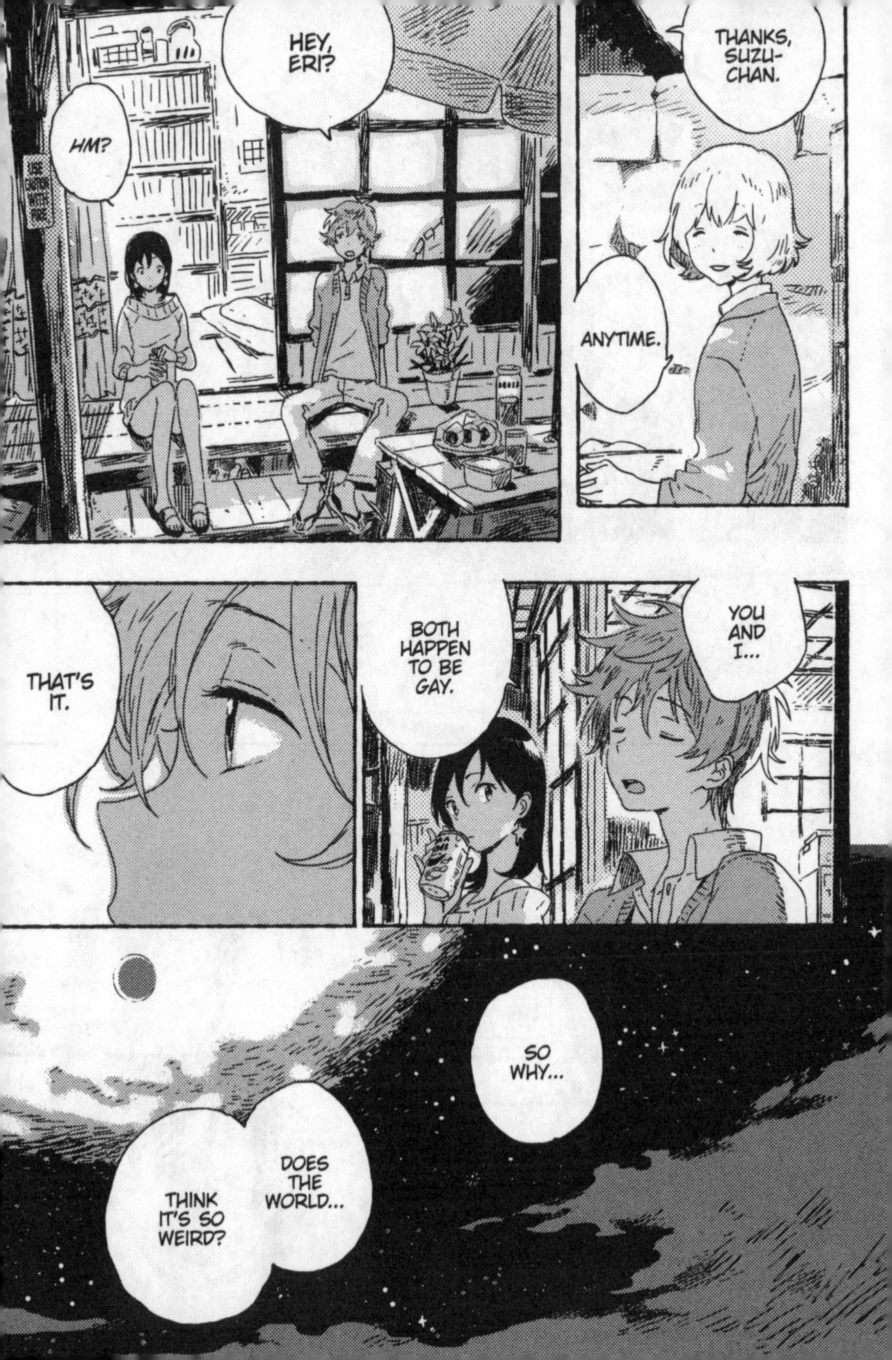
THANKS, SUZU-CHAN.
ANYTIME.
HEY, ERI?
HM?
USE CAUTION WITH FIRE
YOU AND I...
BOTH HAPPEN TO BE GAY.
THAT'S IT.
SO WHY...
DOES THE WORLD...
THINK IT'S SO WEIRD?

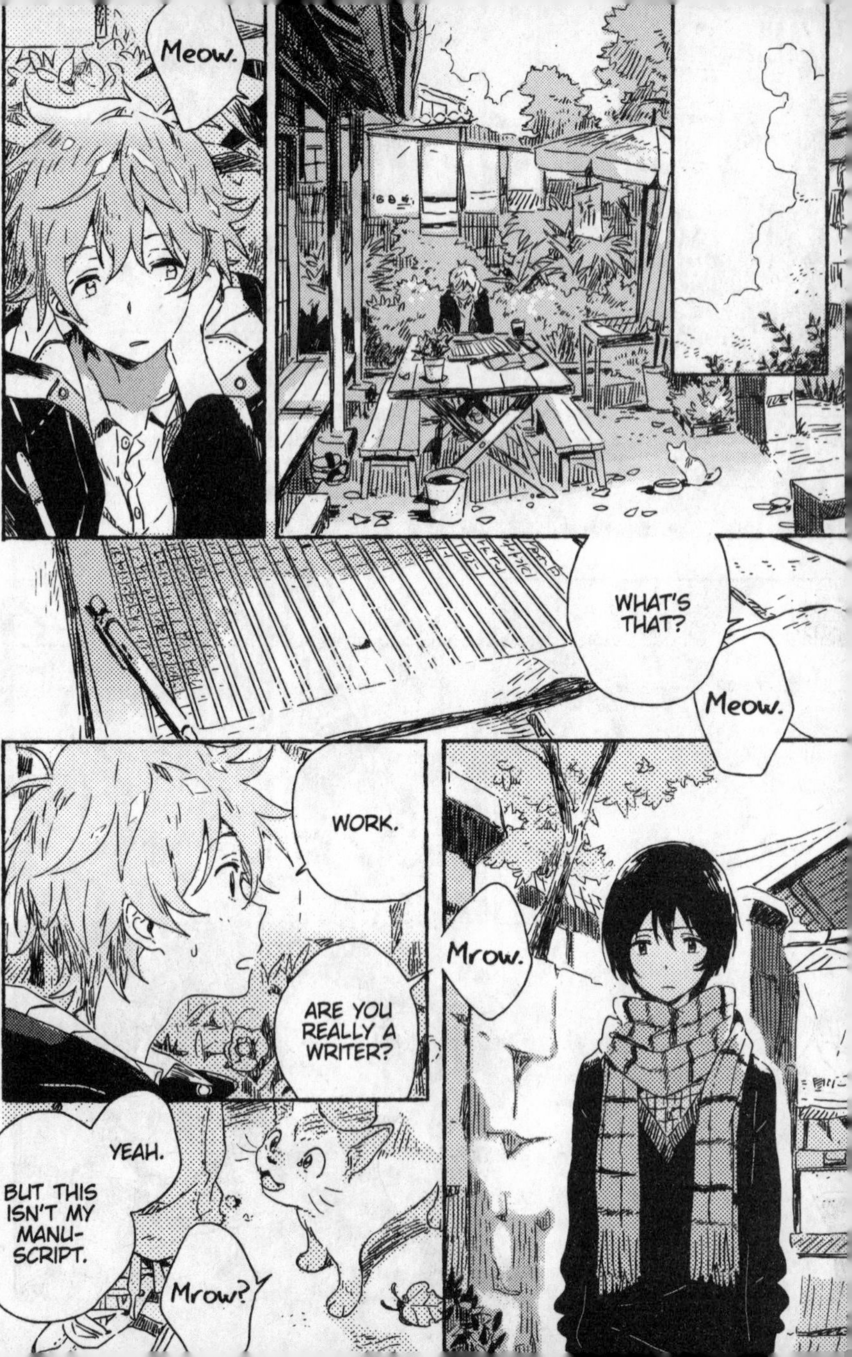
Meow.
WHAT'S THAT?
Meow.
Mrow.
WORK.
ARE YOU REALLY A WRITER?
YEAH.
BUT THIS ISN'T MY MANUSCRIPT.
Mrow?

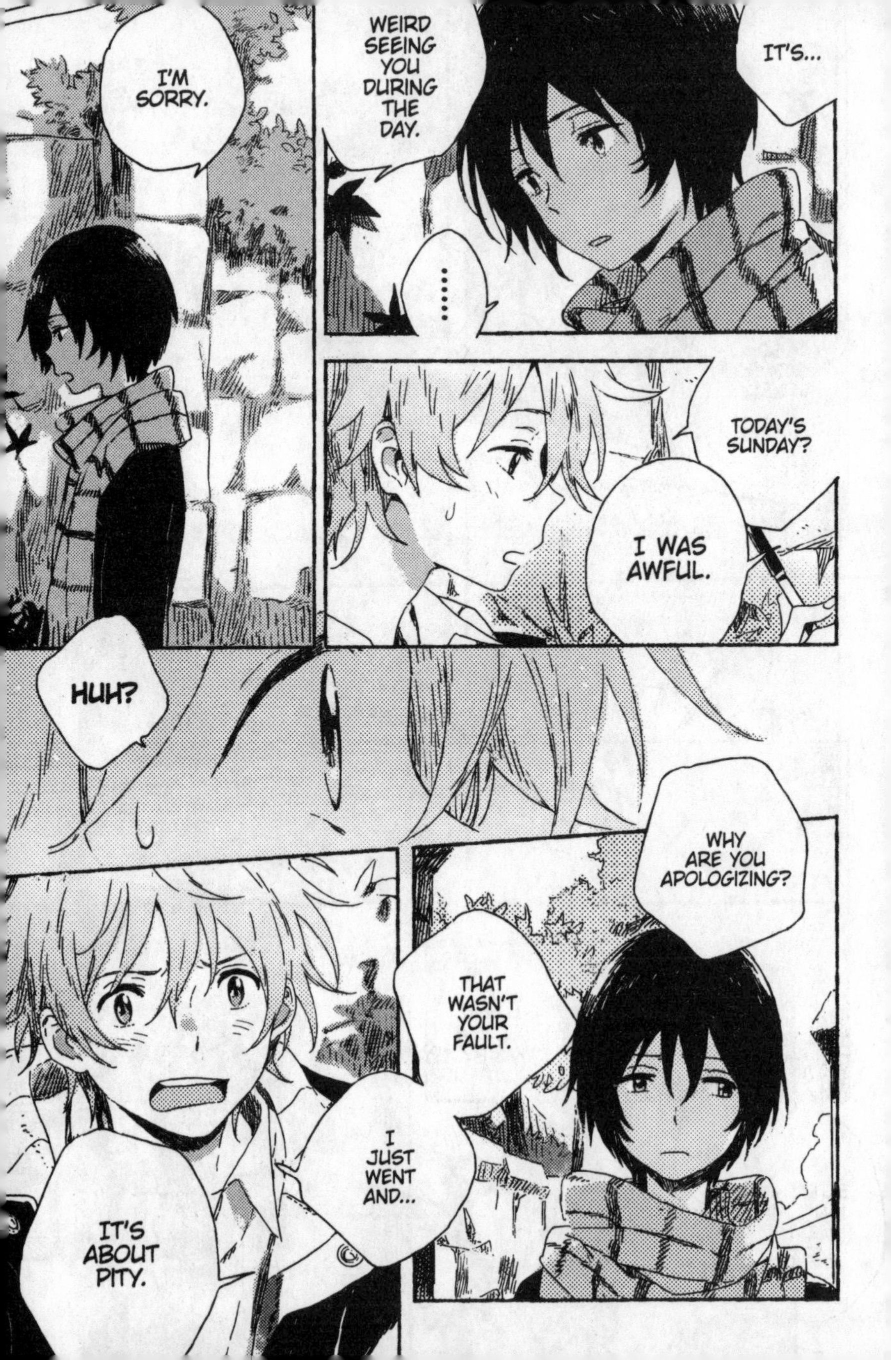
IT'S...
WEIRD SEEING YOU DURING THE DAY.
......
TODAY'S SUNDAY?
I WAS AWFUL.
I'M SORRY.
HUH?
WHY ARE YOU APOLOGIZING?
THAT WASN'T YOUR FAULT.
I JUST WENT AND...
IT'S ABOUT PITY.

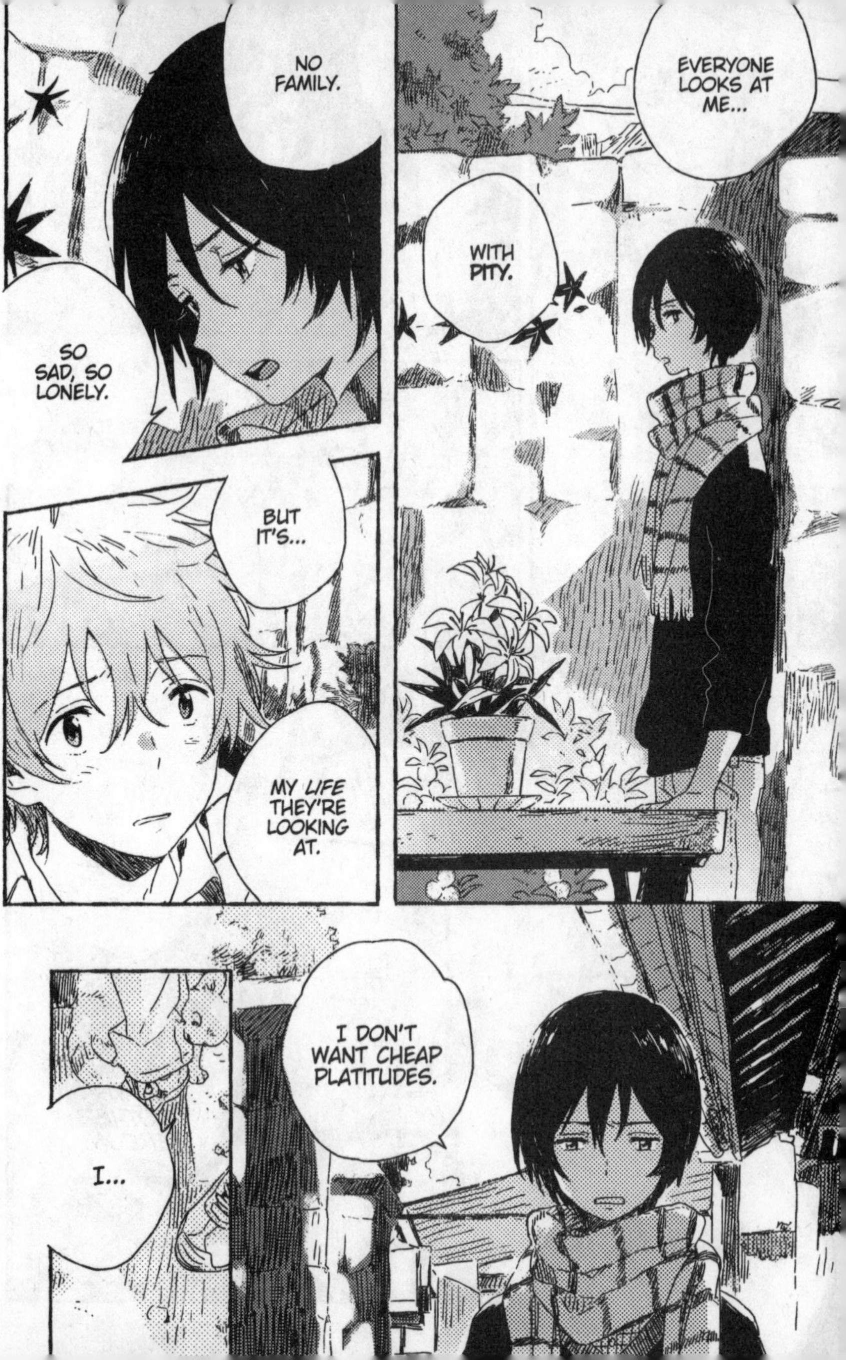
EVERYONE LOOKS AT ME...
WITH PITY.
NO FAMILY.
SO SAD, SO LONELY.
BUT IT'S...
MY *LIFE* THEY'RE LOOKING AT.
I DON'T WANT CHEAP PLATITUDES.
I...

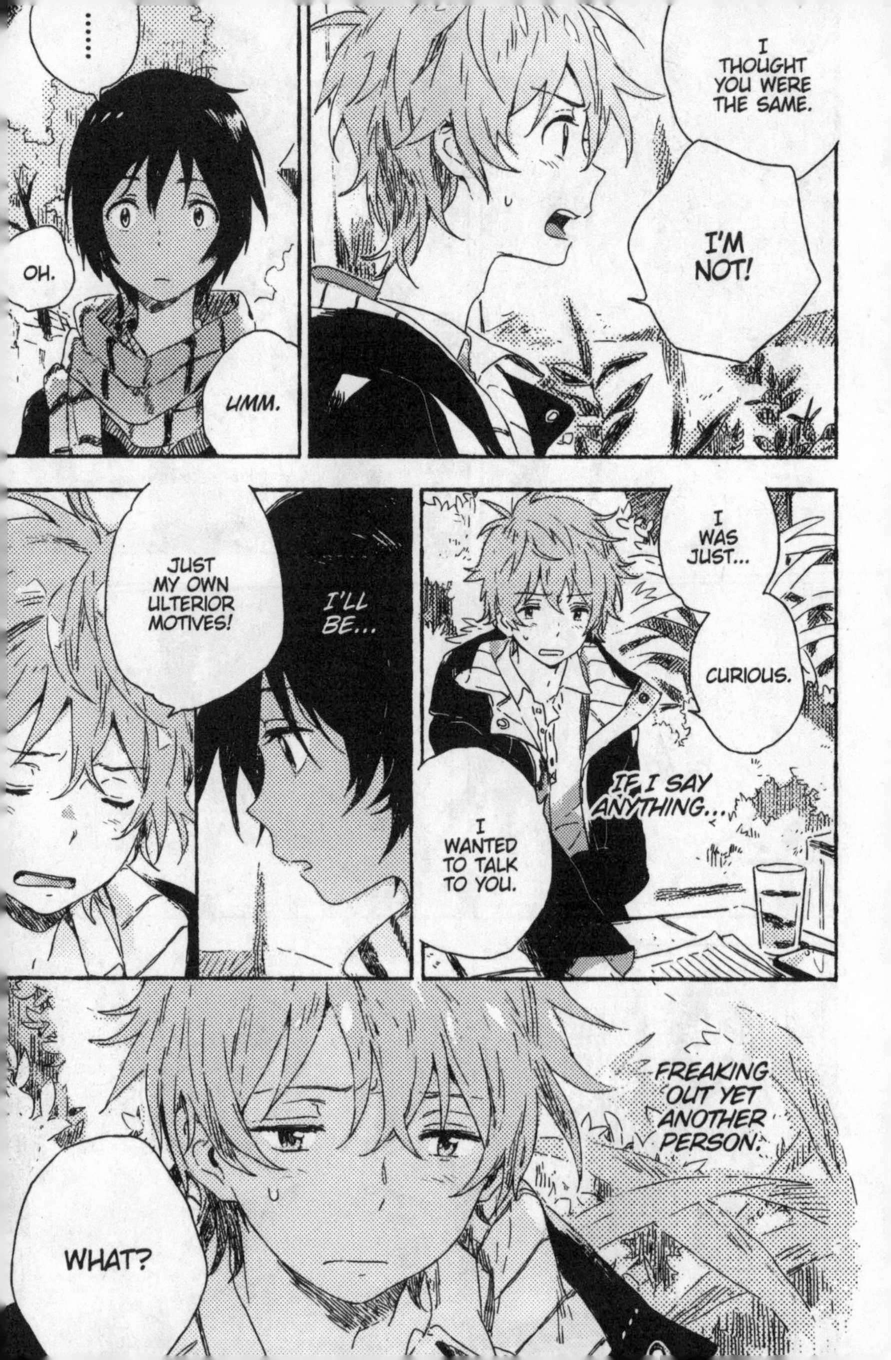
I THOUGHT YOU WERE THE SAME.
I'M NOT!
......
OH.
UMM.
I WAS JUST...
CURIOUS.
IF I SAY ANYTHING...
I WANTED TO TALK TO YOU.
I'LL BE...
JUST MY OWN ULTERIOR MOTIVES!
FREAKING OUT YET ANOTHER PERSON.
WHAT?

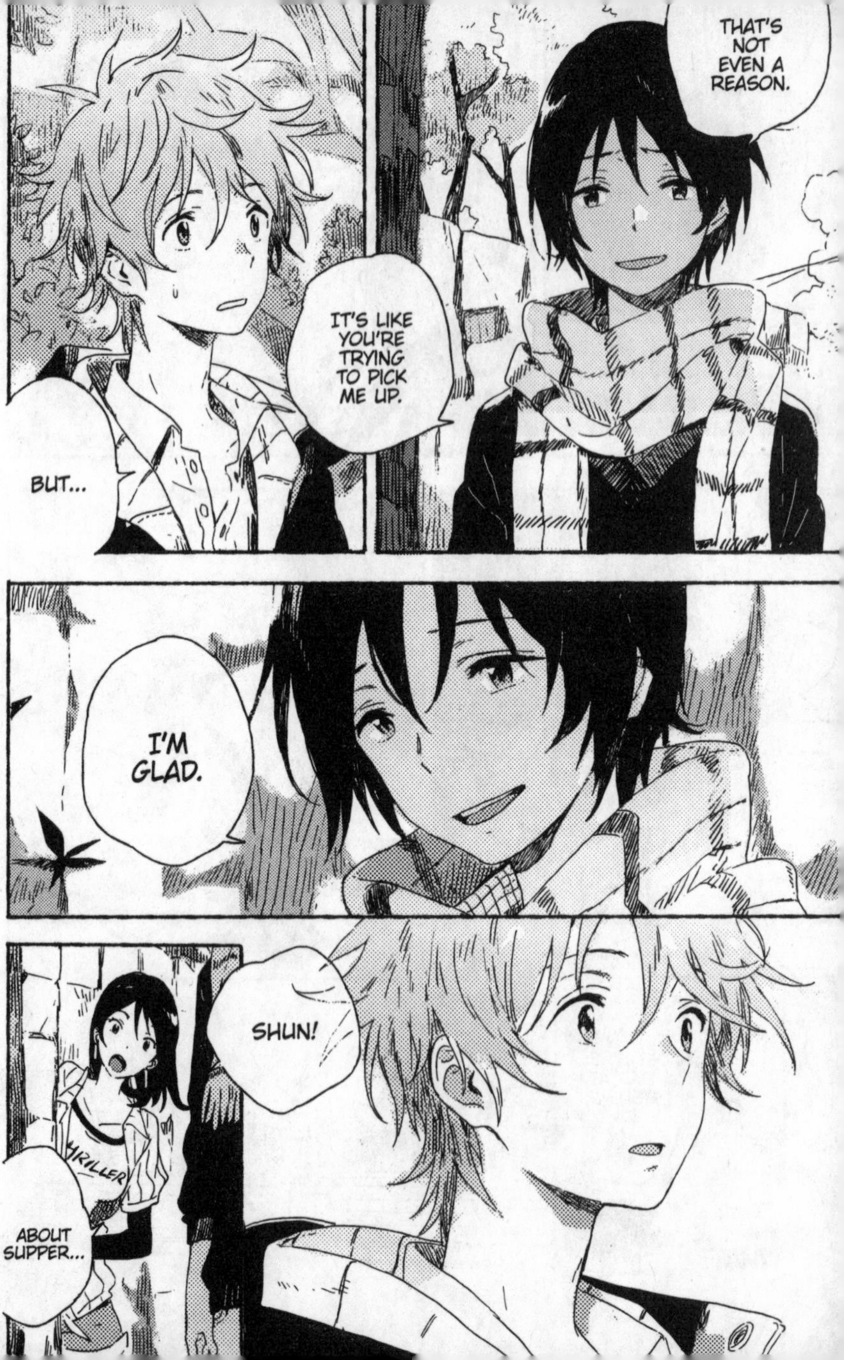
THAT'S NOT EVEN A REASON.
IT'S LIKE YOU'RE TRYING TO PICK ME UP.
BUT...
I'M GLAD.
SHUN!
ABOUT SUPPER...

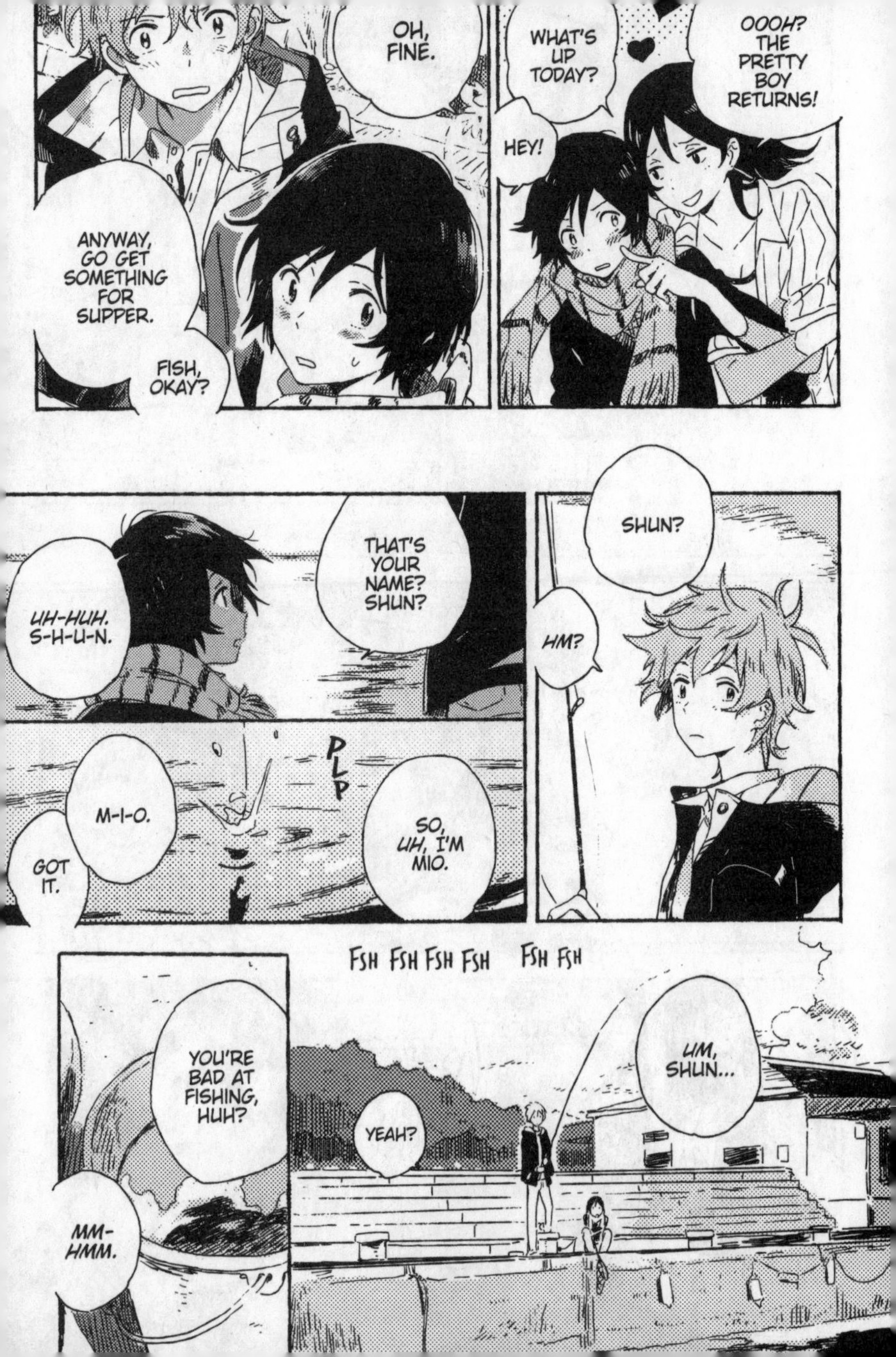
OOOH? THE PRETTY BOY RETURNS!
WHAT'S UP TODAY?
HEY!
OH, FINE.
ANYWAY, GO GET SOMETHING FOR SUPPER.
FISH, OKAY?
SHUN?
HM?
THAT'S YOUR NAME? SHUN?
UH-HUH. S-H-U-N.
PLP
SO, UH, I'M MIO.
M-I-O.
GOT IT.
FSH FSH FSH FSH FSH FSH
UM, SHUN...
YEAH?
YOU'RE BAD AT FISHING, HUH?
MM-HMM.

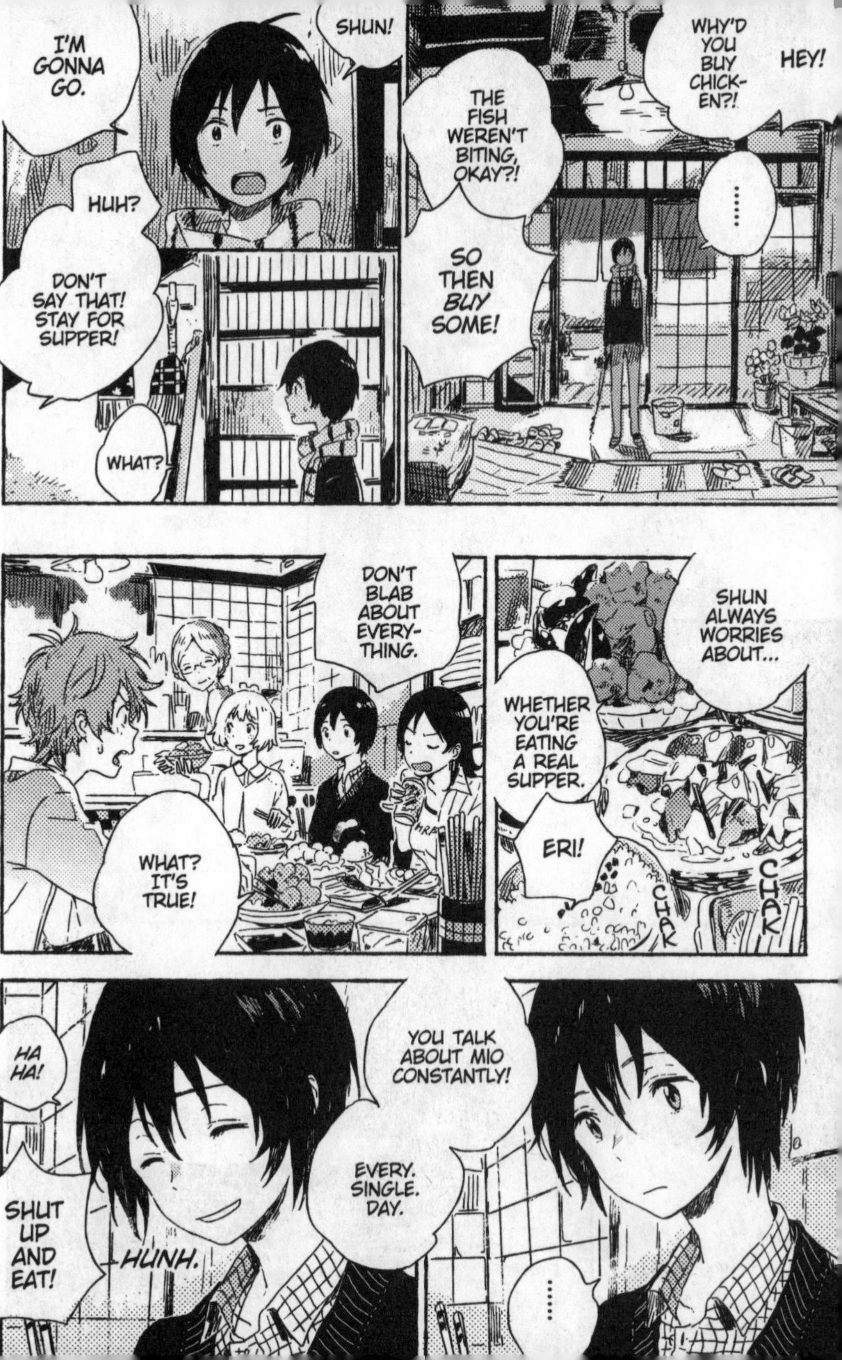
HEY!
WHY'D YOU BUY CHICKEN?!
THE FISH WEREN'T BITING, OKAY?!
......
SO THEN *BUY* SOME!
SHUN!
I'M GONNA GO.
HUH?
DON'T SAY THAT! STAY FOR SUPPER!
WHAT?
SHUN ALWAYS WORRIES ABOUT...
WHETHER YOU'RE EATING A REAL SUPPER.
ERI!
CHAK
CHAK
DON'T BLAB ABOUT EVERYTHING.
WHAT? IT'S TRUE!
YOU TALK ABOUT MIO CONSTANTLY!
EVERY. SINGLE. DAY.
......
HA HA!
SHUT UP AND EAT!
HUNH.

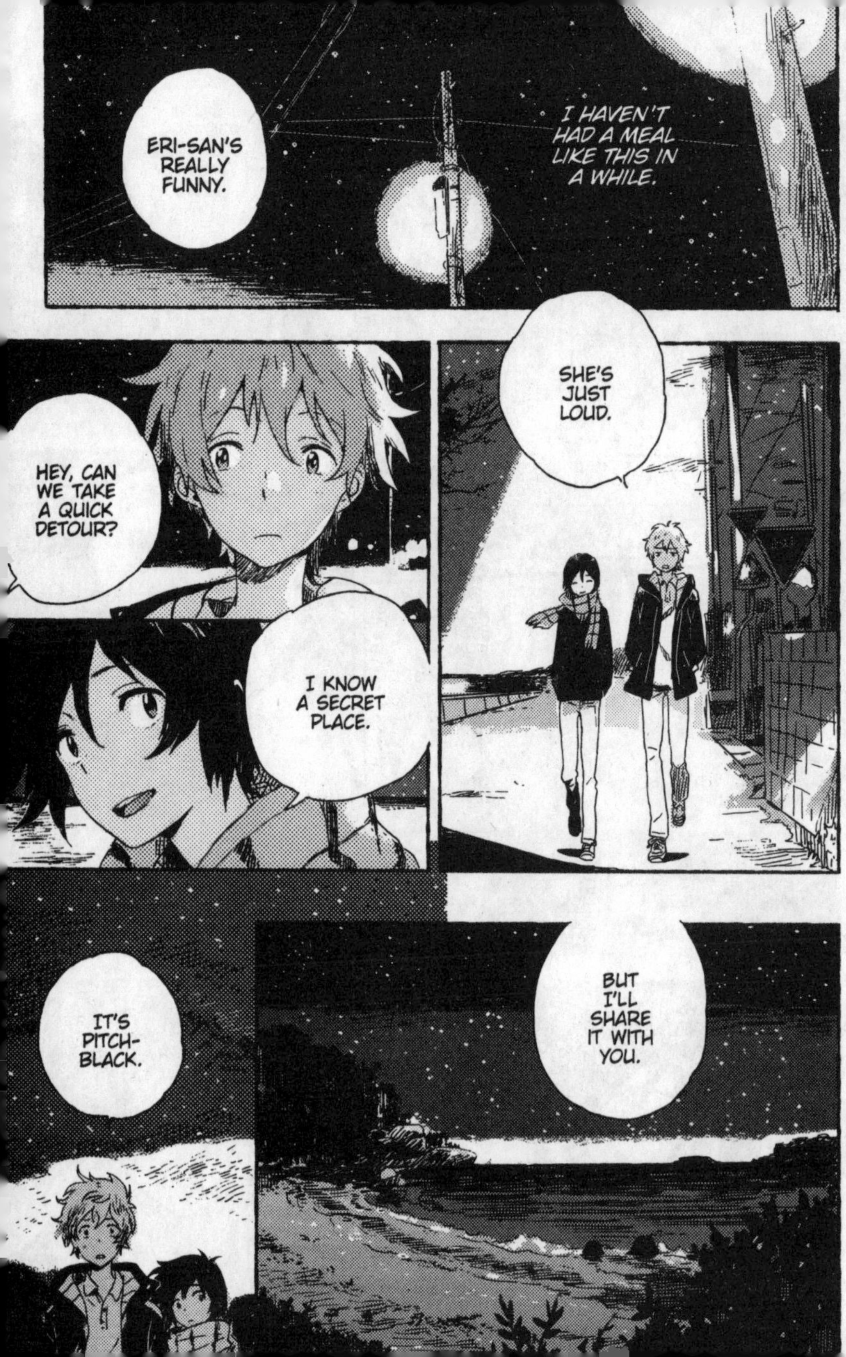
I HAVEN'T HAD A MEAL LIKE THIS IN A WHILE.
ERI-SAN'S REALLY FUNNY.
SHE'S JUST LOUD.
HEY, CAN WE TAKE A QUICK DETOUR?
I KNOW A SECRET PLACE.
BUT I'LL SHARE IT WITH YOU.
IT'S PITCH-BLACK.

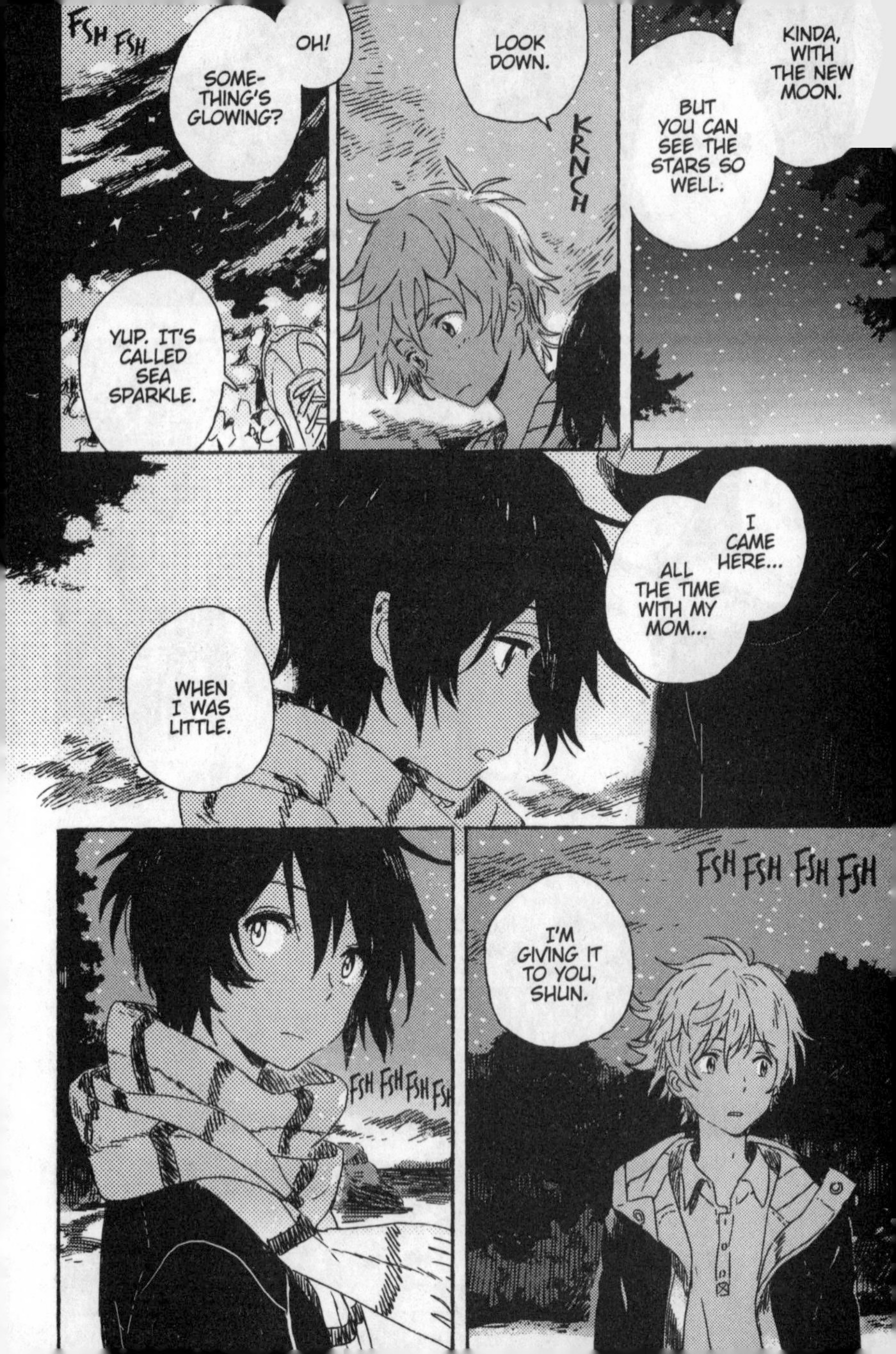
KINDA, WITH THE NEW MOON.
BUT YOU CAN SEE THE STARS SO WELL.
LOOK DOWN.
KRNCH
FSH FSH
OH!
SOME-THING'S GLOWING?
YUP. IT'S CALLED SEA SPARKLE.
I CAME HERE...
ALL THE TIME WITH MY MOM...
WHEN I WAS LITTLE.
FSH FSH FSH FSH
I'M GIVING IT TO YOU, SHUN.
FSH FSH FSH FSH

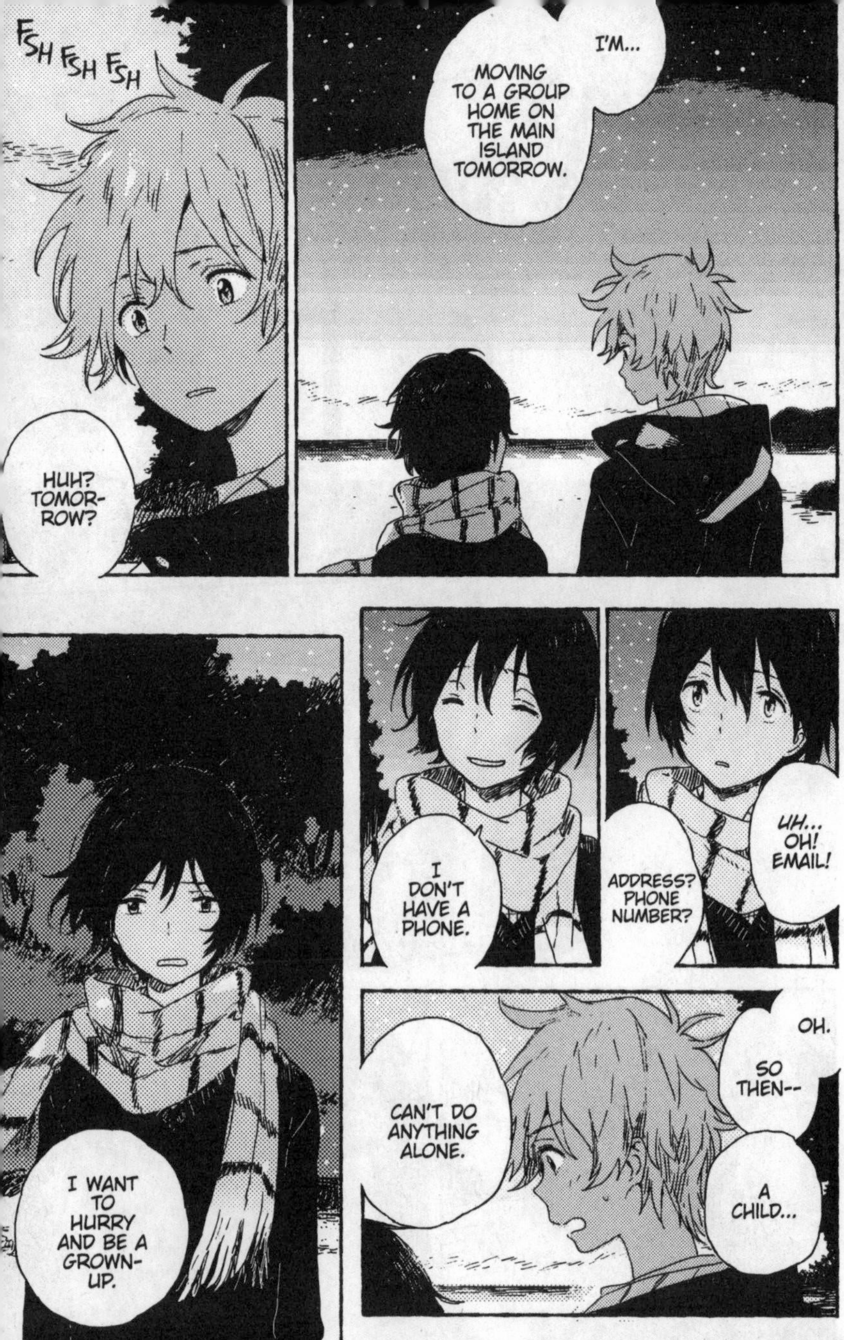
I'M...
MOVING TO A GROUP HOME ON THE MAIN ISLAND TOMORROW.
FSH FSH FSH
HUH? TOMOR-ROW?
UH... OH! EMAIL!
ADDRESS? PHONE NUMBER?
I DON'T HAVE A PHONE.
OH.
SO THEN--
A CHILD...
CAN'T DO ANYTHING ALONE.
I WANT TO HURRY AND BE A GROWN-UP.

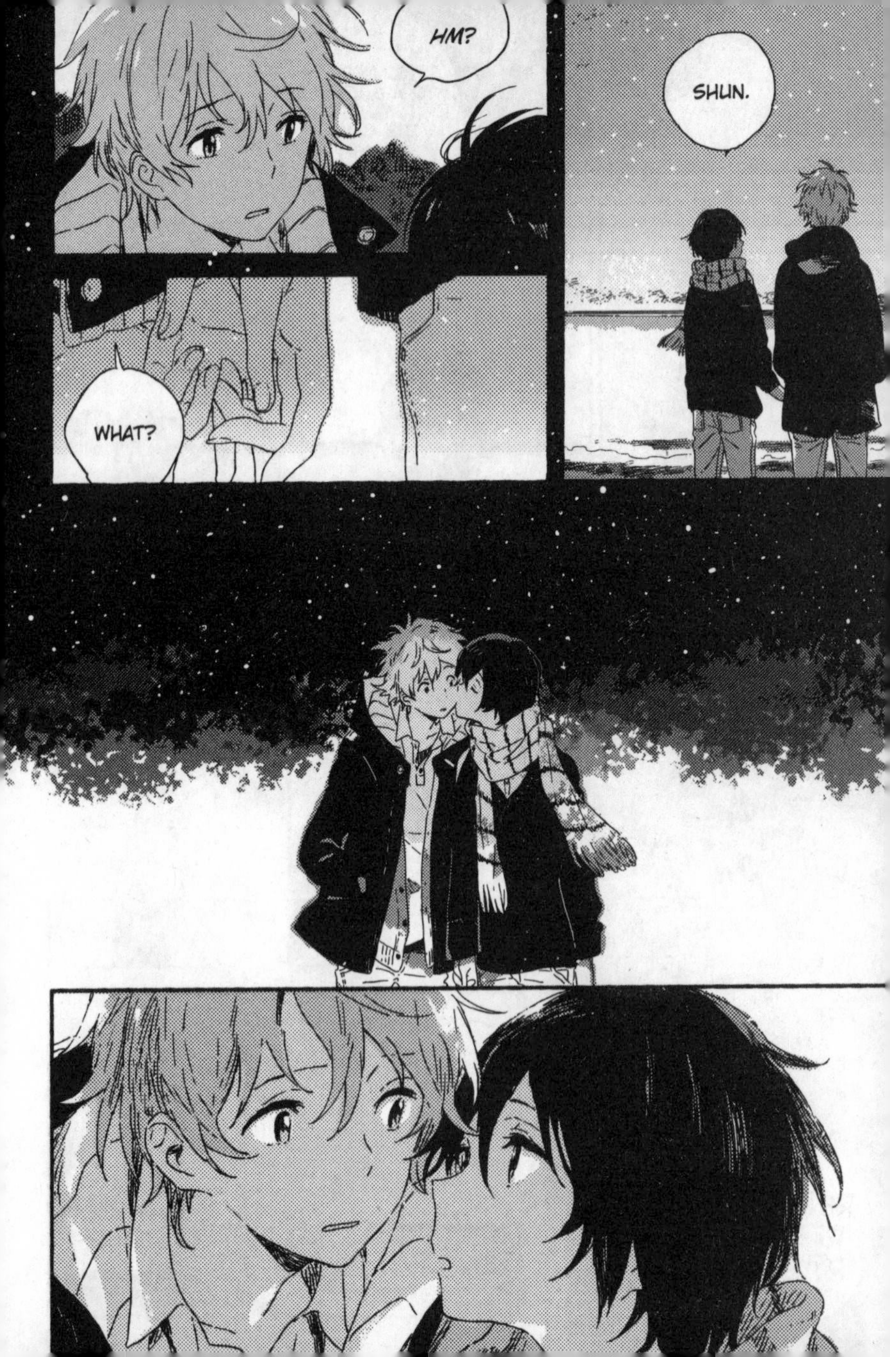
SHUN.
HM?
WHAT?

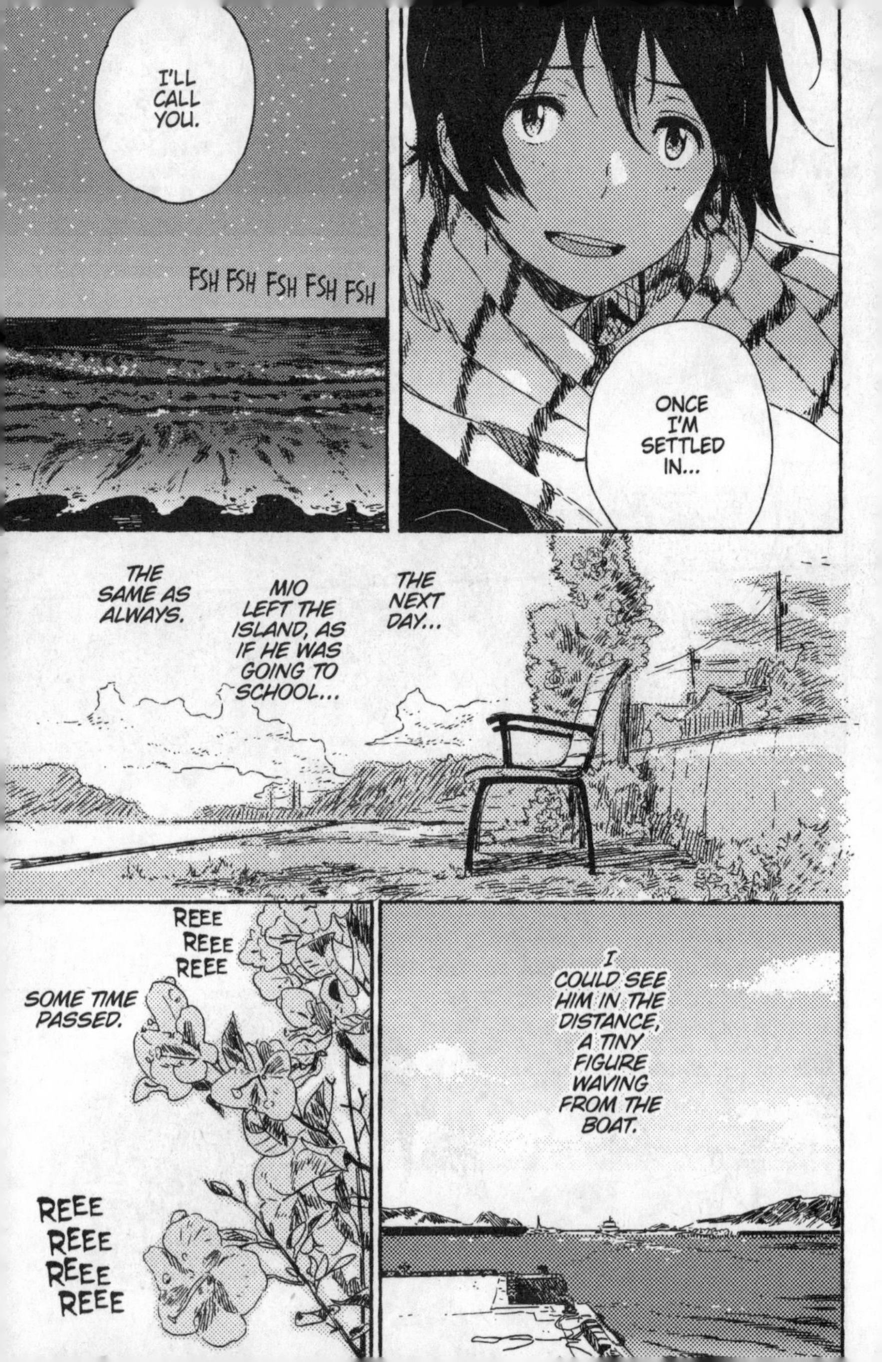
ONCE I'M SETTLED IN...
I'LL CALL YOU.
FSH FSH FSH FSH FSH
THE NEXT DAY...
MIO LEFT THE ISLAND, AS IF HE WAS GOING TO SCHOOL...
THE SAME AS ALWAYS.
I COULD SEE HIM IN THE DISTANCE, A TINY FIGURE WAVING FROM THE BOAT.
REEE REEE REEE
SOME TIME PASSED.
REEE REEE REEE REEE

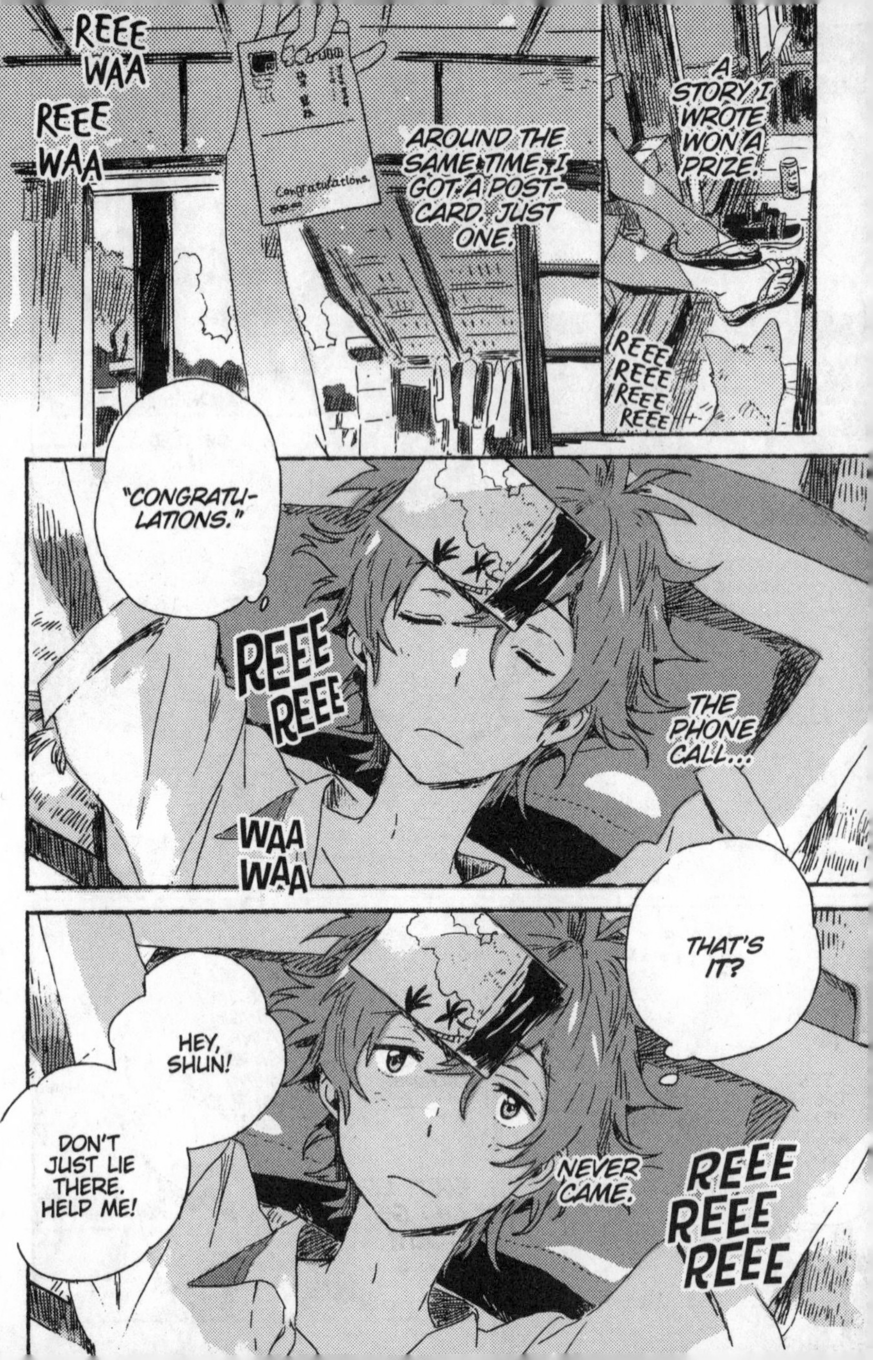
A STORY I WROTE WON A PRIZE.
REEE REEE REEE REEE
AROUND THE SAME TIME, I GOT A POST-CARD. JUST ONE.
Congratulations.
REEE WAA
REEE WAA
"CONGRATULATIONS."
REEE REEE
THE PHONE CALL...
WAA WAA
THAT'S IT?
HEY, SHUN!
NEVER CAME.
REEE REEE REEE
DON'T JUST LIE THERE. HELP ME!

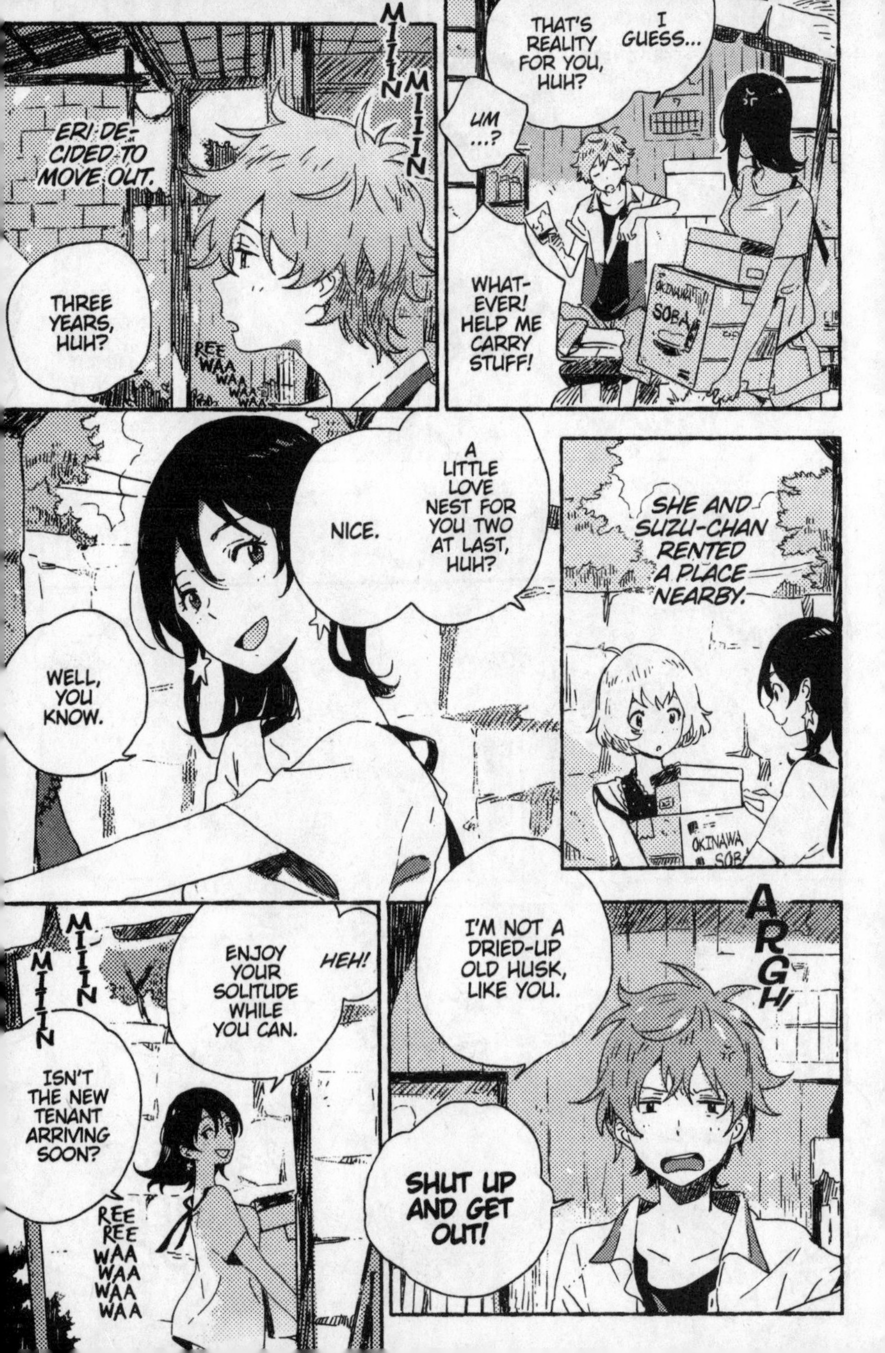
I GUESS...
THAT'S REALITY FOR YOU, HUH?
UM ...?
WHAT-EVER! HELP ME CARRY STUFF!
OKINAWA SOBA
MIIIN MIIIN
ERI DE-CIDED TO MOVE OUT.
THREE YEARS, HUH?
REE WAA WAA WAA WAA
SHE AND SUZU-CHAN RENTED A PLACE NEARBY.
OKINAWA SOB
A LITTLE LOVE NEST FOR YOU TWO AT LAST, HUH?
NICE.
WELL, YOU KNOW.
ARGH
I'M NOT A DRIED-UP OLD HUSK, LIKE YOU.
SHUT UP AND GET OUT!
HEH!
ENJOY YOUR SOLITUDE WHILE YOU CAN.
MIIIN MIIIN
ISN'T THE NEW TENANT ARRIVING SOON?
REE REE WAA WAA WAA WAA

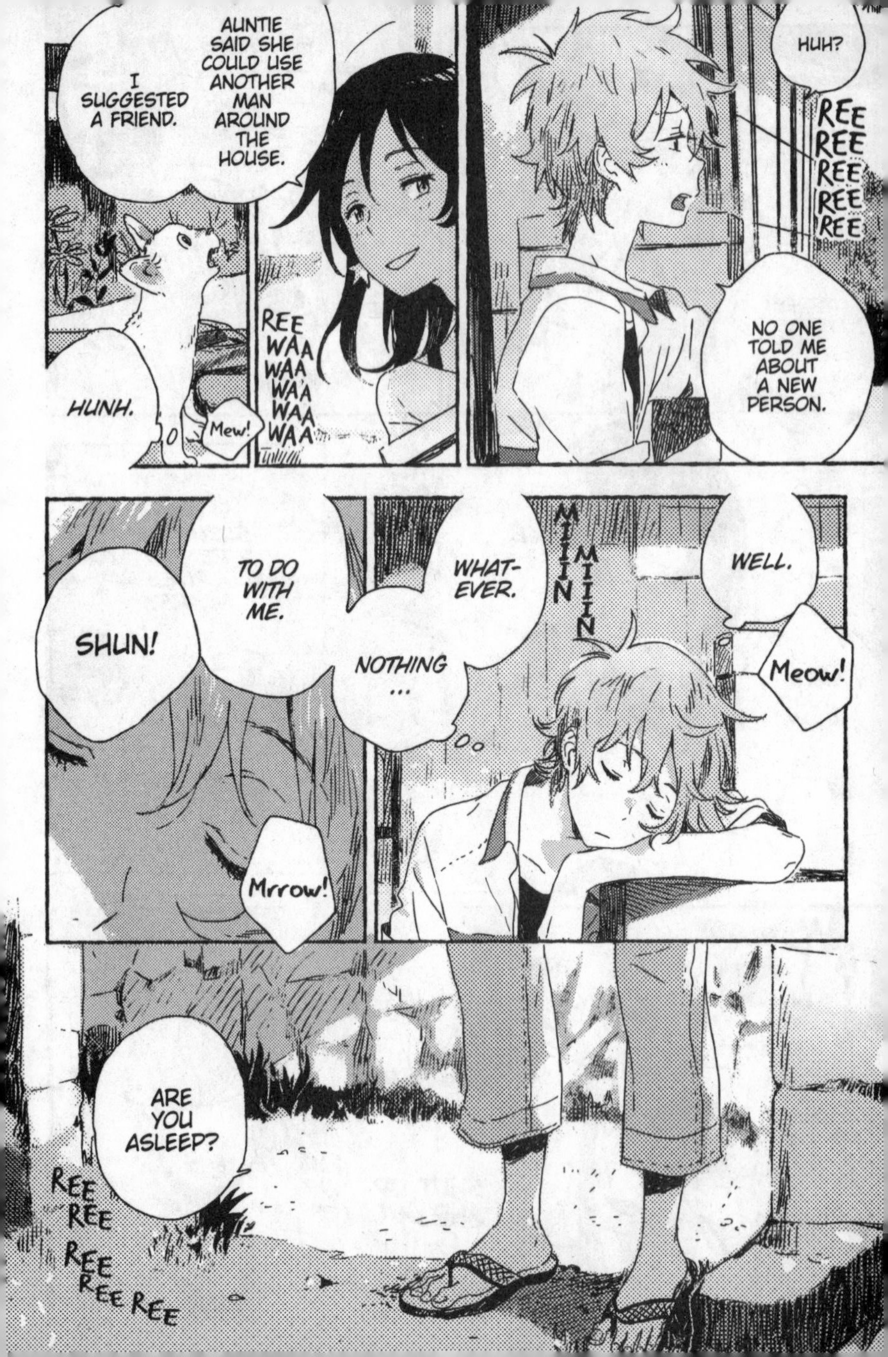
HUH?
REE REE REE REE REE
NO ONE TOLD ME ABOUT A NEW PERSON.
AUNTIE SAID SHE COULD USE ANOTHER MAN AROUND THE HOUSE.
I SUGGESTED A FRIEND.
REE WAA WAA WAA WAA WAA
Mew!
HUNH.
WELL.
Meow!
MIIIN MIIIN
WHAT-EVER.
NOTHING...
TO DO WITH ME.
SHUN!
Mrrow!
ARE YOU ASLEEP?
REE REE REE REE REE

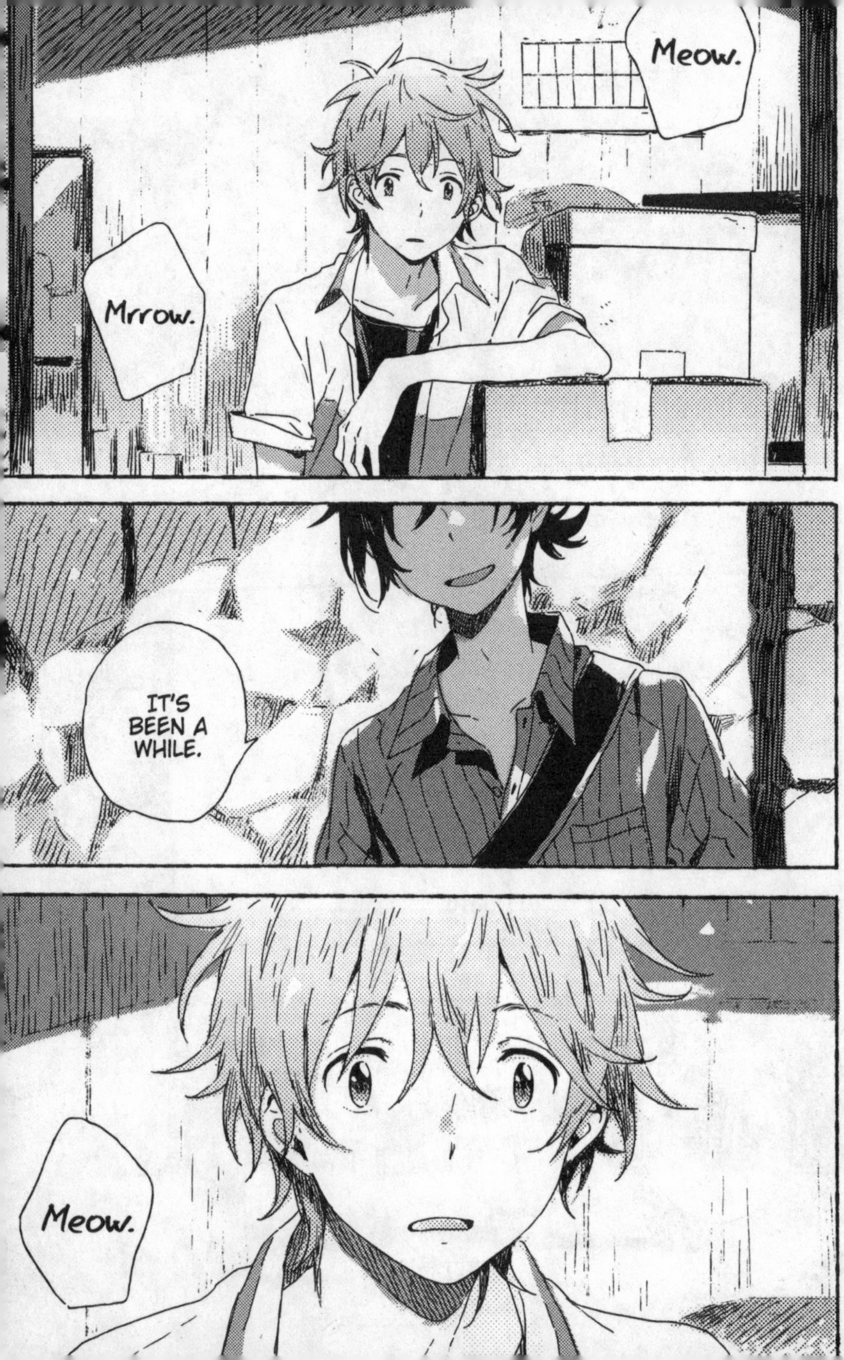
Meow.
Mrrow.
IT'S BEEN A WHILE.
Meow.

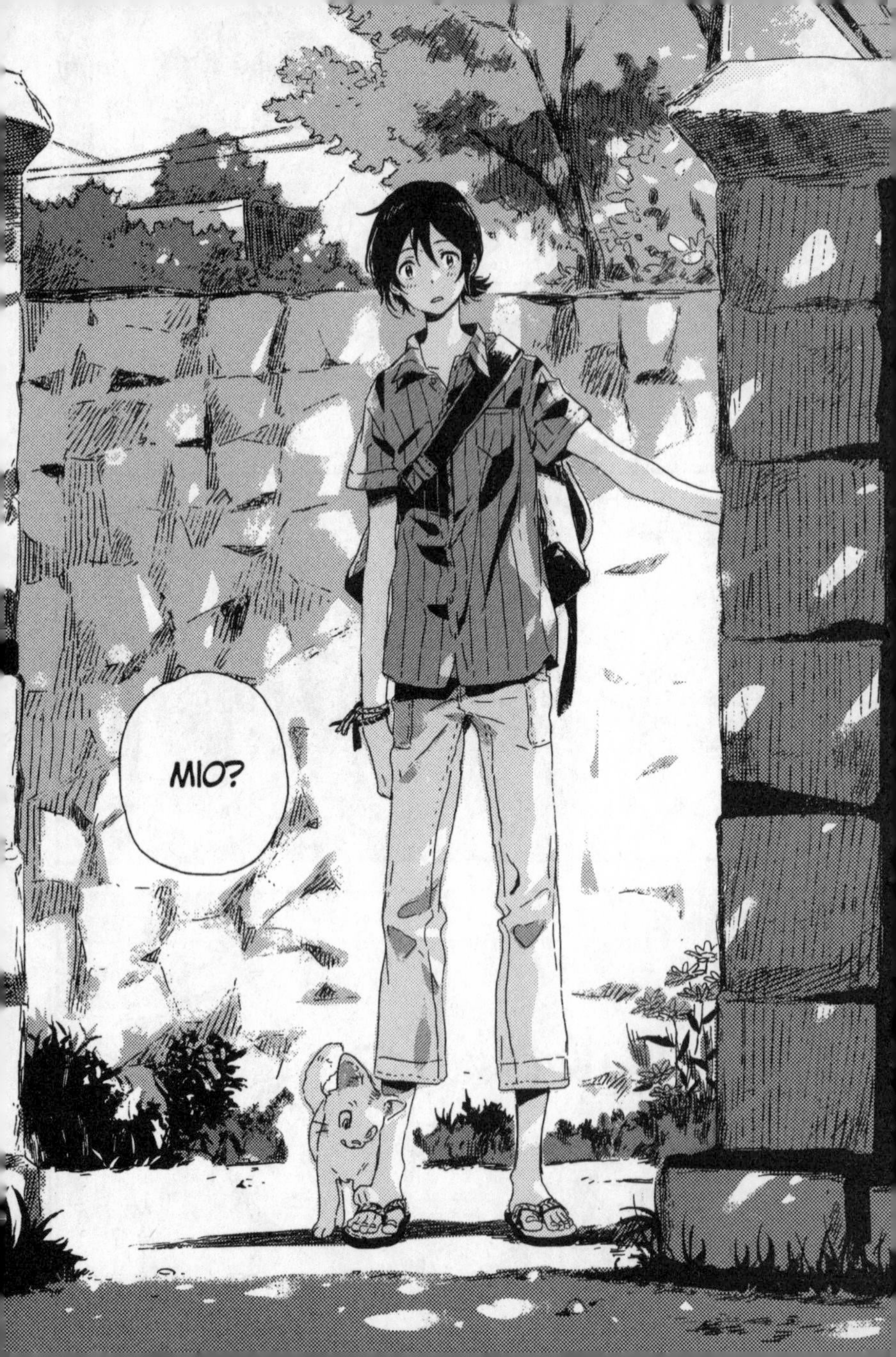
MIO?

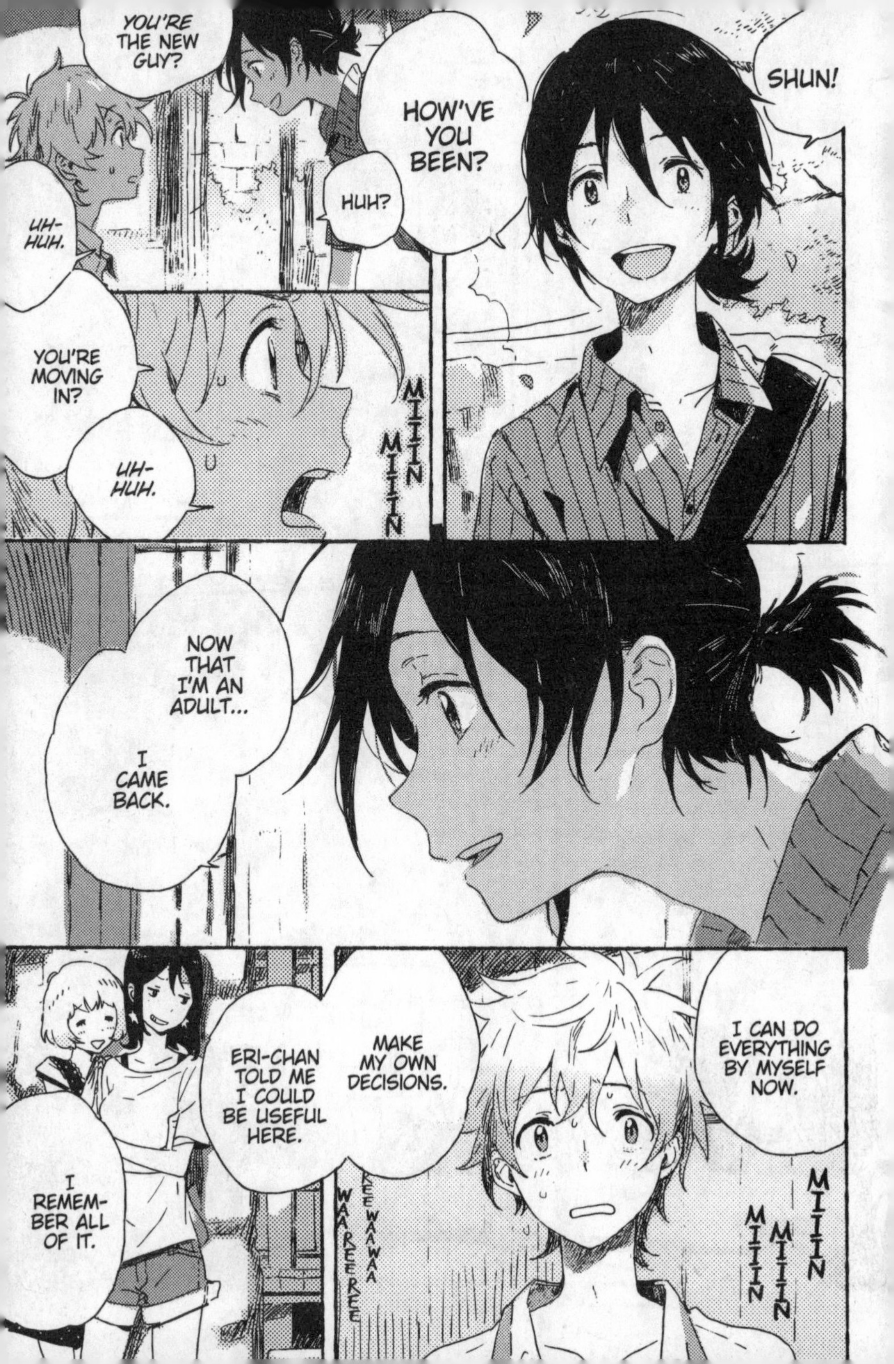
SHUN!
HOW'VE YOU BEEN?
HUH?
YOU'RE THE NEW GUY?
UH-HUH.
YOU'RE MOVING IN?
UH-HUH.
MIIIN MIIIN
NOW THAT I'M AN ADULT...
I CAME BACK.
I CAN DO EVERYTHING BY MYSELF NOW.
MAKE MY OWN DECISIONS.
ERI-CHAN TOLD ME I COULD BE USEFUL HERE.
MIIIN MIIIN MIIIN
REE WAAWAA
WAA REE REE
I REMEMBER ALL OF IT.

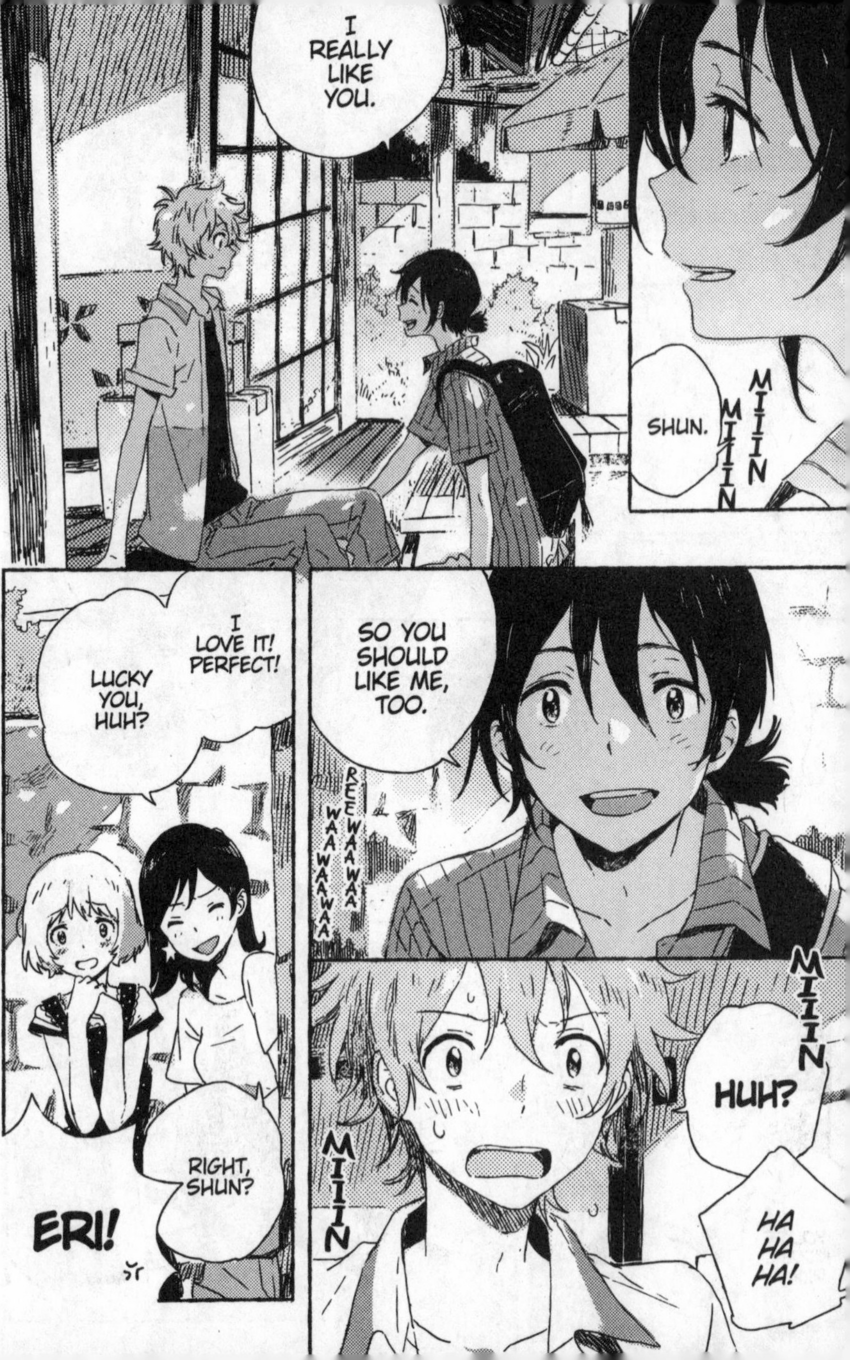
SHUN.
MIIIN
MIIIN
I REALLY LIKE YOU.
SO YOU SHOULD LIKE ME, TOO.
REEWAAAWAA
WAAWAAWAA
MIIIN
HUH?
HA HA HA!
MIIIN
I LOVE IT! PERFECT!
LUCKY YOU, HUH?
RIGHT, SHUN?
ERI!

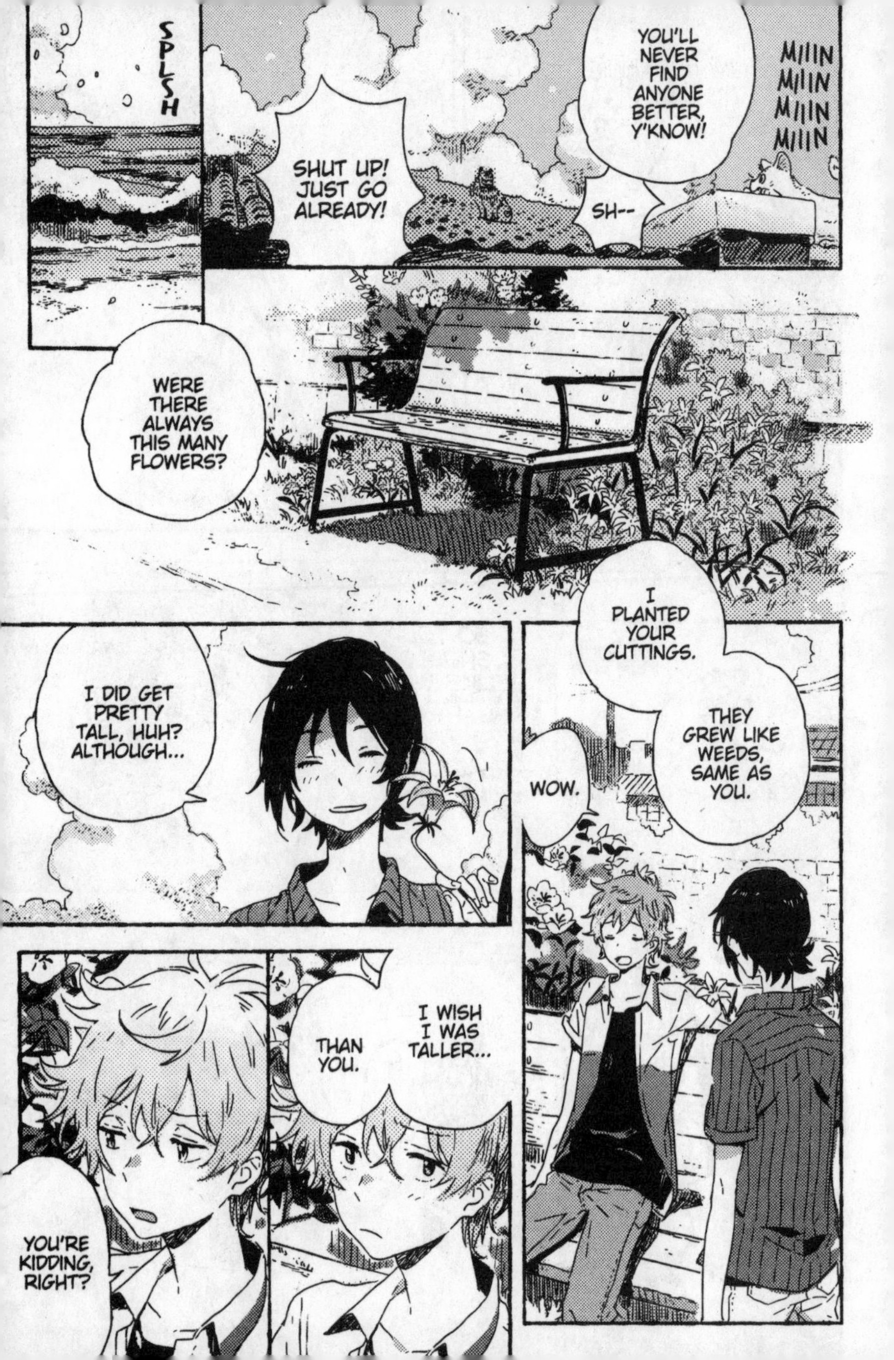
MIIIN MIIIN MIIIN MIIIN
YOU'LL NEVER FIND ANYONE BETTER, Y'KNOW!
SH--
SHUT UP! JUST GO ALREADY!
SPLSH
WERE THERE ALWAYS THIS MANY FLOWERS?
I PLANTED YOUR CUTTINGS.
THEY GREW LIKE WEEDS, SAME AS YOU.
WOW.
I DID GET PRETTY TALL, HUH? ALTHOUGH...
I WISH I WAS TALLER...
THAN YOU.
YOU'RE KIDDING, RIGHT?

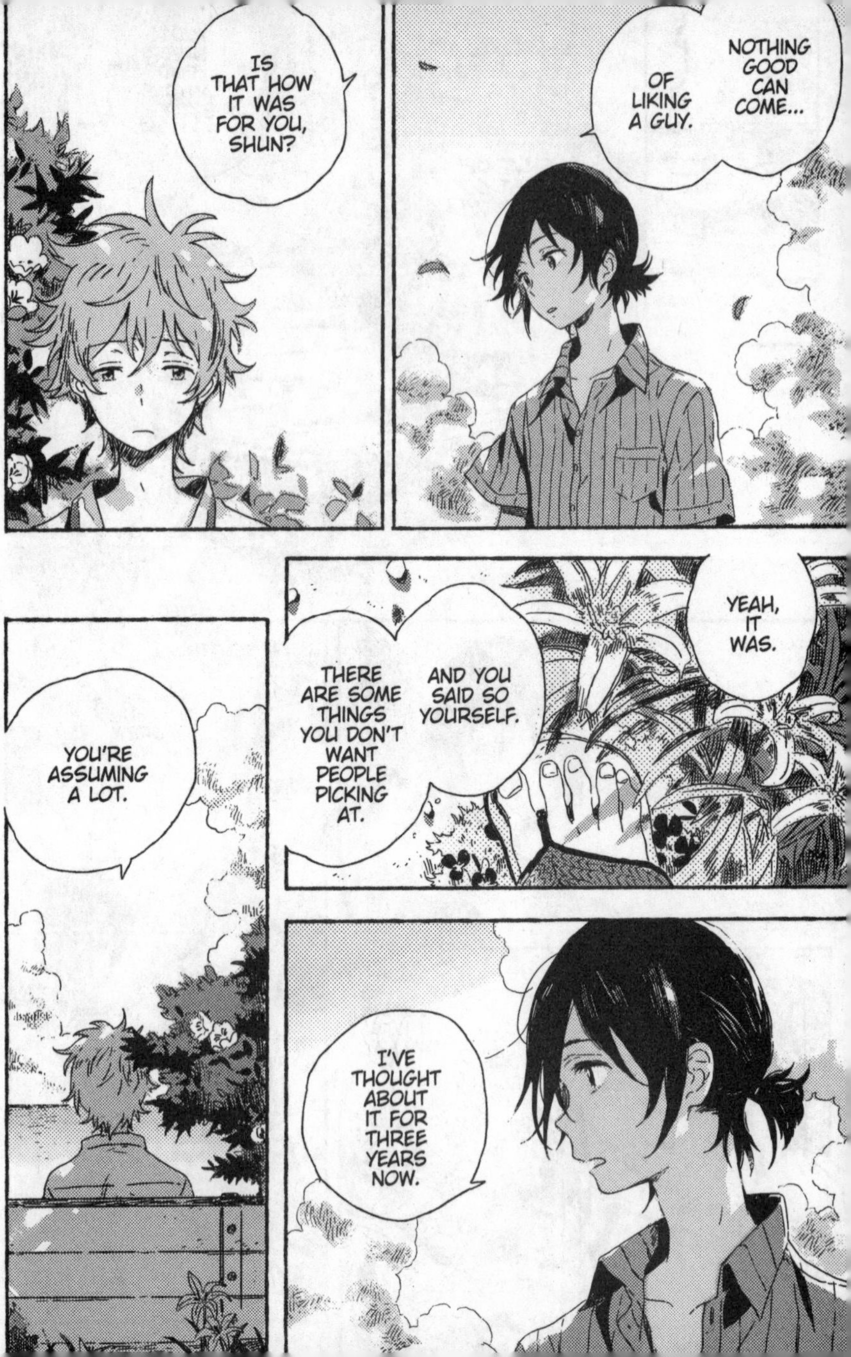
NOTHING GOOD CAN COME...
OF LIKING A GUY.
IS THAT HOW IT WAS FOR YOU, SHUN?
YEAH, IT WAS.
AND YOU SAID SO YOURSELF.
THERE ARE SOME THINGS YOU DON'T WANT PEOPLE PICKING AT.
I'VE THOUGHT ABOUT IT FOR THREE YEARS NOW.
YOU'RE ASSUMING A LOT.

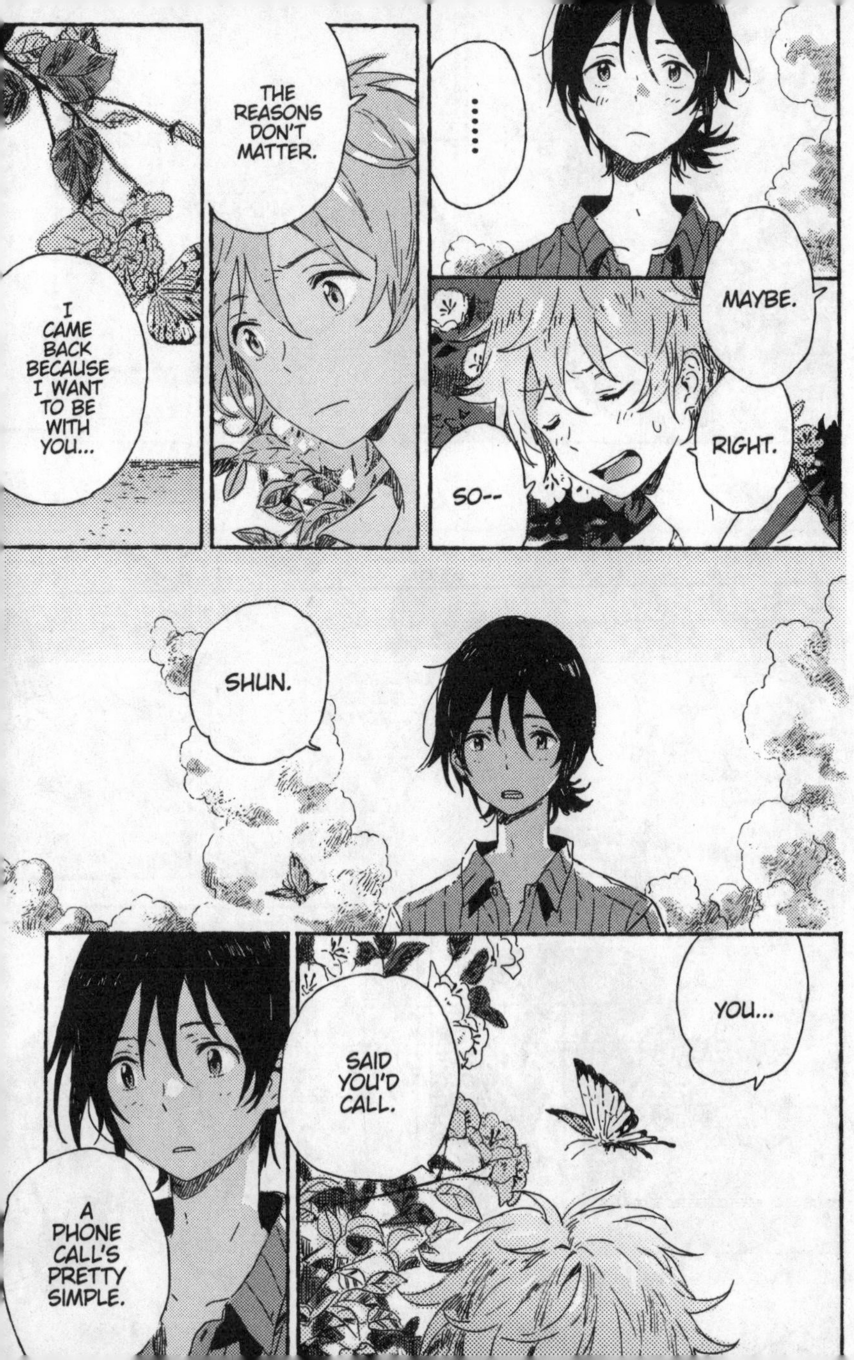
......
MAYBE.
RIGHT.
SO--
THE REASONS DON'T MATTER.
I CAME BACK BECAUSE I WANT TO BE WITH YOU...
SHUN.
YOU...
SAID YOU'D CALL.
A PHONE CALL'S PRETTY SIMPLE.

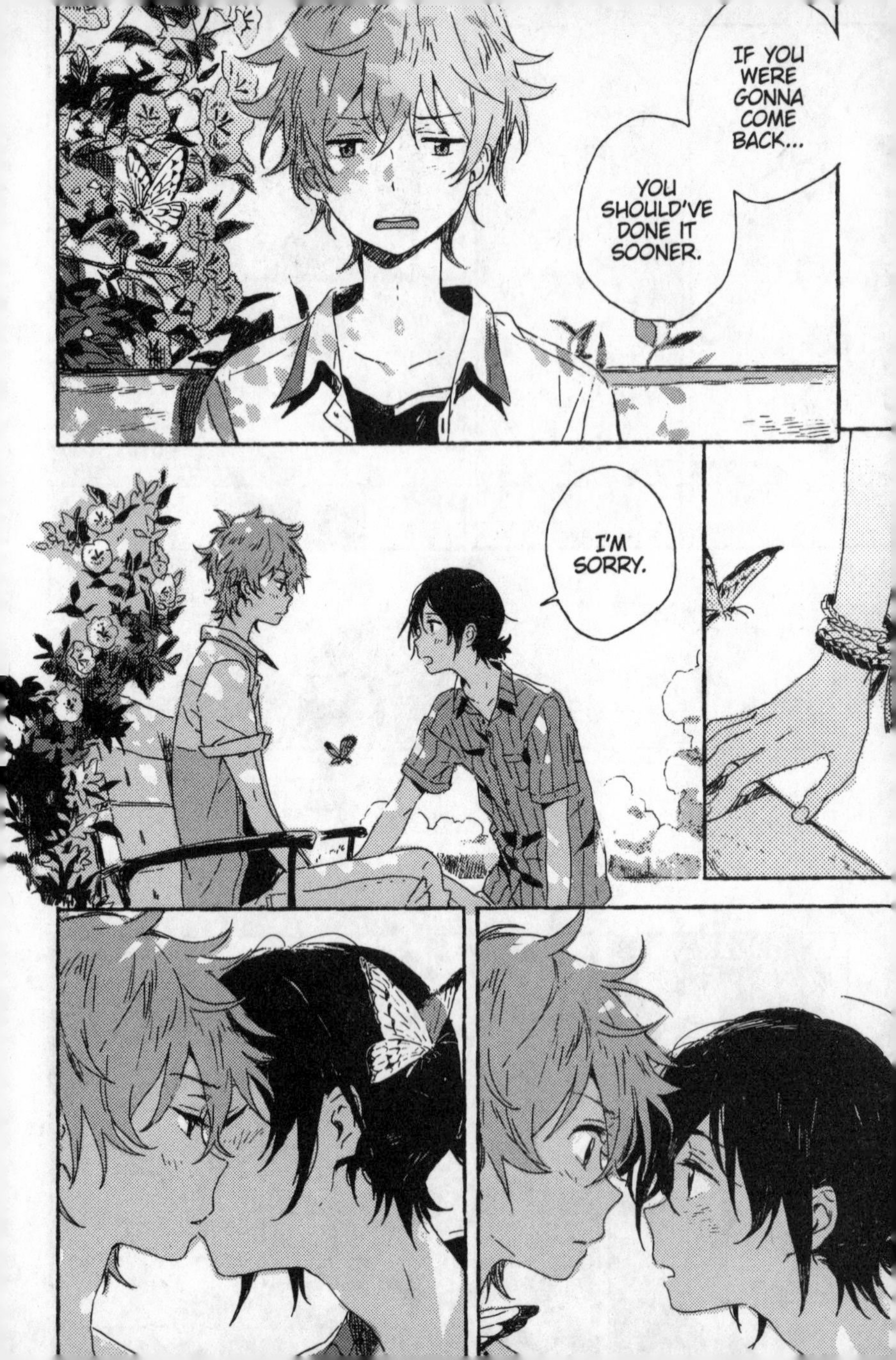
IF YOU WERE GONNA COME BACK...
YOU SHOULD'VE DONE IT SOONER.
I'M SORRY.

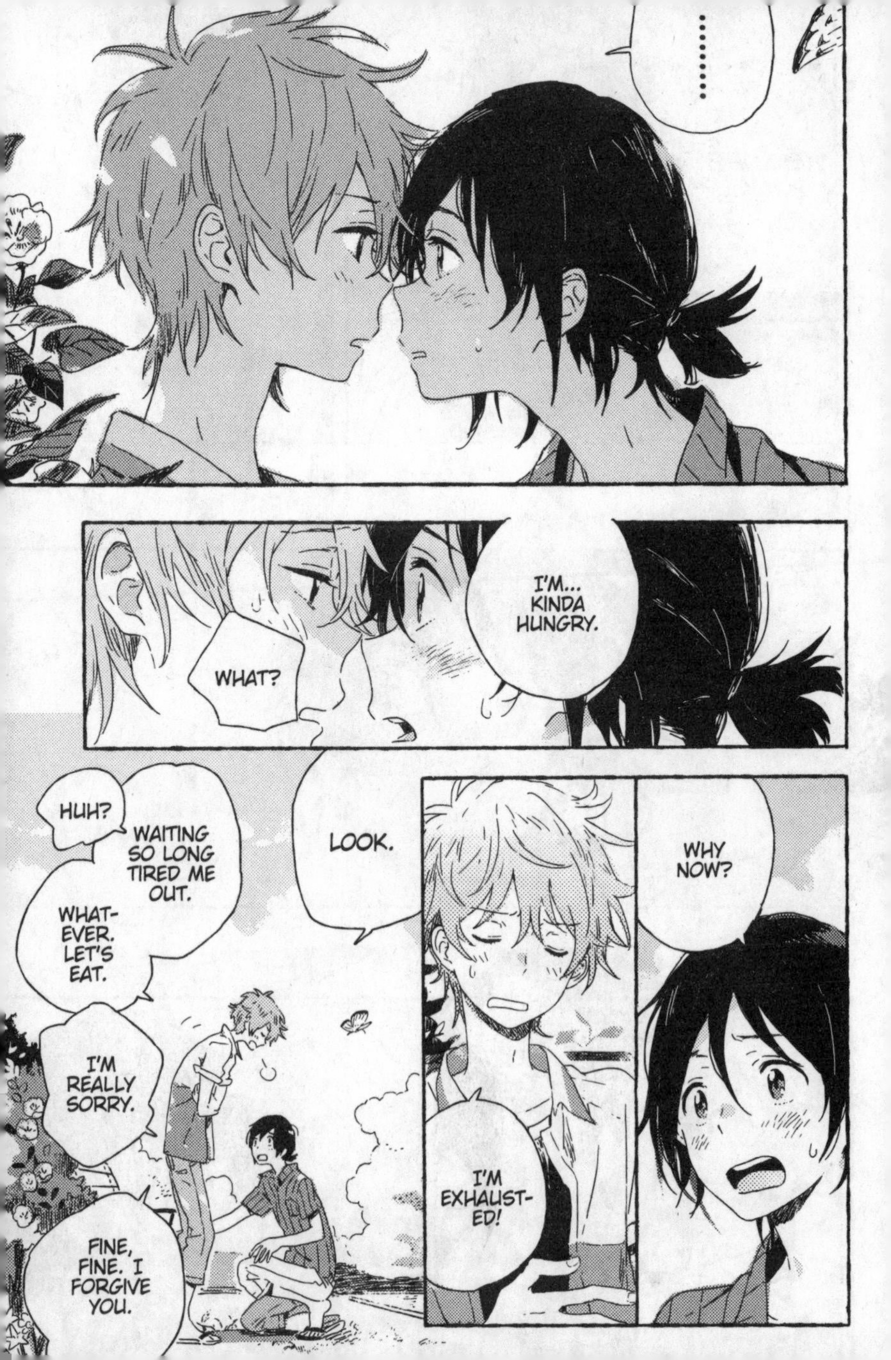
......
I'M... KINDA HUNGRY.
WHAT?
WHY NOW?
I'M EXHAUST-ED!
LOOK.
HUH?
WAITING SO LONG TIRED ME OUT.
WHAT-EVER. LET'S EAT.
I'M REALLY SORRY.
FINE, FINE. I FORGIVE YOU.

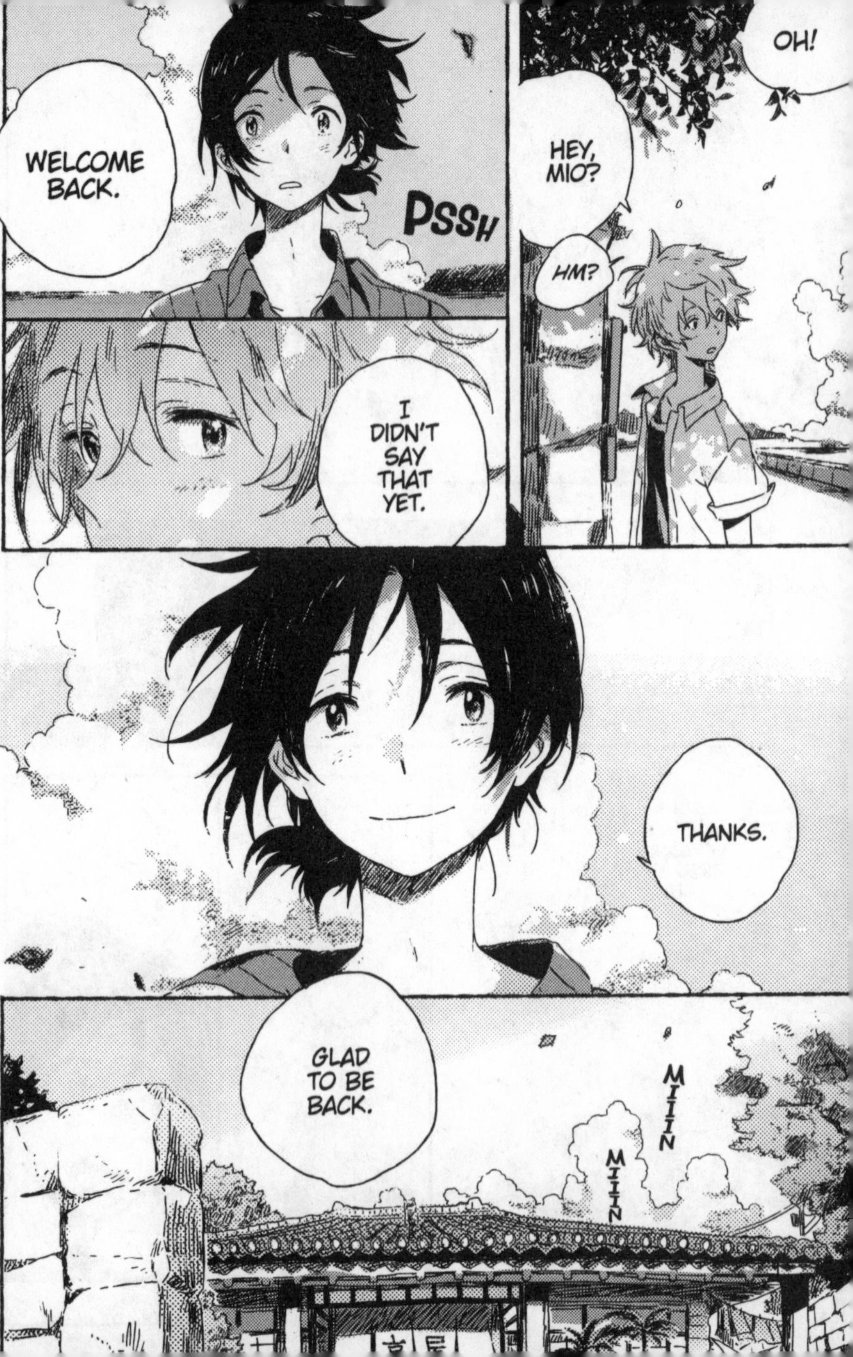
OH!
HEY, MIO?
HM?
WELCOME BACK.
PSSH
I DIDN'T SAY THAT YET.
THANKS.
GLAD TO BE BACK.
MIIIN
MIIIN

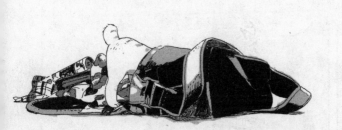

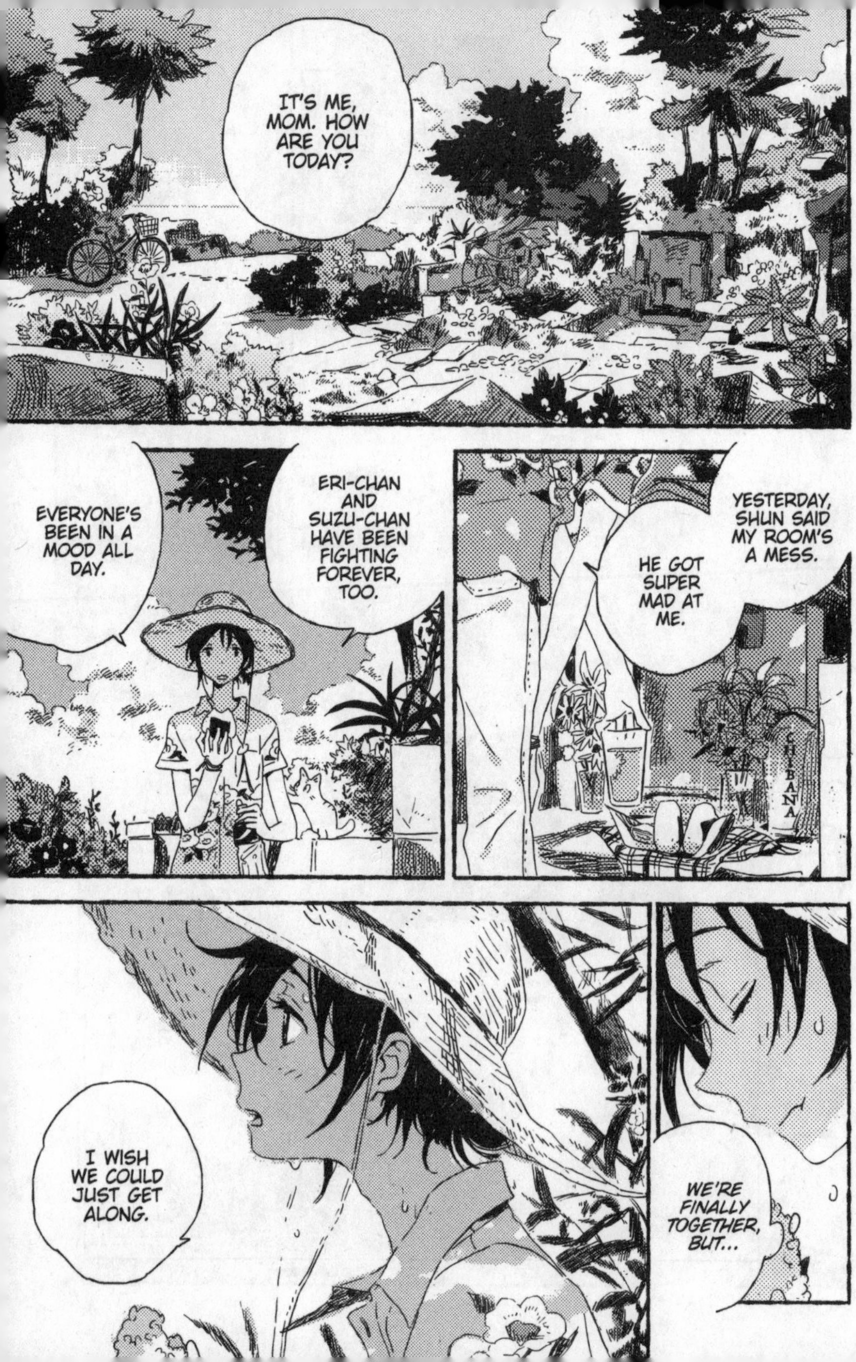
IT'S ME, MOM. HOW ARE YOU TODAY?
YESTERDAY, SHUN SAID MY ROOM'S A MESS.
HE GOT SUPER MAD AT ME.
CHIBANA
ERI-CHAN AND SUZU-CHAN HAVE BEEN FIGHTING FOREVER, TOO.
EVERYONE'S BEEN IN A MOOD ALL DAY.
WE'RE FINALLY TOGETHER, BUT...
I WISH WE COULD JUST GET ALONG.

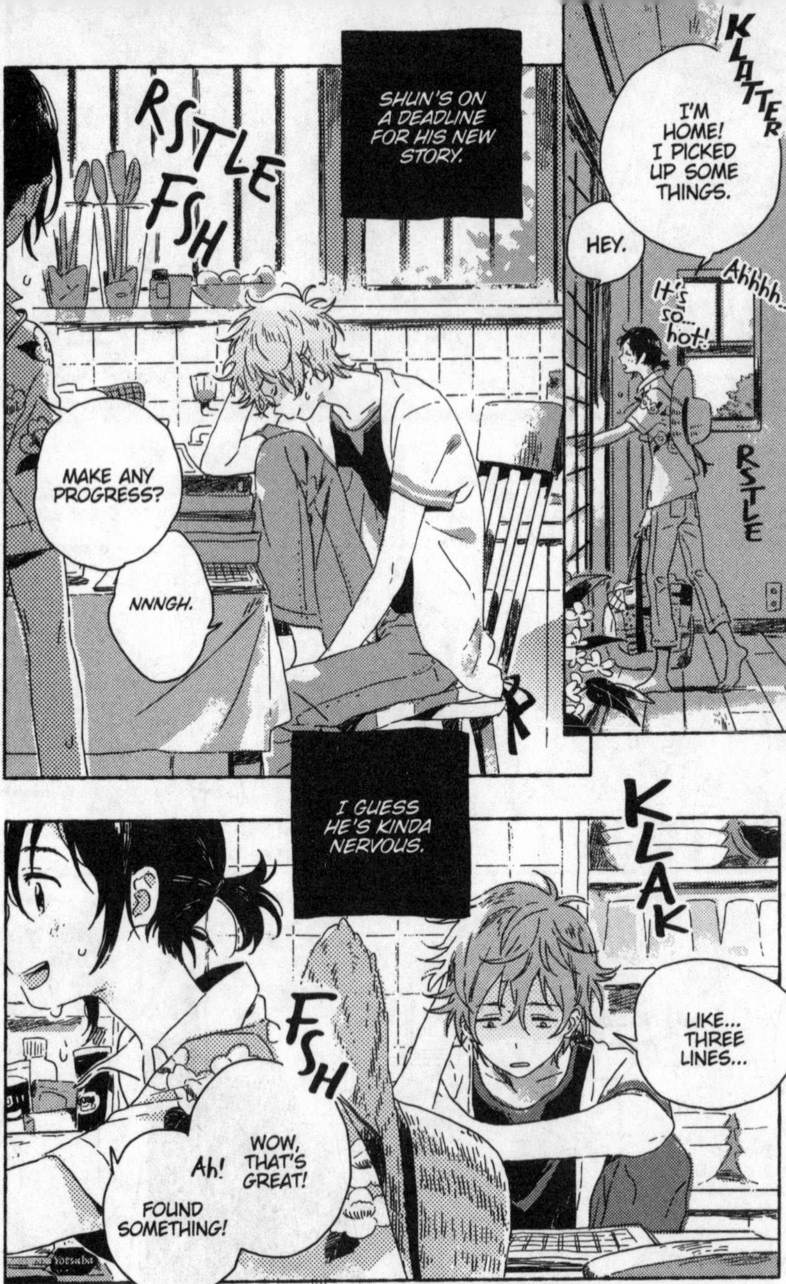
KLATTER
I'M HOME! I PICKED UP SOME THINGS.
HEY.
Ahhhh... It's so... hot!
RSTLE
SHUN'S ON A DEADLINE FOR HIS NEW STORY.
RSTLE
FSH
MAKE ANY PROGRESS?
NNNGH.
I GUESS HE'S KINDA NERVOUS.
KLAK
LIKE... THREE LINES...
FSH
WOW, THAT'S GREAT!
Ah!
FOUND SOMETHING!

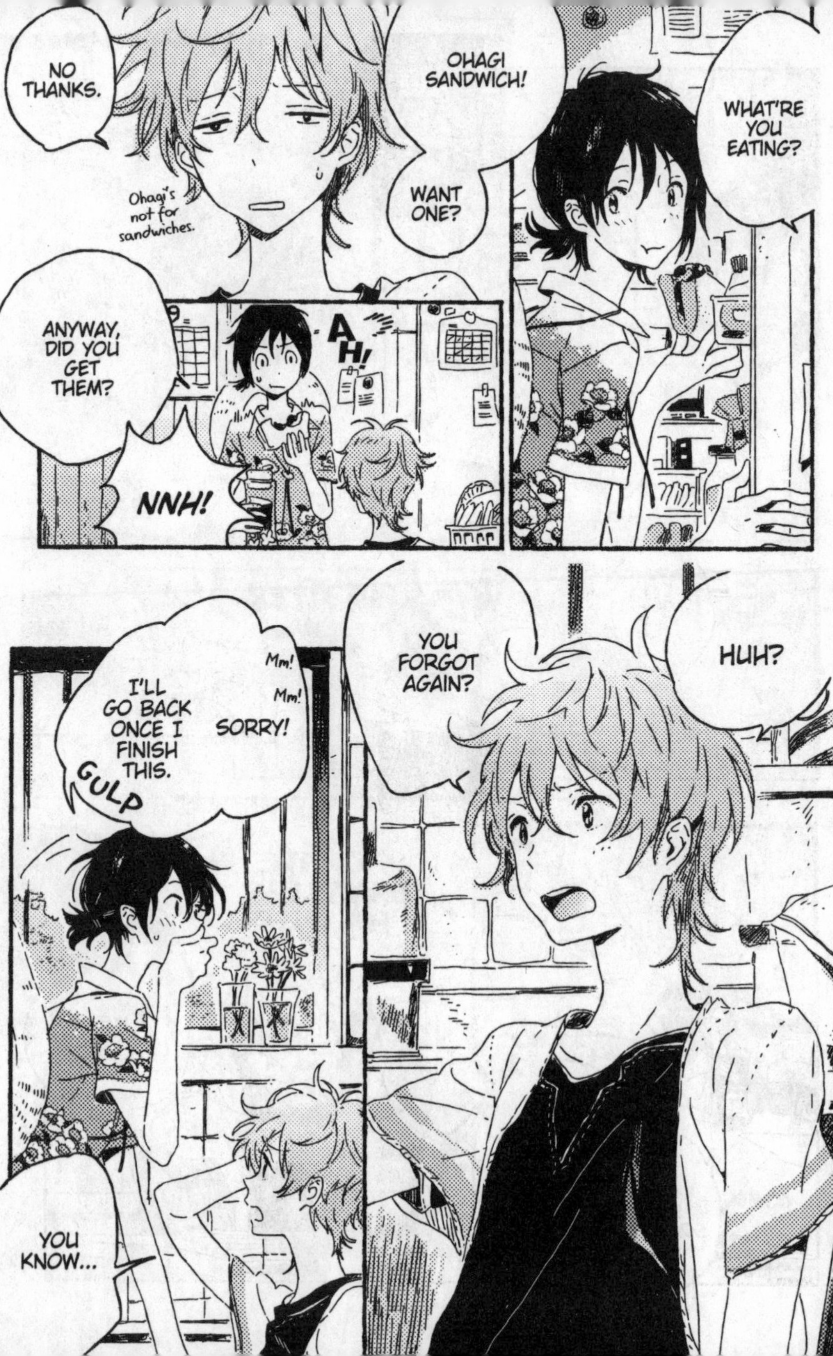
WHAT'RE YOU EATING?
OHAGI SANDWICH!
WANT ONE?
NO THANKS.
Ohagi's not for sandwiches.
ANYWAY, DID YOU GET THEM?
AH!
NNH!
HUH?
YOU FORGOT AGAIN?
Mm!
Mm!
SORRY!
I'LL GO BACK ONCE I FINISH THIS.
GULP
YOU KNOW...

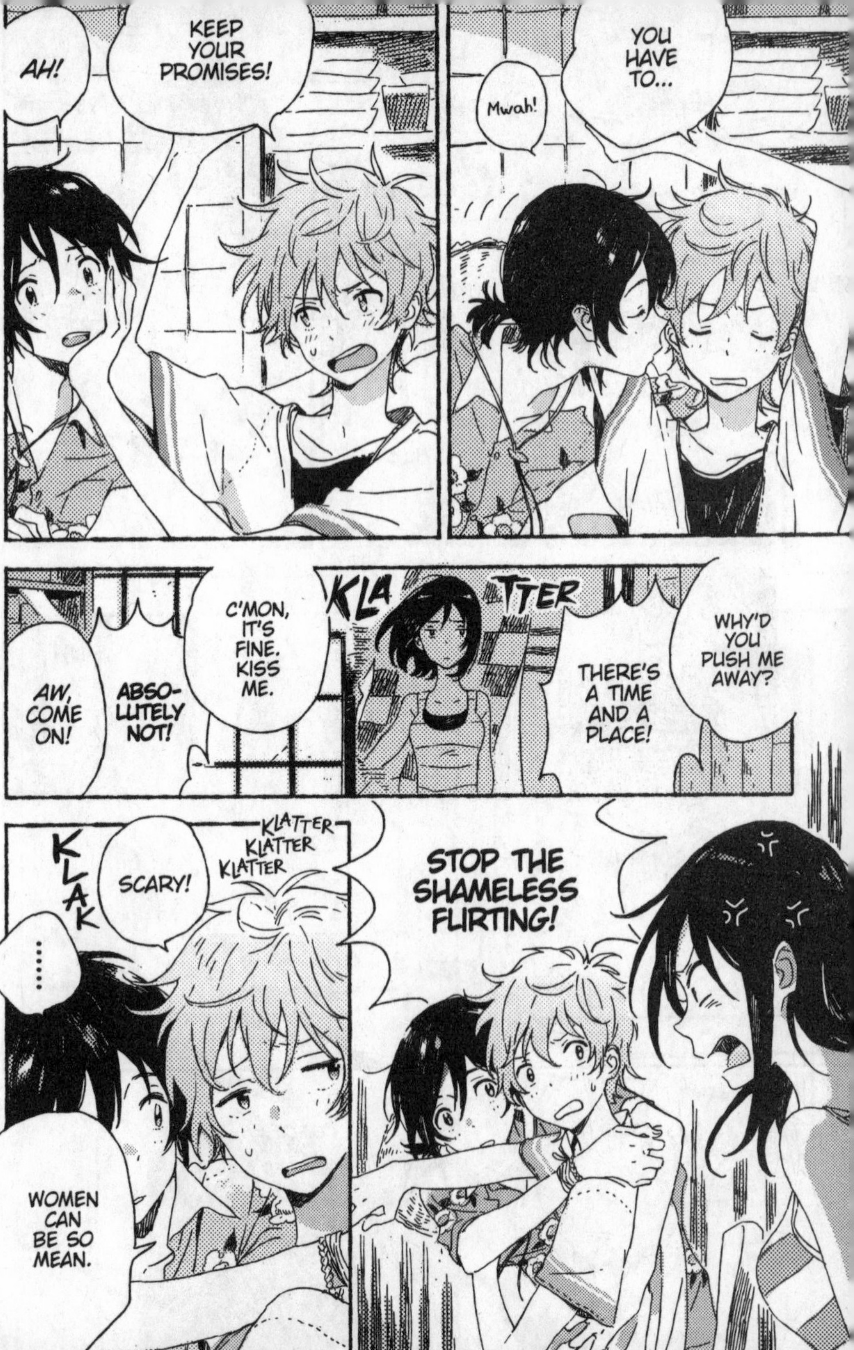
YOU HAVE TO...
Mwah!
KEEP YOUR PROMISES!
AH!
WHY'D YOU PUSH ME AWAY?
THERE'S A TIME AND A PLACE!
KLATTER
C'MON, IT'S FINE. KISS ME.
ABSO-LUTELY NOT!
AW, COME ON!
STOP THE SHAMELESS FLIRTING!
KLATTER KLATTER KLATTER
SCARY!
KLAK
......
WOMEN CAN BE SO MEAN.

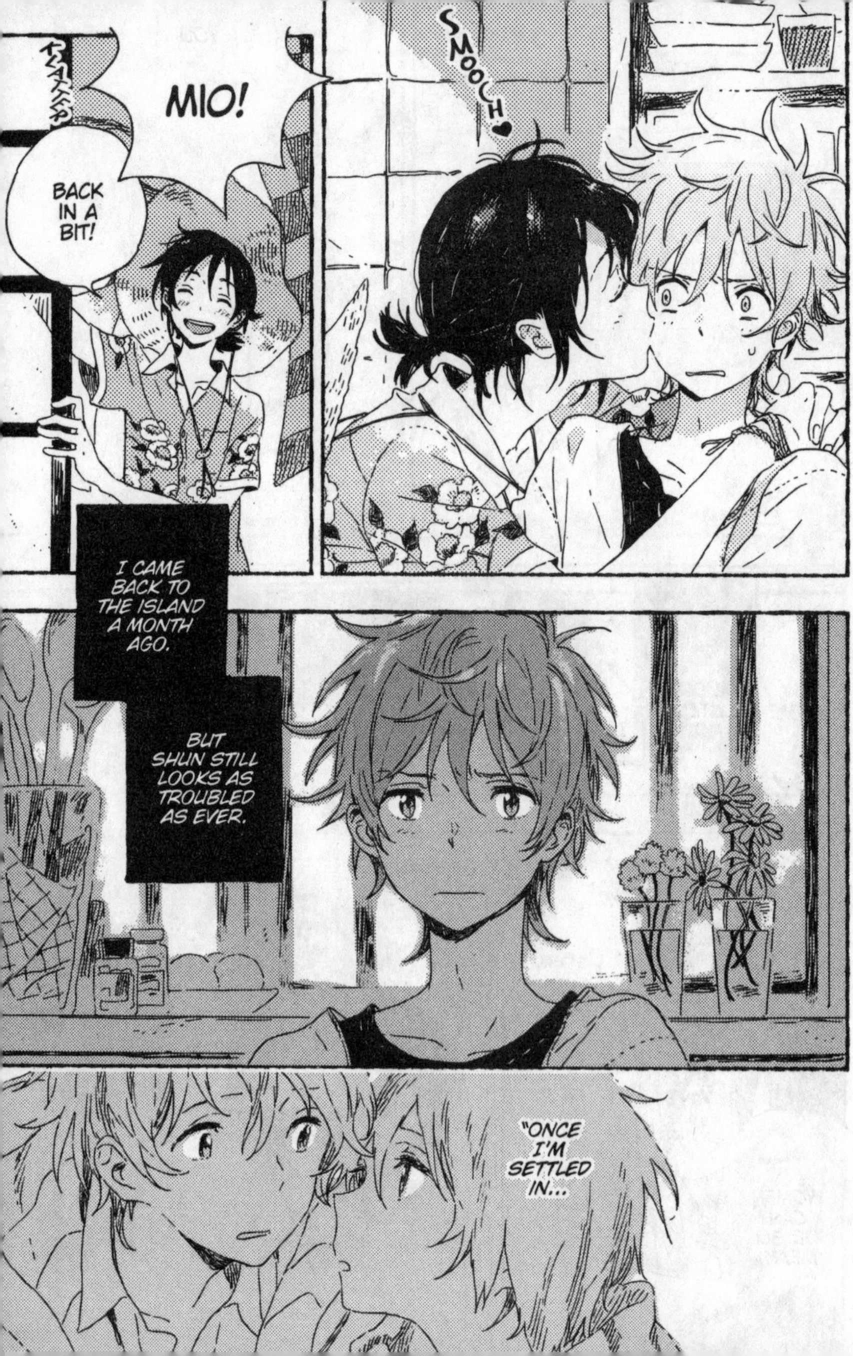
SMOOCH♥
KLATTER
MIO!
BACK IN A BIT!
I CAME BACK TO THE ISLAND A MONTH AGO.
BUT SHUN STILL LOOKS AS TROUBLED AS EVER.
"ONCE I'M SETTLED IN...

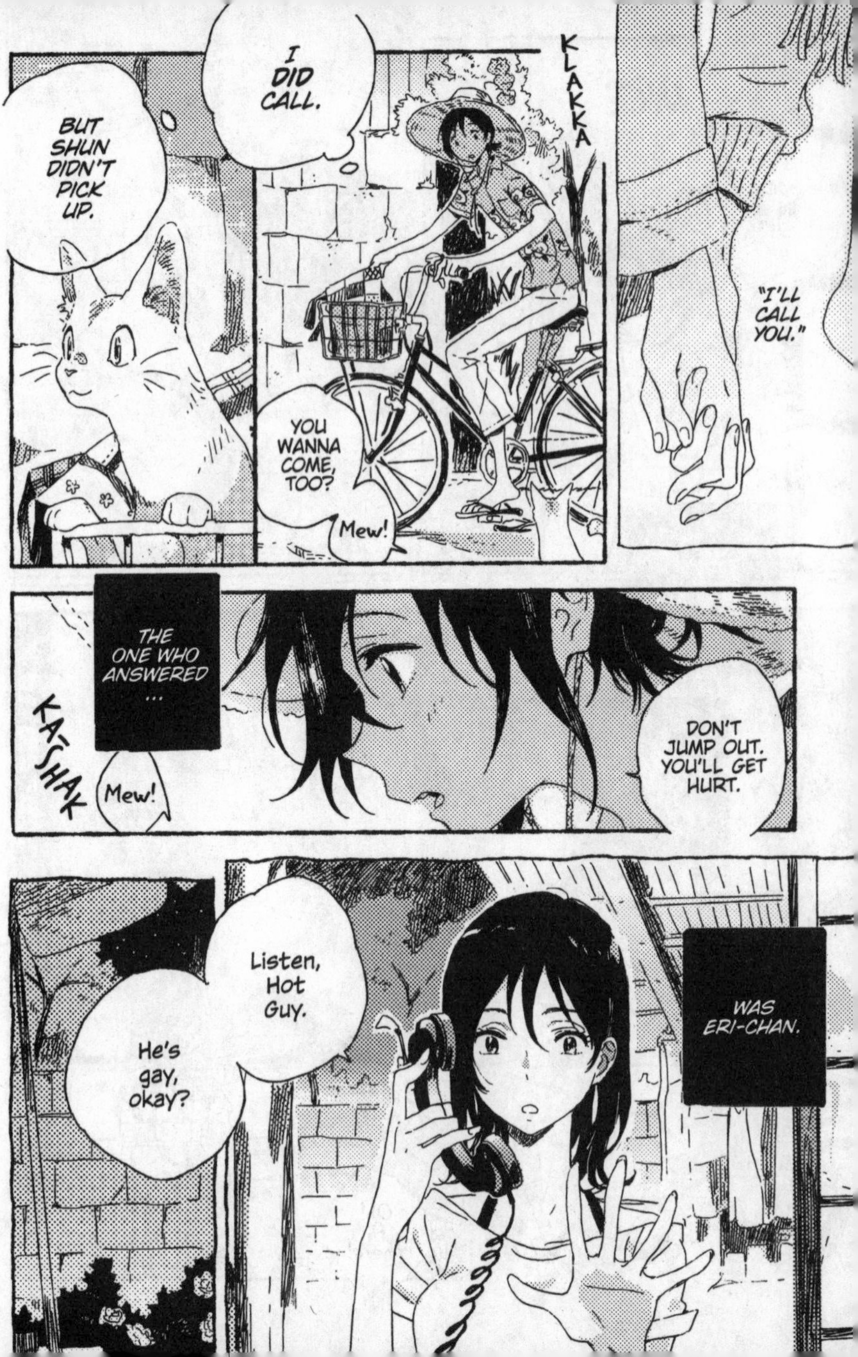
"I'LL CALL YOU."
KLAKKA
YOU WANNA COME, TOO?
Mew!
I DID CALL.
BUT SHUN DIDN'T PICK UP.
DON'T JUMP OUT. YOU'LL GET HURT.
THE ONE WHO ANSWERED ...
KA'SHAK
Mew!
WAS ERI-CHAN.
Listen, Hot Guy.
He's gay, okay?

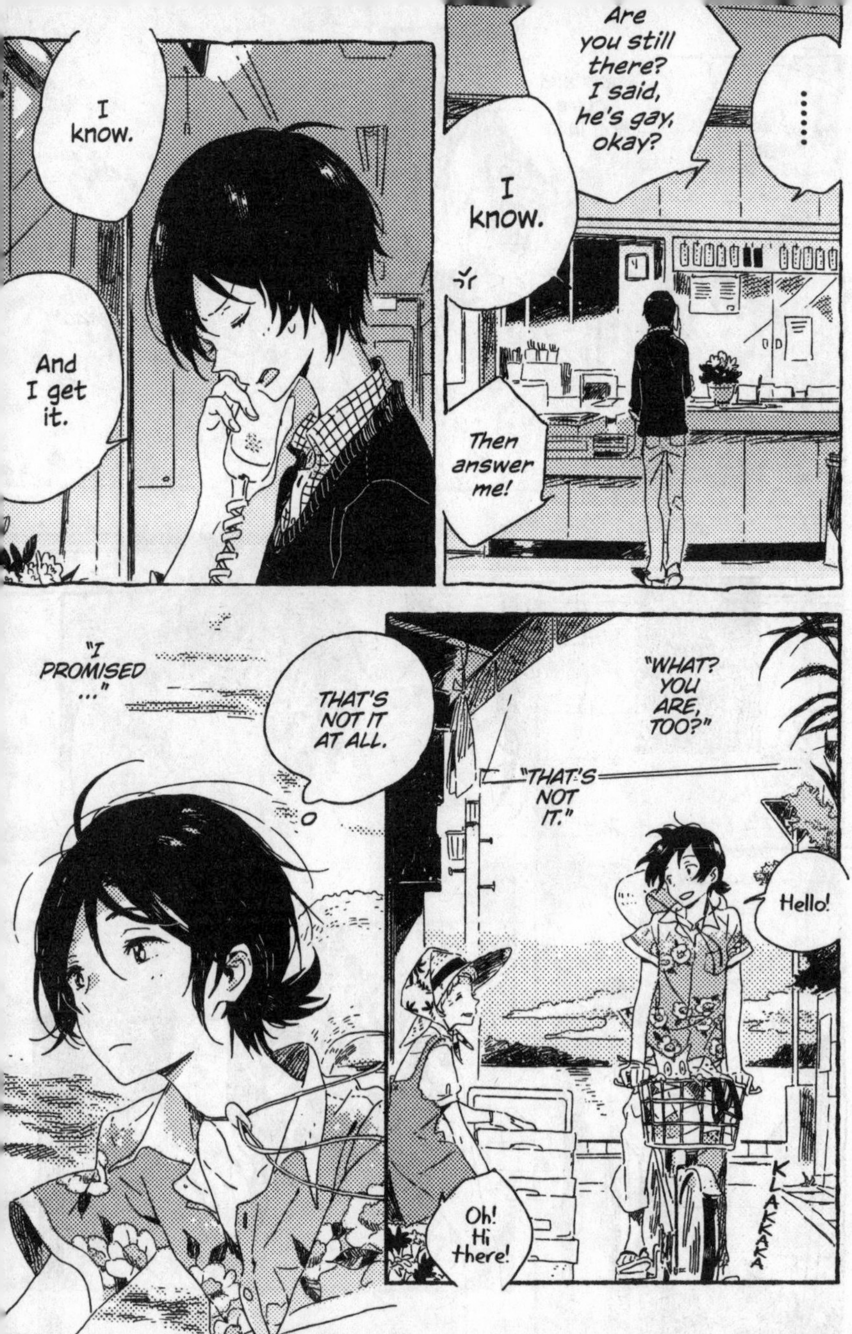

......
Are you still there? I said, he's gay, okay?
I know.
Then answer me!
I know.
And I get it.
"WHAT? YOU ARE, TOO?"
"THAT'S NOT IT."
Hello!
Oh! Hi there!
KLAKKAKA
THAT'S NOT IT AT ALL.
"I PROMISED ..."

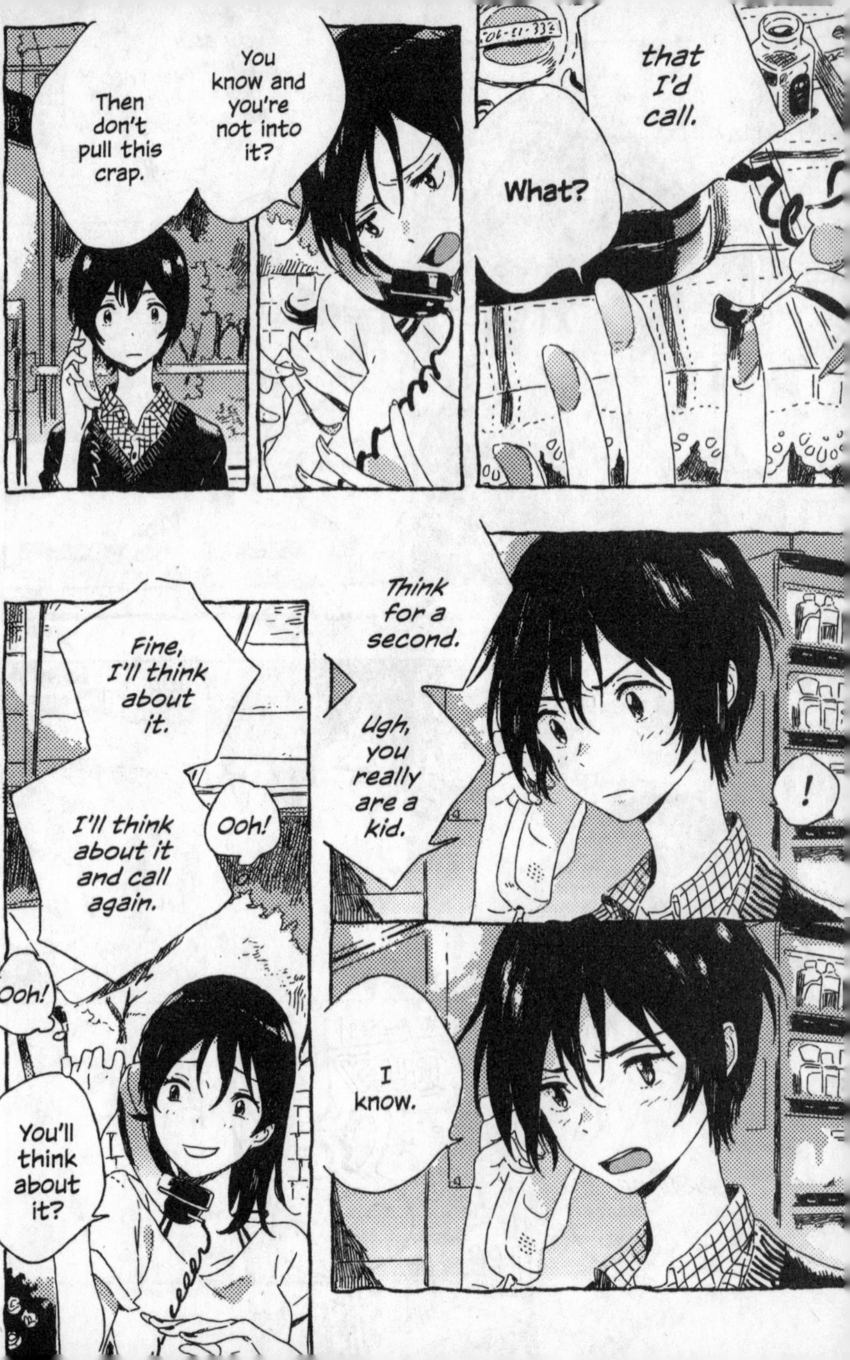

that I'd call.
What?
You know and you're not into it?
Then don't pull this crap.
Think for a second.
Ugh, you really are a kid.
!
I know.
Fine, I'll think about it.
Ooh!
I'll think about it and call again.
Ooh!
You'll think about it?

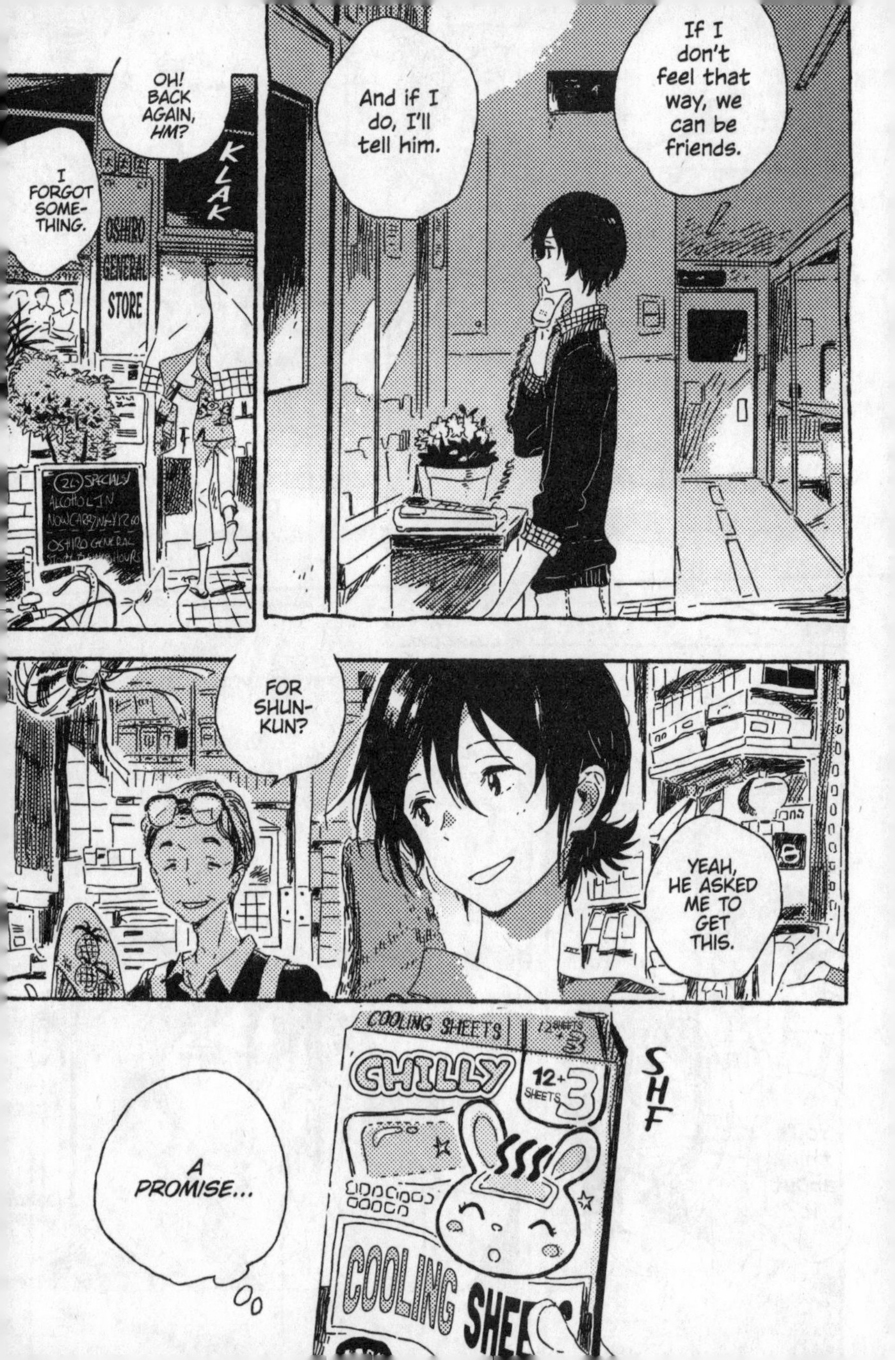
If I don't feel that way, we can be friends.
And if I do, I'll tell him.
OH! BACK AGAIN, HM?
KLAK
I FORGOT SOMETHING.
OSHIRO GENERAL STORE
FOR SHUN-KUN?
YEAH, HE ASKED ME TO GET THIS.
COOLING SHEETS
CHILLY
12+3 SHEETS
SHF
A PROMISE...

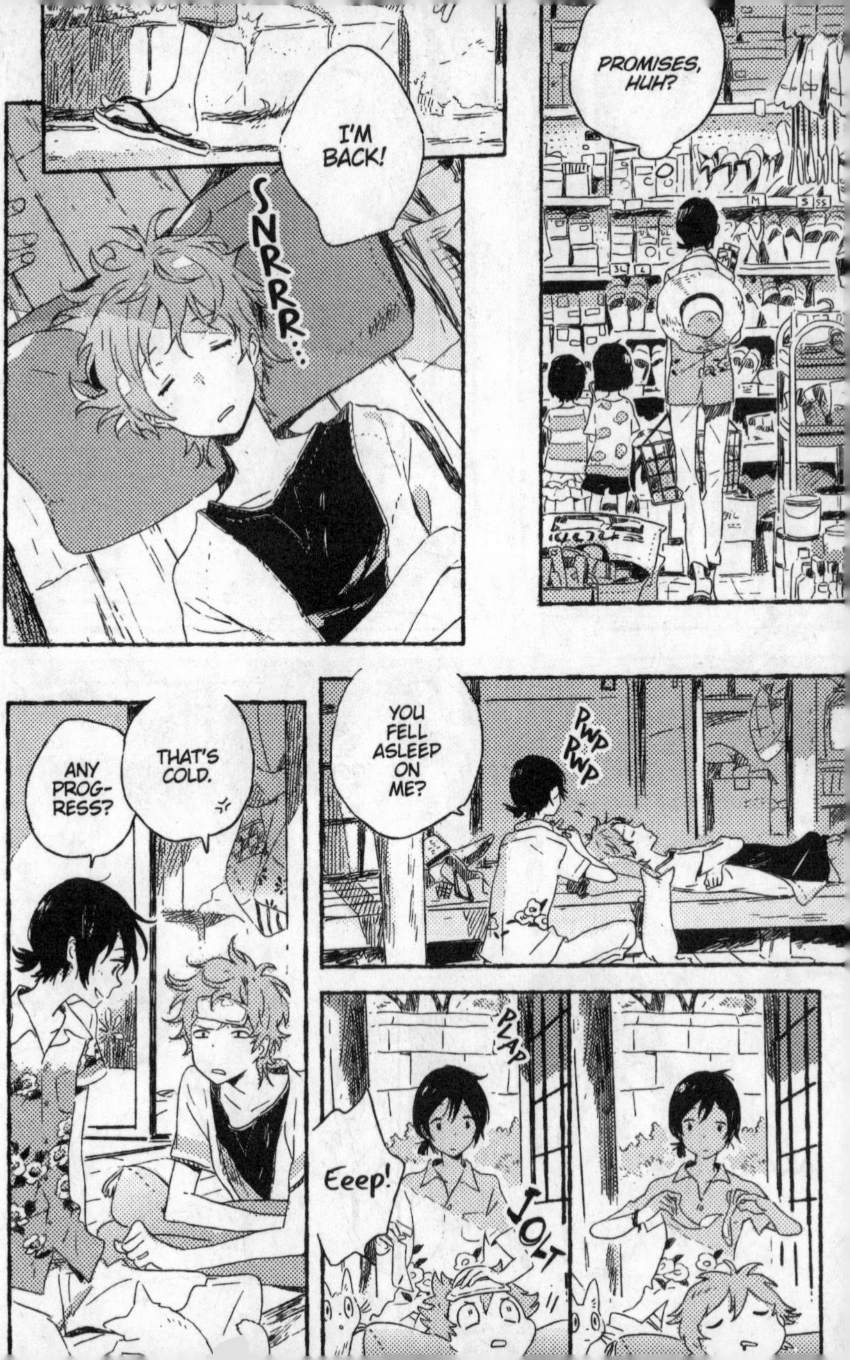
PROMISES, HUH?
I'M BACK!
SNRRR...
YOU FELL ASLEEP ON ME?
PWP RWP
PLAP
Eeep!
JOLT
THAT'S COLD.
ANY PROG-RESS?

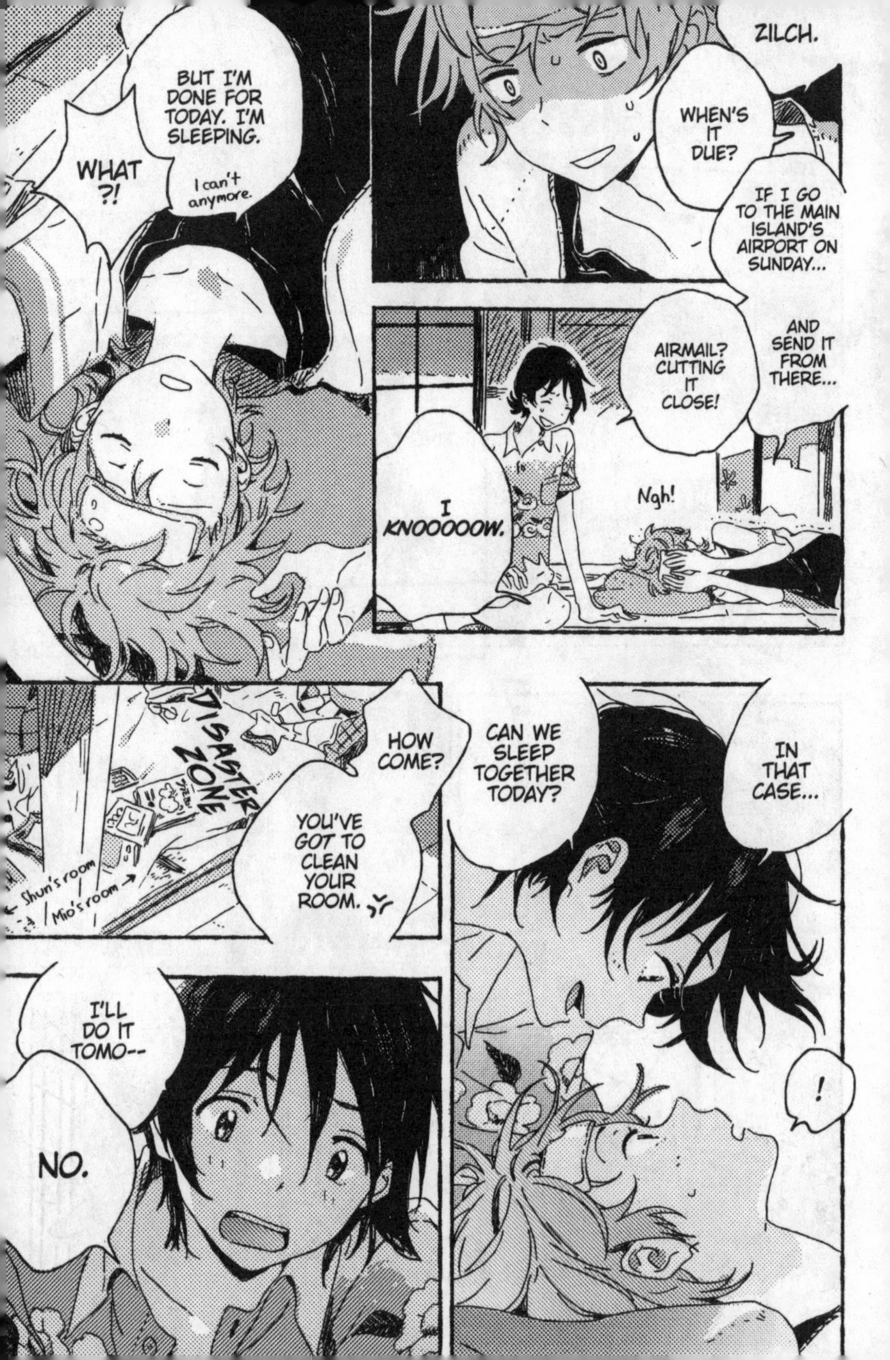
ZILCH.
WHEN'S IT DUE?
IF I GO TO THE MAIN ISLAND'S AIRPORT ON SUNDAY...
AND SEND IT FROM THERE...
AIRMAIL? CUTTING IT CLOSE!
Ngh!
I KNOOOOOW.
BUT I'M DONE FOR TODAY. I'M SLEEPING.
I can't anymore.
WHAT?!
IN THAT CASE...
CAN WE SLEEP TOGETHER TODAY?
!
HOW COME?
YOU'VE GOT TO CLEAN YOUR ROOM.
DISASTER ZONE
← Shun's room
Mio's room →
I'LL DO IT TOMO--
NO.

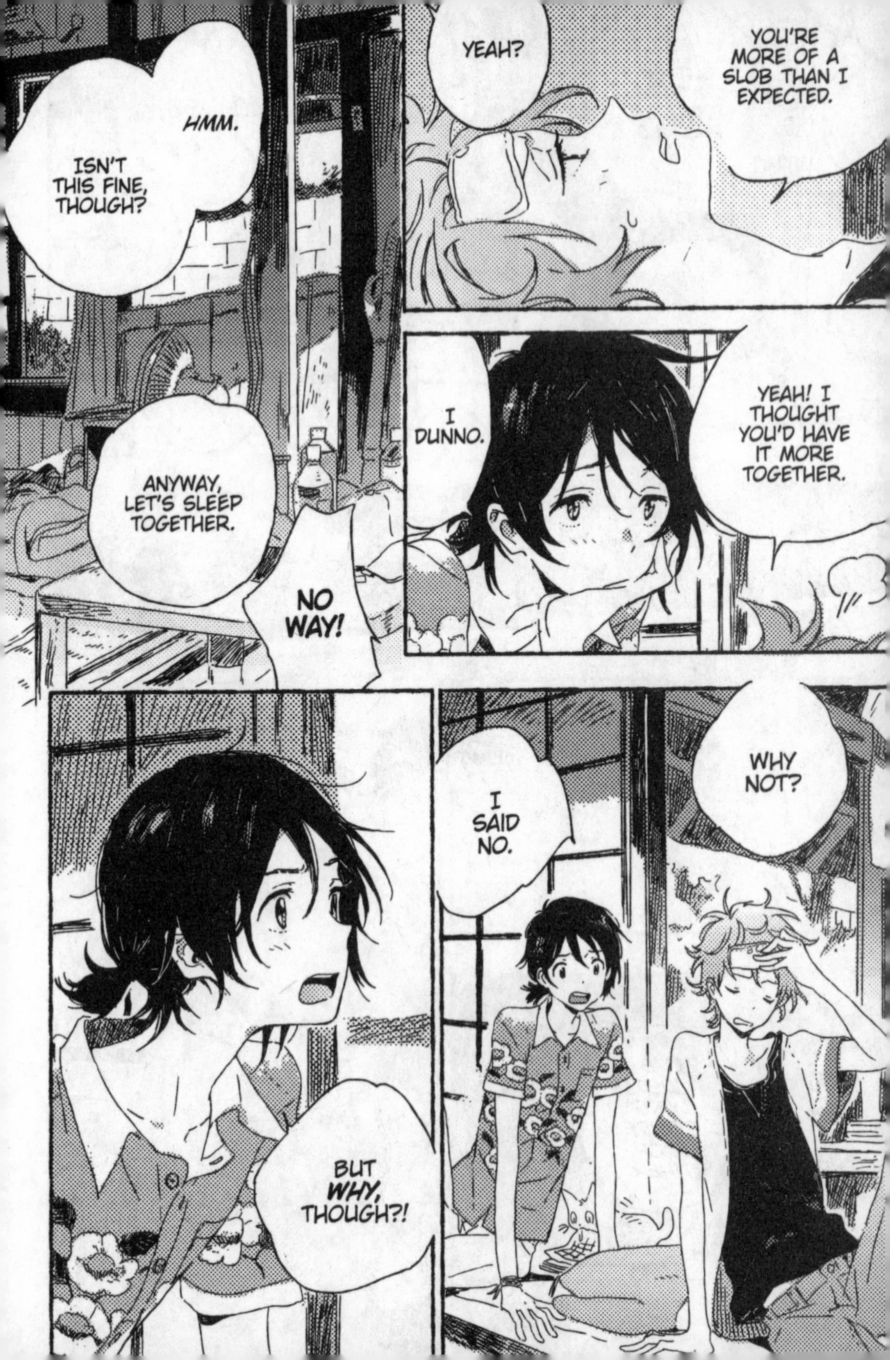
YOU'RE MORE OF A SLOB THAN I EXPECTED.
YEAH?
YEAH! I THOUGHT YOU'D HAVE IT MORE TOGETHER.
I DUNNO.
HMM.
ISN'T THIS FINE, THOUGH?
ANYWAY, LET'S SLEEP TOGETHER.
NO WAY!
WHY NOT?
I SAID NO.
BUT WHY, THOUGH?!

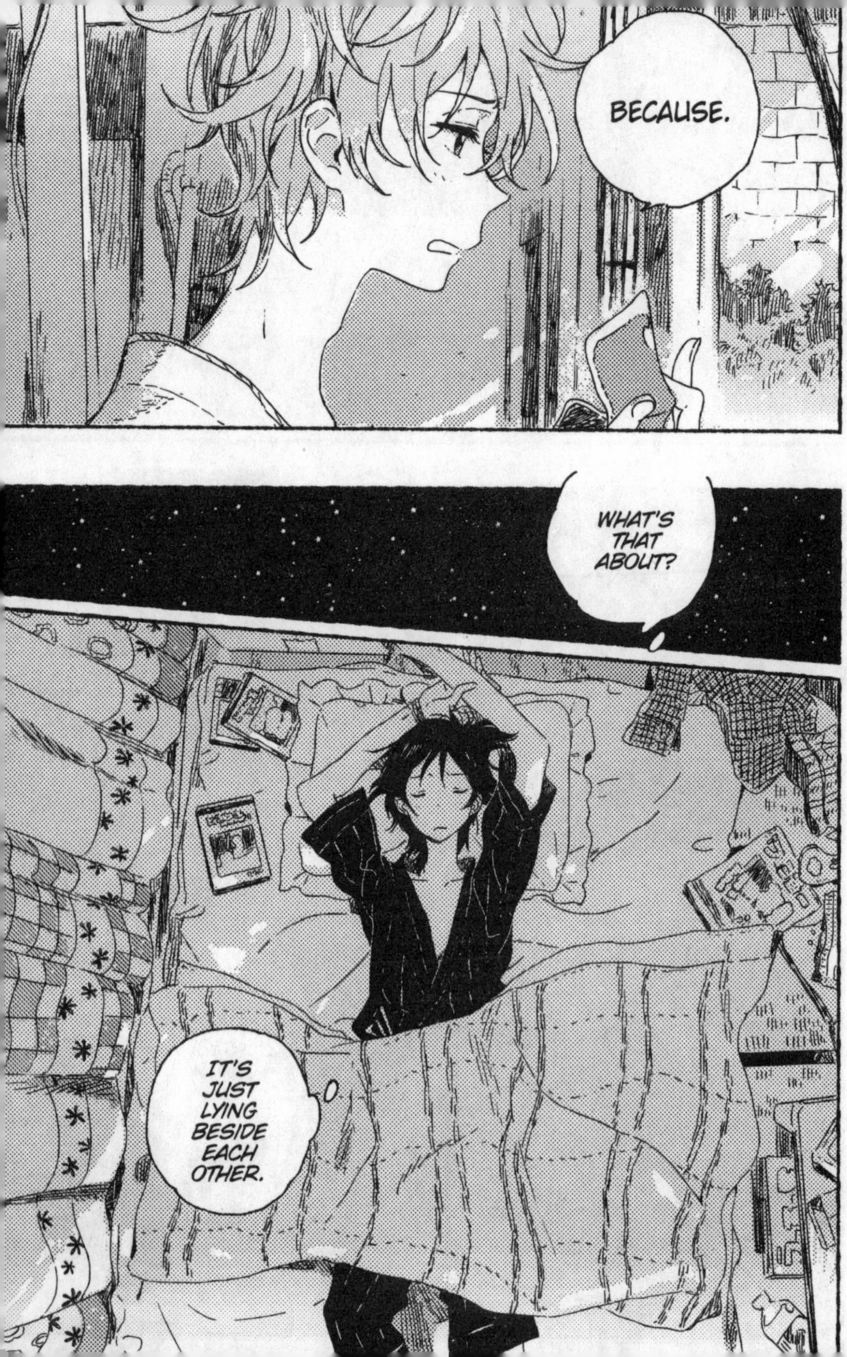
BECAUSE.
WHAT'S THAT ABOUT?
IT'S JUST LYING BESIDE EACH OTHER.

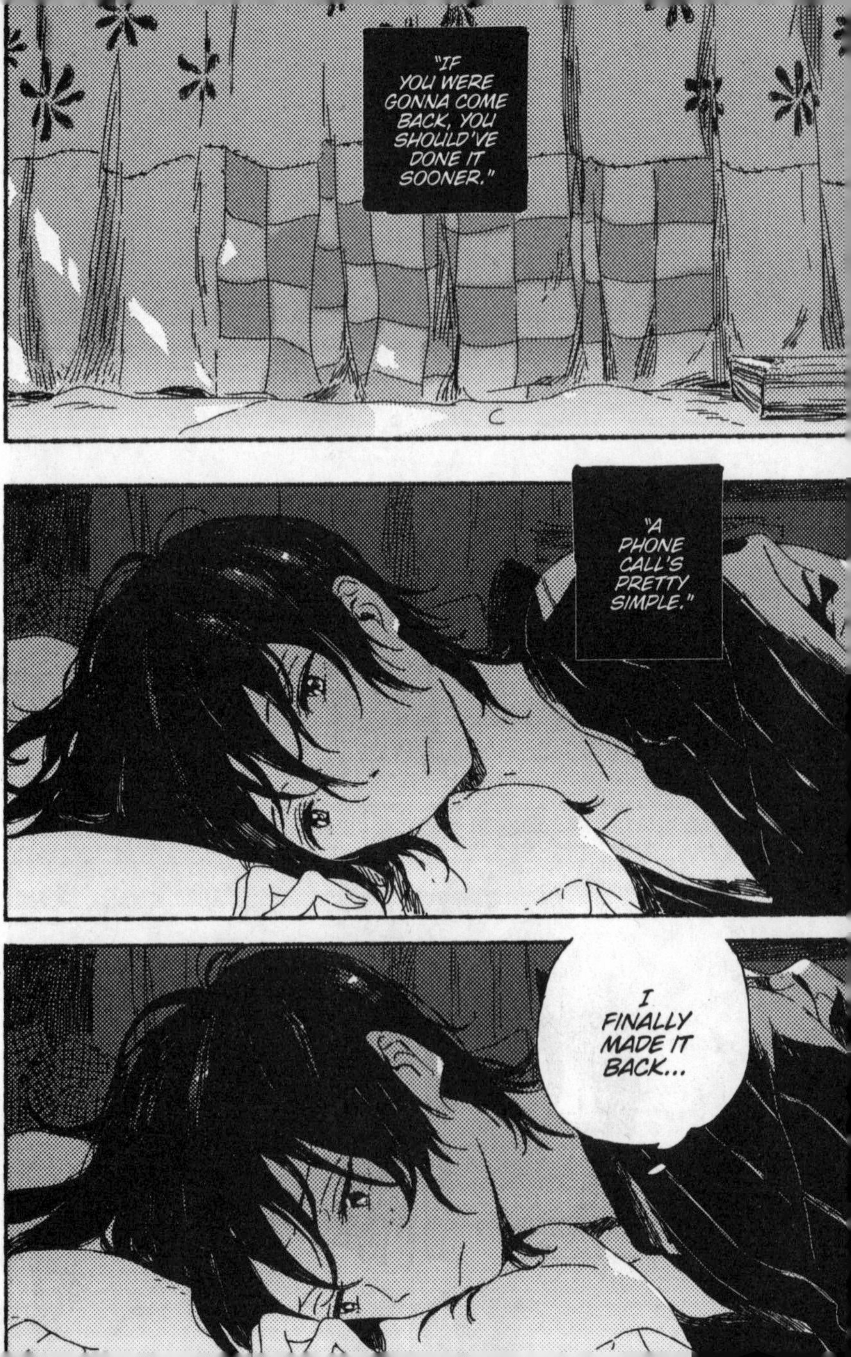
"IF YOU WERE GONNA COME BACK, YOU SHOULD'VE DONE IT SOONER."
"A PHONE CALL'S PRETTY SIMPLE."
I FINALLY MADE IT BACK...

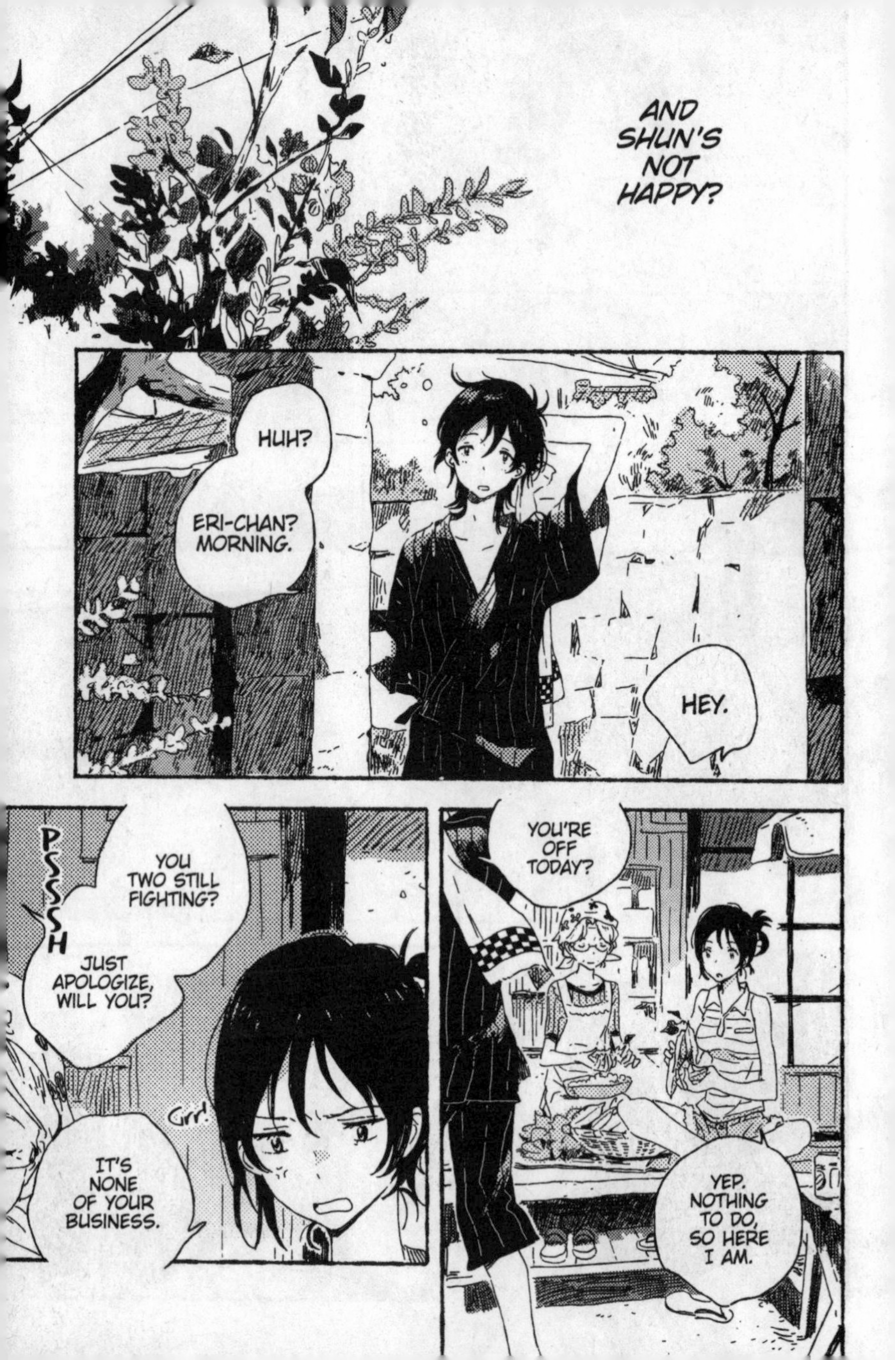
AND SHUN'S NOT HAPPY?
HEY.
HUH?
ERI-CHAN? MORNING.
YOU'RE OFF TODAY?
YEP. NOTHING TO DO, SO HERE I AM.
YOU TWO STILL FIGHTING?
PSSSH
JUST APOLOGIZE, WILL YOU?
Grr!
IT'S NONE OF YOUR BUSINESS.

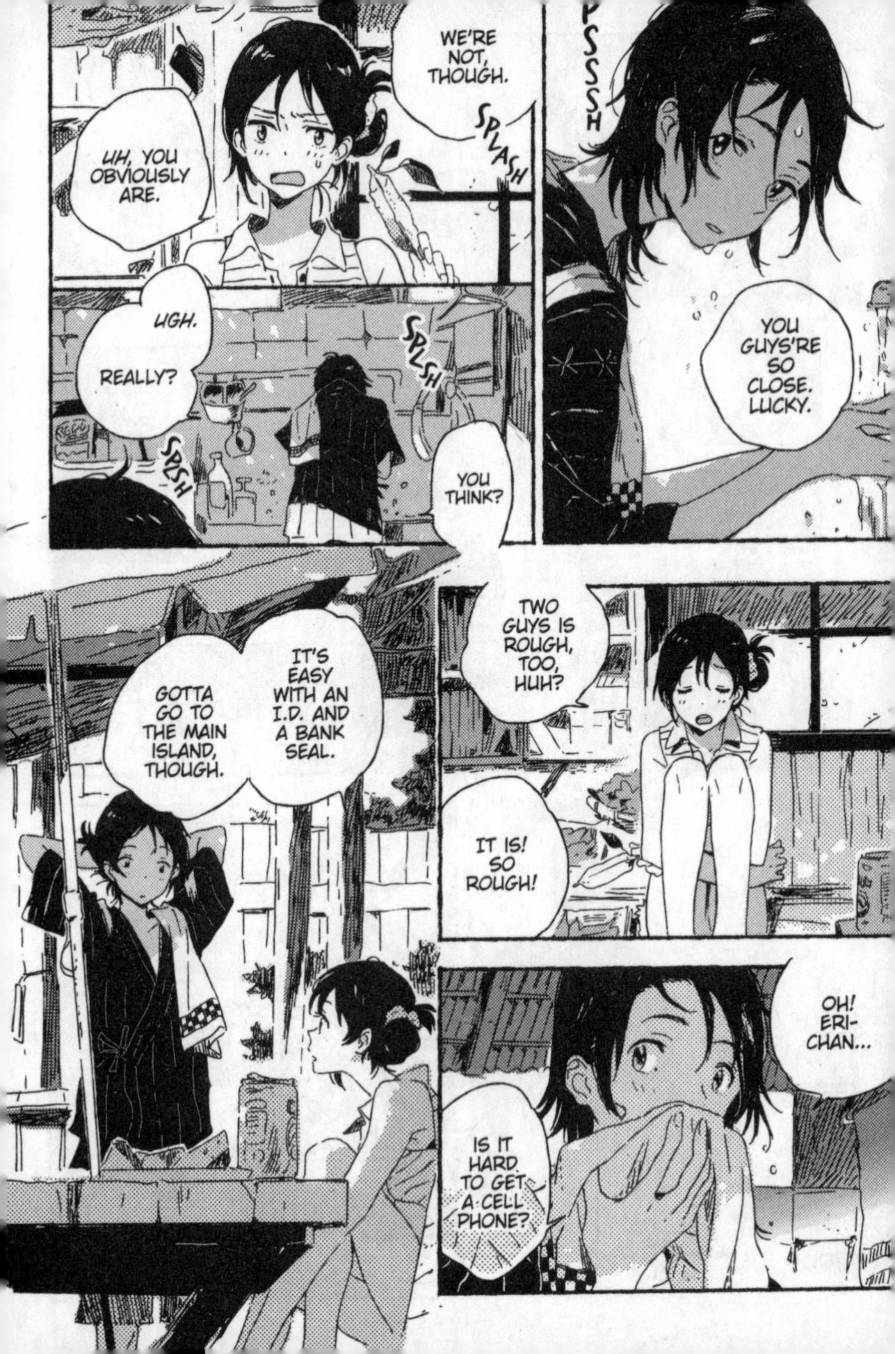
PSSSH
YOU GUYS'RE SO CLOSE. LUCKY.
WE'RE NOT, THOUGH.
SPLASH
UH, YOU OBVIOUSLY ARE.
SPLSH
UGH.
REALLY?
SPLSH
YOU THINK?
TWO GUYS IS ROUGH, TOO, HUH?
IT IS! SO ROUGH!
OH! ERI-CHAN...
IS IT HARD TO GET A CELL PHONE?
IT'S EASY WITH AN I.D. AND A BANK SEAL.
GOTTA GO TO THE MAIN ISLAND, THOUGH.

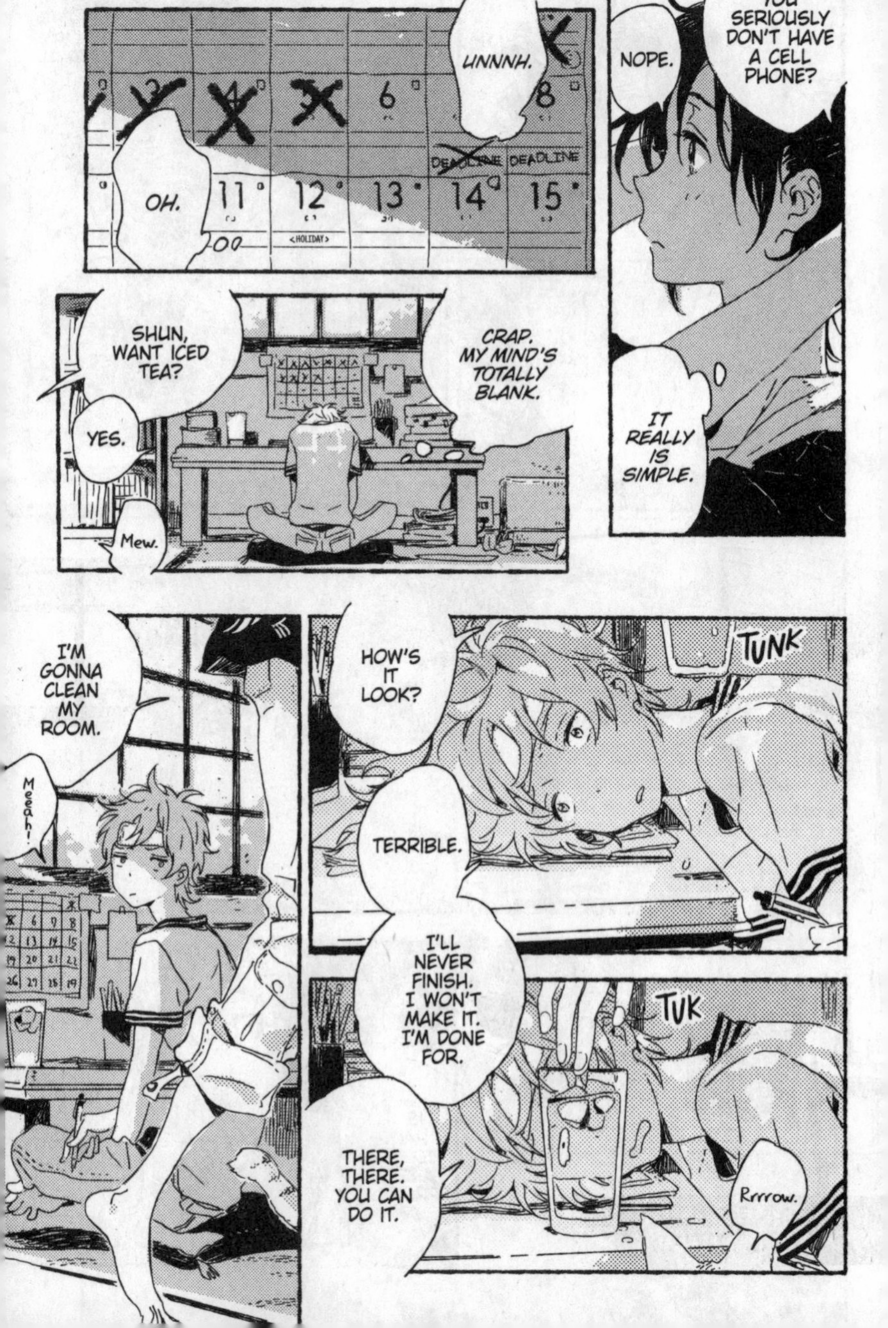
YOU SERIOUSLY DON'T HAVE A CELL PHONE?
NOPE.
IT REALLY IS SIMPLE.
UNNNH.
DEADLINE
DEADLINE
OH.
<HOLIDAY>
CRAP. MY MIND'S TOTALLY BLANK.
SHUN, WANT ICED TEA?
YES.
Mew.
TUNK
HOW'S IT LOOK?
TERRIBLE.
TUK
I'LL NEVER FINISH. I WON'T MAKE IT. I'M DONE FOR.
Rrrrow.
THERE, THERE. YOU CAN DO IT.
I'M GONNA CLEAN MY ROOM.
Meeah!

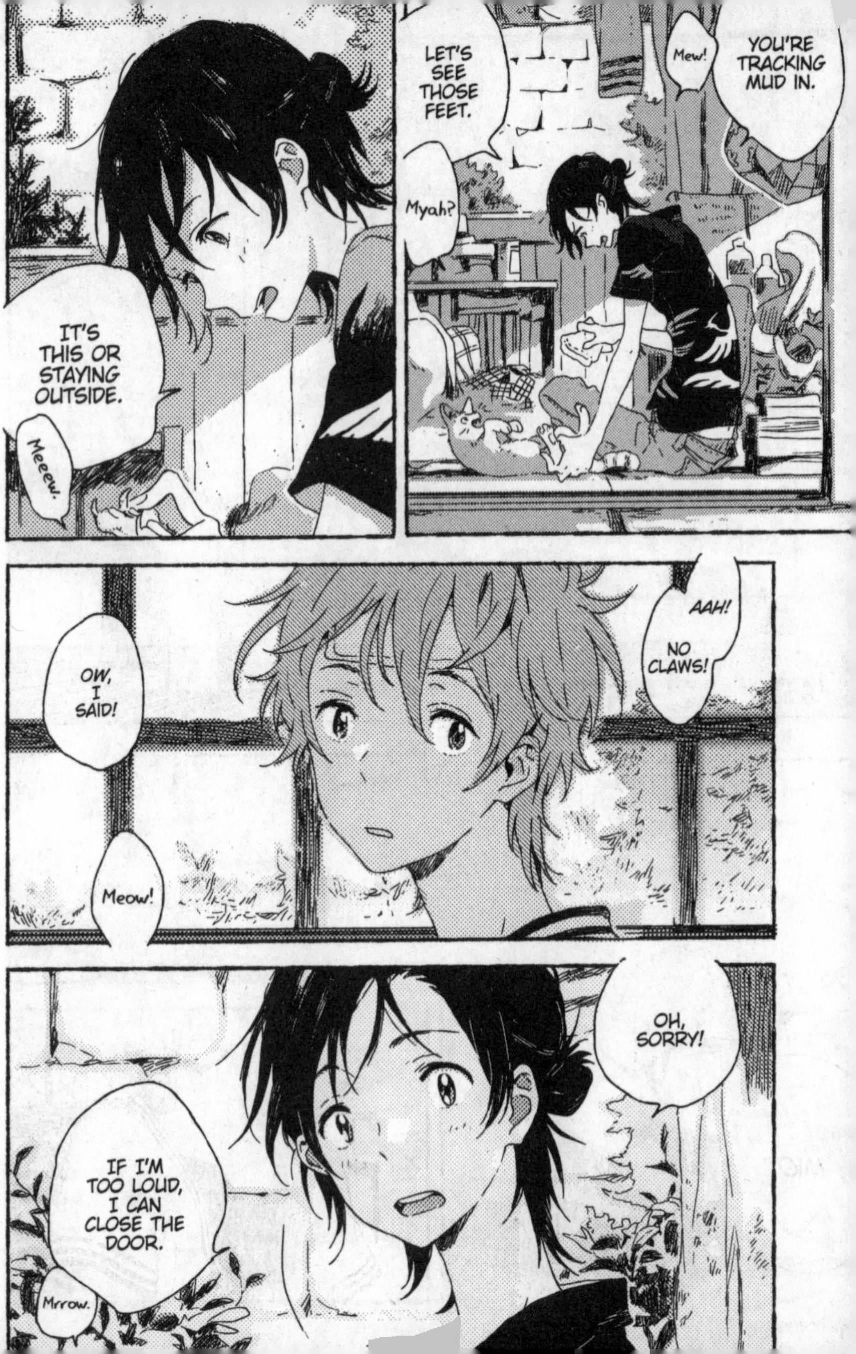
YOU'RE TRACKING MUD IN.
Mew!
LET'S SEE THOSE FEET.
Myah?
IT'S THIS OR STAYING OUTSIDE.
Meeew.
AAH!
NO CLAWS!
OW, I SAID!
Meow!
OH, SORRY!
IF I'M TOO LOUD, I CAN CLOSE THE DOOR.
Mrrow.

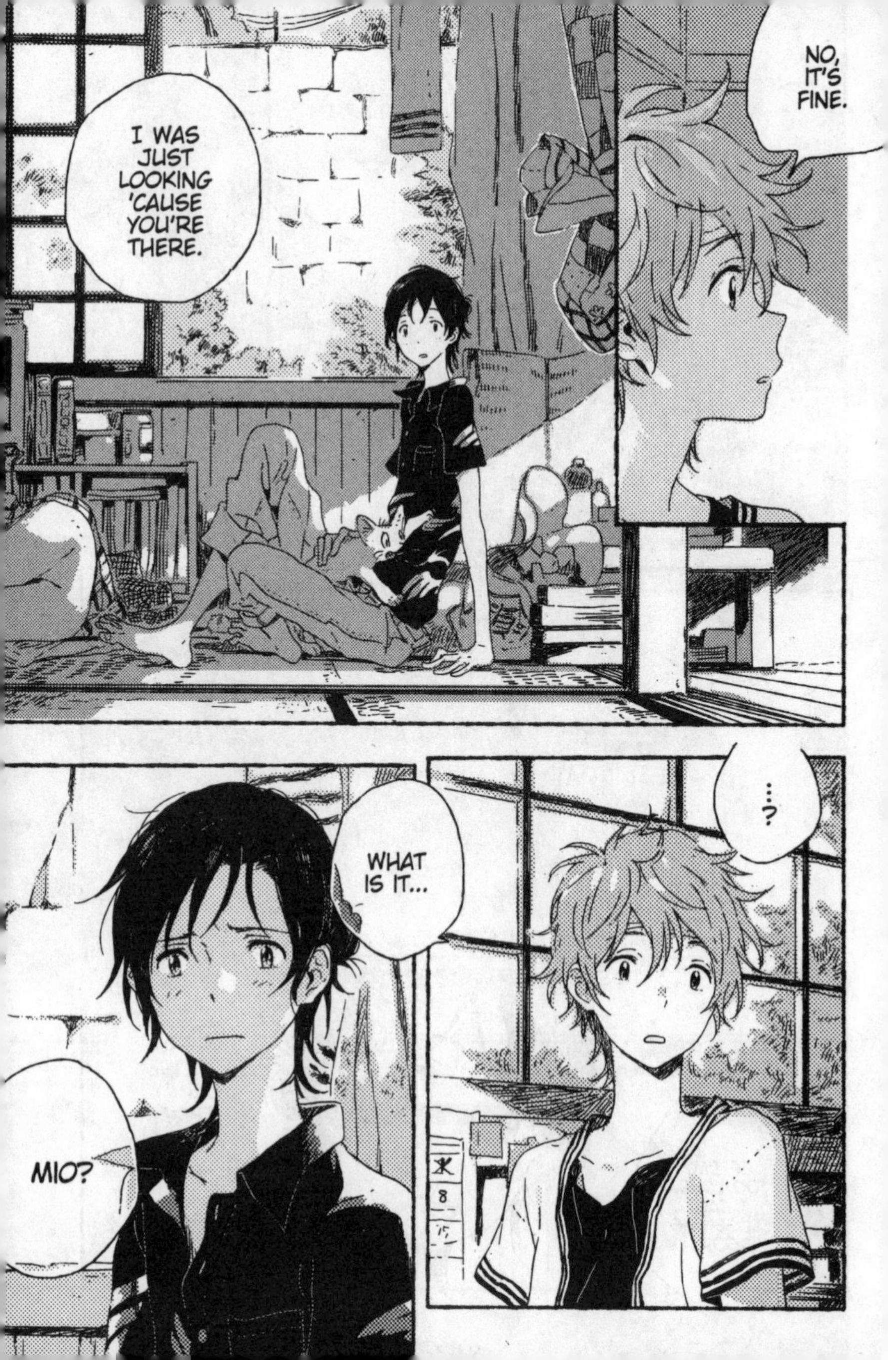
NO, IT'S FINE.
I WAS JUST LOOKING 'CAUSE YOU'RE THERE.
...?
WHAT IS IT...
MIO?

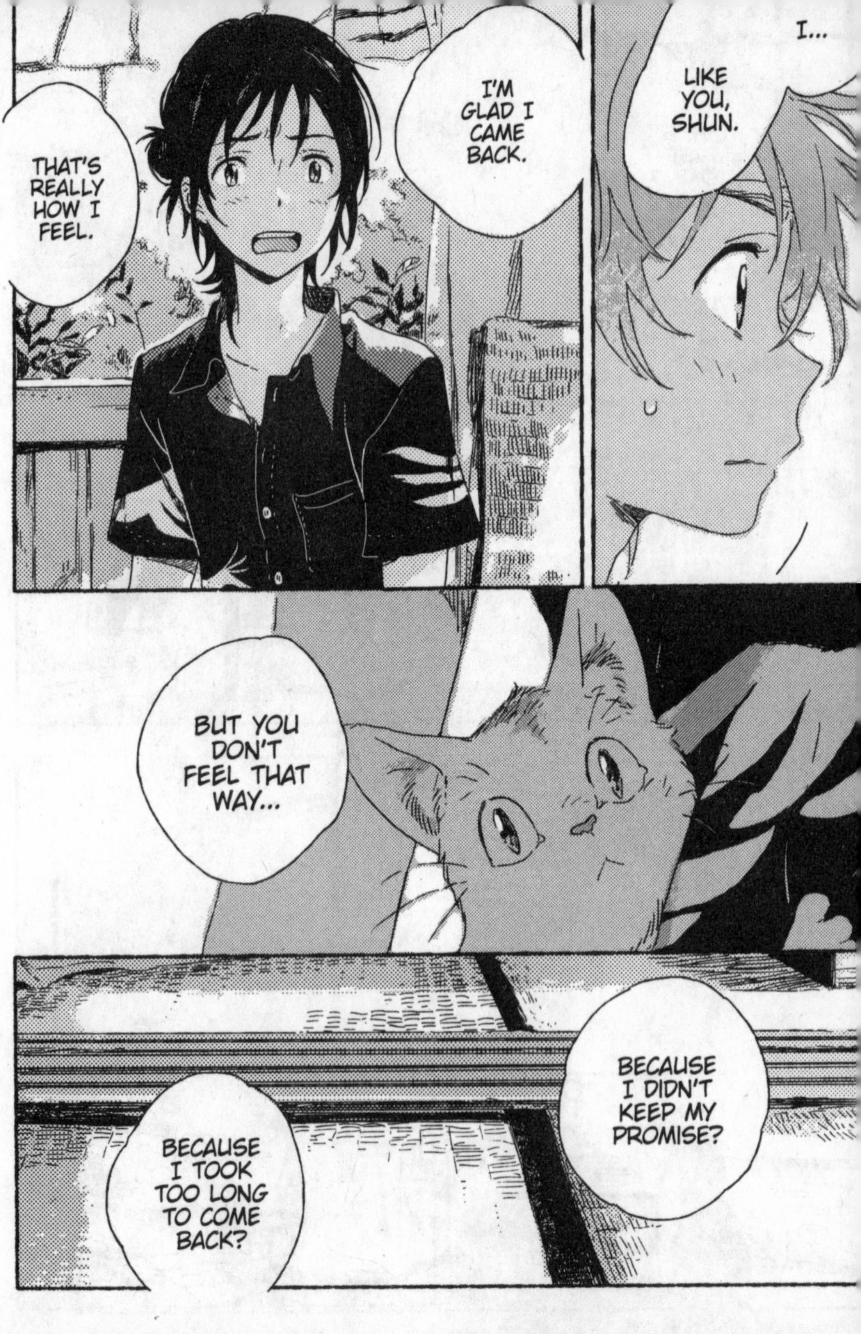
I...
LIKE YOU, SHUN.
I'M GLAD I CAME BACK.
THAT'S REALLY HOW I FEEL.
BUT YOU DON'T FEEL THAT WAY...
BECAUSE I DIDN'T KEEP MY PROMISE?
BECAUSE I TOOK TOO LONG TO COME BACK?

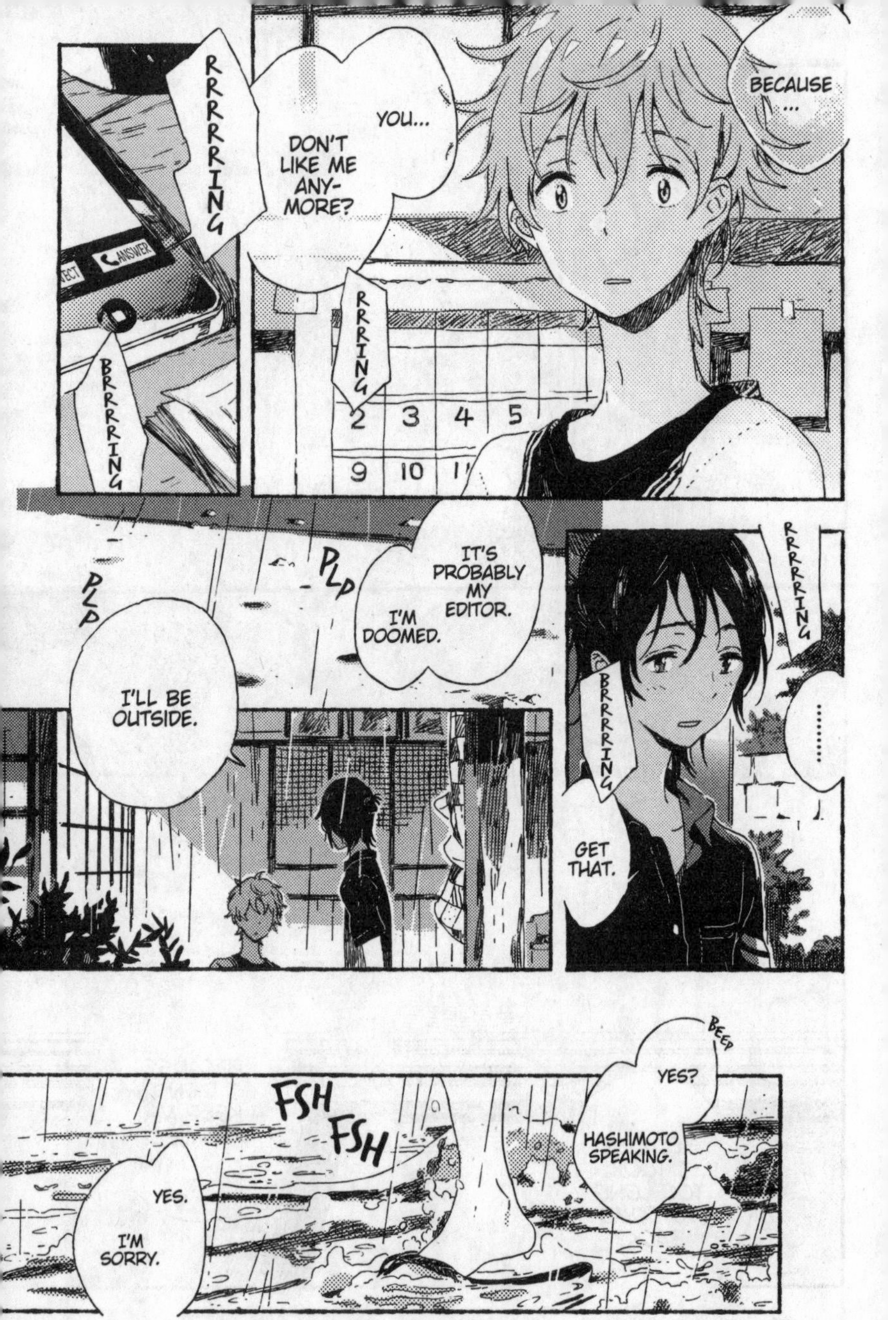
BECAUSE ...
YOU...
DON'T LIKE ME ANY-MORE?
RRRING
RRRRRRING
ANSWER
BRRRRRING
RRRRRING
......
IT'S PROBABLY MY EDITOR.
I'M DOOMED.
BRRRRRING
GET THAT.
PLP
PLP
I'LL BE OUTSIDE.
BEEP
YES?
HASHIMOTO SPEAKING.
FSH
FSH
YES.
I'M SORRY.

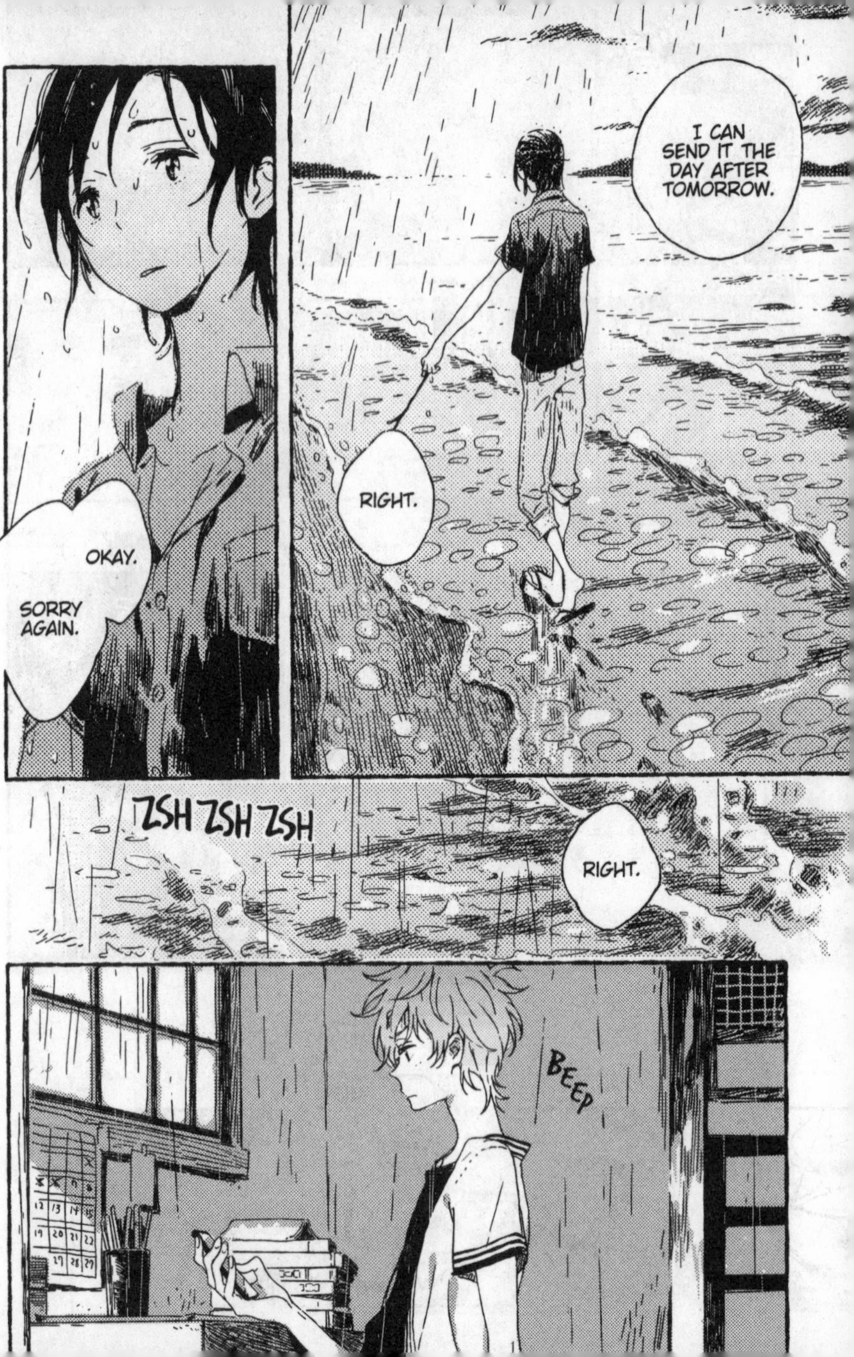
I CAN SEND IT THE DAY AFTER TOMORROW.
RIGHT.
OKAY.
SORRY AGAIN.
RIGHT.
ZSH ZSH ZSH
BEEP

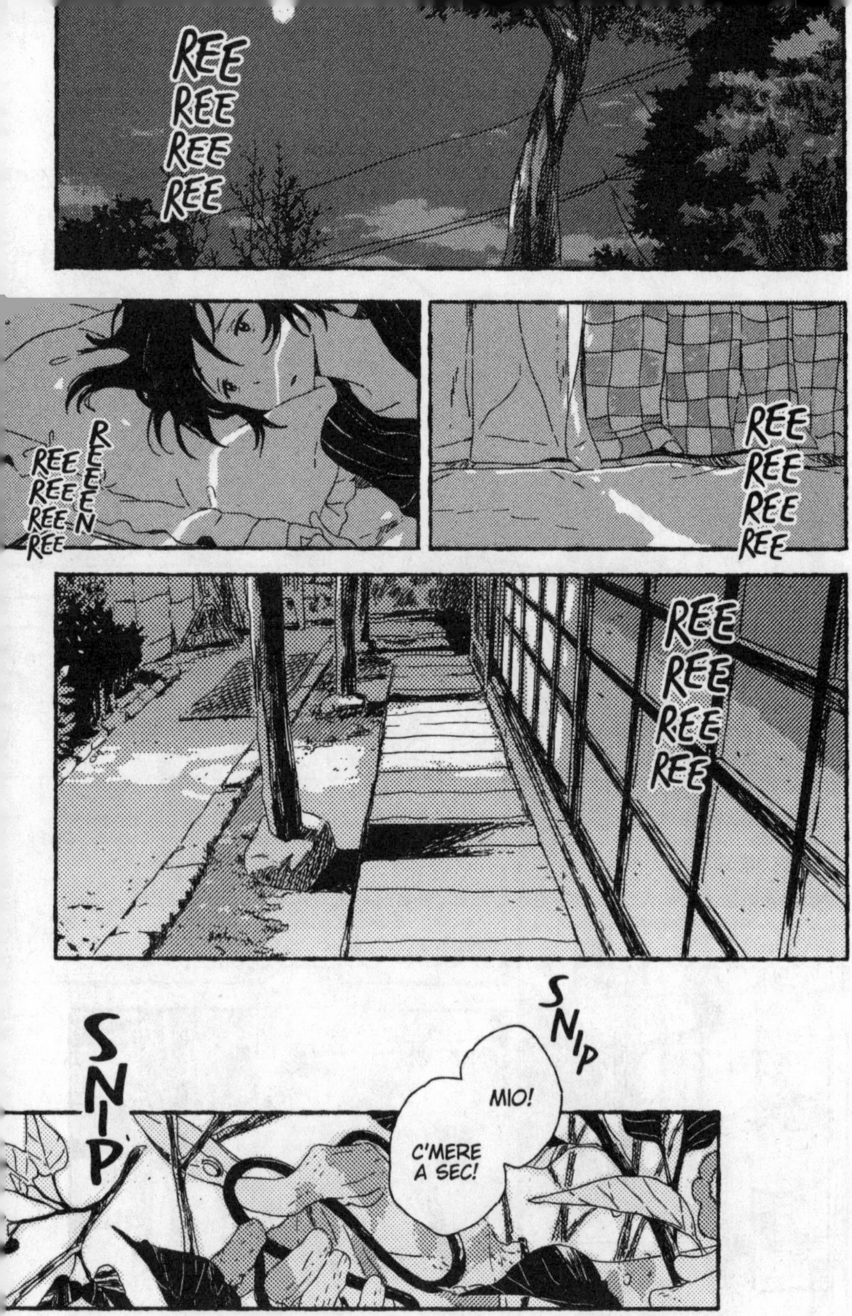
REE
REE
REE
REE
REE
REE
REE
REE
REEEEN
REE
REE
REE
REE
REE
REE
REE
REE
SNIP
MIO!
C'MERE A SEC!
SNIP

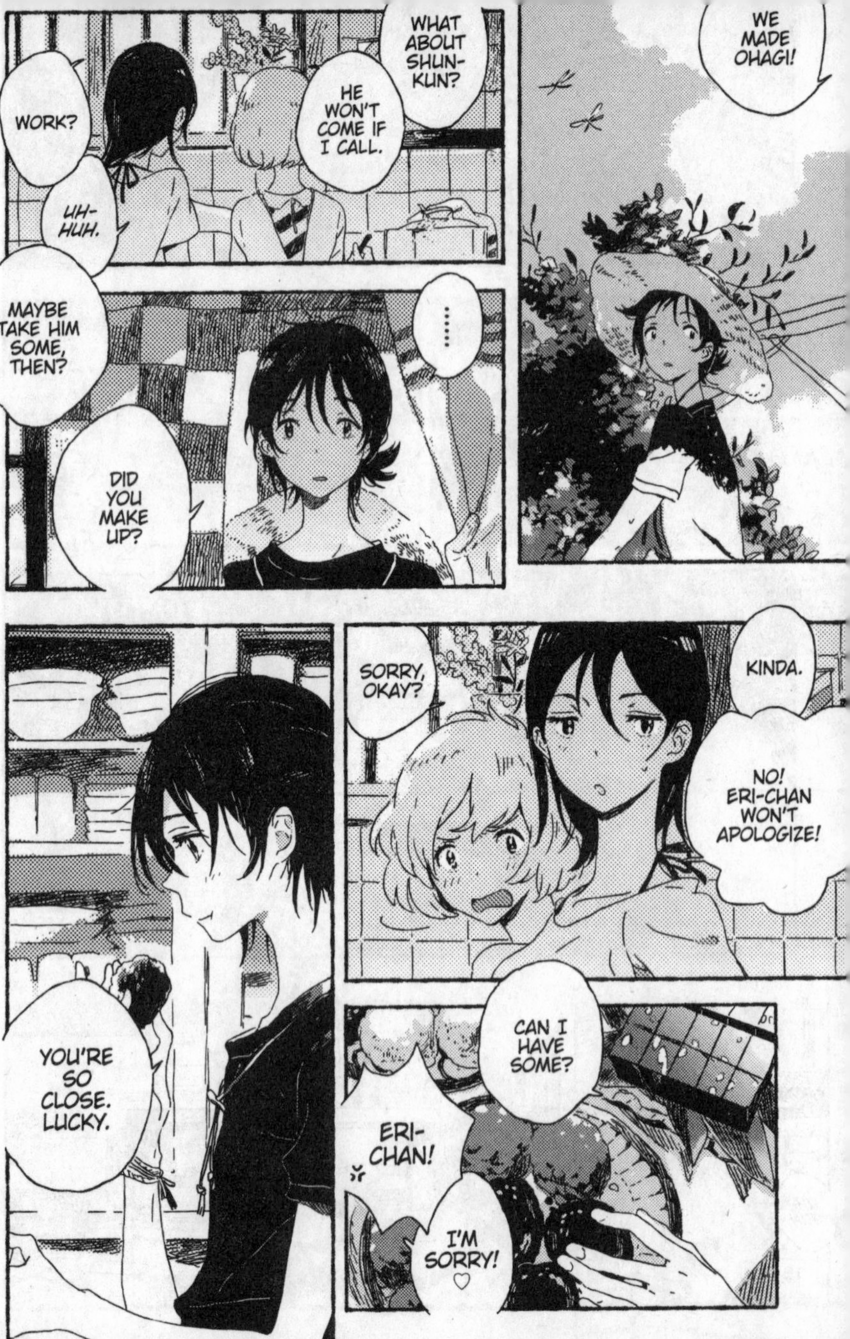
WE MADE OHAGI!
WHAT ABOUT SHUN-KUN?
HE WON'T COME IF I CALL.
WORK?
UH-HUH.
......
MAYBE TAKE HIM SOME, THEN?
DID YOU MAKE UP?
KINDA.
SORRY, OKAY?
NO! ERI-CHAN WON'T APOLOGIZE!
CAN I HAVE SOME?
ERI-CHAN!
I'M SORRY! ♡
YOU'RE SO CLOSE. LUCKY.

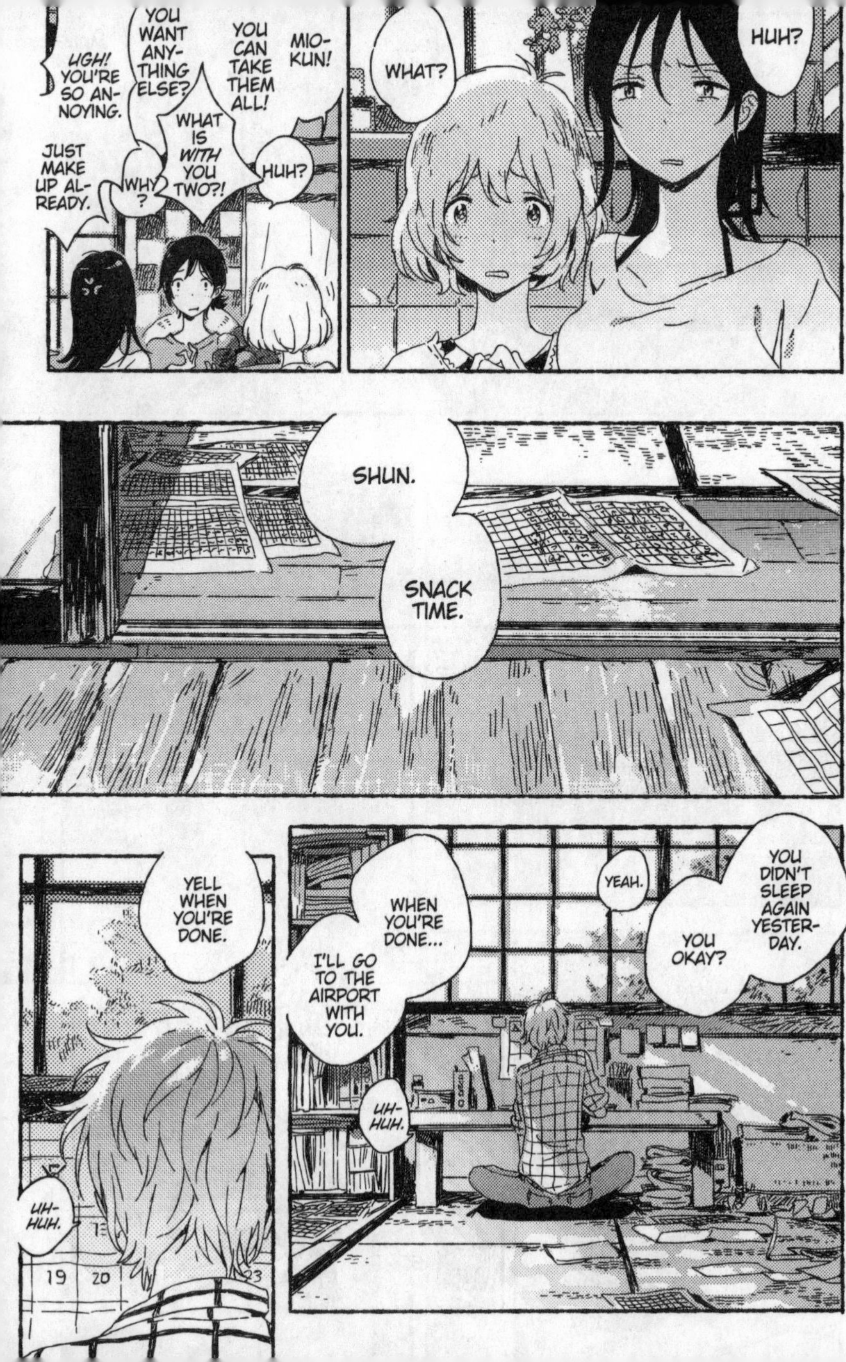
HUH?
WHAT?
MIO-KUN!
YOU CAN TAKE THEM ALL!
YOU WANT ANYTHING ELSE?
HUH?
WHAT IS WITH YOU TWO?!
WHY?
UGH! YOU'RE SO ANNOYING.
JUST MAKE UP ALREADY.
SHUN.
SNACK TIME.
YOU DIDN'T SLEEP AGAIN YESTERDAY.
YEAH.
YOU OKAY?
WHEN YOU'RE DONE...
I'LL GO TO THE AIRPORT WITH YOU.
UH-HUH.
YELL WHEN YOU'RE DONE.
UH-HUH.

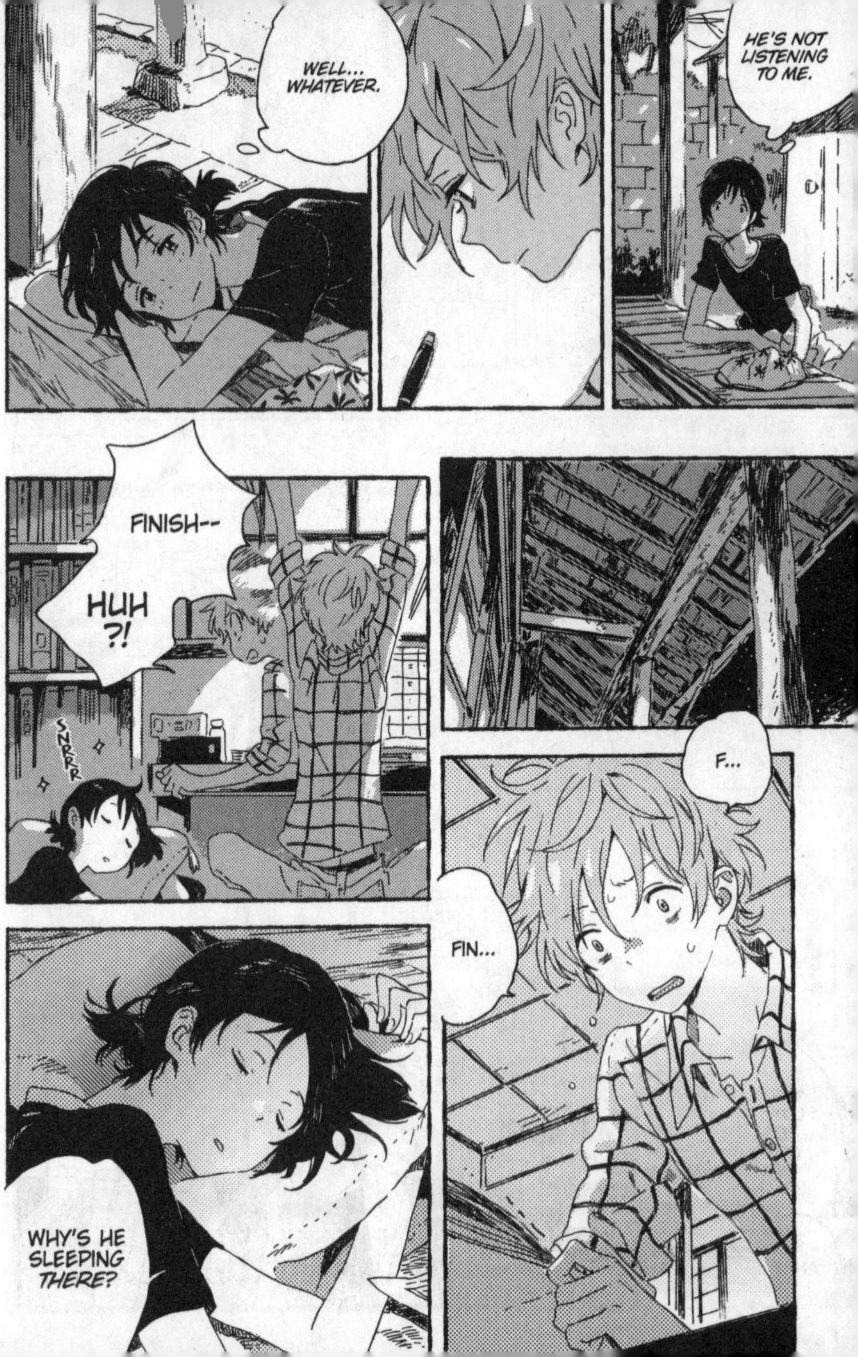
HE'S NOT LISTENING TO ME.
WELL... WHATEVER.
FINISH--
HUH ?!
SNRRR
F...
FIN...
WHY'S HE SLEEPING THERE?

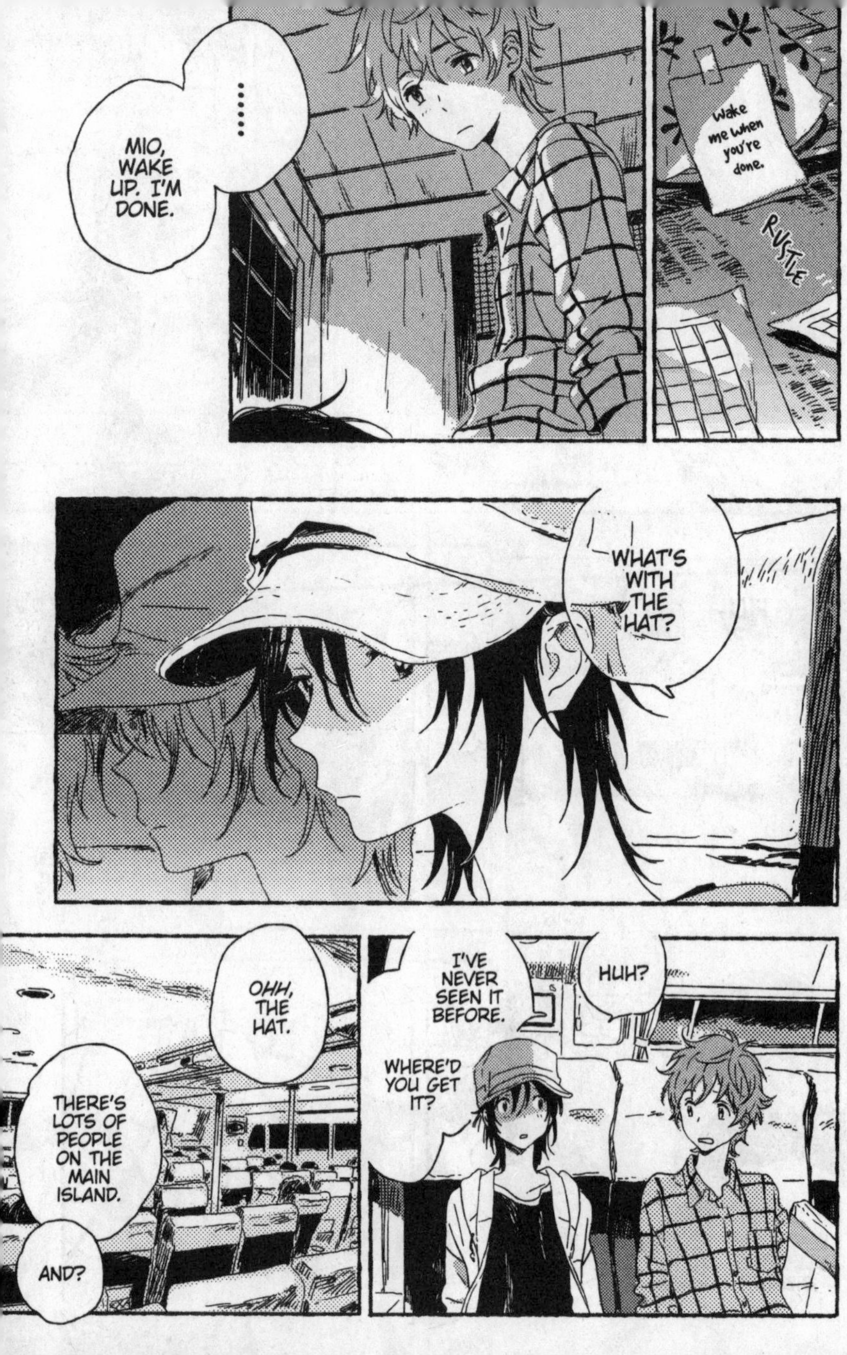
Wake me when you're done.
RUSTLE
......
MIO, WAKE UP. I'M DONE.
WHAT'S WITH THE HAT?
HUH?
I'VE NEVER SEEN IT BEFORE.
WHERE'D YOU GET IT?
OHH, THE HAT.
THERE'S LOTS OF PEOPLE ON THE MAIN ISLAND.
AND?

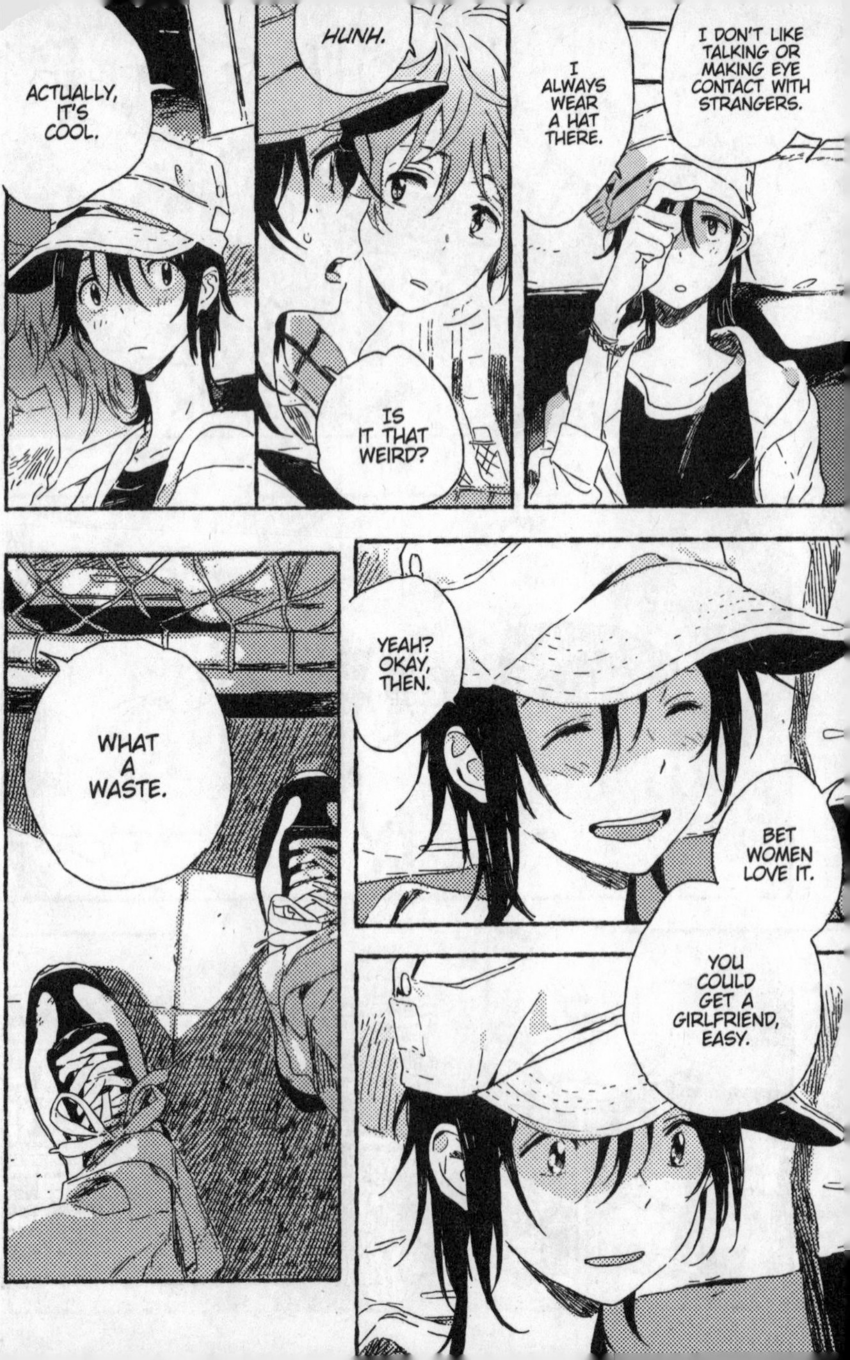
I DON'T LIKE TALKING OR MAKING EYE CONTACT WITH STRANGERS.
I ALWAYS WEAR A HAT THERE.
HUNH.
IS IT THAT WEIRD?
ACTUALLY, IT'S COOL.
YEAH? OKAY, THEN.
BET WOMEN LOVE IT.
YOU COULD GET A GIRLFRIEND, EASY.
WHAT A WASTE.

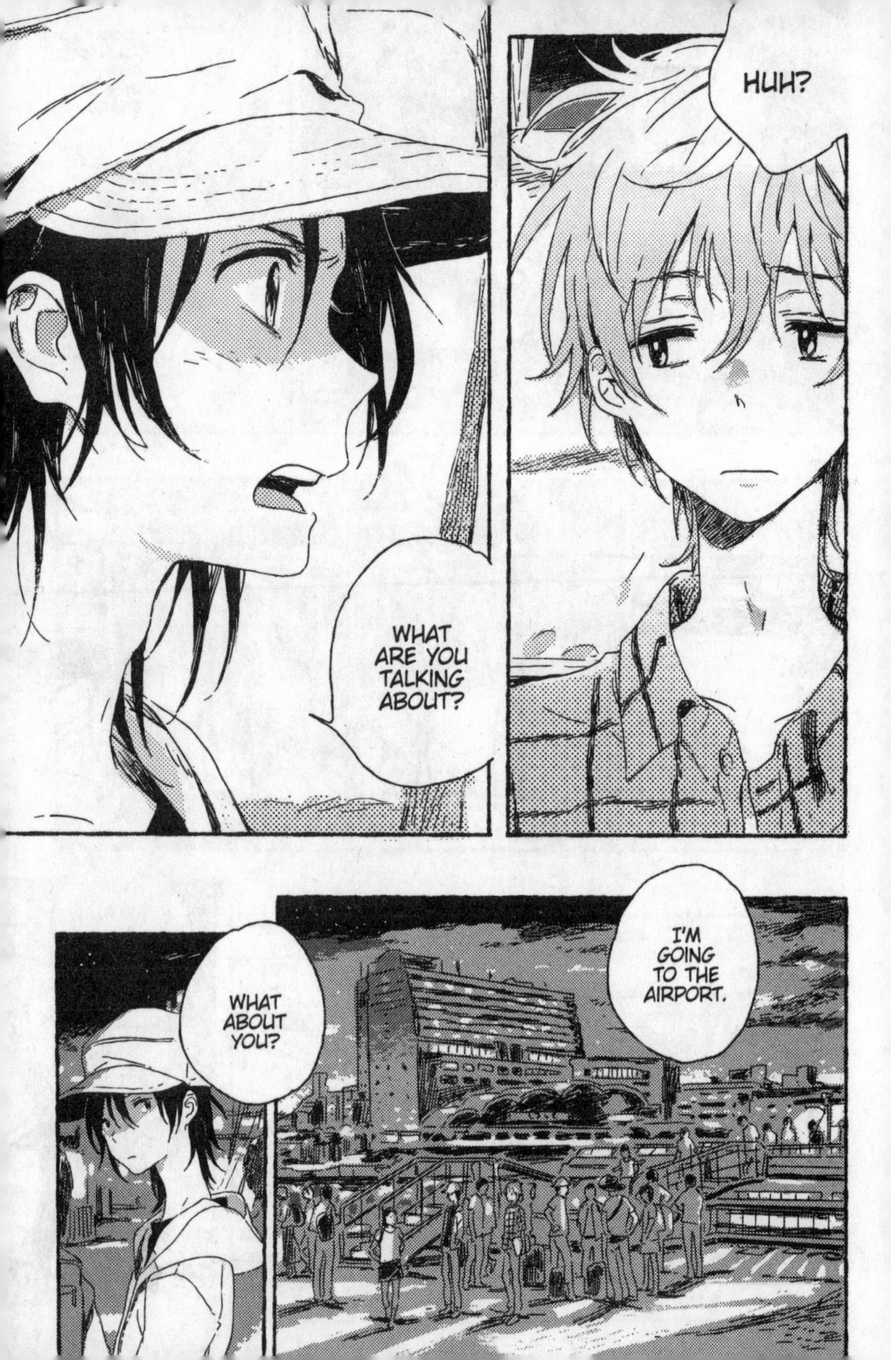
HUH?
WHAT ARE YOU TALKING ABOUT?
I'M GOING TO THE AIRPORT.
WHAT ABOUT YOU?

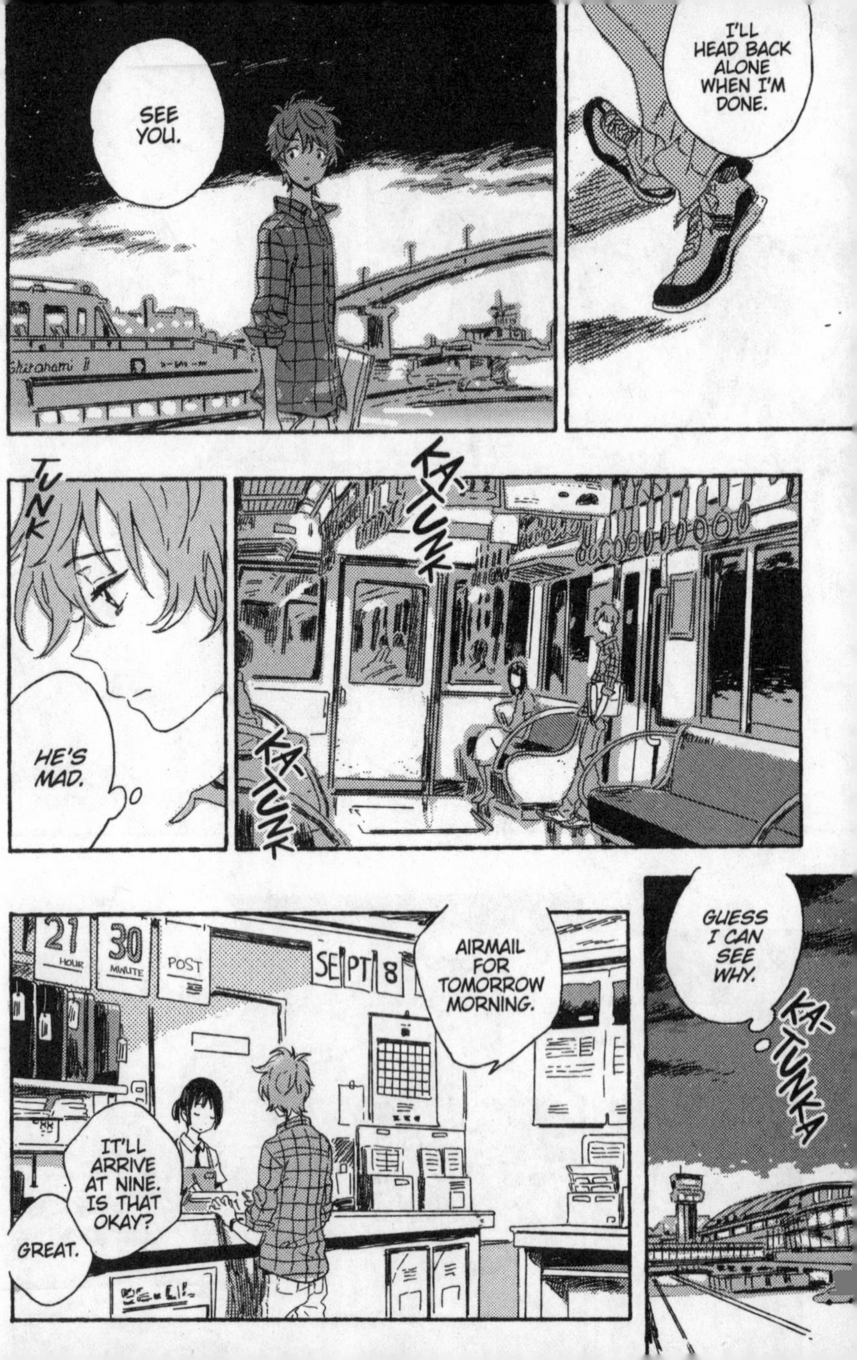
I'LL HEAD BACK ALONE WHEN I'M DONE.
SEE YOU.
KA-TUNK
KA-TUNK
TUNK
HE'S MAD.
GUESS I CAN SEE WHY.
KA-TUNKA
21 HOUR
30 MINUTE
POST
SEPT 8
AIRMAIL FOR TOMORROW MORNING.
IT'LL ARRIVE AT NINE. IS THAT OKAY?
GREAT.

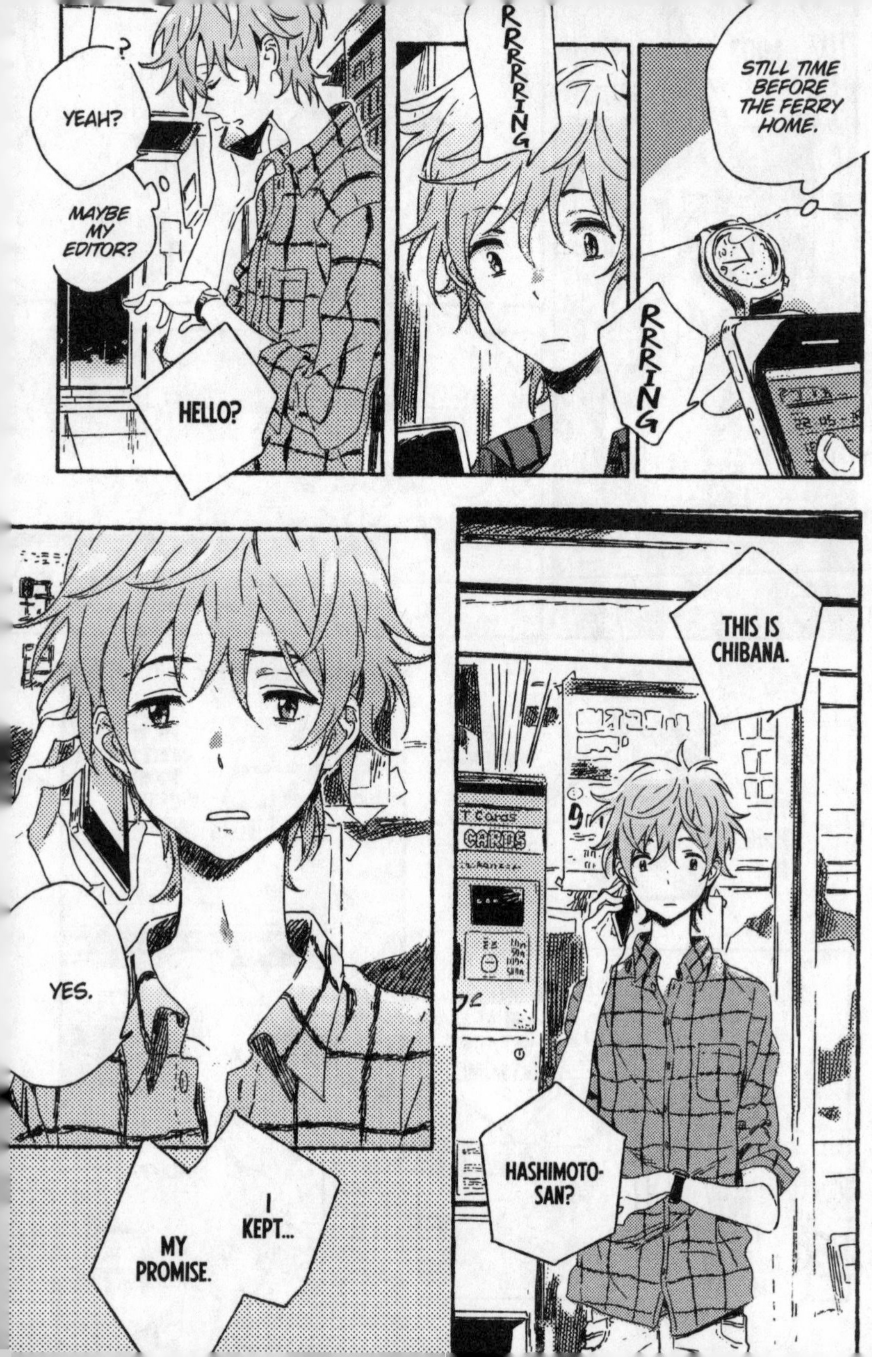
STILL TIME BEFORE THE FERRY HOME.
RRRING
RRRRRING
?
YEAH?
MAYBE MY EDITOR?
HELLO?
THIS IS CHIBANA.
HASHIMOTO-SAN?
YES.
I KEPT...
MY PROMISE.

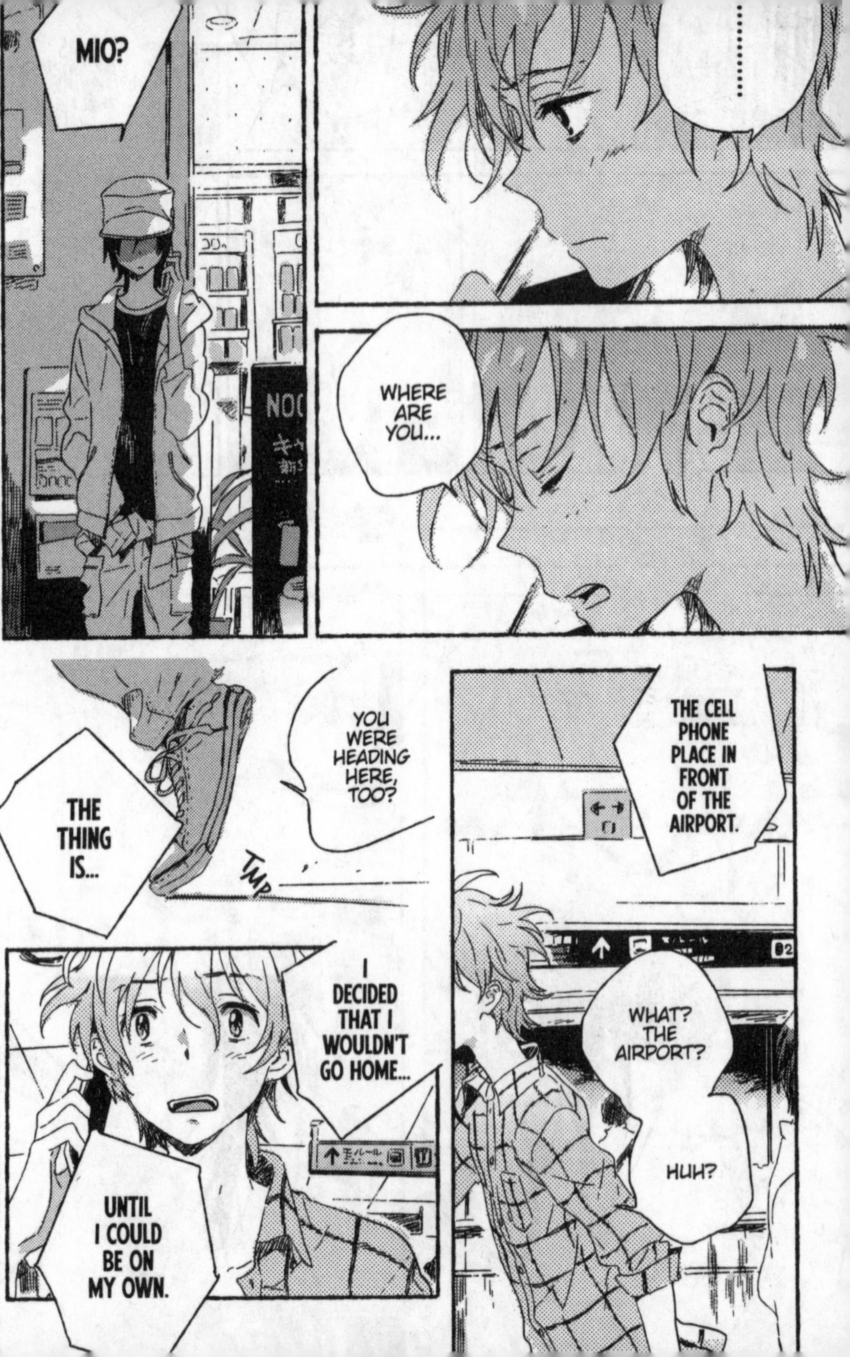
......
WHERE ARE YOU...
MIO?
THE CELL PHONE PLACE IN FRONT OF THE AIRPORT.
WHAT? THE AIRPORT?
HUH?
YOU WERE HEADING HERE, TOO?
TMP
THE THING IS...
I DECIDED THAT I WOULDN'T GO HOME...
UNTIL I COULD BE ON MY OWN.

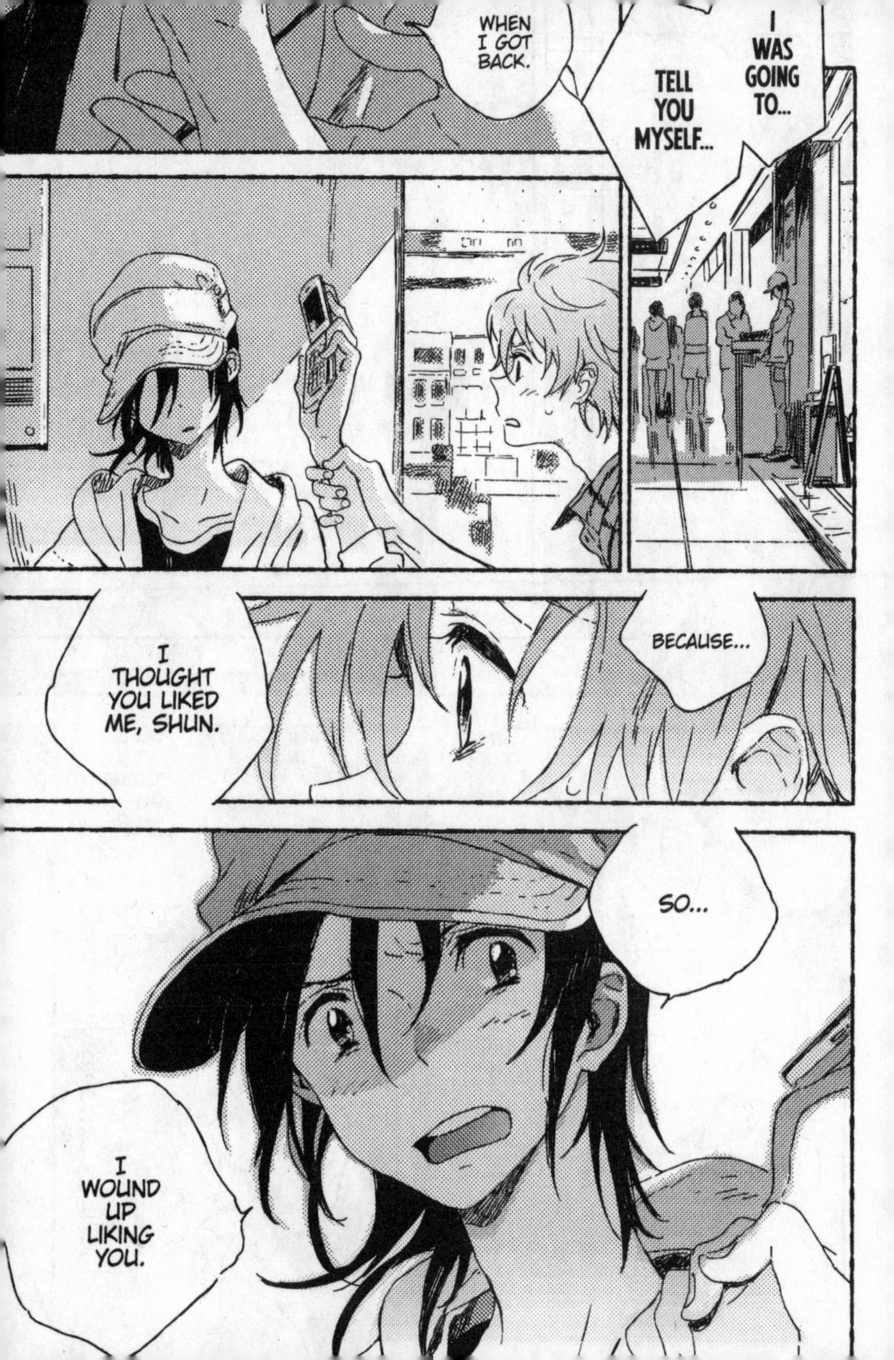
I WAS GOING TO...
TELL YOU MYSELF...
WHEN I GOT BACK.
BECAUSE...
I THOUGHT YOU LIKED ME, SHUN.
SO...
I WOUND UP LIKING YOU.

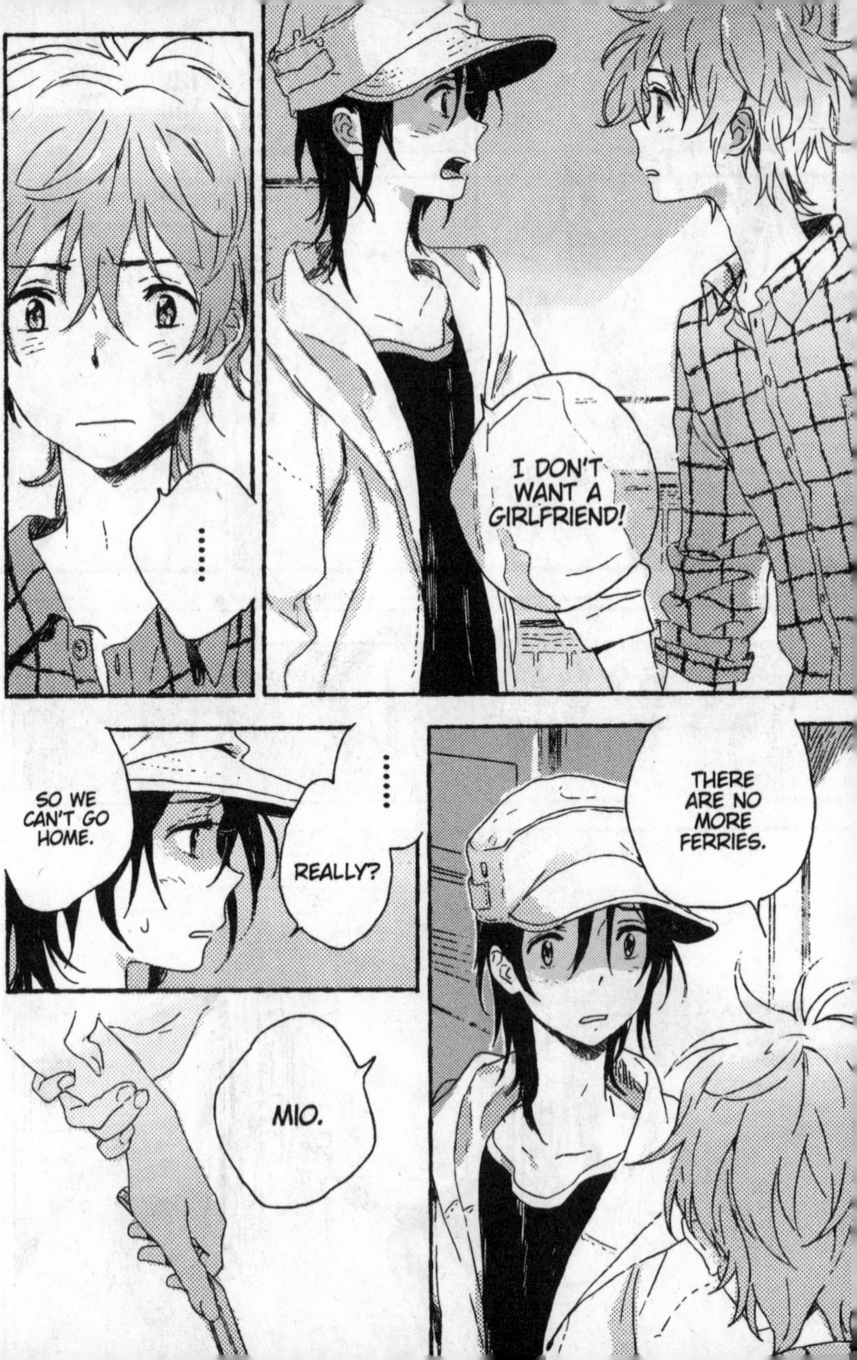
I DON'T WANT A GIRLFRIEND!
......
THERE ARE NO MORE FERRIES.
......
SO WE CAN'T GO HOME.
REALLY?
MIO.

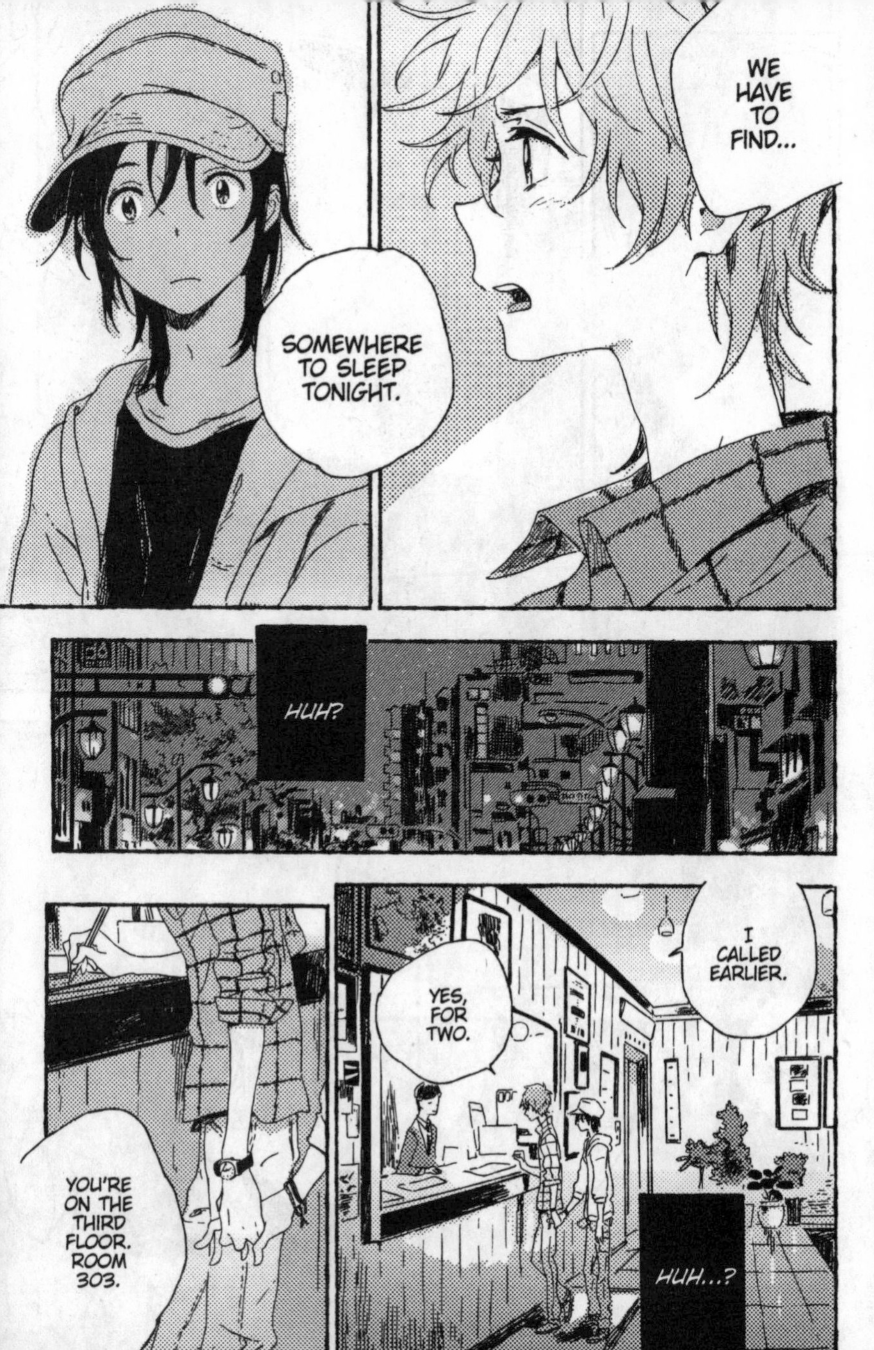
WE HAVE TO FIND...
SOMEWHERE TO SLEEP TONIGHT.
HUH?
I CALLED EARLIER.
YES, FOR TWO.
HUH...?
YOU'RE ON THE THIRD FLOOR. ROOM 303.

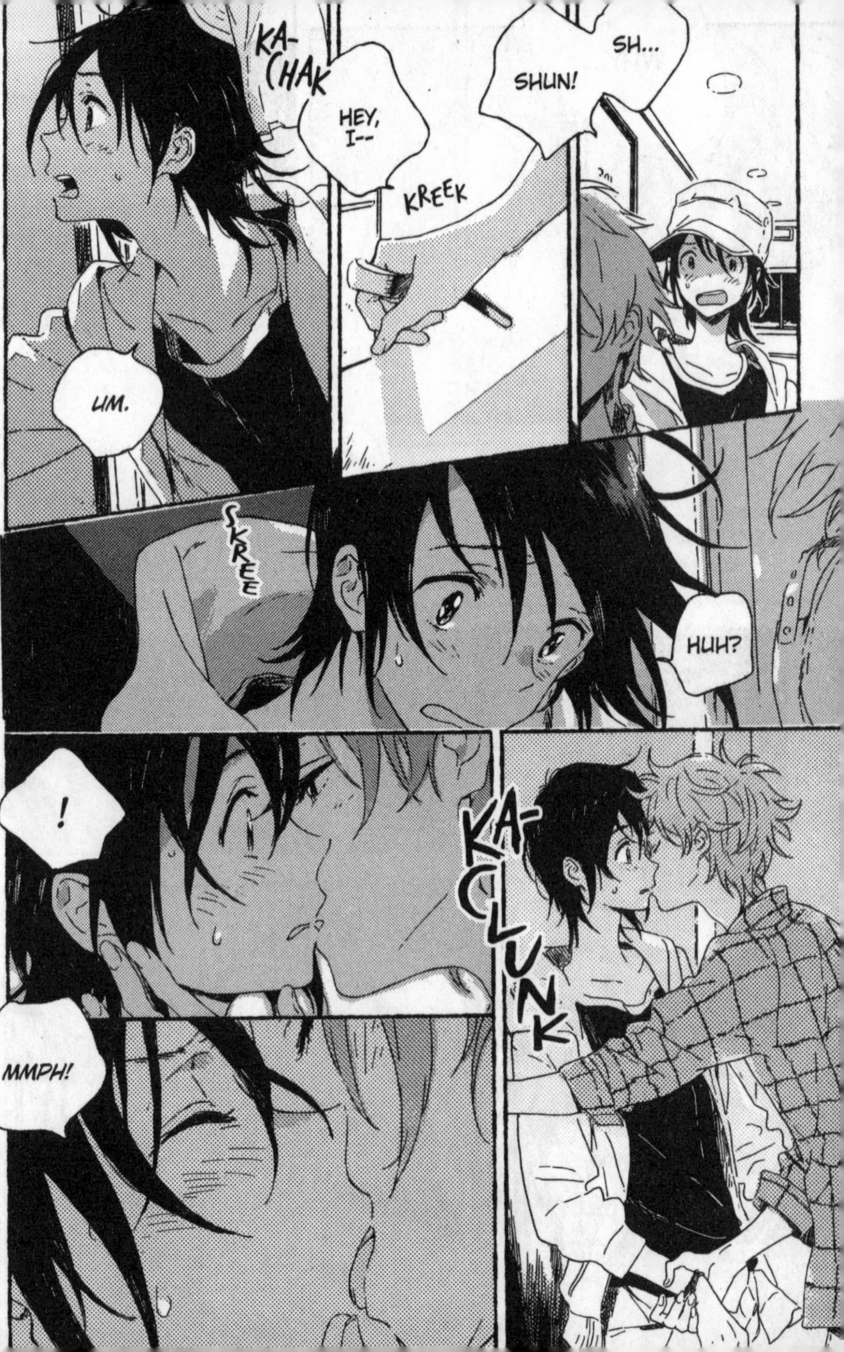
SH...
SHUN!
HEY, I--
KREEK
KA-CHAK
UM.
HUH?
SKREE
KA-CLUNK
!
MMPH!

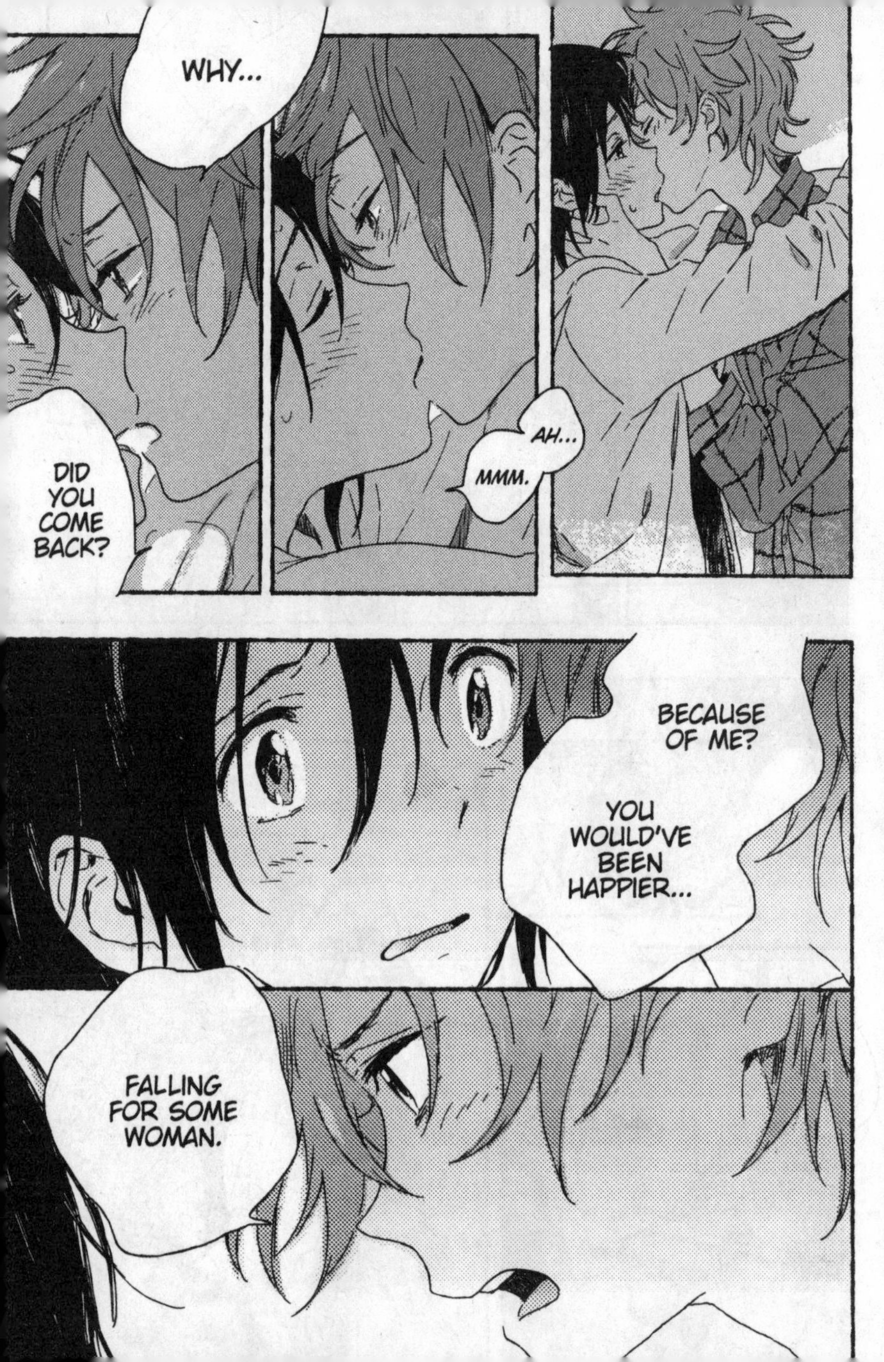
AH...
MMM.
WHY...
DID YOU COME BACK?
BECAUSE OF ME?
YOU WOULD'VE BEEN HAPPIER...
FALLING FOR SOME WOMAN.

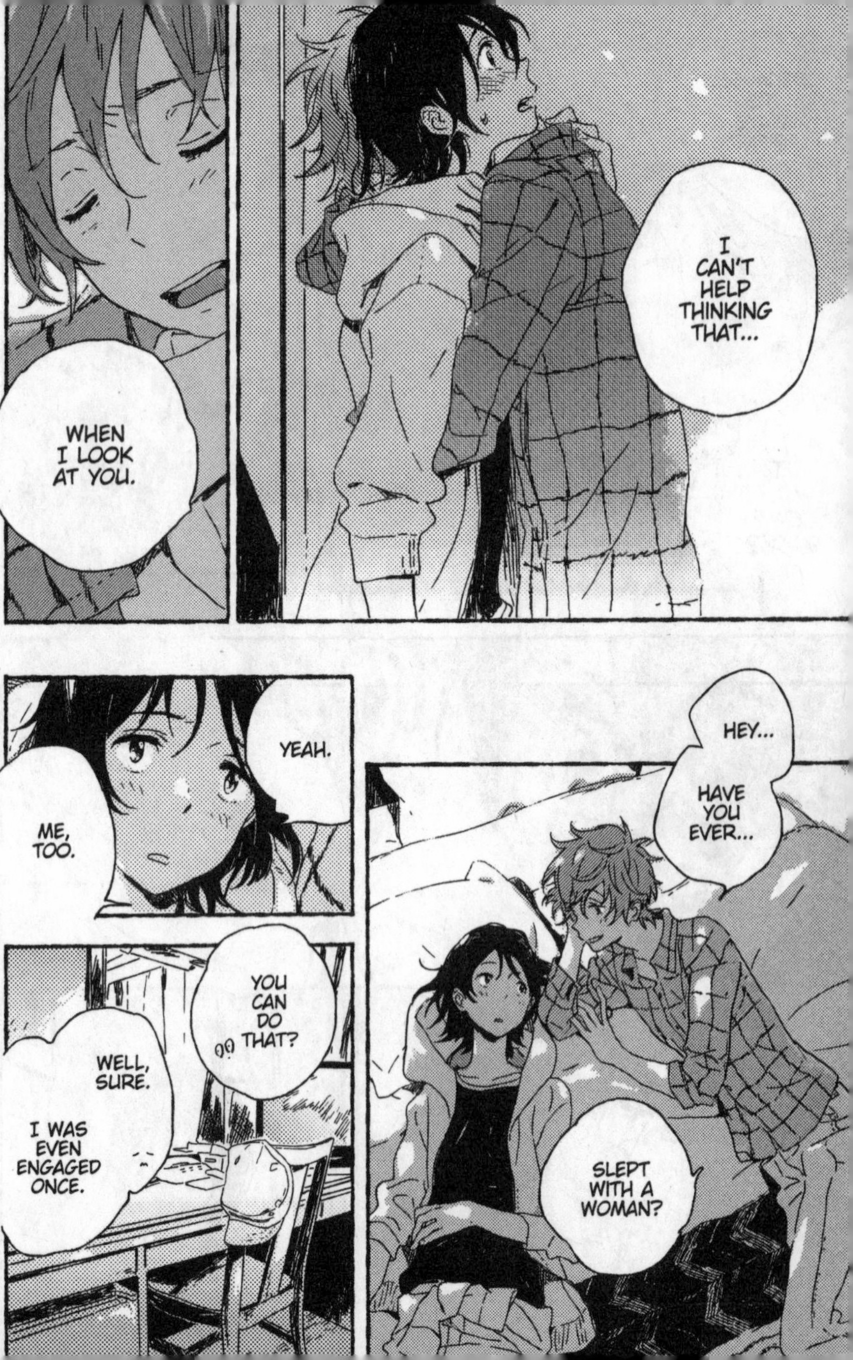
I CAN'T HELP THINKING THAT...
WHEN I LOOK AT YOU.
YEAH.
ME, TOO.
HEY...
HAVE YOU EVER...
SLEPT WITH A WOMAN?
YOU CAN DO THAT?
WELL, SURE.
I WAS EVEN ENGAGED ONCE.

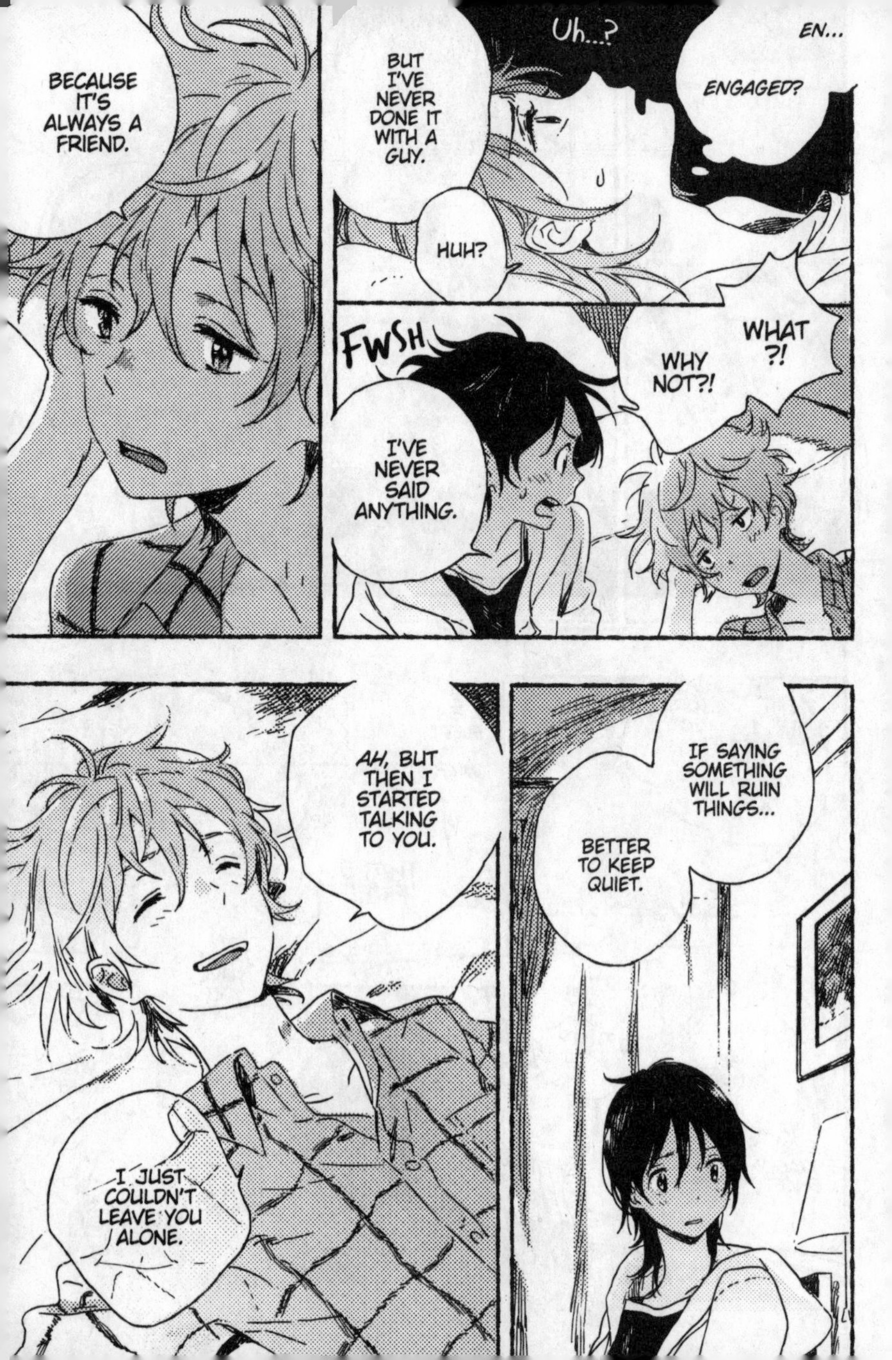
EN...
ENGAGED?
Uh...?
BUT I'VE NEVER DONE IT WITH A GUY.
HUH?
WHAT?!
WHY NOT?!
FWSH
I'VE NEVER SAID ANYTHING.
BECAUSE IT'S ALWAYS A FRIEND.
IF SAYING SOMETHING WILL RUIN THINGS...
BETTER TO KEEP QUIET.
AH, BUT THEN I STARTED TALKING TO YOU.
I JUST COULDN'T LEAVE YOU ALONE.

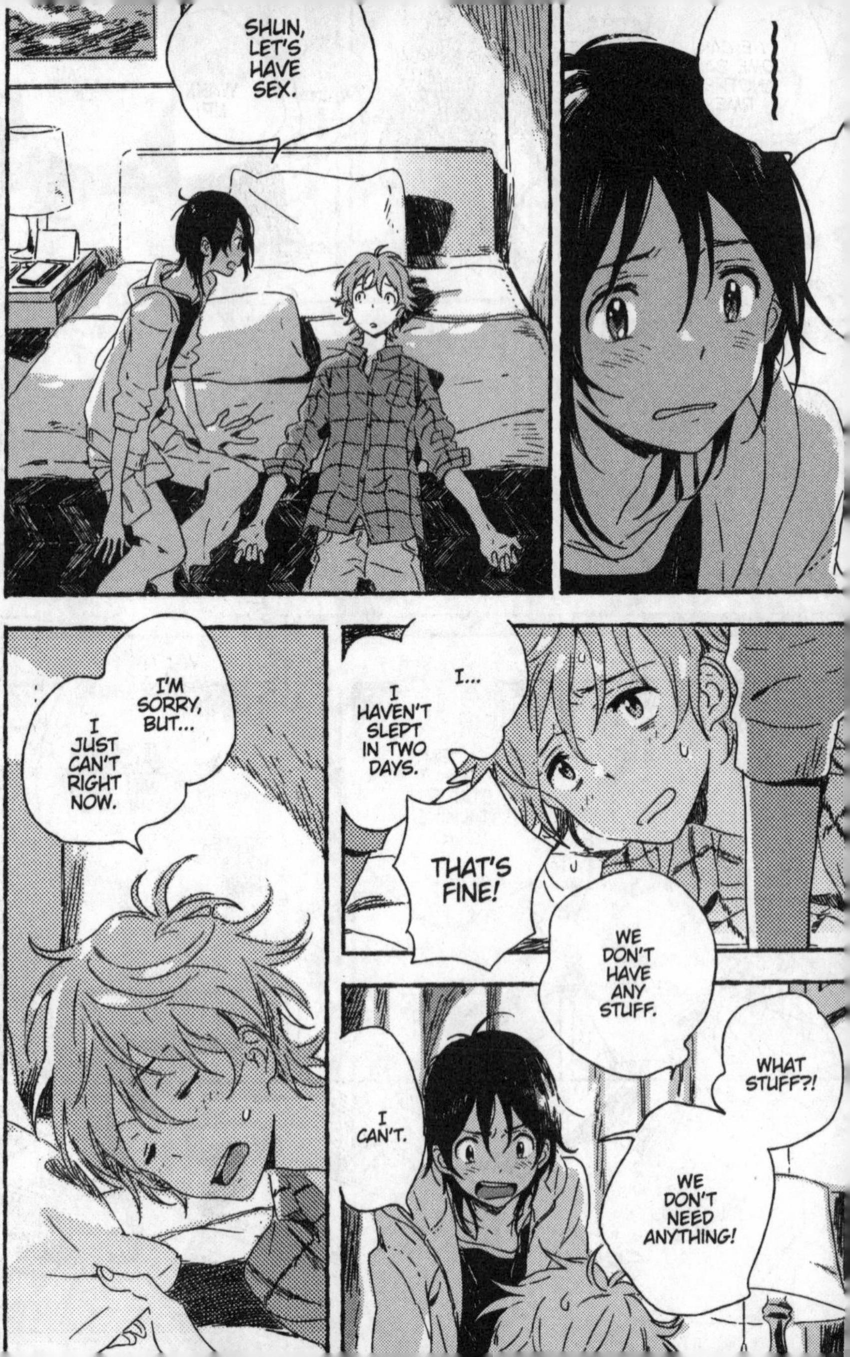

SHUN, LET'S HAVE SEX.
I...
I HAVEN'T SLEPT IN TWO DAYS.
THAT'S FINE!
WE DON'T HAVE ANY STUFF.
WHAT STUFF?!
I CAN'T.
WE DON'T NEED ANYTHING!
I'M SORRY, BUT...
I JUST CAN'T RIGHT NOW.

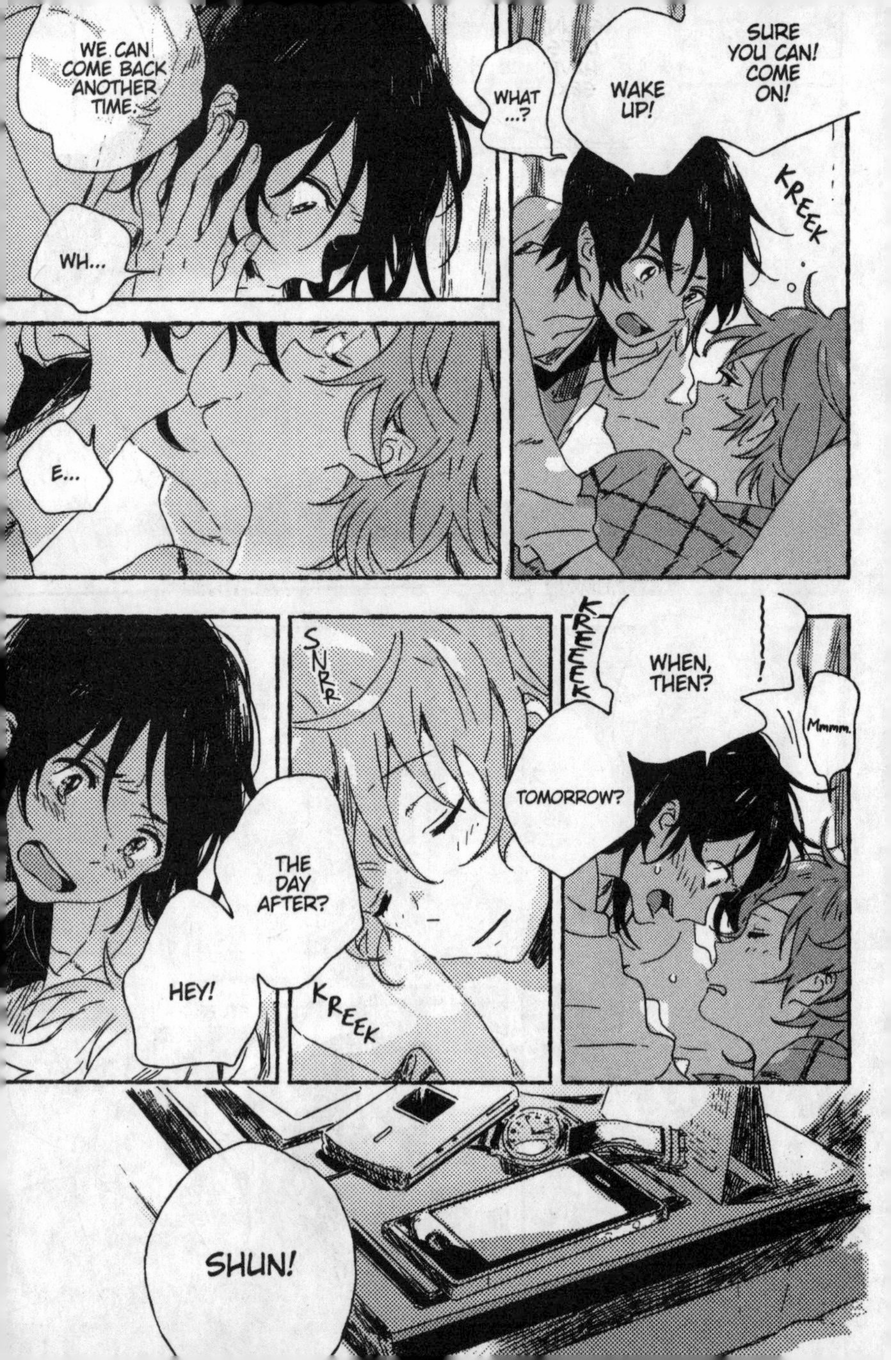

SURE YOU CAN! COME ON!
WAKE UP!
WHAT ...?
KREEK
WE CAN COME BACK ANOTHER TIME.
WH...
E...
!
WHEN, THEN?
Mmmm.
KREEEK
TOMORROW?
SNRR
KREEK
THE DAY AFTER?
HEY!
SHUN!

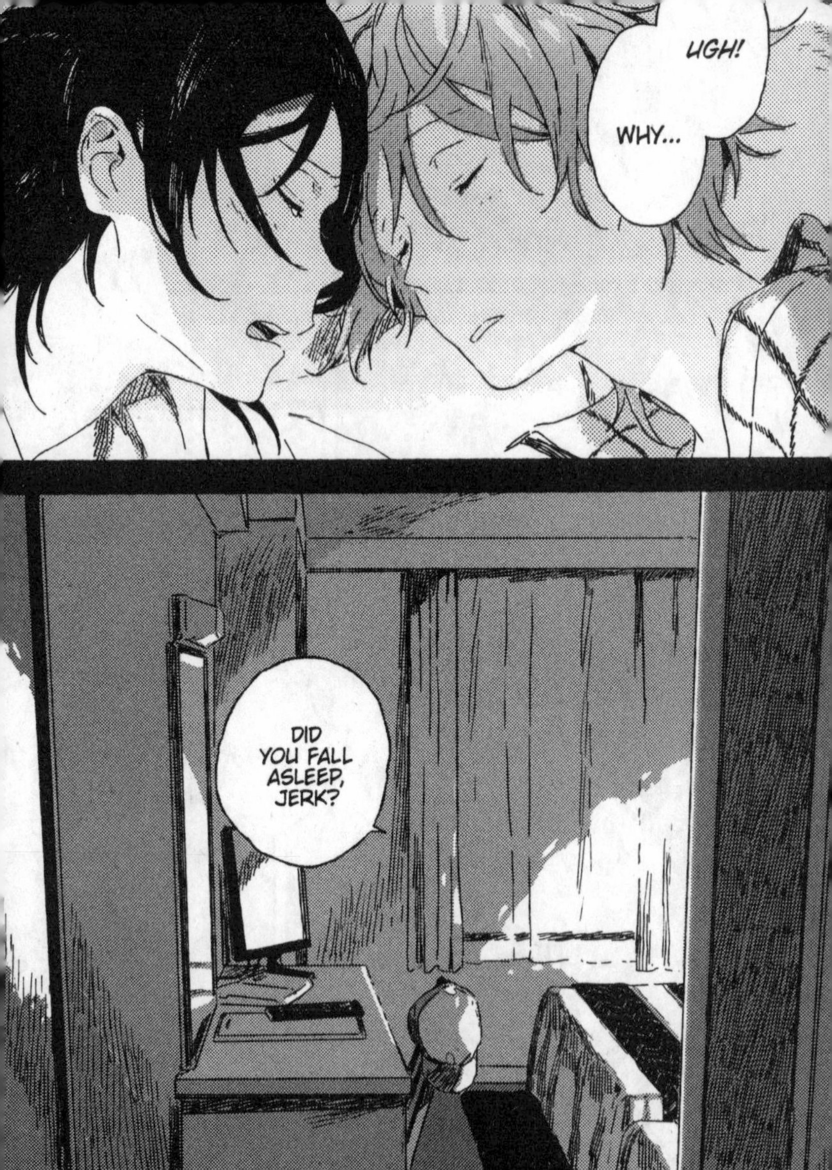
UGH!
WHY...
DID YOU FALL ASLEEP, JERK?

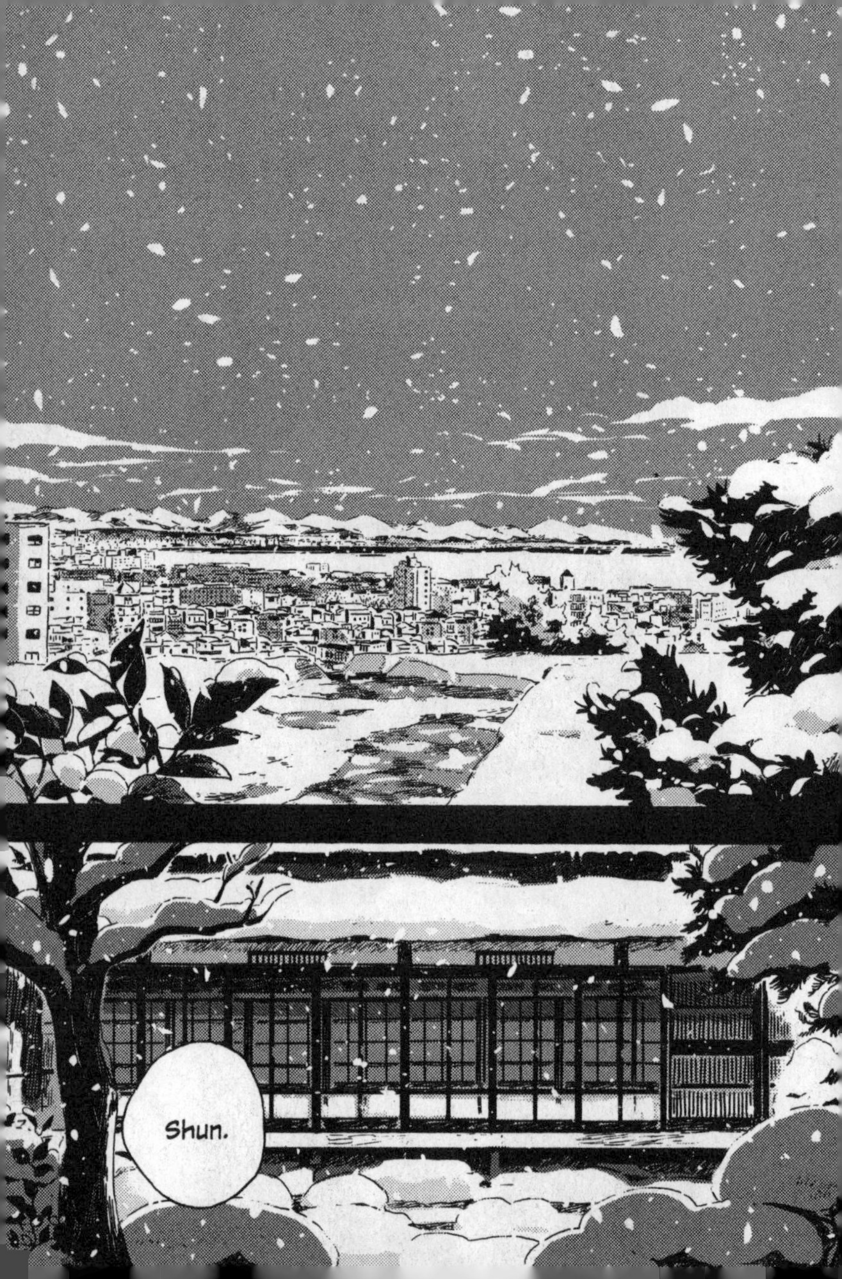
Shun.

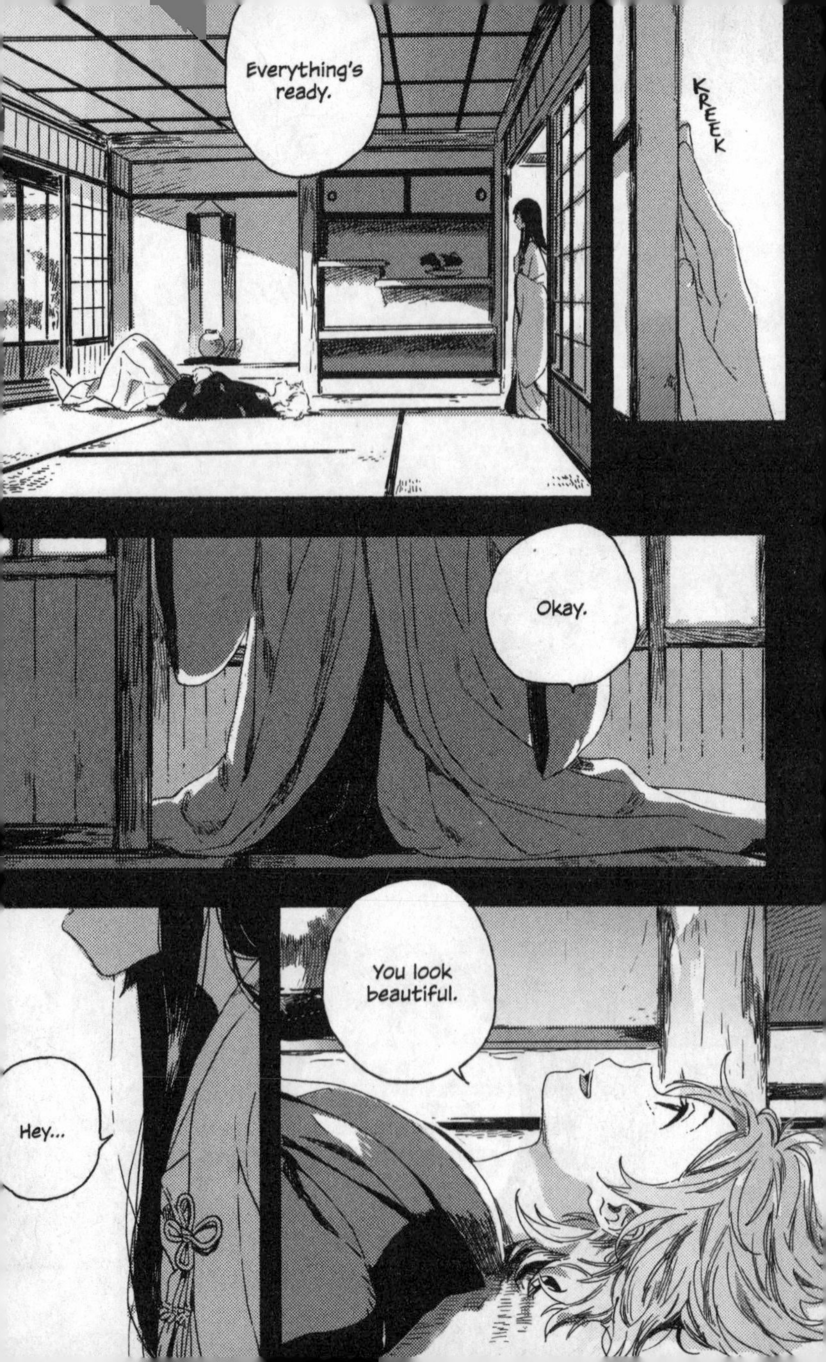
KREEK
Everything's ready.
Okay.
You look beautiful.
Hey...

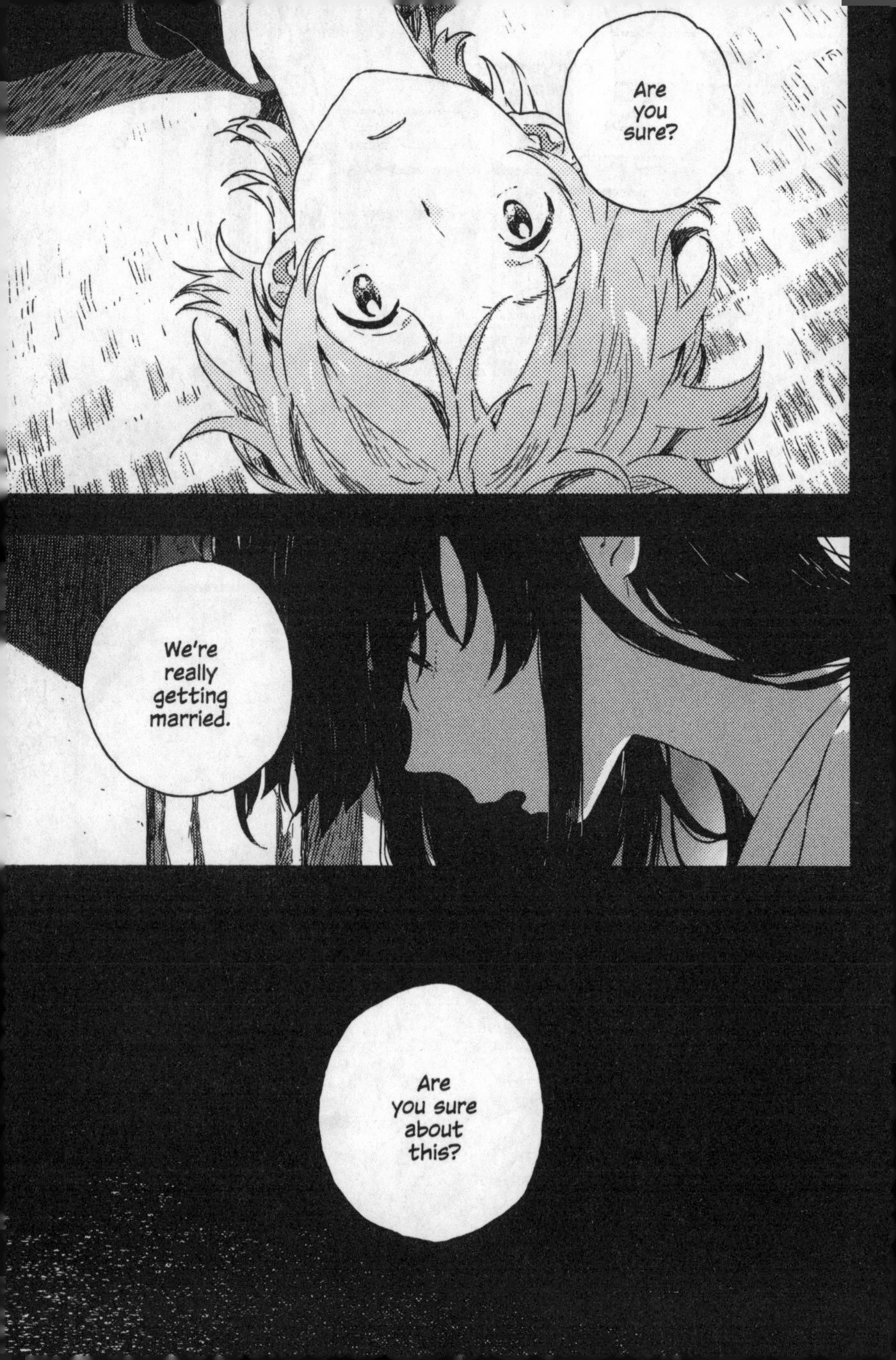
Are you sure?
We're really getting married.
Are you sure about this?

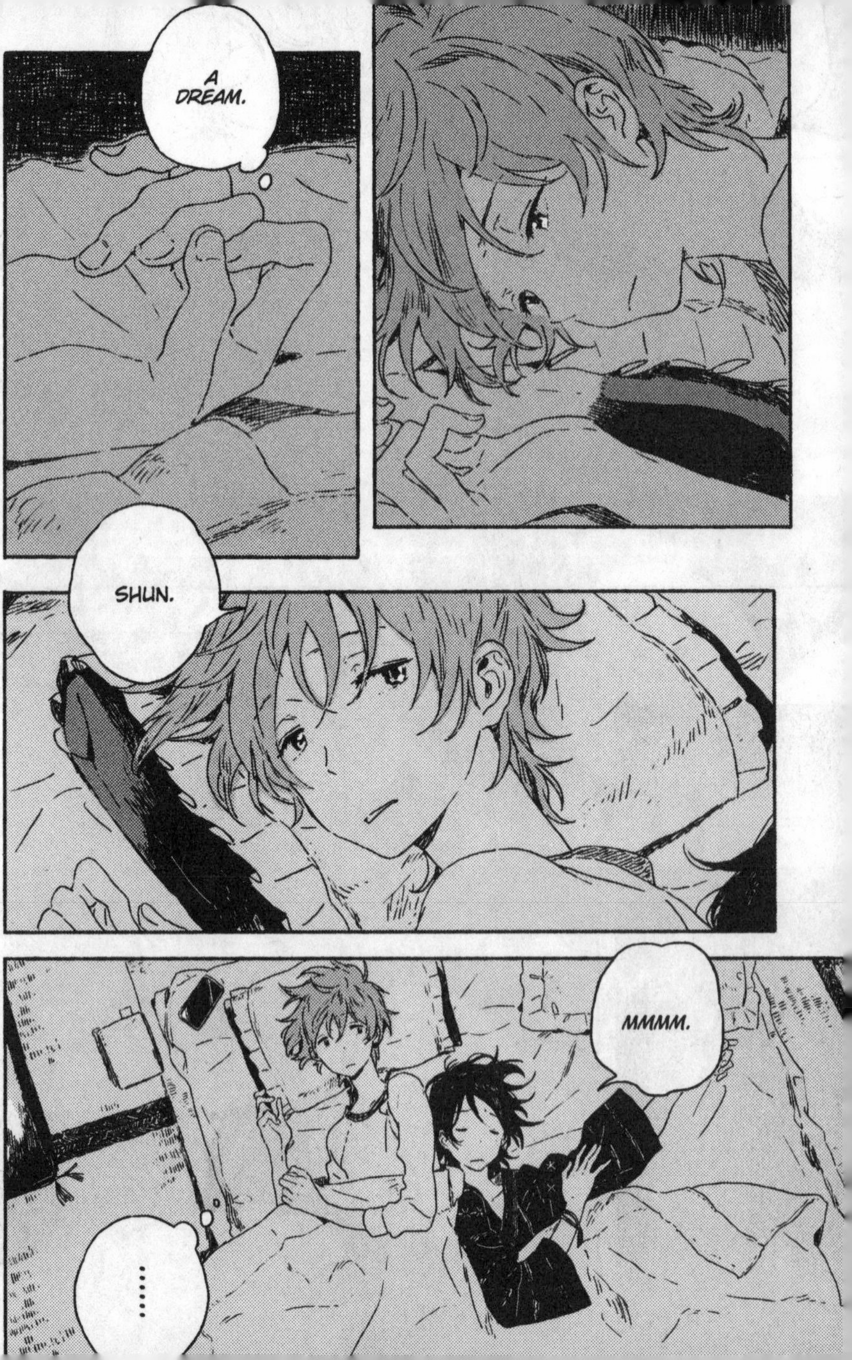
A DREAM.
SHUN.
MMMM.
......

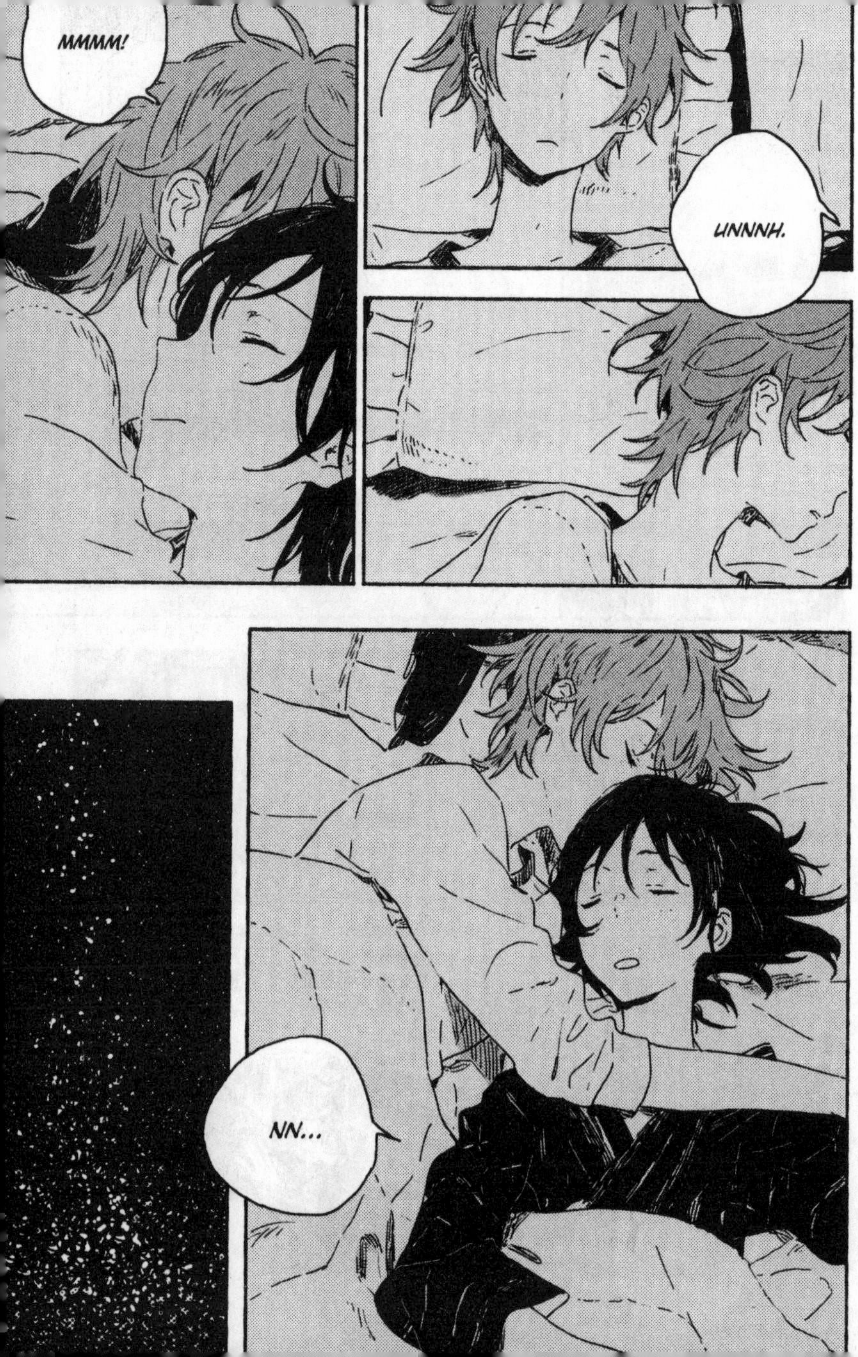
UNNH.
MMMM!
NN...

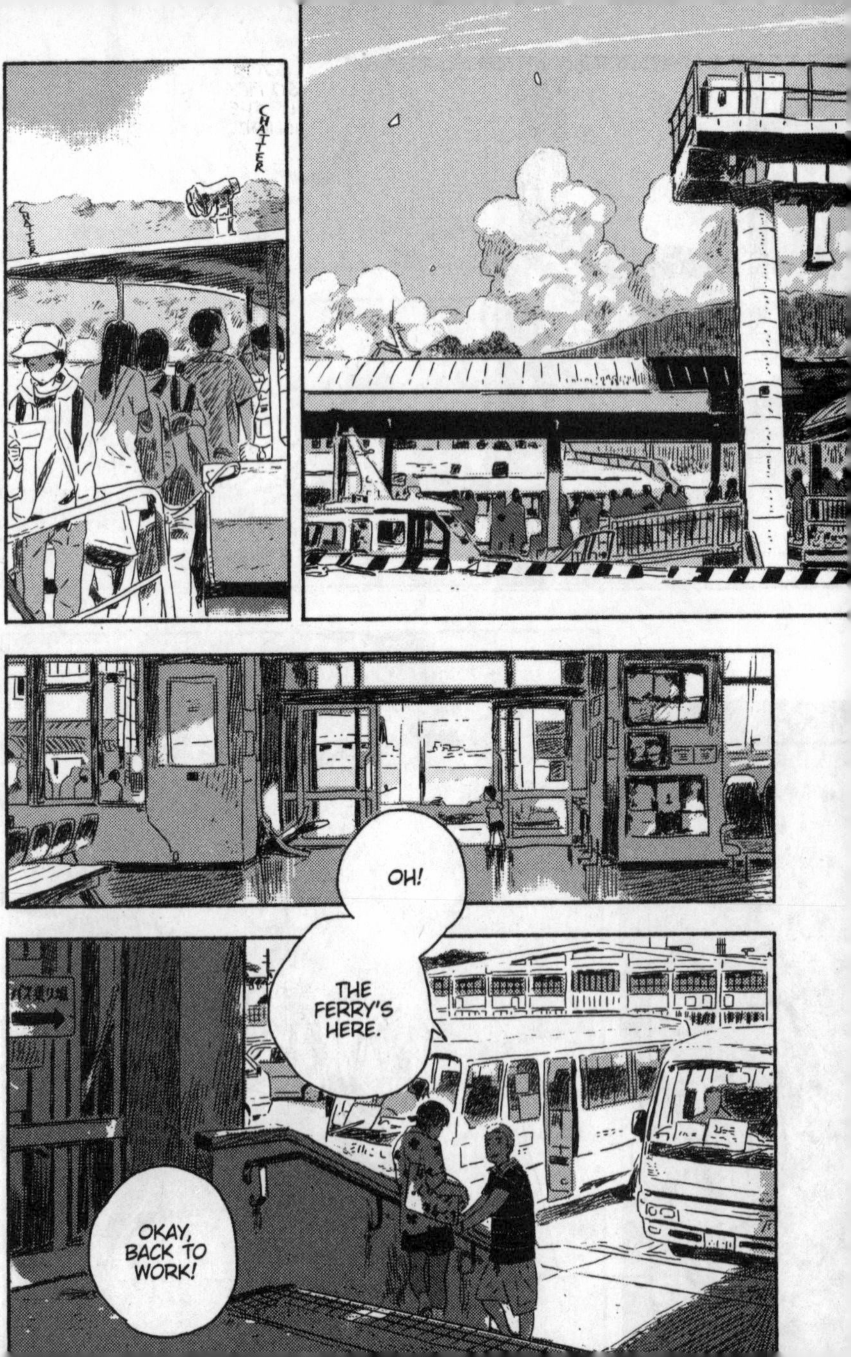
CHATTER
CHATTER
OH!
THE FERRY'S HERE.
バス乗り場
OKAY, BACK TO WORK!

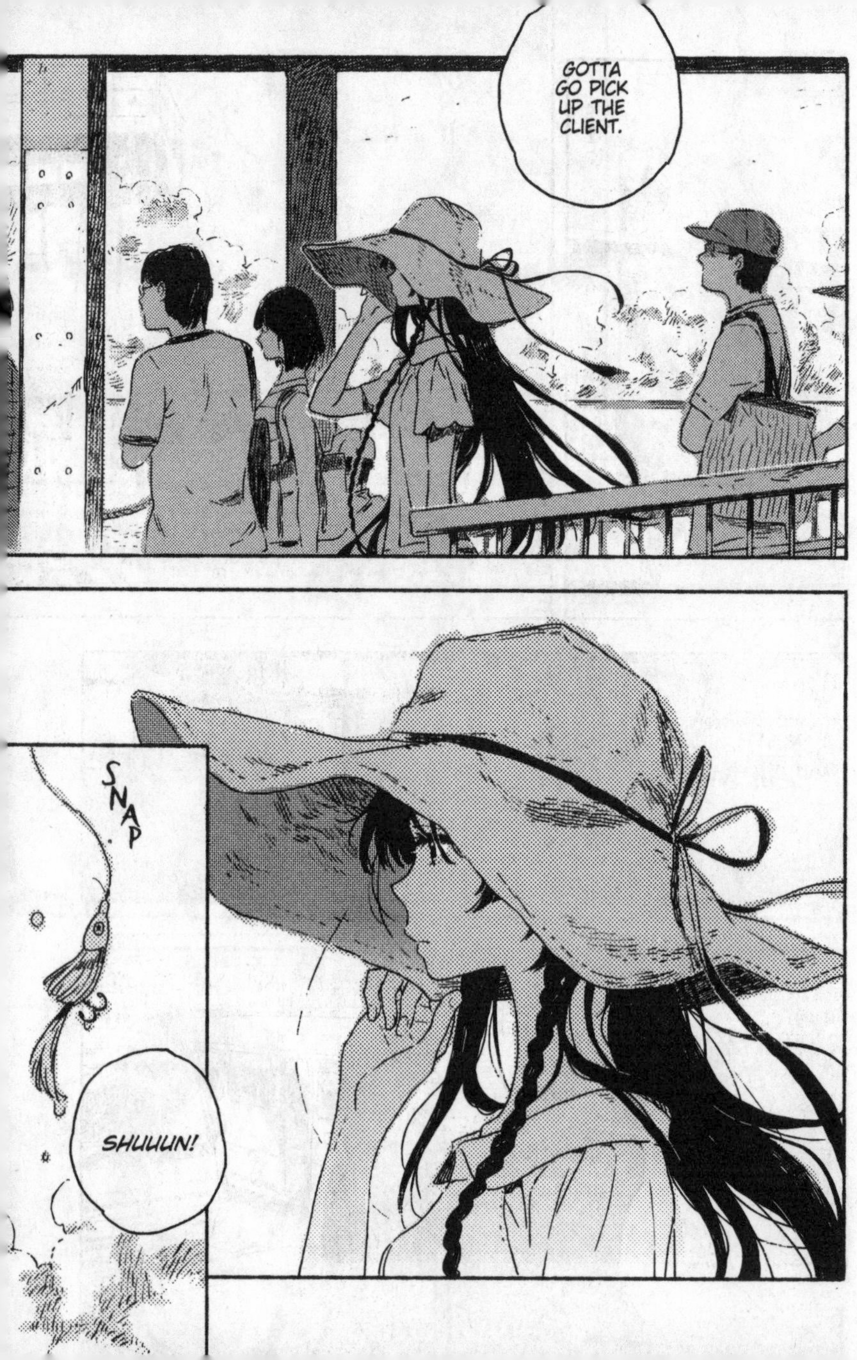
GOTTA GO PICK UP THE CLIENT.
SNAP
SHUUUN!

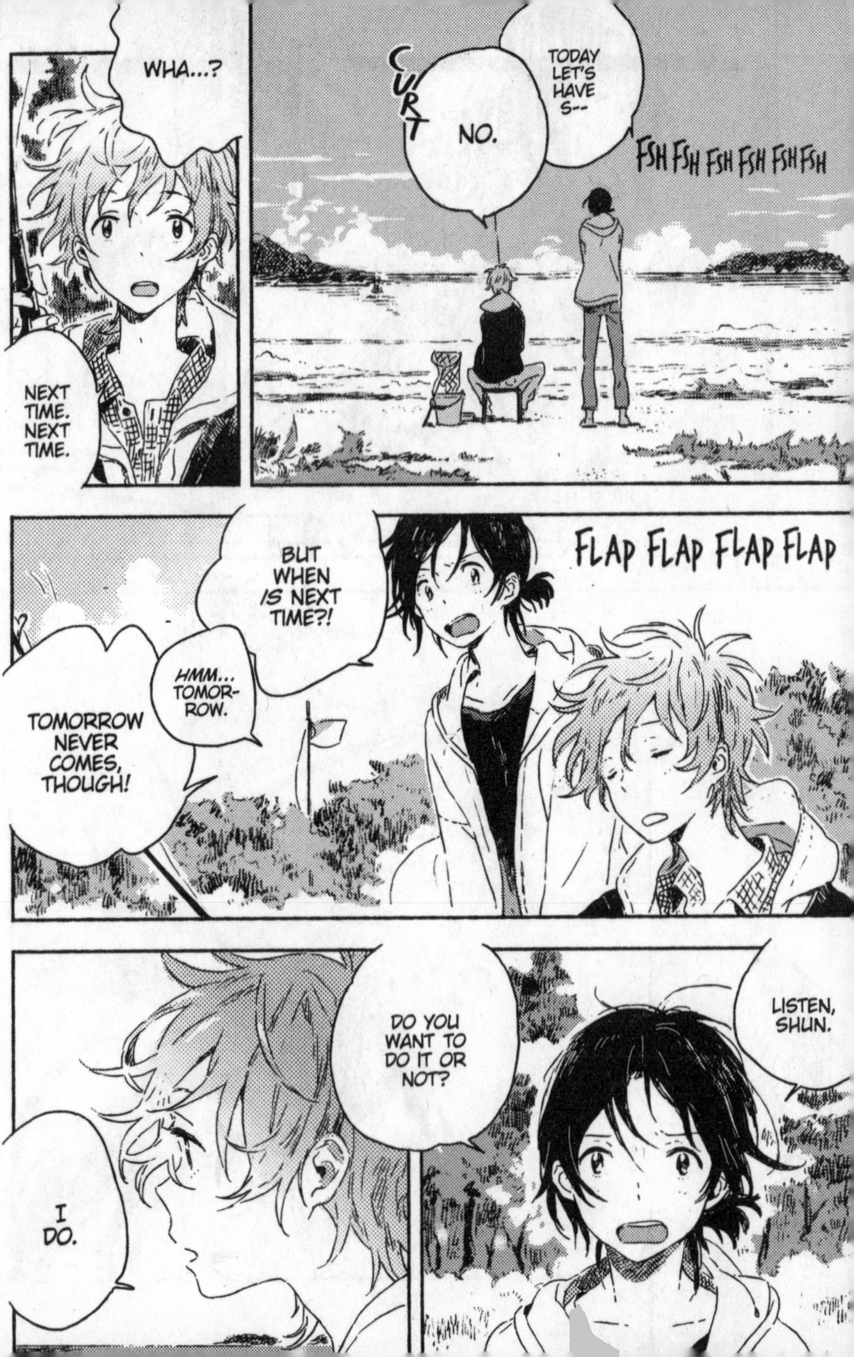

FSH FSH FSH FSH FSH FSH
TODAY LET'S HAVE S--
CURT
NO.
WHA...?
NEXT TIME. NEXT TIME.
FLAP FLAP FLAP FLAP
BUT WHEN IS NEXT TIME?!
HMM... TOMORROW.
TOMORROW NEVER COMES, THOUGH!
LISTEN, SHUN.
DO YOU WANT TO DO IT OR NOT?
I DO.

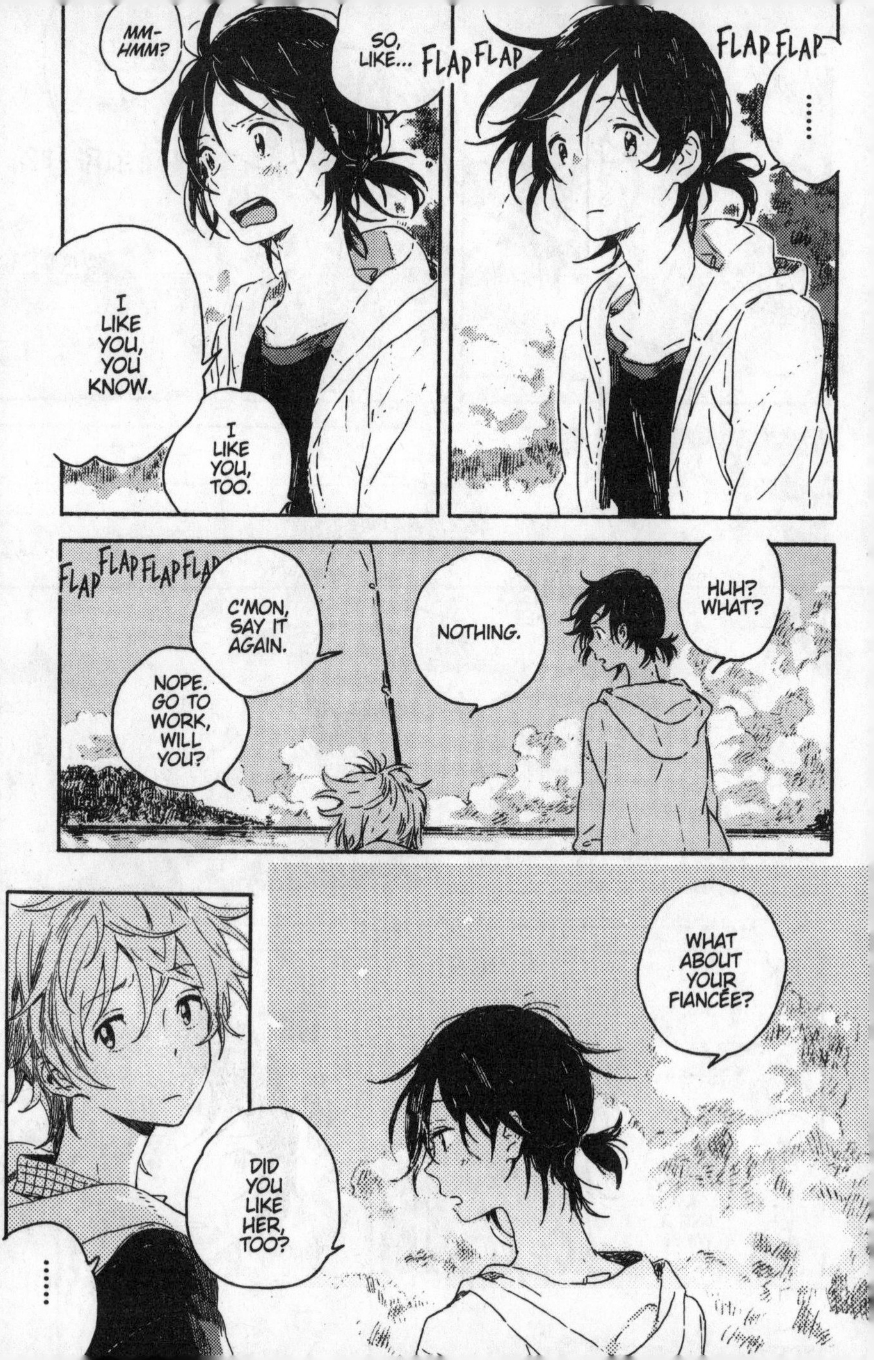
FLAP FLAP
......
SO, LIKE...
FLAP FLAP
MM-HMM?
I LIKE YOU, YOU KNOW.
I LIKE YOU, TOO.
HUH? WHAT?
NOTHING.
C'MON, SAY IT AGAIN.
FLAP FLAP FLAP FLAP
NOPE. GO TO WORK, WILL YOU?
WHAT ABOUT YOUR FIANCÉE?
DID YOU LIKE HER, TOO?
......

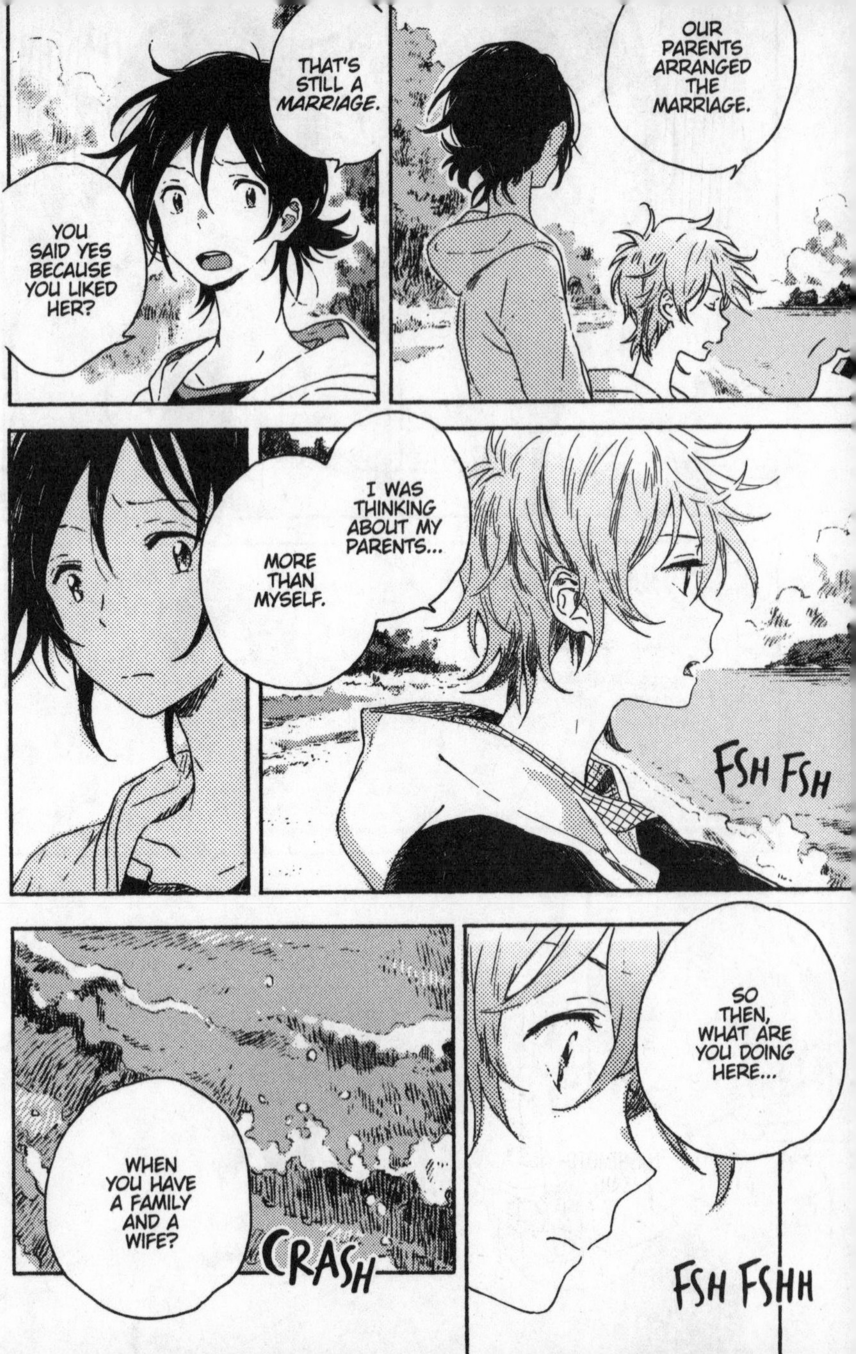
OUR PARENTS ARRANGED THE MARRIAGE.
THAT'S STILL A *MARRIAGE*.
YOU SAID YES BECAUSE YOU LIKED HER?
I WAS THINKING ABOUT MY PARENTS...
MORE THAN MYSELF.
FSH FSH
SO THEN, WHAT ARE YOU DOING HERE...
FSH FSHH
WHEN YOU HAVE A FAMILY AND A WIFE?
CRASH

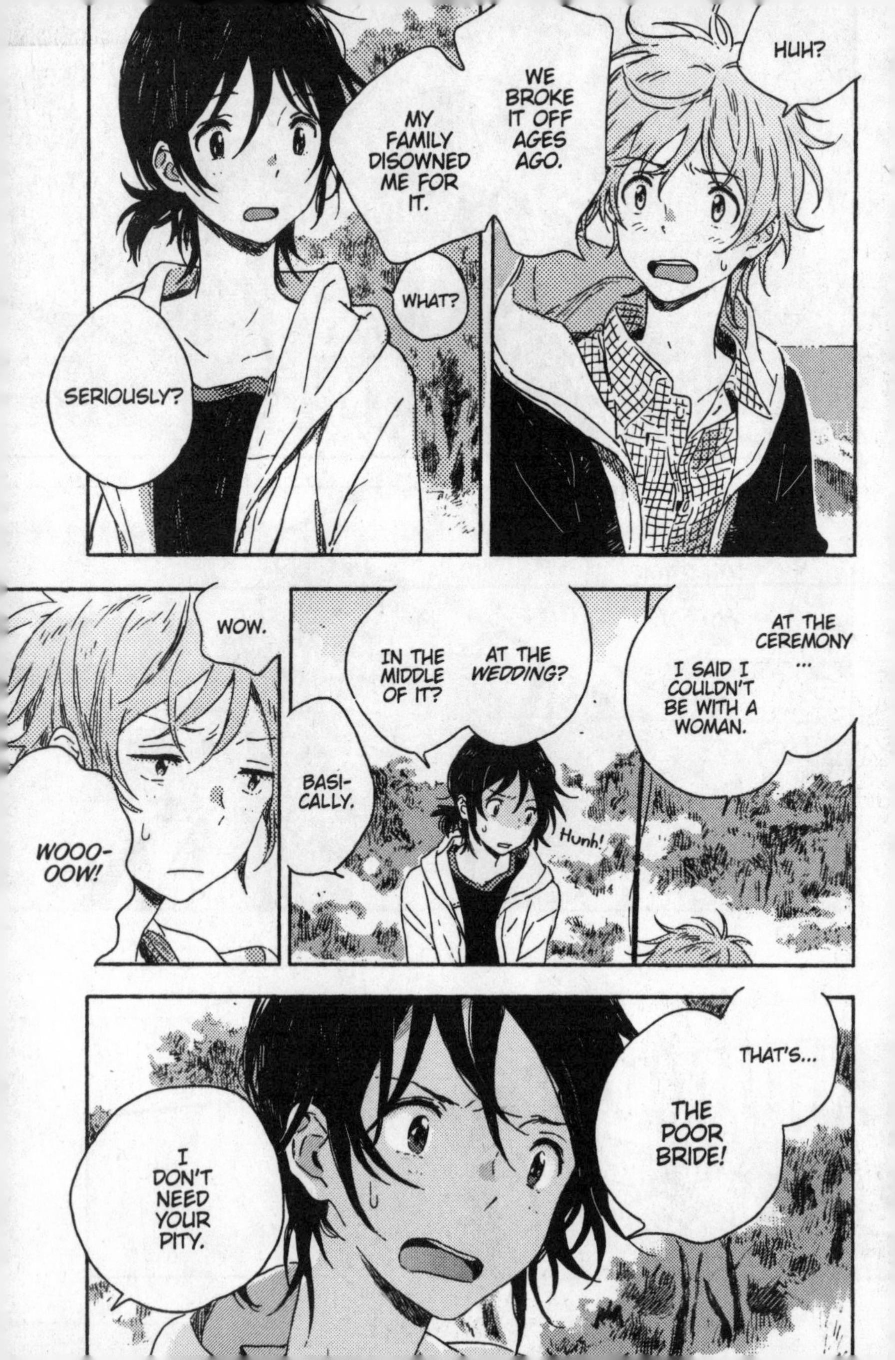
HUH?
WE BROKE IT OFF AGES AGO.
MY FAMILY DISOWNED ME FOR IT.
WHAT?
SERIOUSLY?
AT THE CEREMONY...
I SAID I COULDN'T BE WITH A WOMAN.
AT THE *WEDDING?*
IN THE MIDDLE OF IT?
Hunh!
BASI-CALLY.
WOW.
WOOO-OOW!
THAT'S...
THE POOR BRIDE!
I DON'T NEED YOUR PITY.

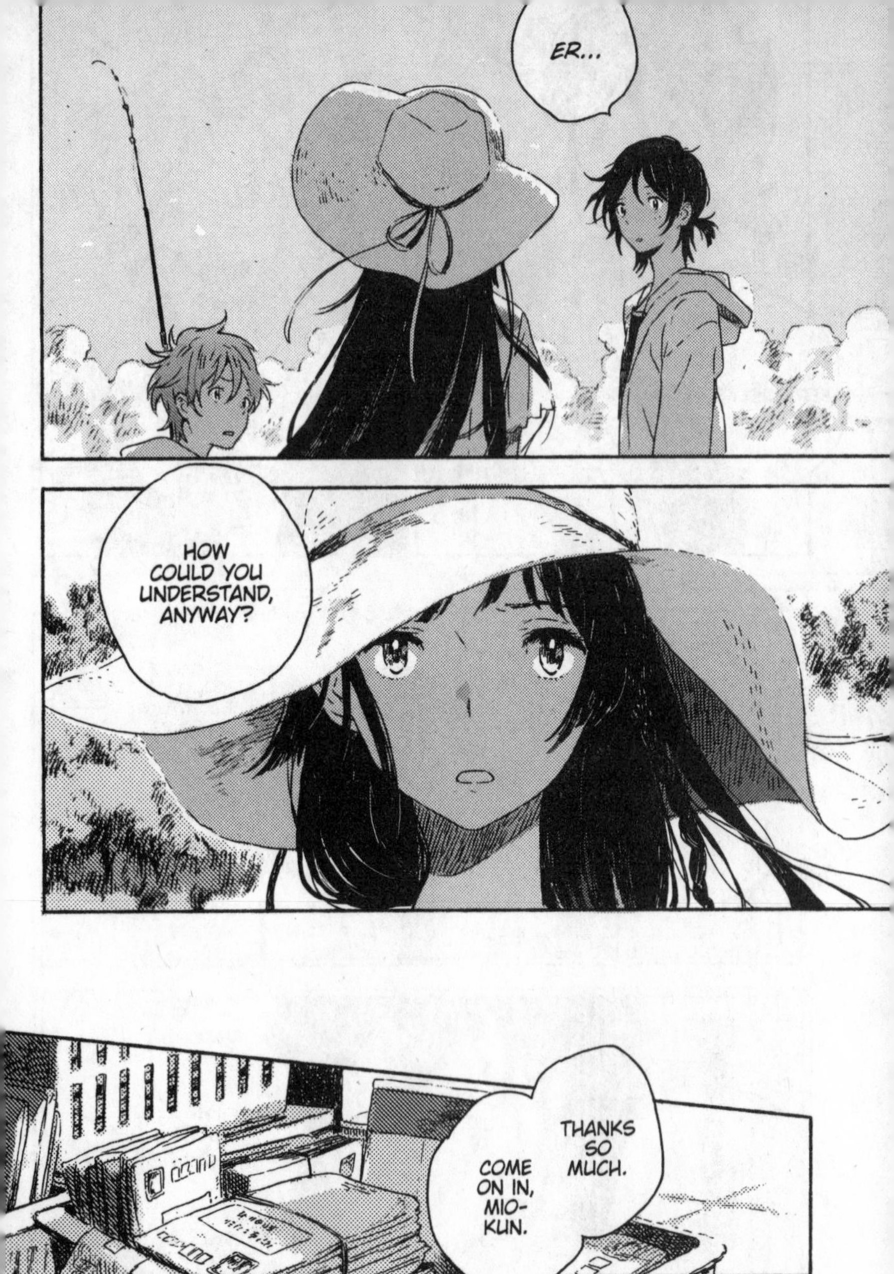
ER...
HOW COULD YOU UNDERSTAND, ANYWAY?
THANKS SO MUCH.
COME ON IN, MIO-KUN.

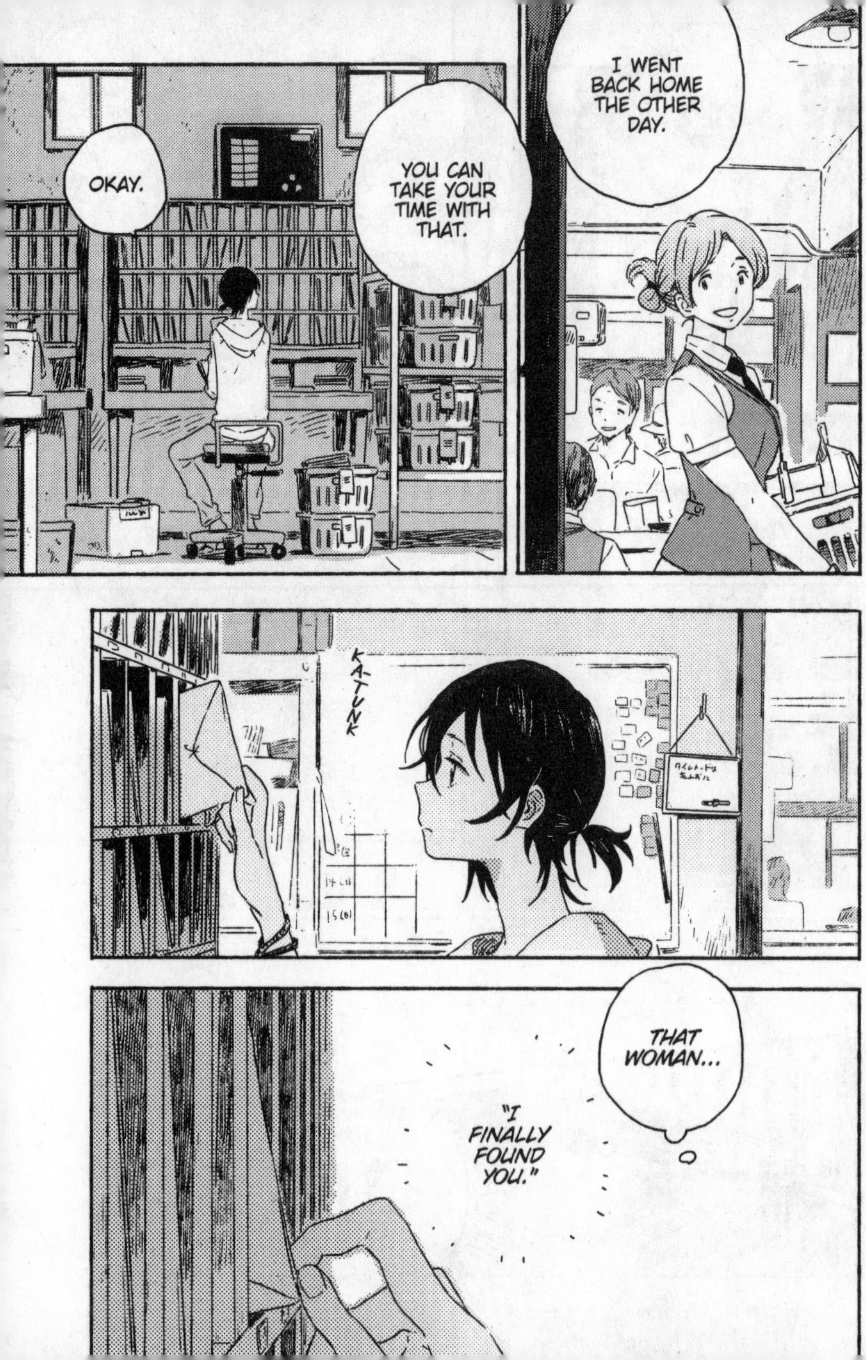
I WENT BACK HOME THE OTHER DAY.
YOU CAN TAKE YOUR TIME WITH THAT.
OKAY.
KA-TUNK
THAT WOMAN...
"I FINALLY FOUND YOU."

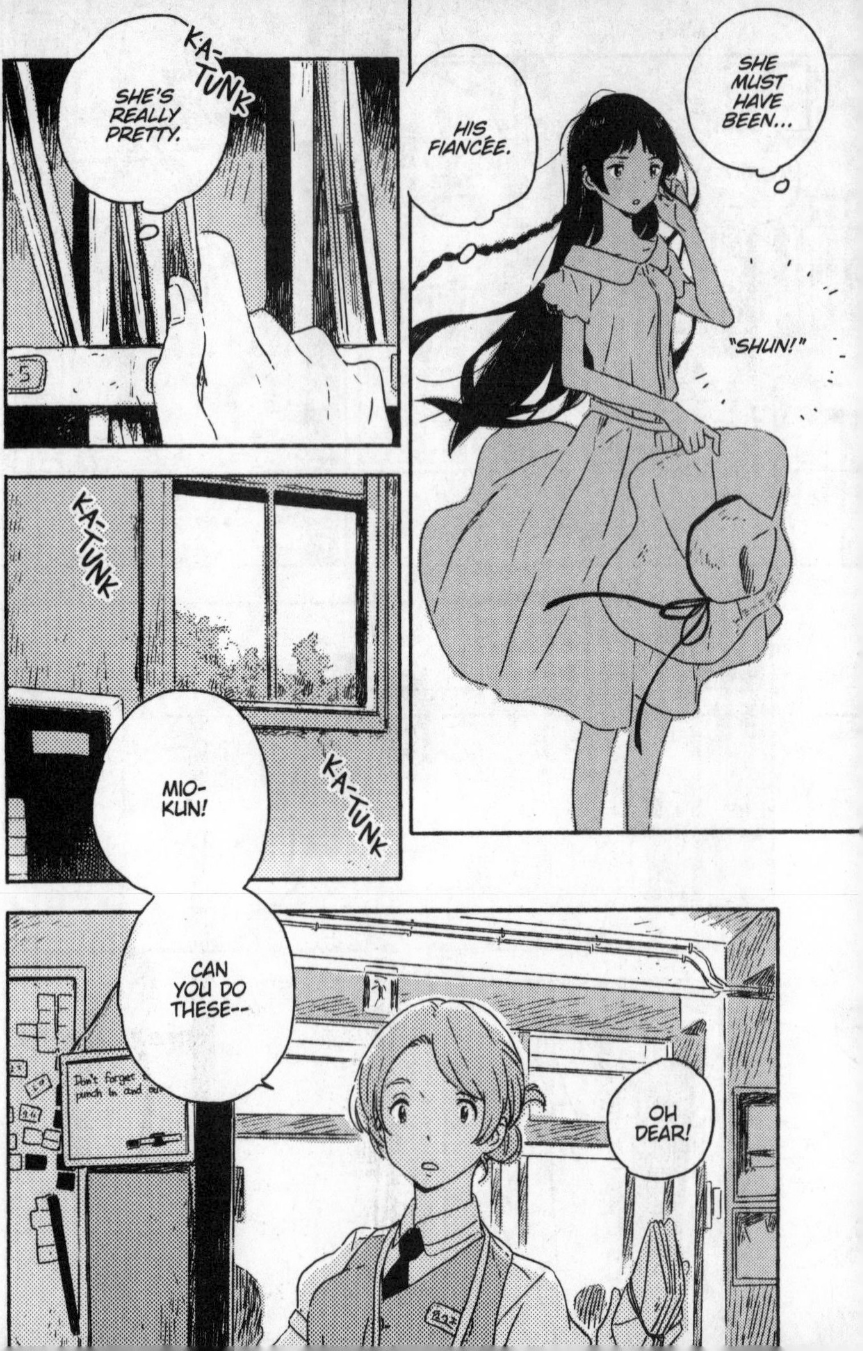
SHE MUST HAVE BEEN...
HIS FIANCÉE.
"SHUN!"
KA-TUNK
SHE'S REALLY PRETTY.
KA-TUNK
MIO-KUN!
KA-TUNK
CAN YOU DO THESE--
OH DEAR!
Don't forget
punch in and

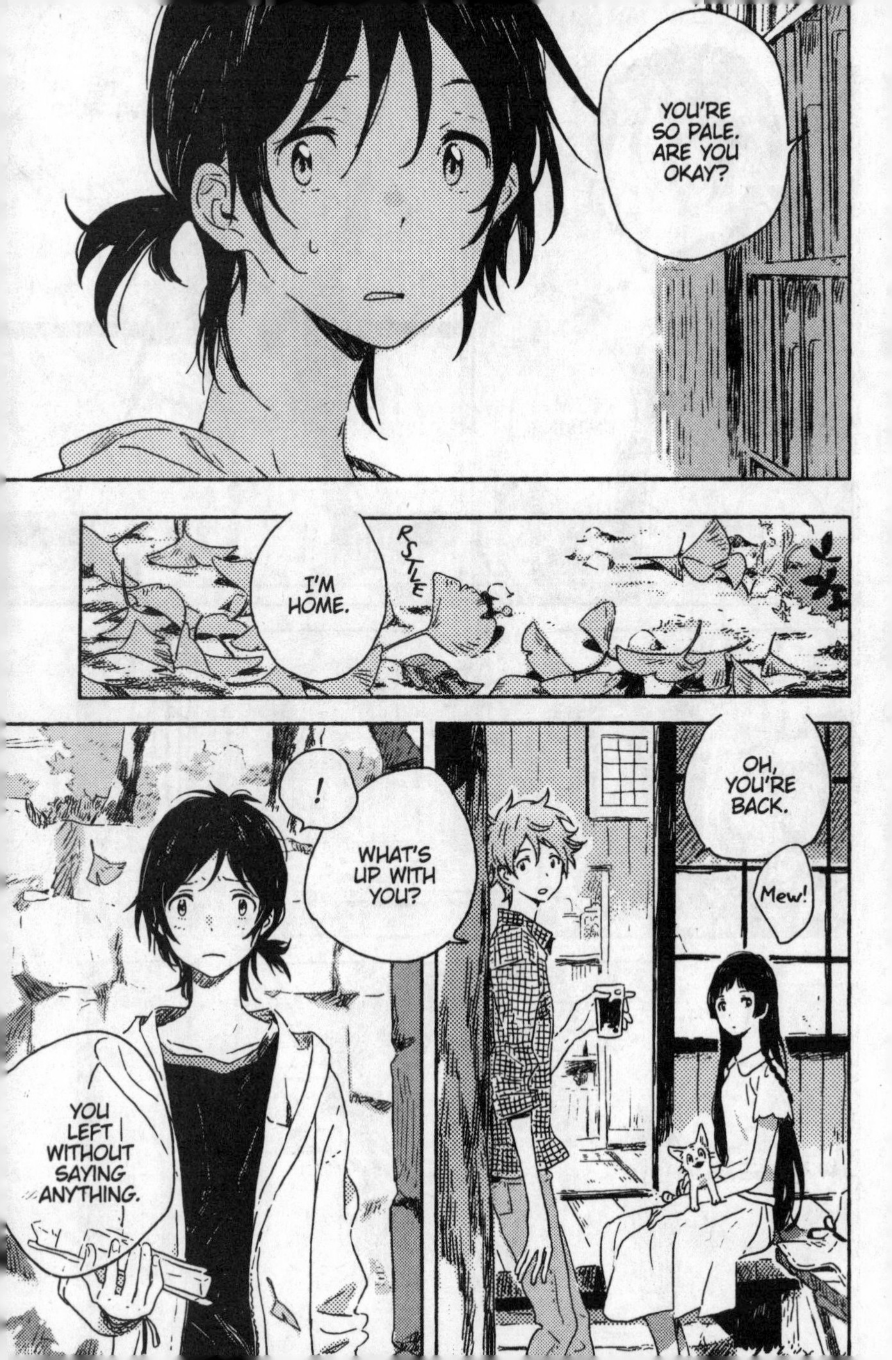
YOU'RE SO PALE. ARE YOU OKAY?
RSTLE
I'M HOME.
OH, YOU'RE BACK.
Mew!
!
WHAT'S UP WITH YOU?
YOU LEFT WITHOUT SAYING ANYTHING.

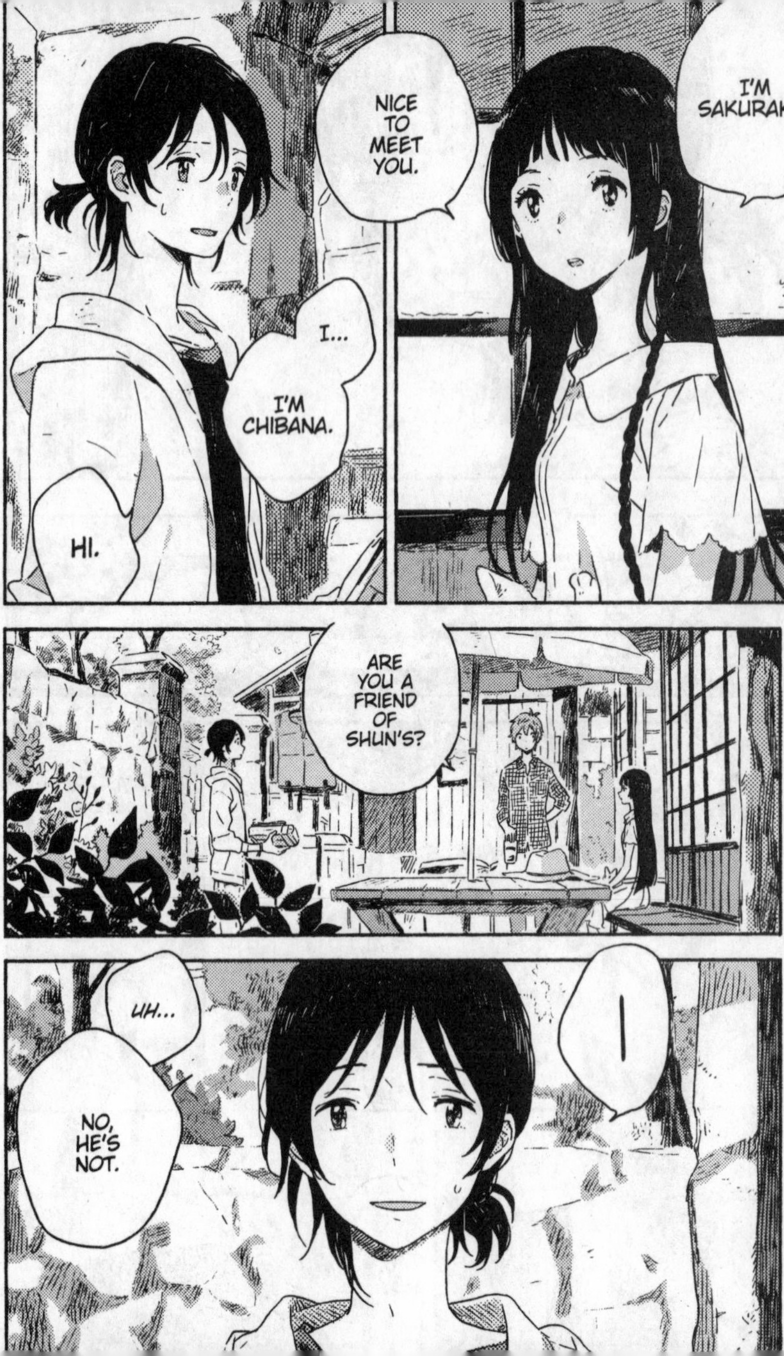
I'M SAKURAKO.
NICE TO MEET YOU.
I...
I'M CHIBANA.
HI.
ARE YOU A FRIEND OF SHUN'S?
UH...
NO, HE'S NOT.

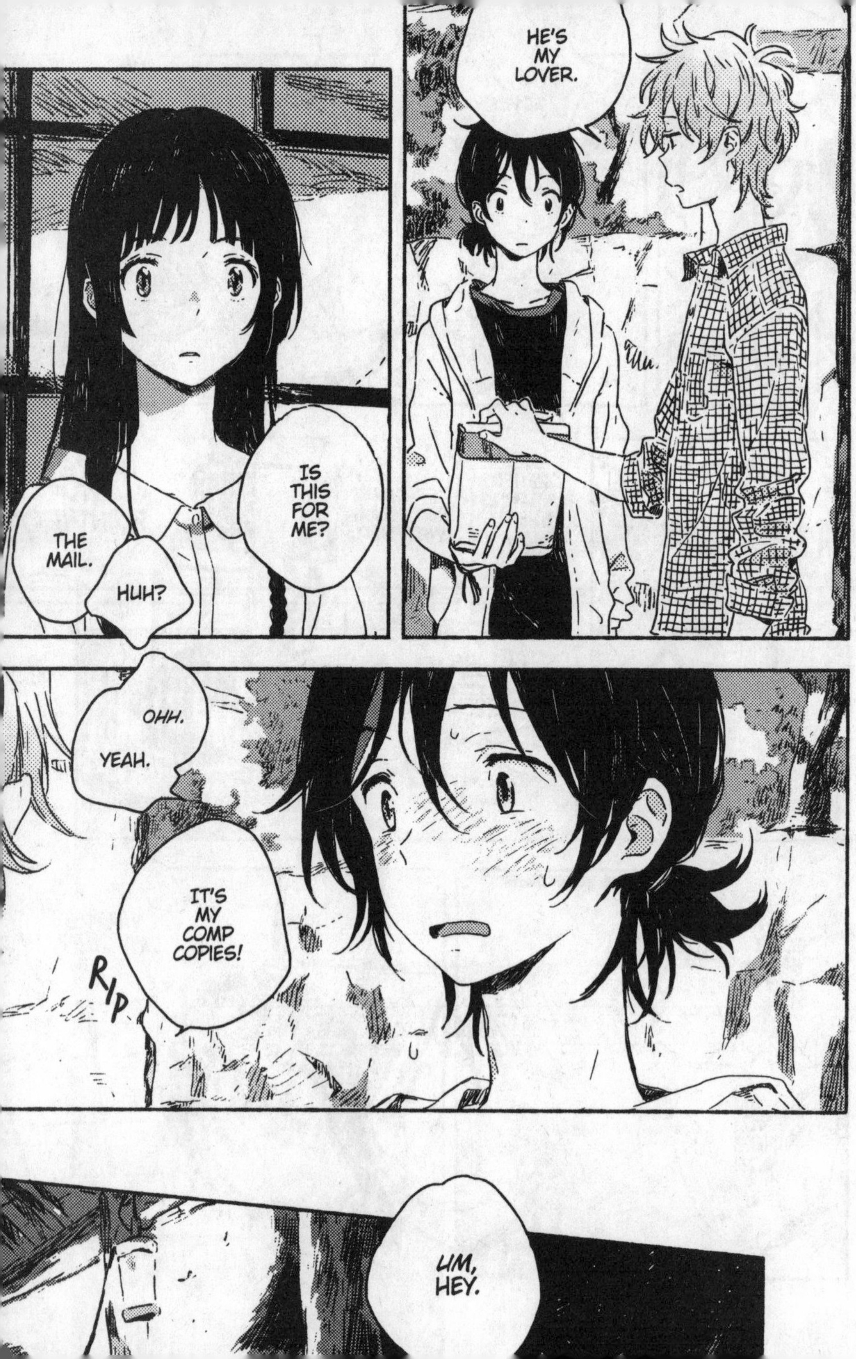
HE'S MY LOVER.
IS THIS FOR ME?
HUH?
THE MAIL.
OHH. YEAH.
IT'S MY COMP COPIES!
RIP
UM, HEY.

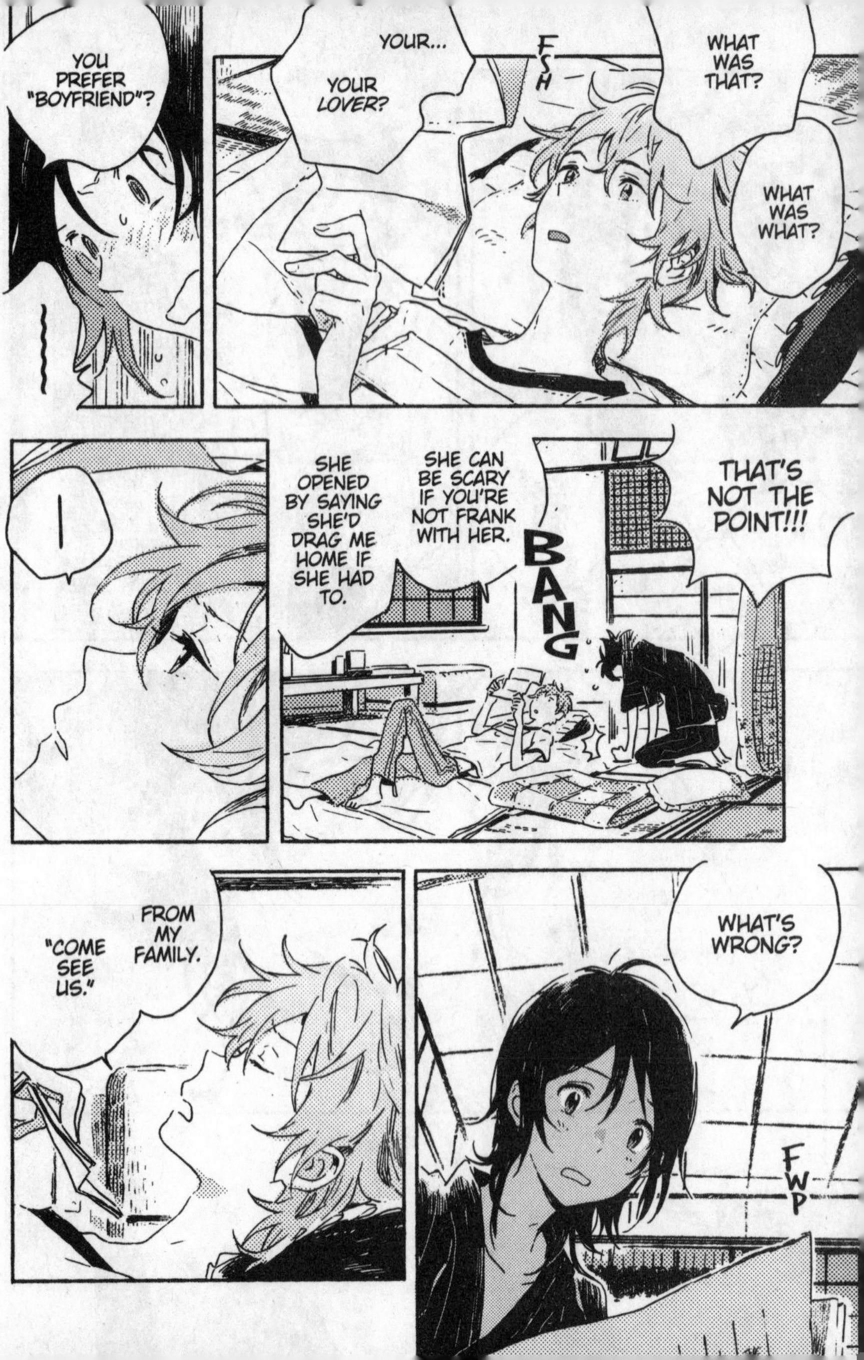
WHAT WAS THAT?
WHAT WAS WHAT?
YOUR...
YOUR LOVER?
FSH
YOU PREFER "BOYFRIEND"?
THAT'S NOT THE POINT!!!
BANG
SHE CAN BE SCARY IF YOU'RE NOT FRANK WITH HER.
SHE OPENED BY SAYING SHE'D DRAG ME HOME IF SHE HAD TO.
WHAT'S WRONG?
FWP
FROM MY FAMILY.
"COME SEE US."

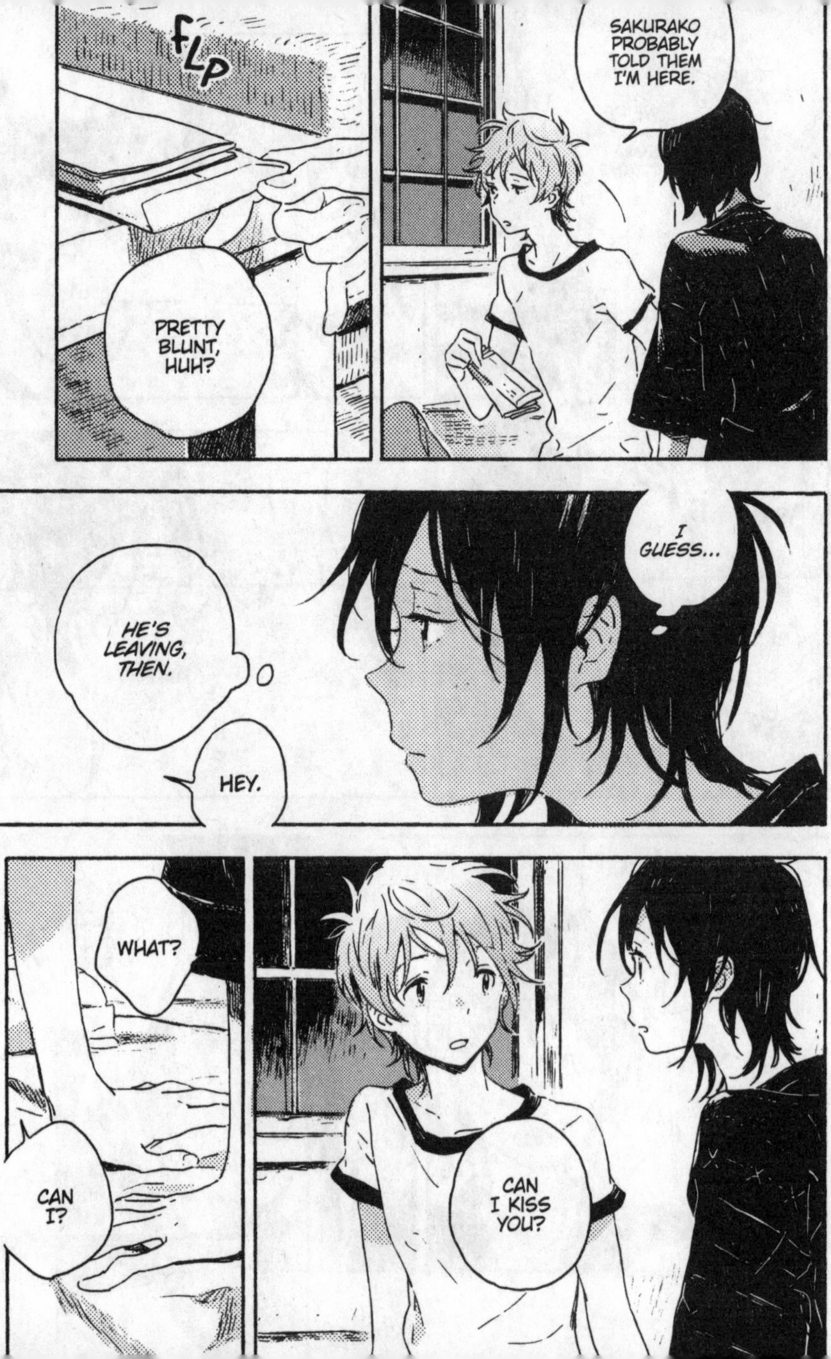
SAKURAKO PROBABLY TOLD THEM I'M HERE.
FLP
PRETTY BLUNT, HUH?
I GUESS...
HE'S LEAVING, THEN.
HEY.
CAN I KISS YOU?
WHAT?
CAN I?

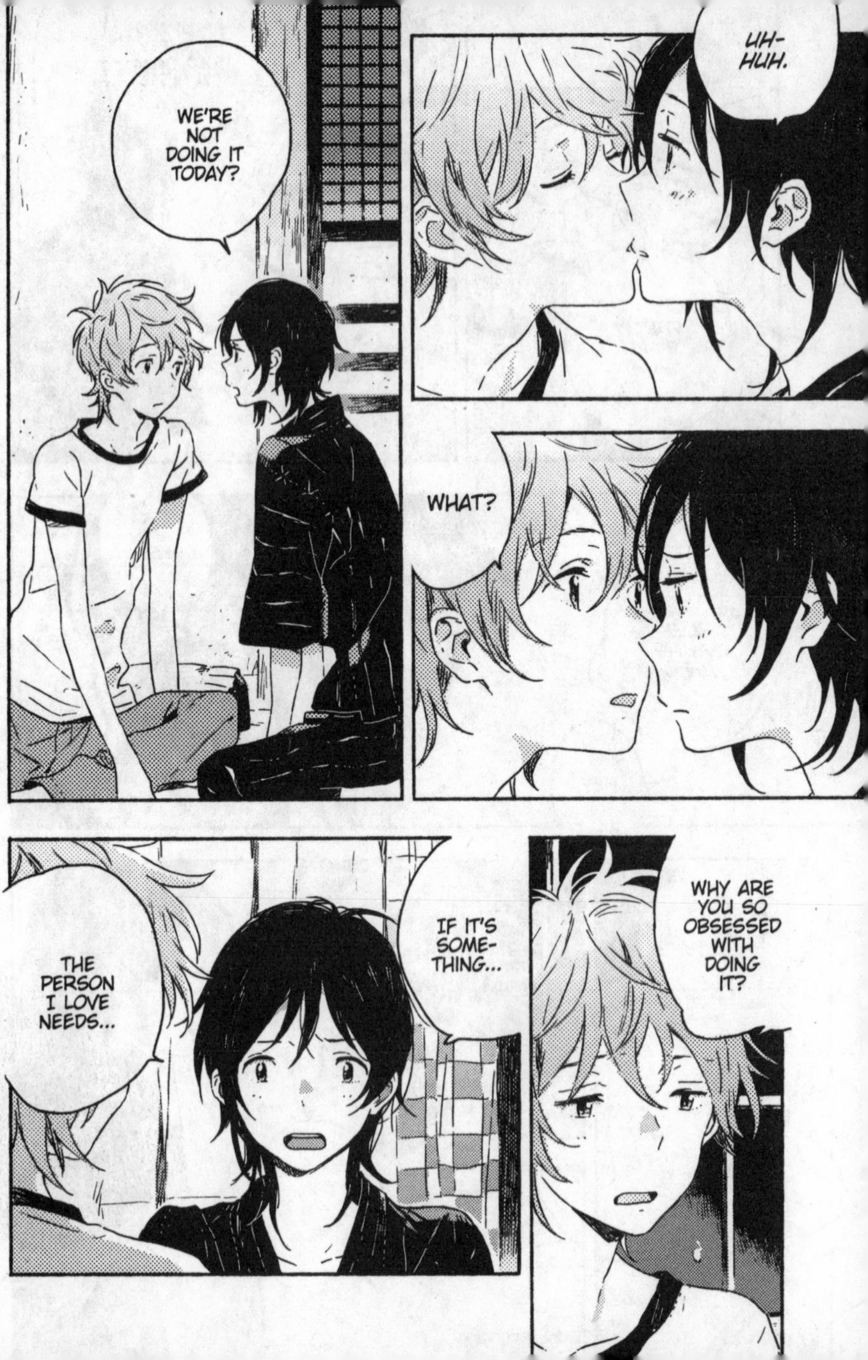
UH-HUH.
WHAT?
WE'RE NOT DOING IT TODAY?
WHY ARE YOU SO OBSESSED WITH DOING IT?
IF IT'S SOME-THING...
THE PERSON I LOVE NEEDS...

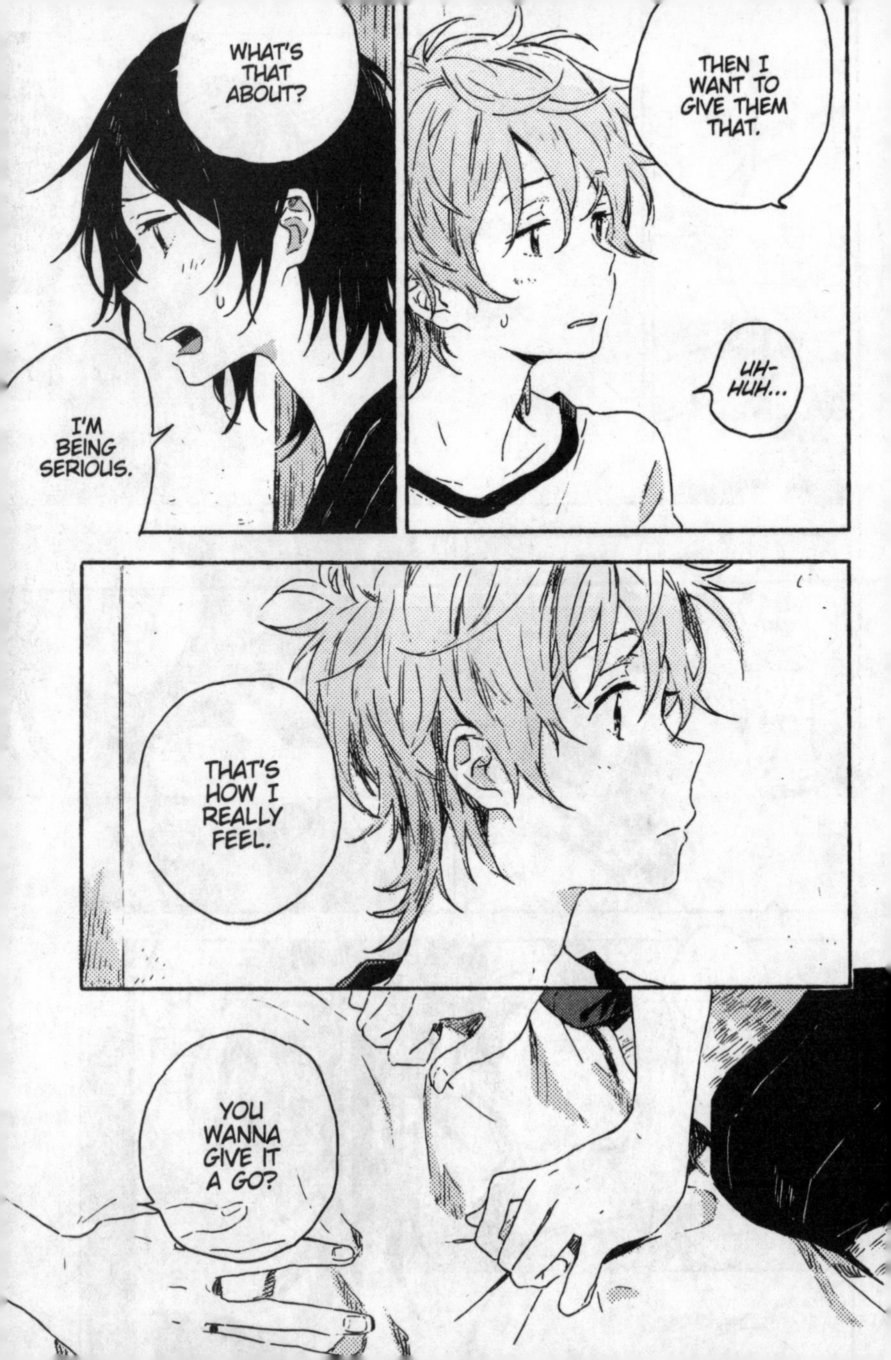
THEN I WANT TO GIVE THEM THAT.
UH-HUH...
WHAT'S THAT ABOUT?
I'M BEING SERIOUS.
THAT'S HOW I REALLY FEEL.
YOU WANNA GIVE IT A GO?

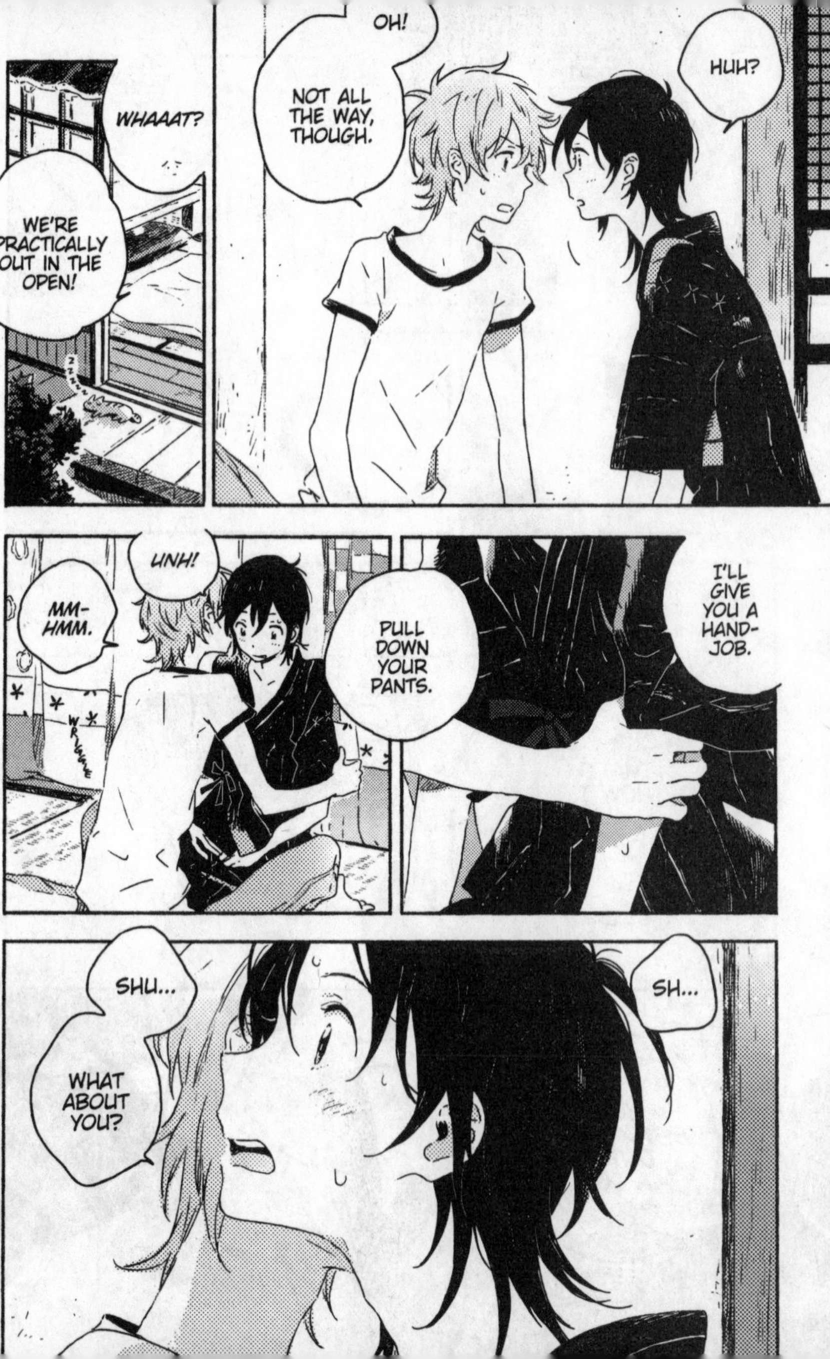
HUH?
OH!
NOT ALL THE WAY, THOUGH.
WHAAAT?
WE'RE PRACTICALLY OUT IN THE OPEN!
I'LL GIVE YOU A HAND-JOB.
PULL DOWN YOUR PANTS.
UNH!
MM-HMM.
WRIGGLE
SH...
SHU...
WHAT ABOUT YOU?

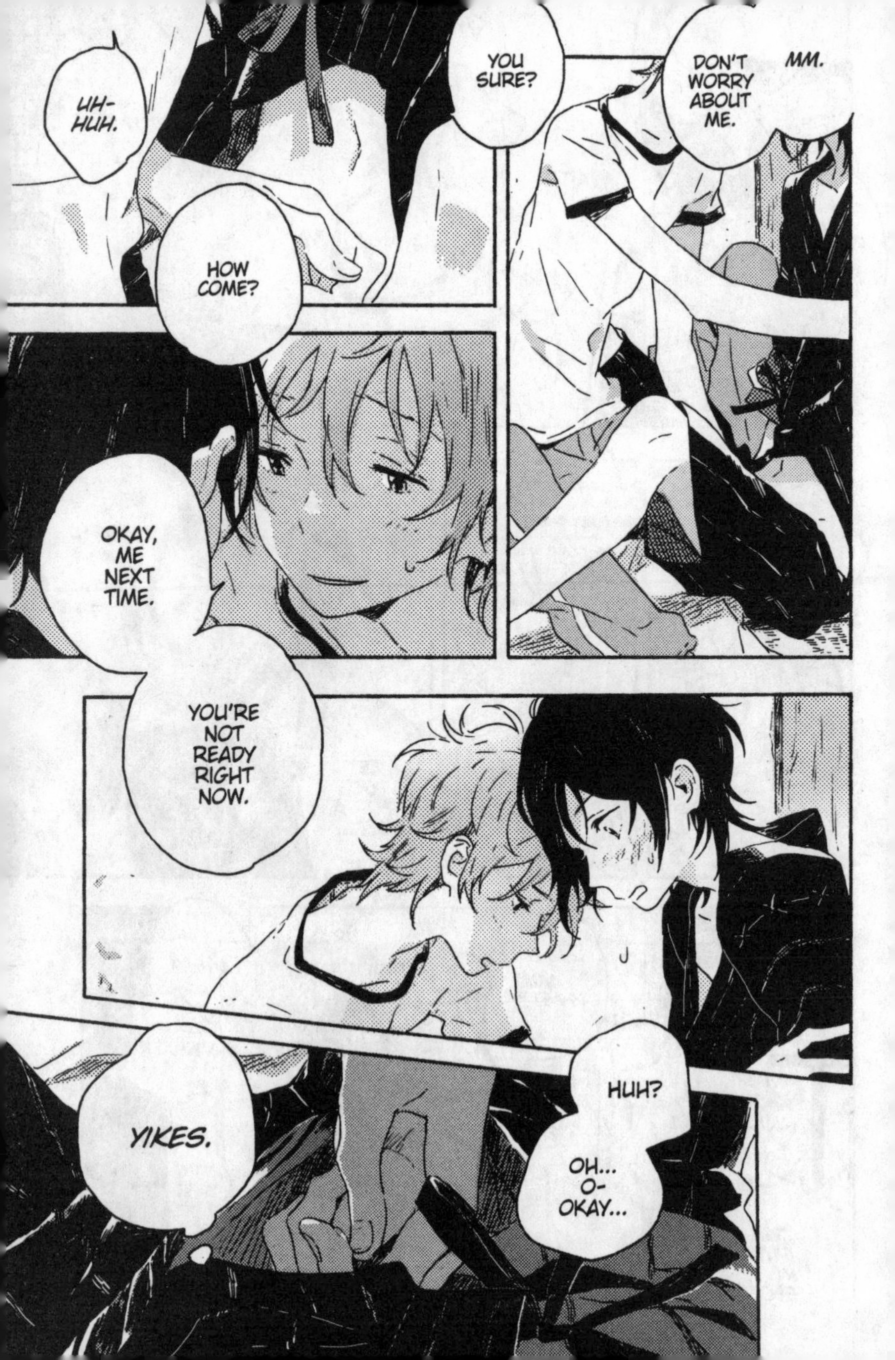
MM.
DON'T WORRY ABOUT ME.
YOU SURE?
UH-HUH.
HOW COME?
OKAY, ME NEXT TIME.
YOU'RE NOT READY RIGHT NOW.
HUH?
OH... O-OKAY...
YIKES.

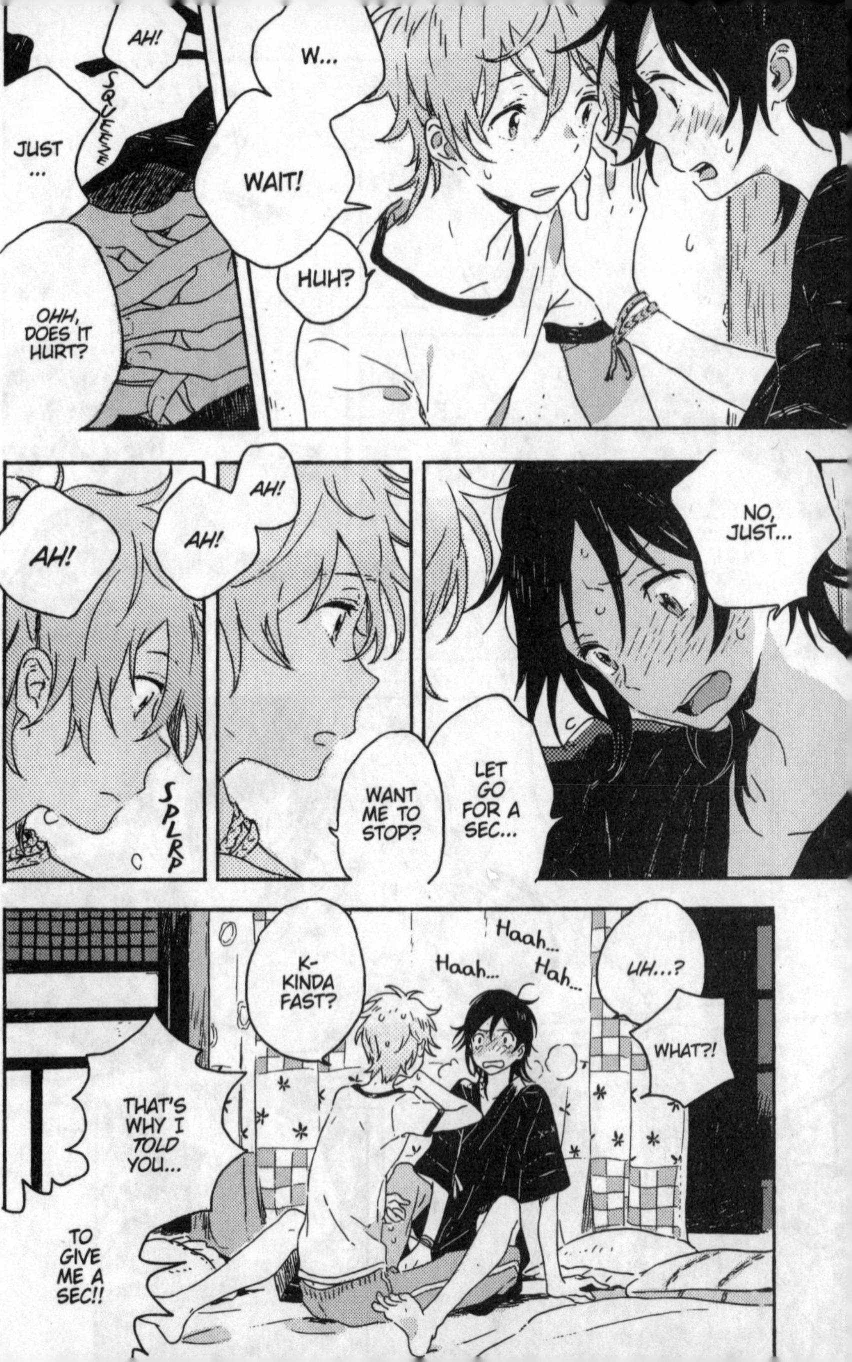
W...
WAIT!
AH!
SQUEEZE
JUST ...
HUH?
OHH, DOES IT HURT?
NO, JUST...
LET GO FOR A SEC...
WANT ME TO STOP?
AH!
AH!
AH!
SPLRP
UH...?
WHAT?!
Haaah...
Hah...
Haaah...
K-KINDA FAST?
THAT'S WHY I *TOLD* YOU...
TO GIVE ME A SEC!!

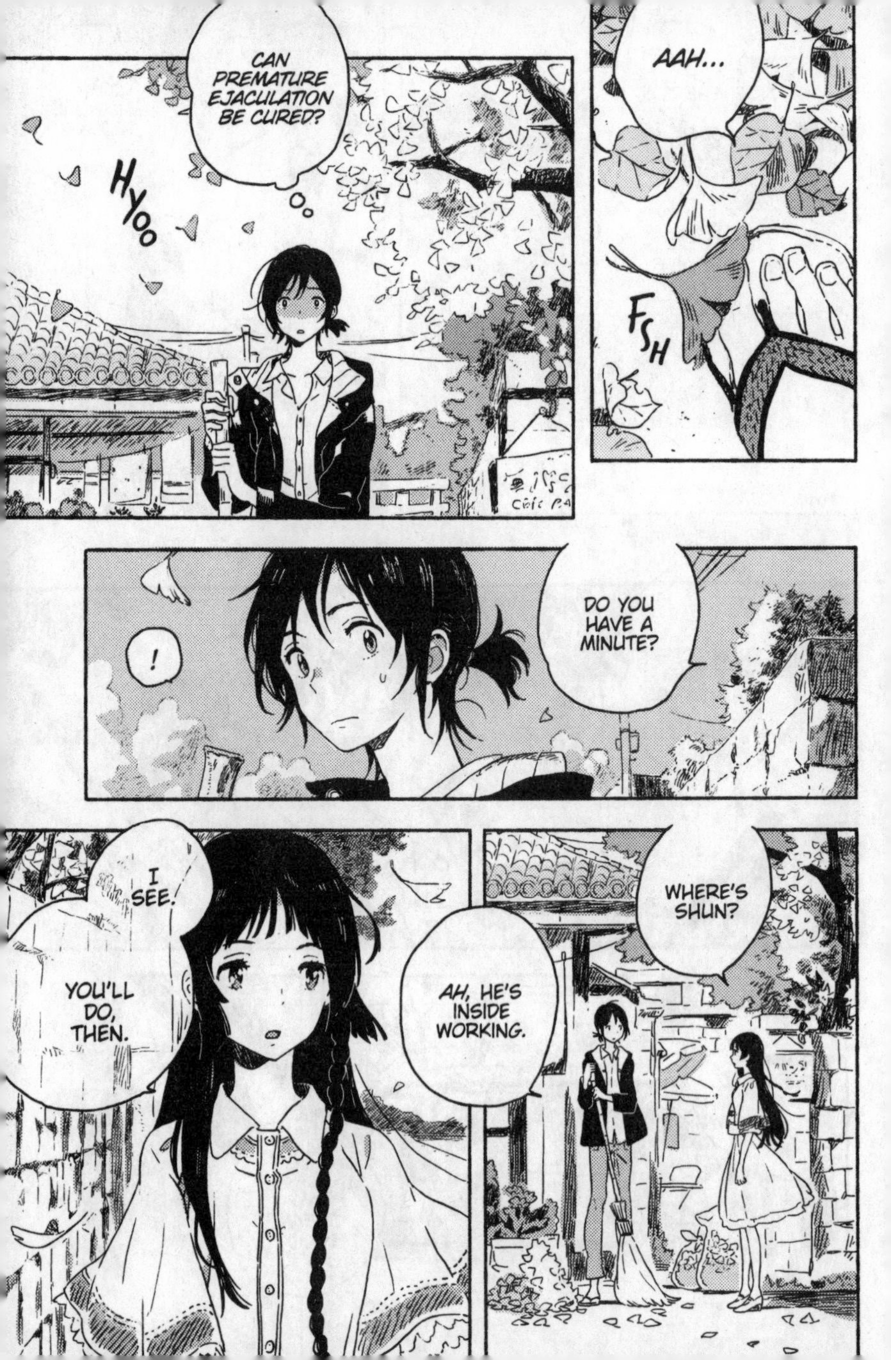
AAH...
FSH
CAN PREMATURE EJACULATION BE CURED?
HYOO
DO YOU HAVE A MINUTE?
!
WHERE'S SHUN?
AH, HE'S INSIDE WORKING.
I SEE.
YOU'LL DO, THEN.

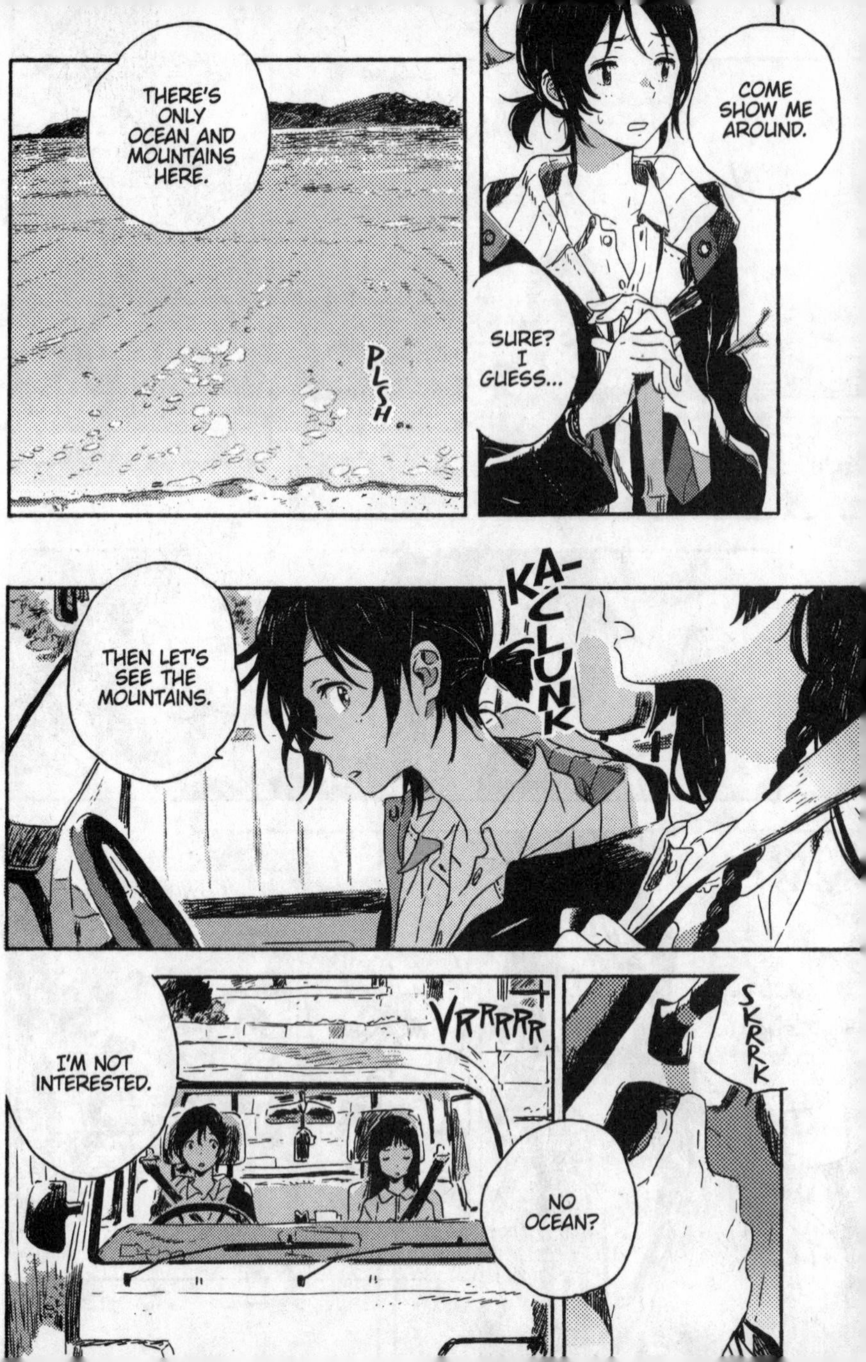
COME SHOW ME AROUND.
SURE? I GUESS...
THERE'S ONLY OCEAN AND MOUNTAINS HERE.
PLSH
KA-CLUNK
THEN LET'S SEE THE MOUNTAINS.
SKRRK
NO OCEAN?
VRRRRR
I'M NOT INTERESTED.

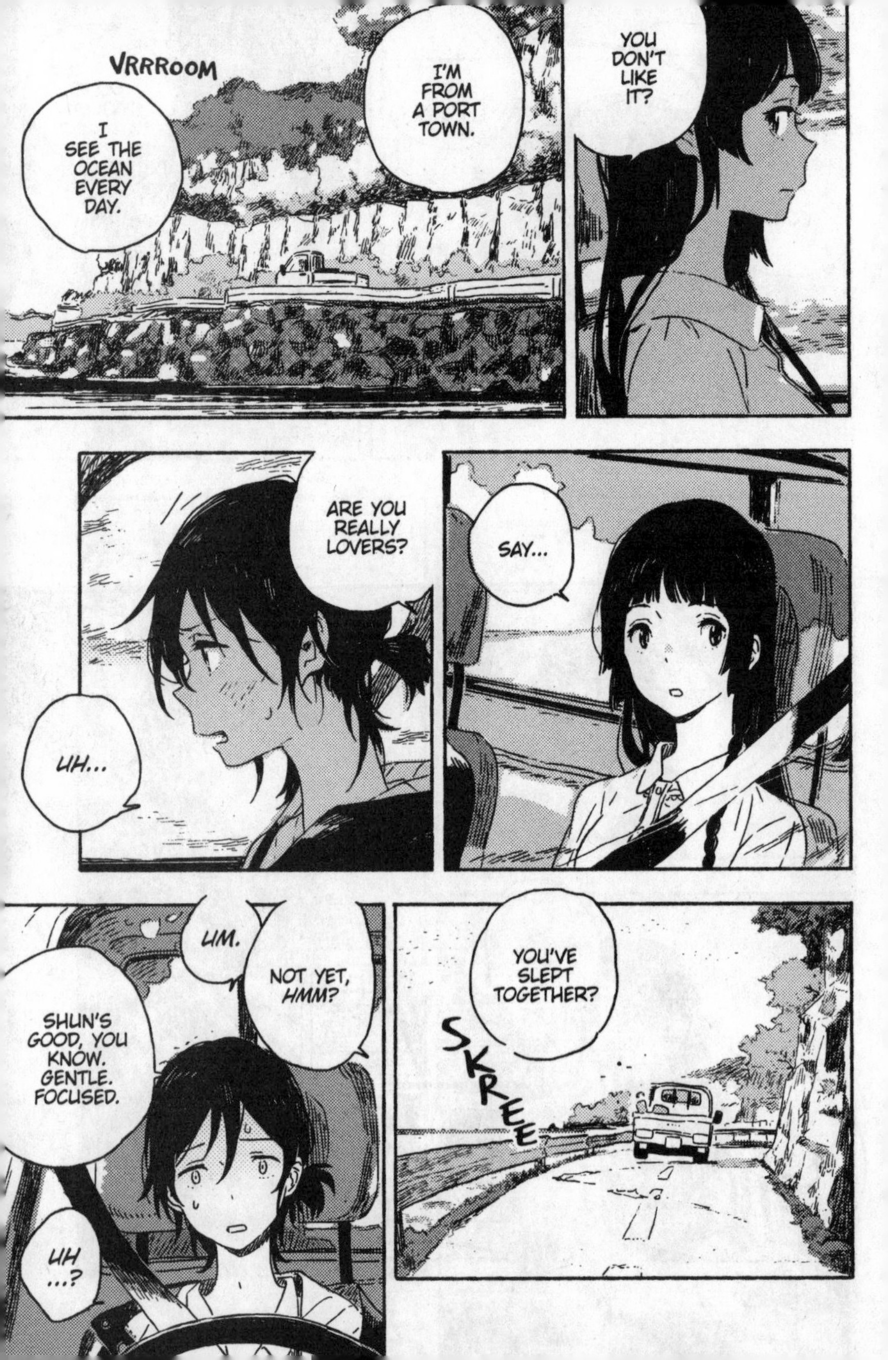
YOU DON'T LIKE IT?
I'M FROM A PORT TOWN.
VRRROOM
I SEE THE OCEAN EVERY DAY.
SAY...
ARE YOU REALLY LOVERS?
UH...
YOU'VE SLEPT TOGETHER?
SKREE
UM.
NOT YET, HMM?
SHUN'S GOOD, YOU KNOW. GENTLE. FOCUSED.
UH ...?

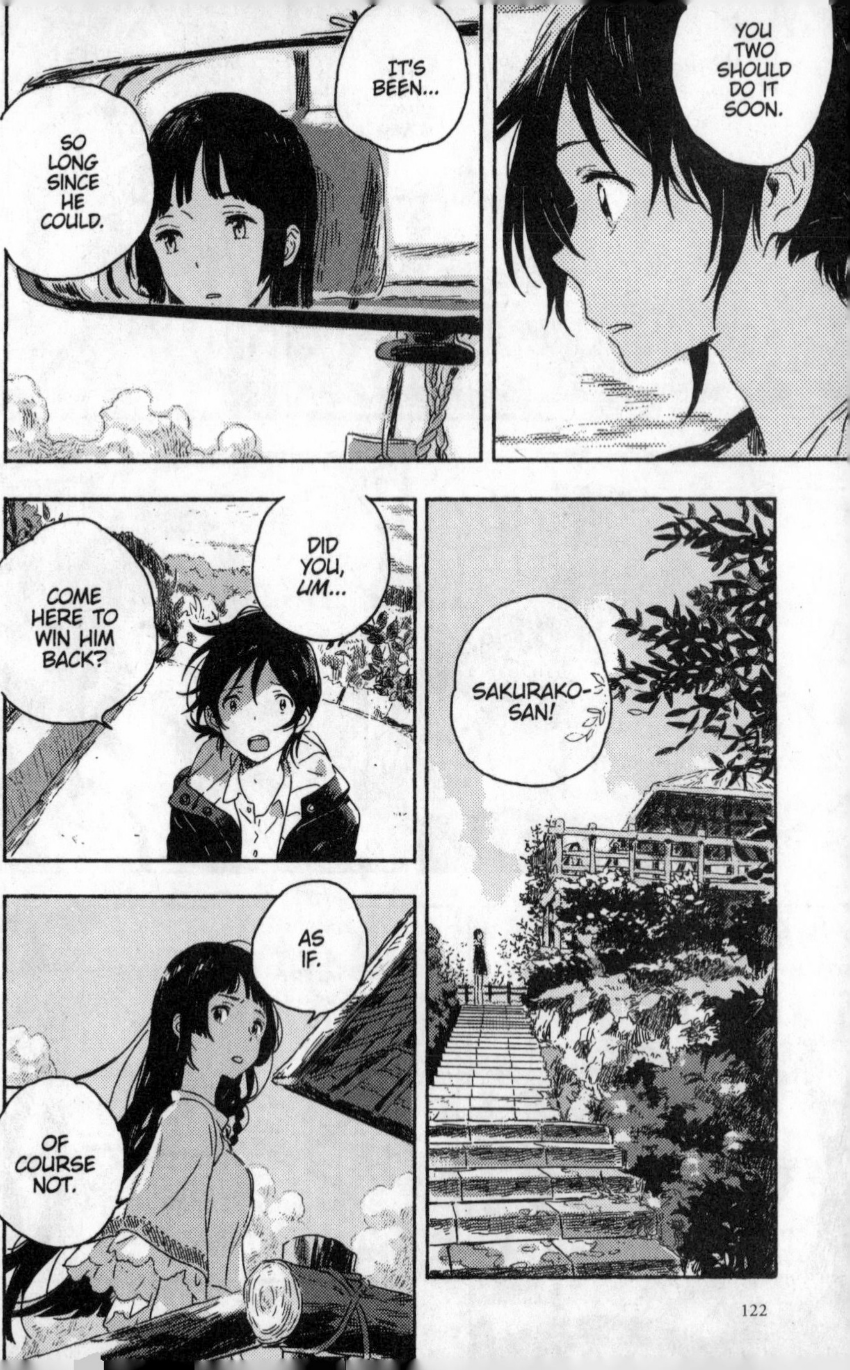
YOU TWO SHOULD DO IT SOON.
IT'S BEEN...
SO LONG SINCE HE COULD.
SAKURAKO-SAN!
DID YOU, UM...
COME HERE TO WIN HIM BACK?
AS IF.
OF COURSE NOT.

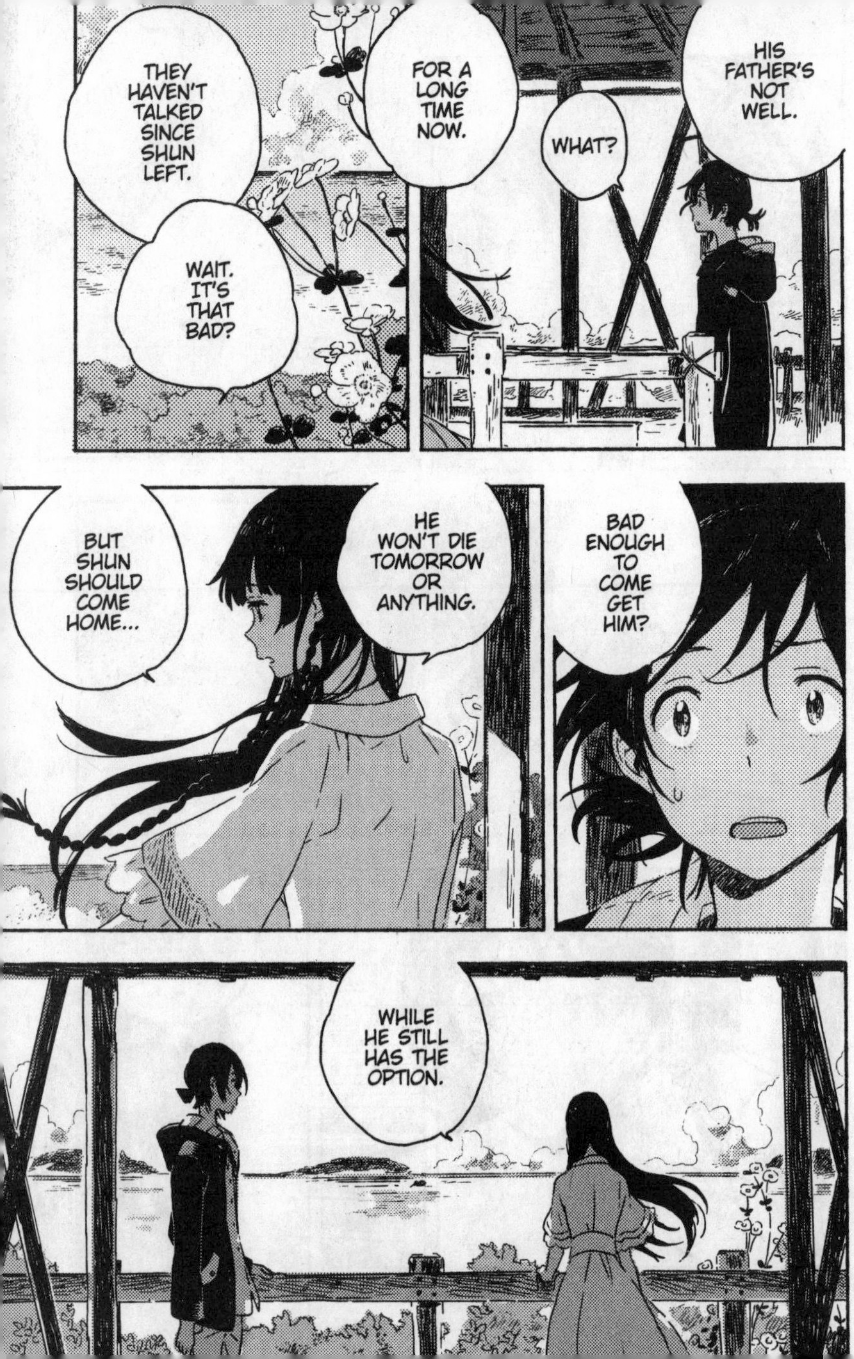
HIS FATHER'S NOT WELL.
WHAT?
FOR A LONG TIME NOW.
THEY HAVEN'T TALKED SINCE SHUN LEFT.
WAIT. IT'S THAT BAD?
BAD ENOUGH TO COME GET HIM?
HE WON'T DIE TOMORROW OR ANYTHING.
BUT SHUN SHOULD COME HOME...
WHILE HE STILL HAS THE OPTION.

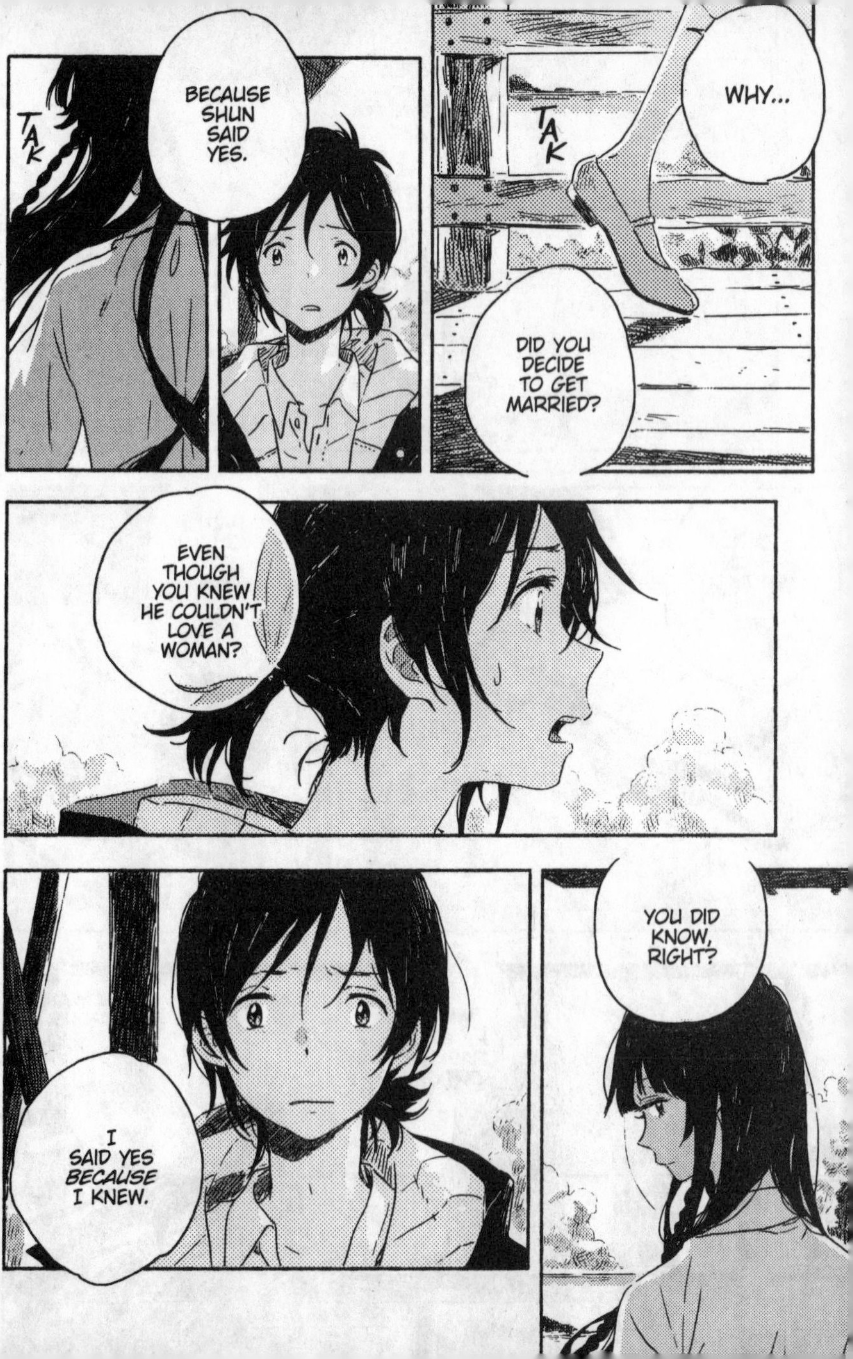
WHY...
TAK
DID YOU DECIDE TO GET MARRIED?
BECAUSE SHUN SAID YES.
TAK
EVEN THOUGH YOU KNEW HE COULDN'T LOVE A WOMAN?
YOU DID KNOW, RIGHT?
I SAID YES *BECAUSE* I KNEW.

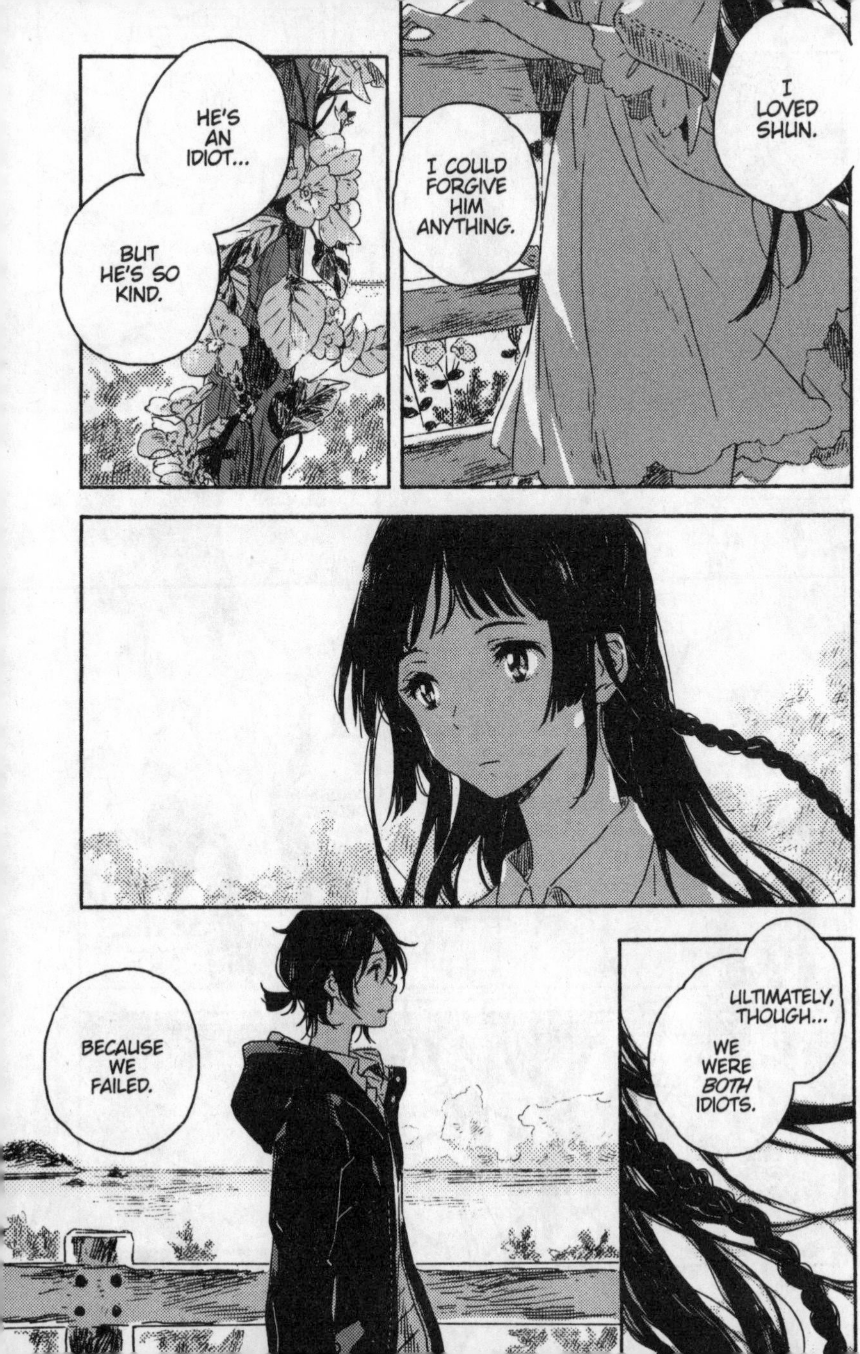
I LOVED SHUN.
I COULD FORGIVE HIM ANYTHING.
HE'S AN IDIOT...
BUT HE'S SO KIND.
ULTIMATELY, THOUGH...
WE WERE *BOTH* IDIOTS.
BECAUSE WE FAILED.

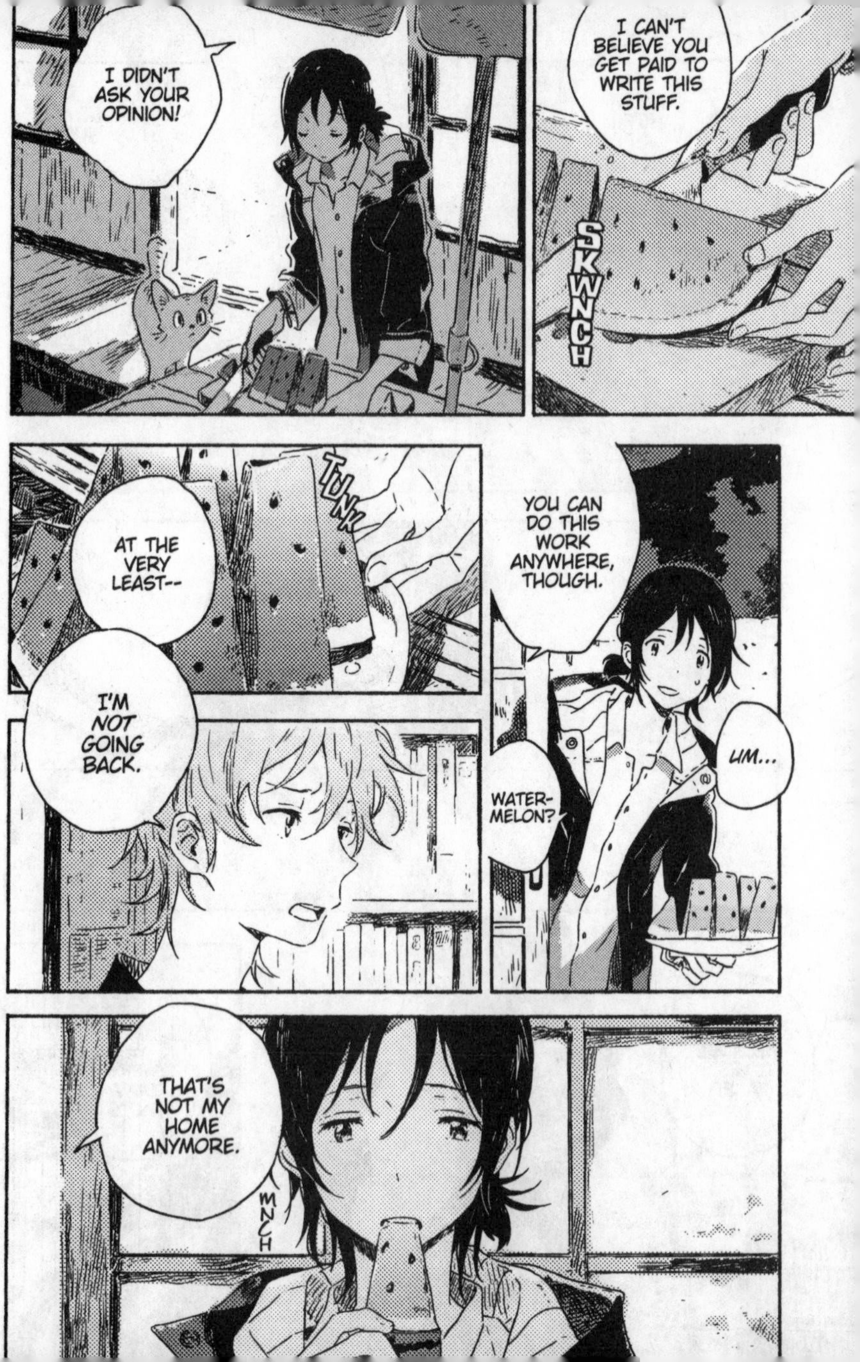
I CAN'T BELIEVE YOU GET PAID TO WRITE THIS STUFF.
SKWNCH
I DIDN'T ASK YOUR OPINION!
YOU CAN DO THIS WORK ANYWHERE, THOUGH.
UM...
WATER-MELON?
AT THE VERY LEAST--
TUNK
I'M *NOT* GOING BACK.
THAT'S NOT MY HOME ANYMORE.
MNCH

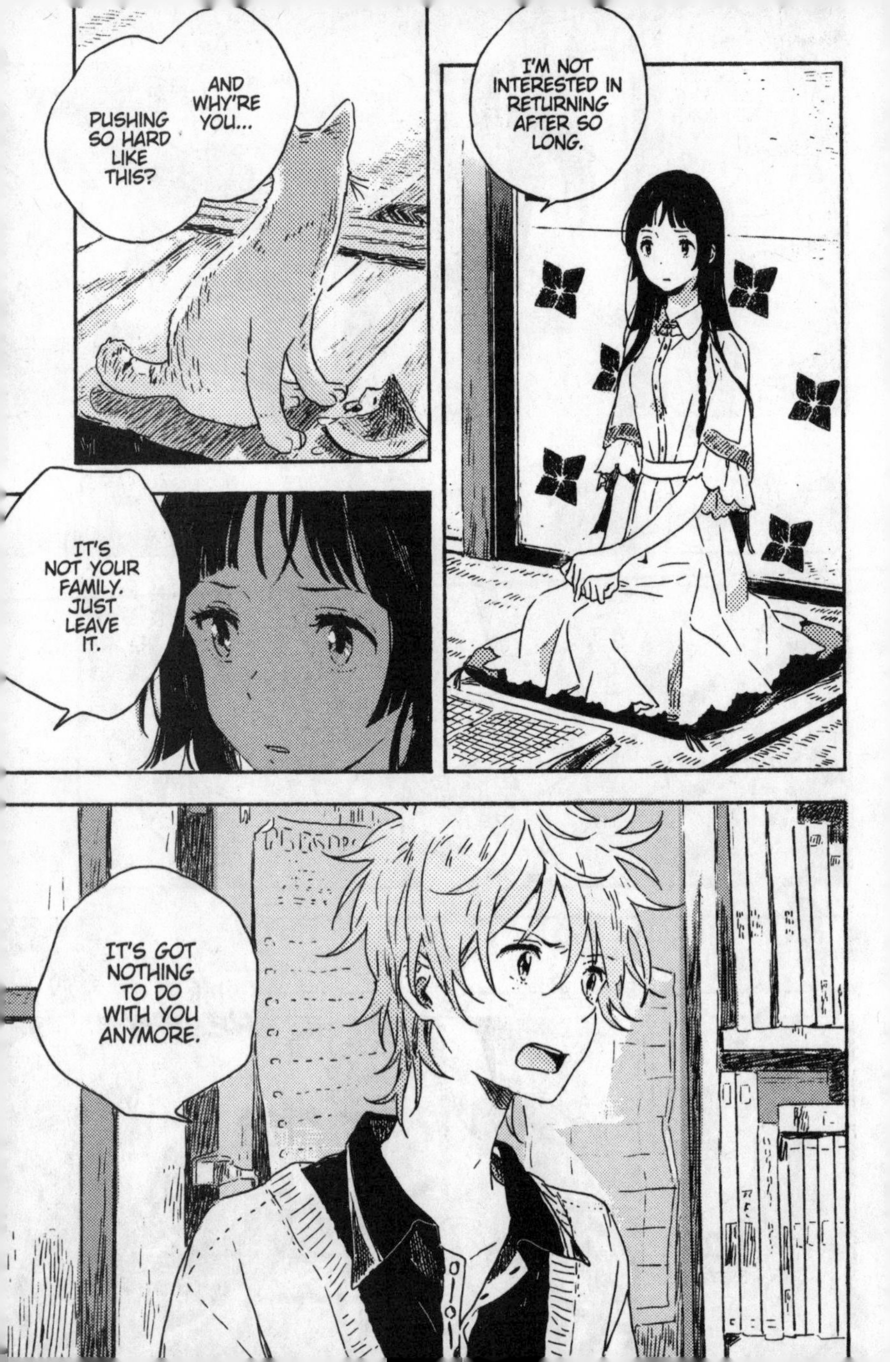
I'M NOT INTERESTED IN RETURNING AFTER SO LONG.
AND WHY'RE YOU...
PUSHING SO HARD LIKE THIS?
IT'S NOT YOUR FAMILY. JUST LEAVE IT.
IT'S GOT NOTHING TO DO WITH YOU ANYMORE.

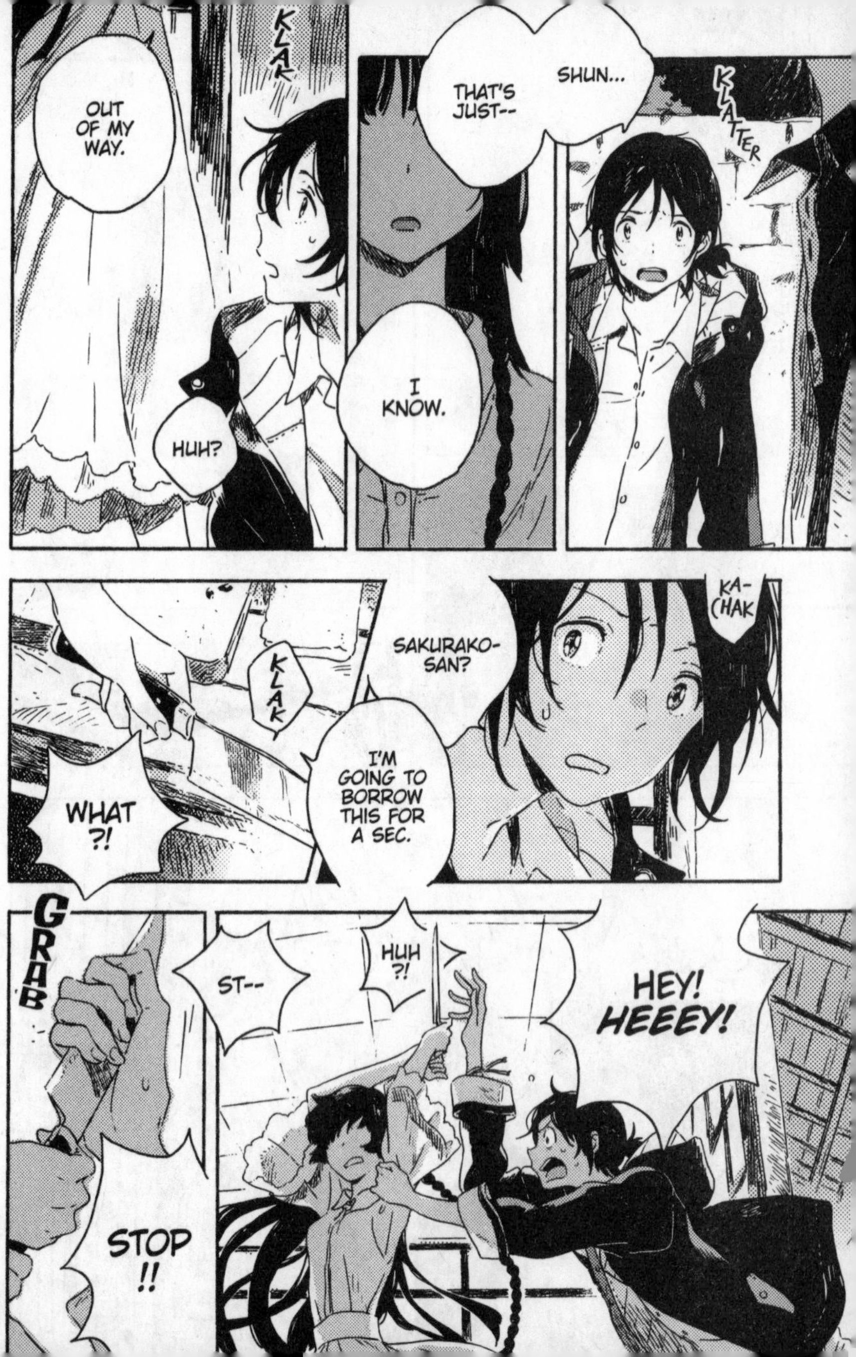
KLATTER
SHUN... THAT'S JUST--
I KNOW.
KLAK
OUT OF MY WAY.
HUH?
KA-CHAK
SAKURAKO-SAN?
I'M GOING TO BORROW THIS FOR A SEC.
KLAK
WHAT ?!
HEY! HEEEY!
HUH ?!
ST--
GRAB
STOP !!

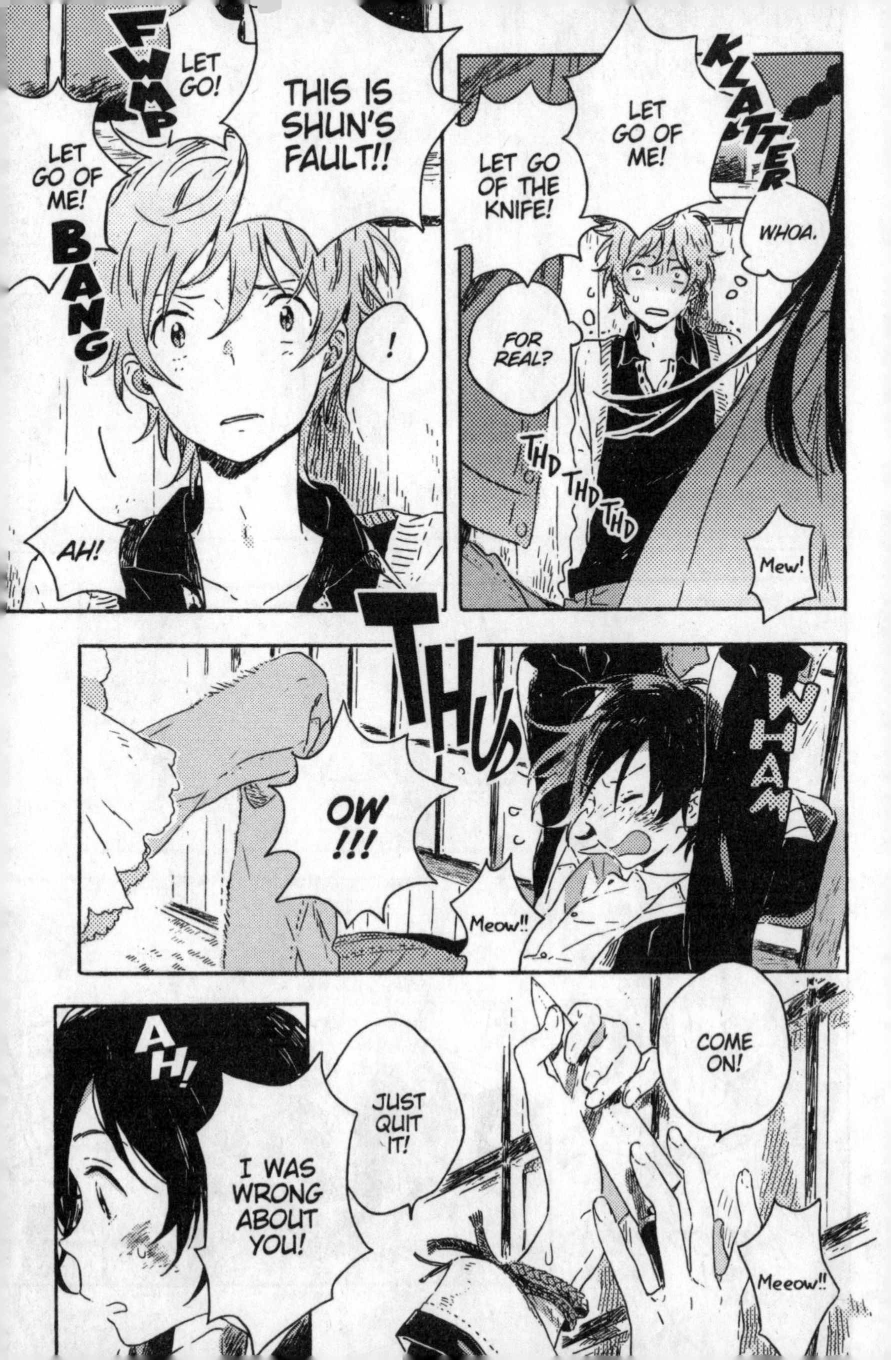
KLATTER
LET GO OF ME!
LET GO OF THE KNIFE!
WHOA.
FOR REAL?
THD THD THD
Mew!
THIS IS SHUN'S FAULT!!
LET GO!
FWMP
LET GO OF ME!
BANG
!
AH!
WHAM
THUD
OW !!!
Meow!!
COME ON!
Meeow!!
JUST QUIT IT!
I WAS WRONG ABOUT YOU!
AH!

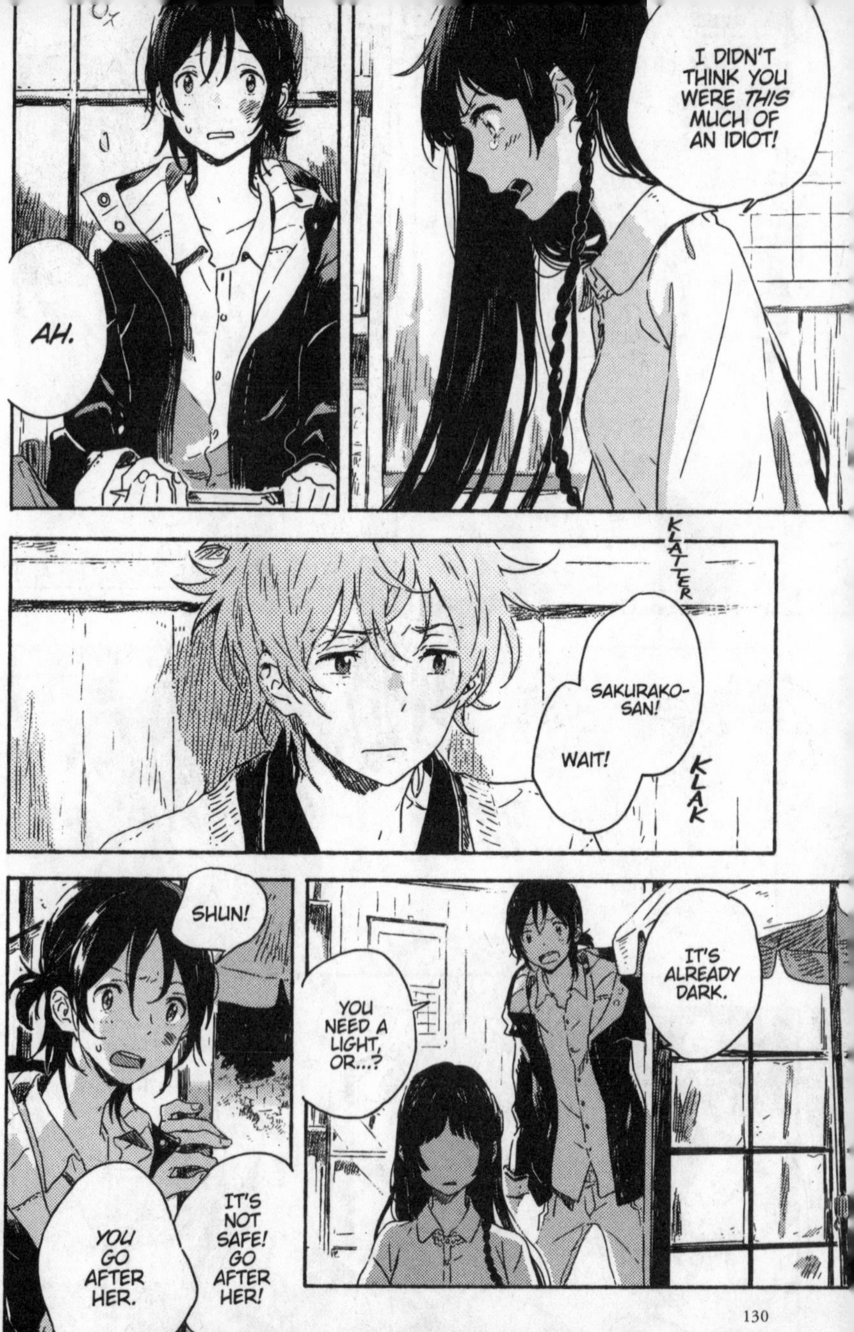
I DIDN'T THINK YOU WERE *THIS* MUCH OF AN IDIOT!
AH.
KLATTER
SAKURAKO-SAN!
WAIT!
KLAK
IT'S ALREADY DARK.
YOU NEED A LIGHT, OR...?
SHUN!
IT'S NOT SAFE! GO AFTER HER!
YOU GO AFTER HER.

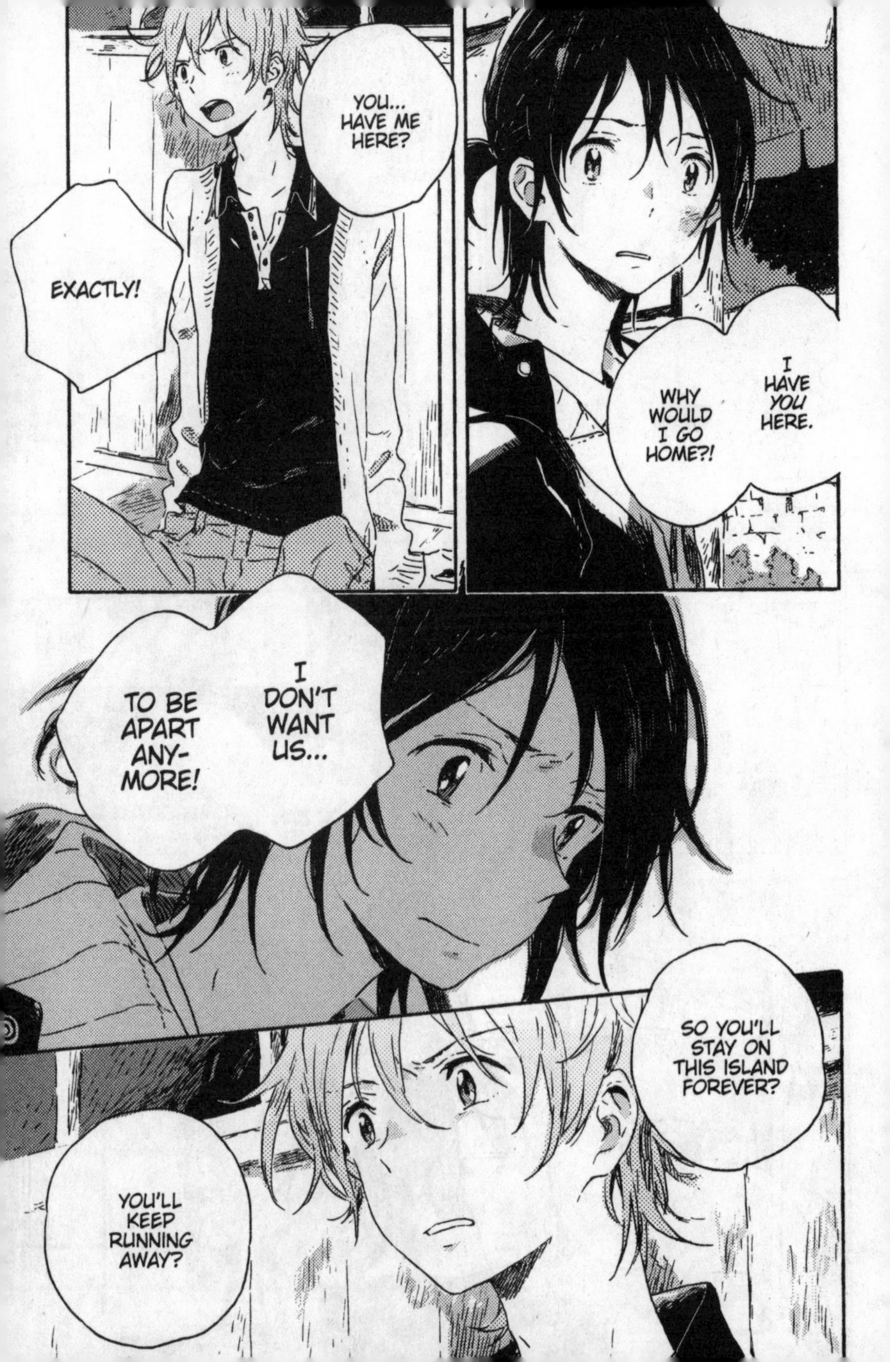
I HAVE YOU HERE.
WHY WOULD I GO HOME?!
YOU... HAVE ME HERE?
EXACTLY!
I DON'T WANT US...
TO BE APART ANY-MORE!
SO YOU'LL STAY ON THIS ISLAND FOREVER?
YOU'LL KEEP RUNNING AWAY?

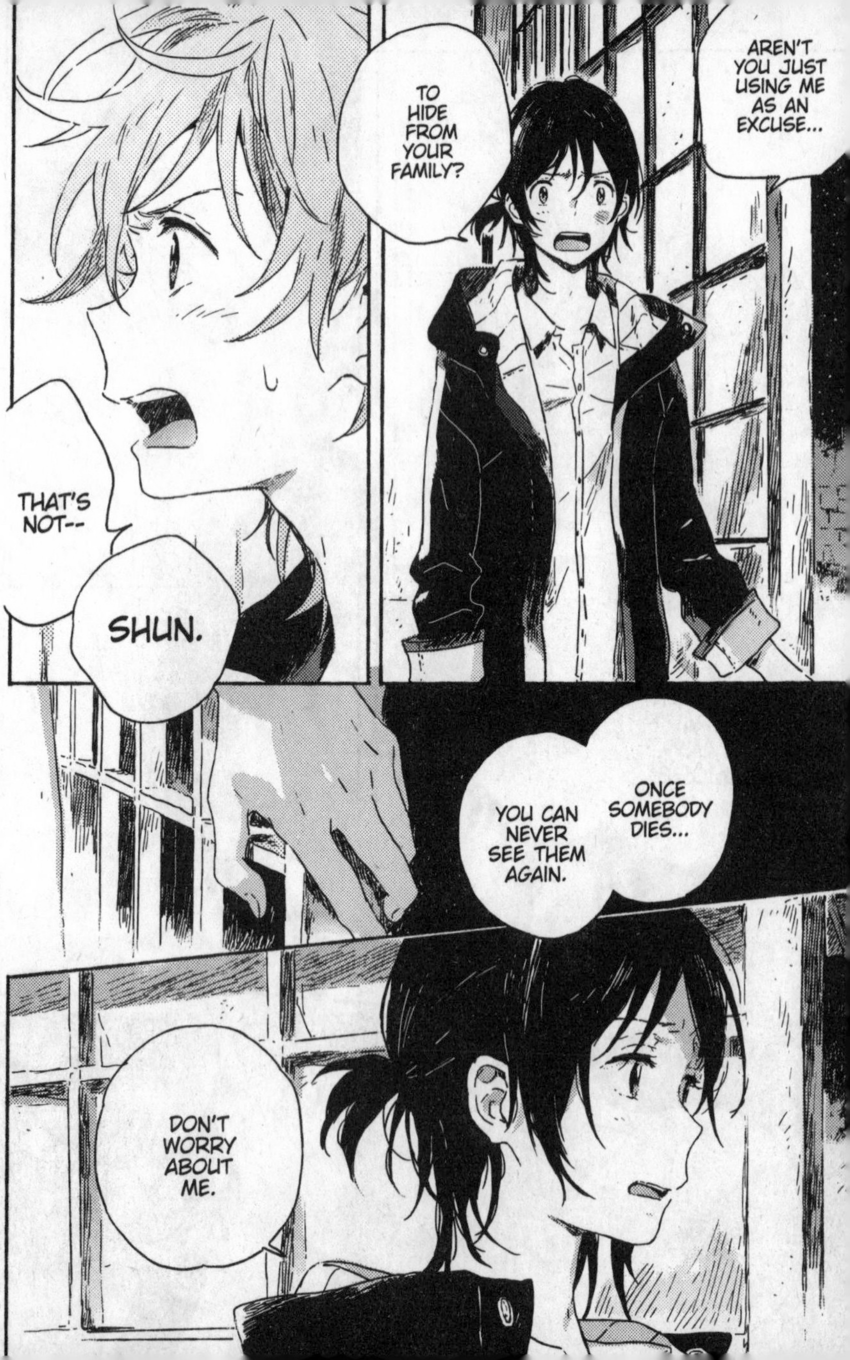
AREN'T YOU JUST USING ME AS AN EXCUSE...
TO HIDE FROM YOUR FAMILY?
THAT'S NOT--
SHUN.
ONCE SOMEBODY DIES...
YOU CAN NEVER SEE THEM AGAIN.
DON'T WORRY ABOUT ME.

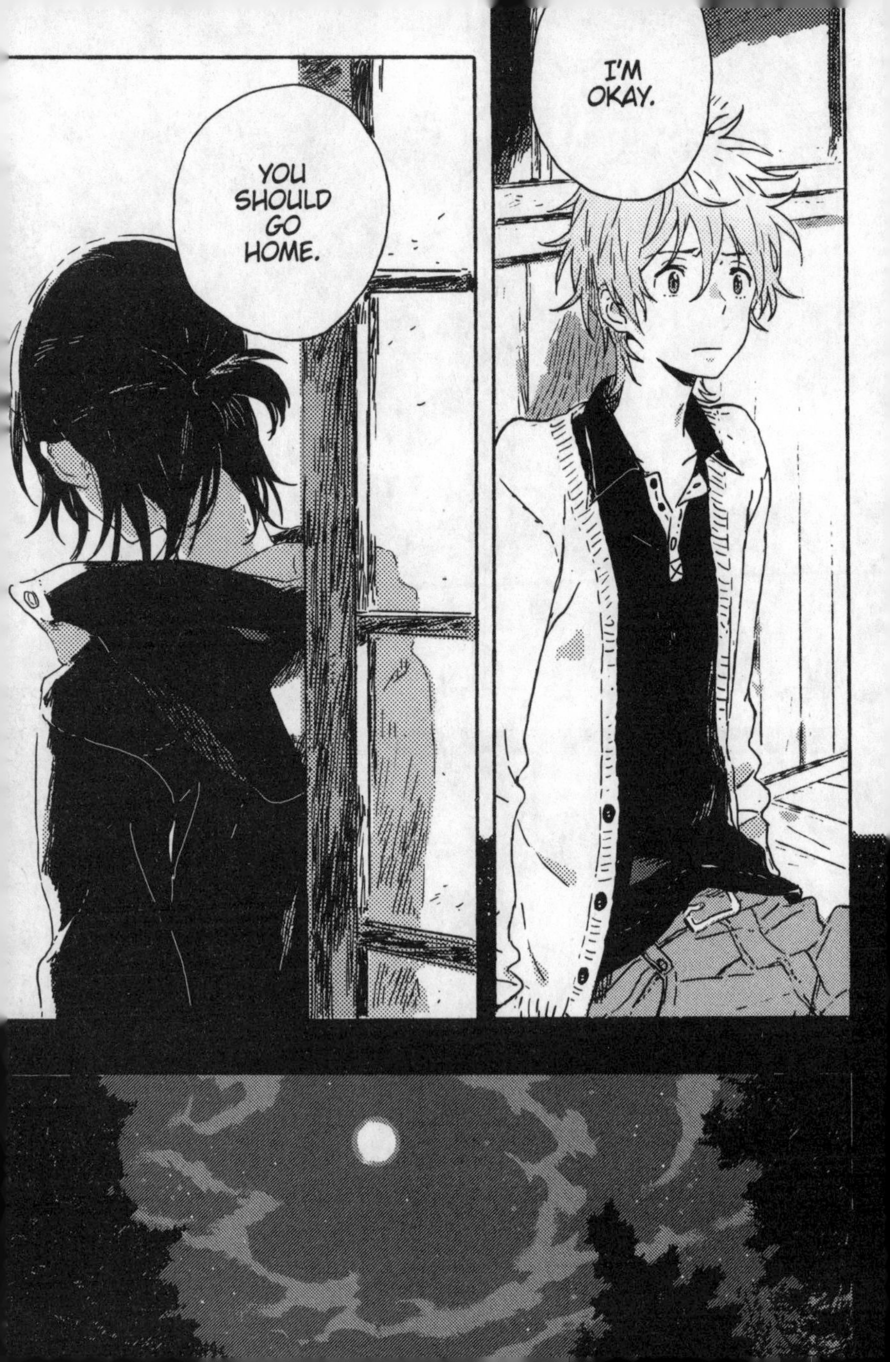
I'M OKAY.
YOU SHOULD GO HOME.

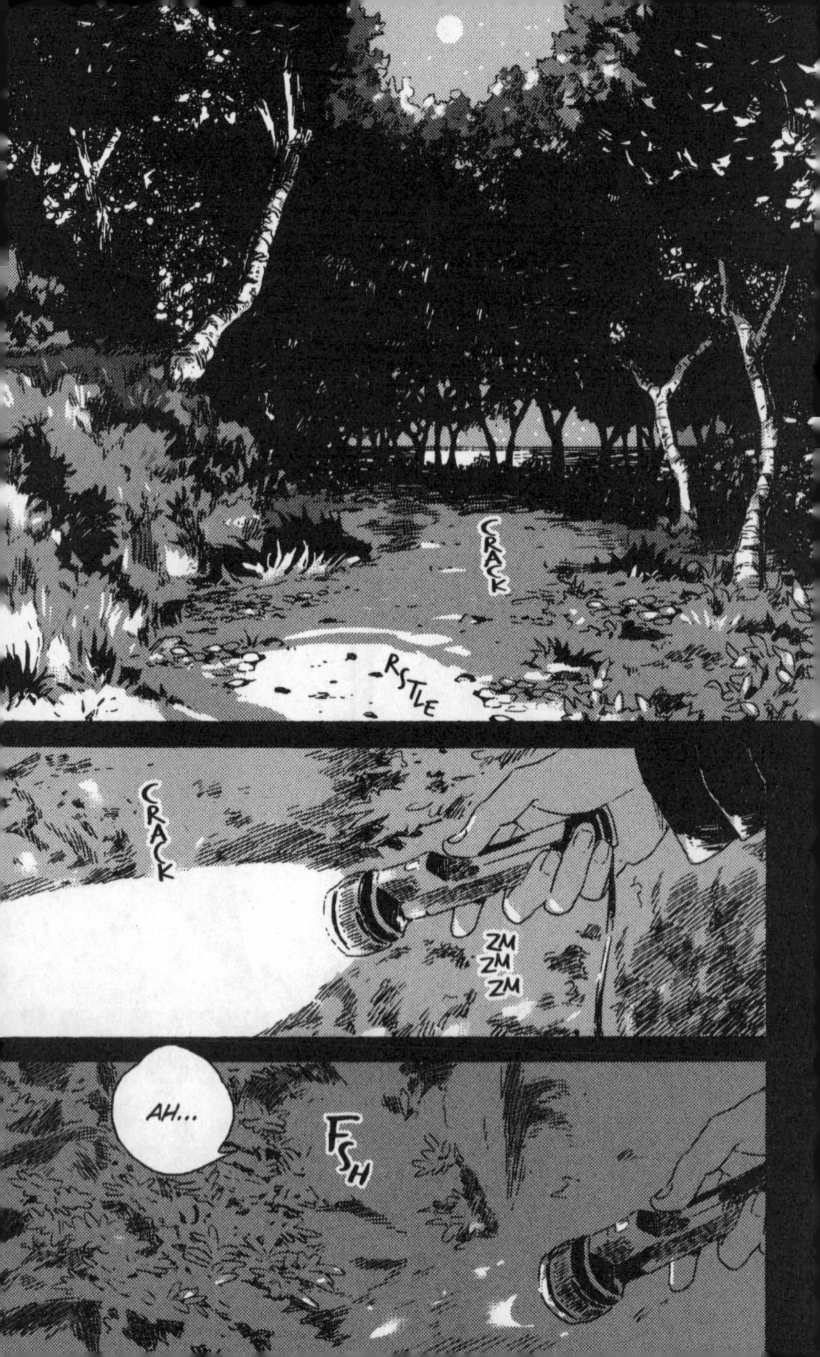
CRACK
RSTLE
CRACK
ZM ZM ZM
FSH
AH...

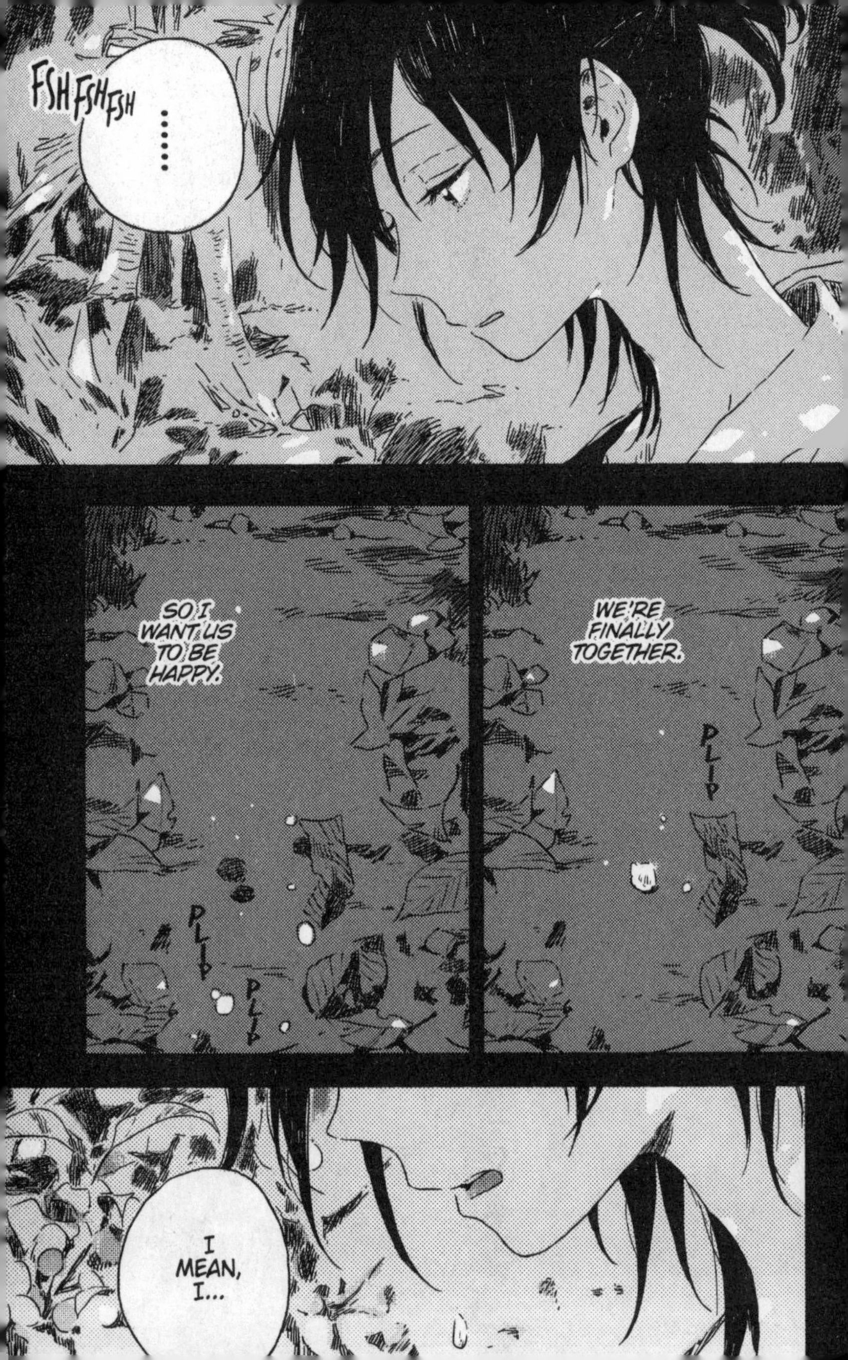
FSH FSH FSH
......
WE'RE FINALLY TOGETHER.
PLIP
SO I WANT US TO BE HAPPY.
PLIP
PLIP
I MEAN, I...

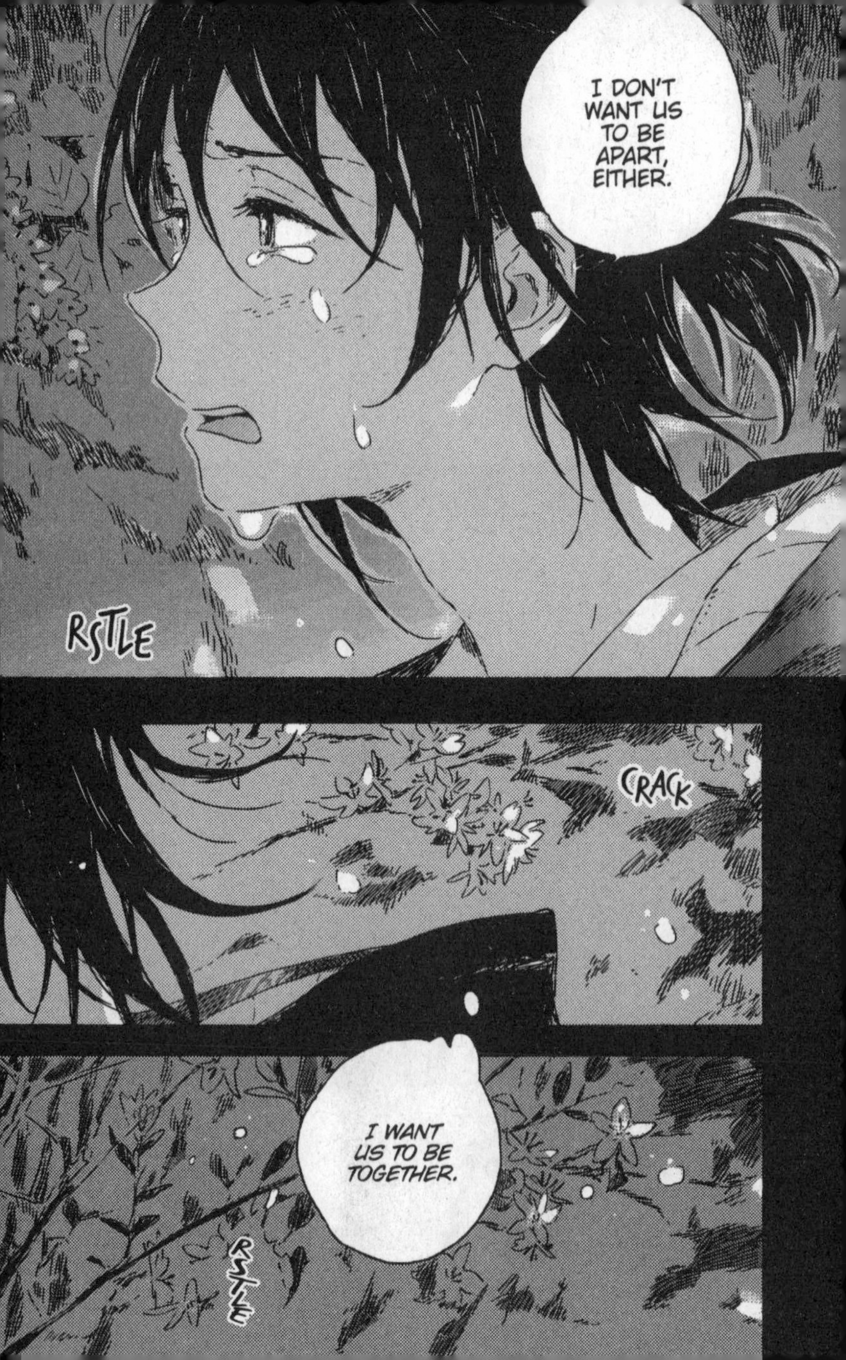
I DON'T WANT US TO BE APART, EITHER.
RSTLE
CRACK
I WANT US TO BE TOGETHER.
RSTLE

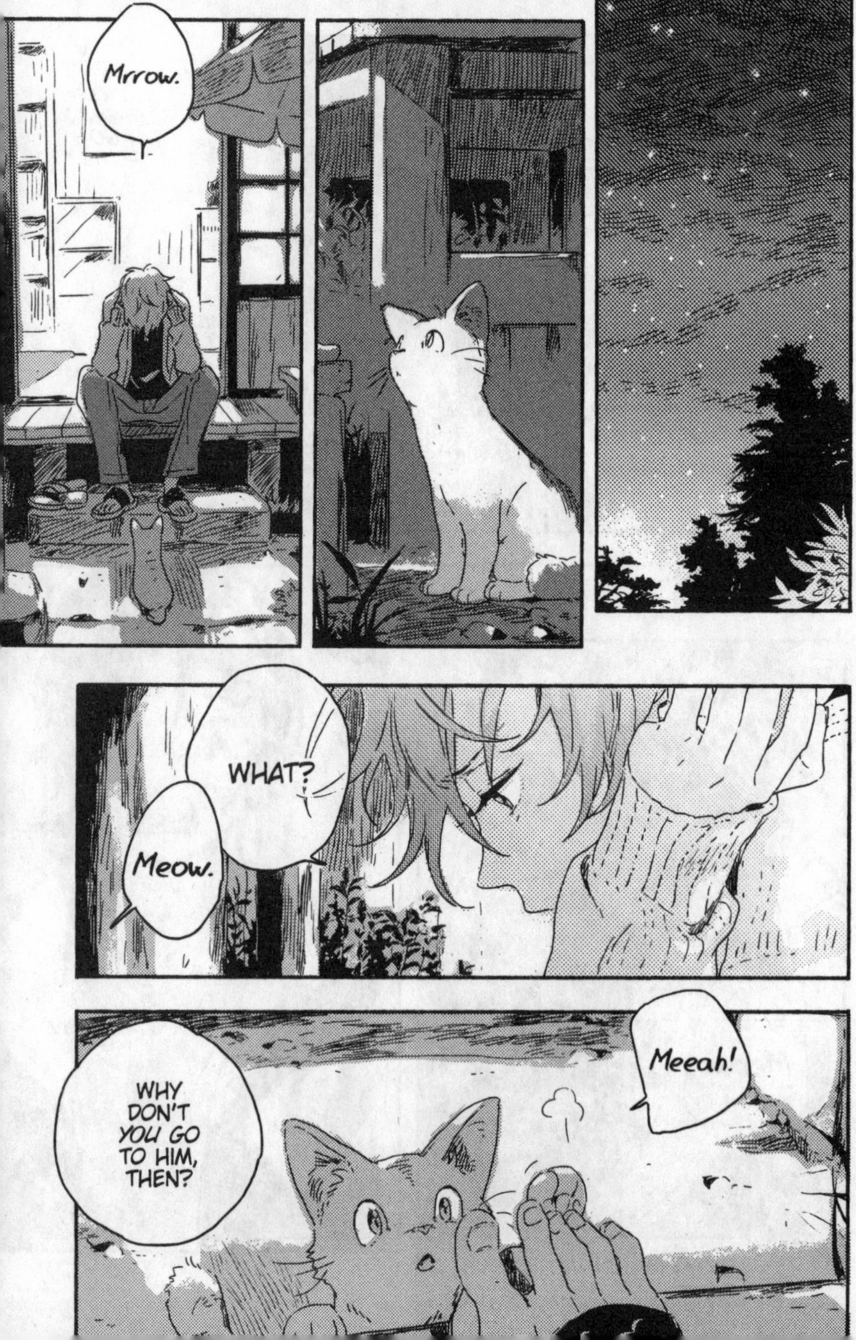
Mrrow.
WHAT?
Meow.
Meeah!
WHY DON'T YOU GO TO HIM, THEN?

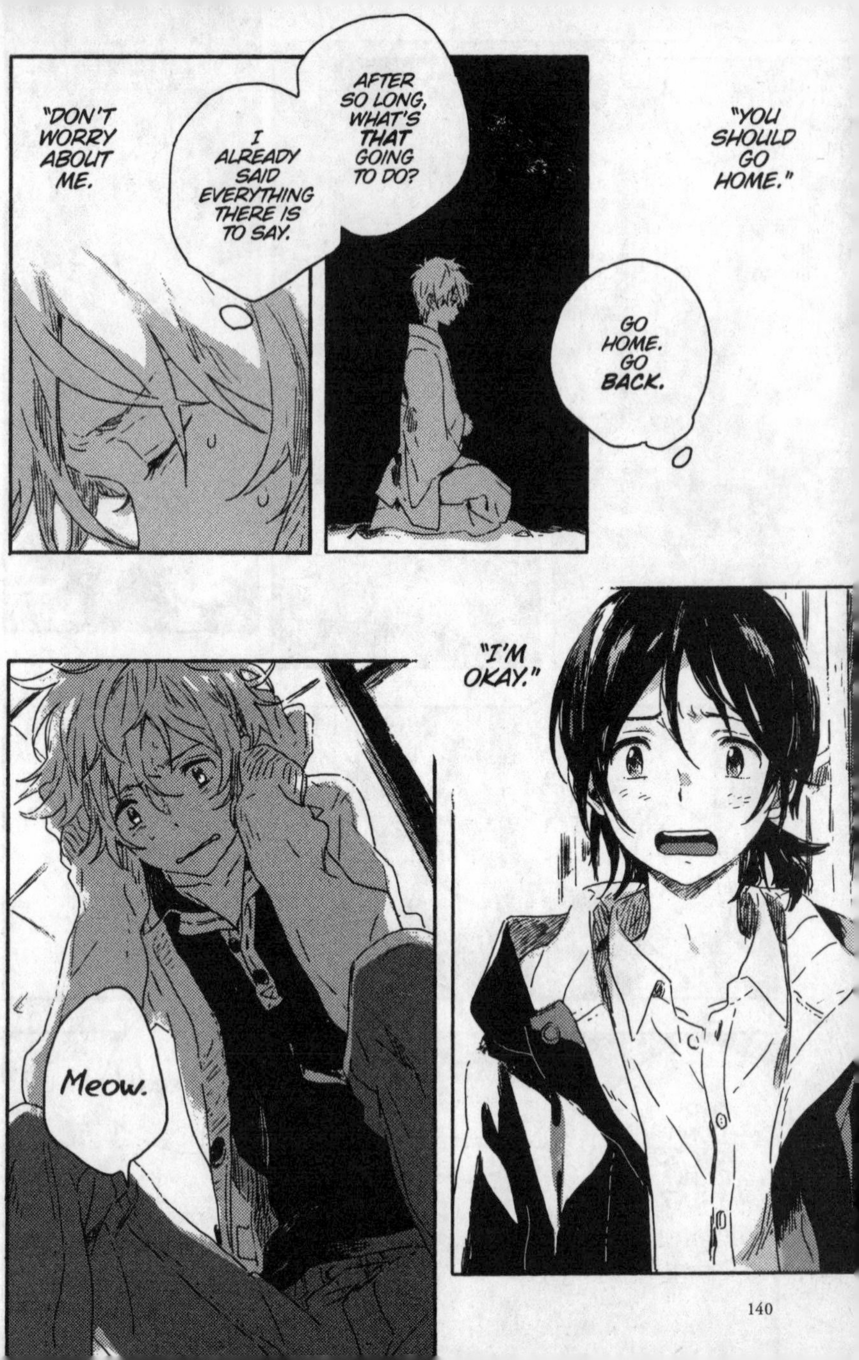
"YOU SHOULD GO HOME."
GO HOME. GO BACK.
AFTER SO LONG, WHAT'S THAT GOING TO DO?
I ALREADY SAID EVERYTHING THERE IS TO SAY.
"DON'T WORRY ABOUT ME.
"I'M OKAY."
Meow.

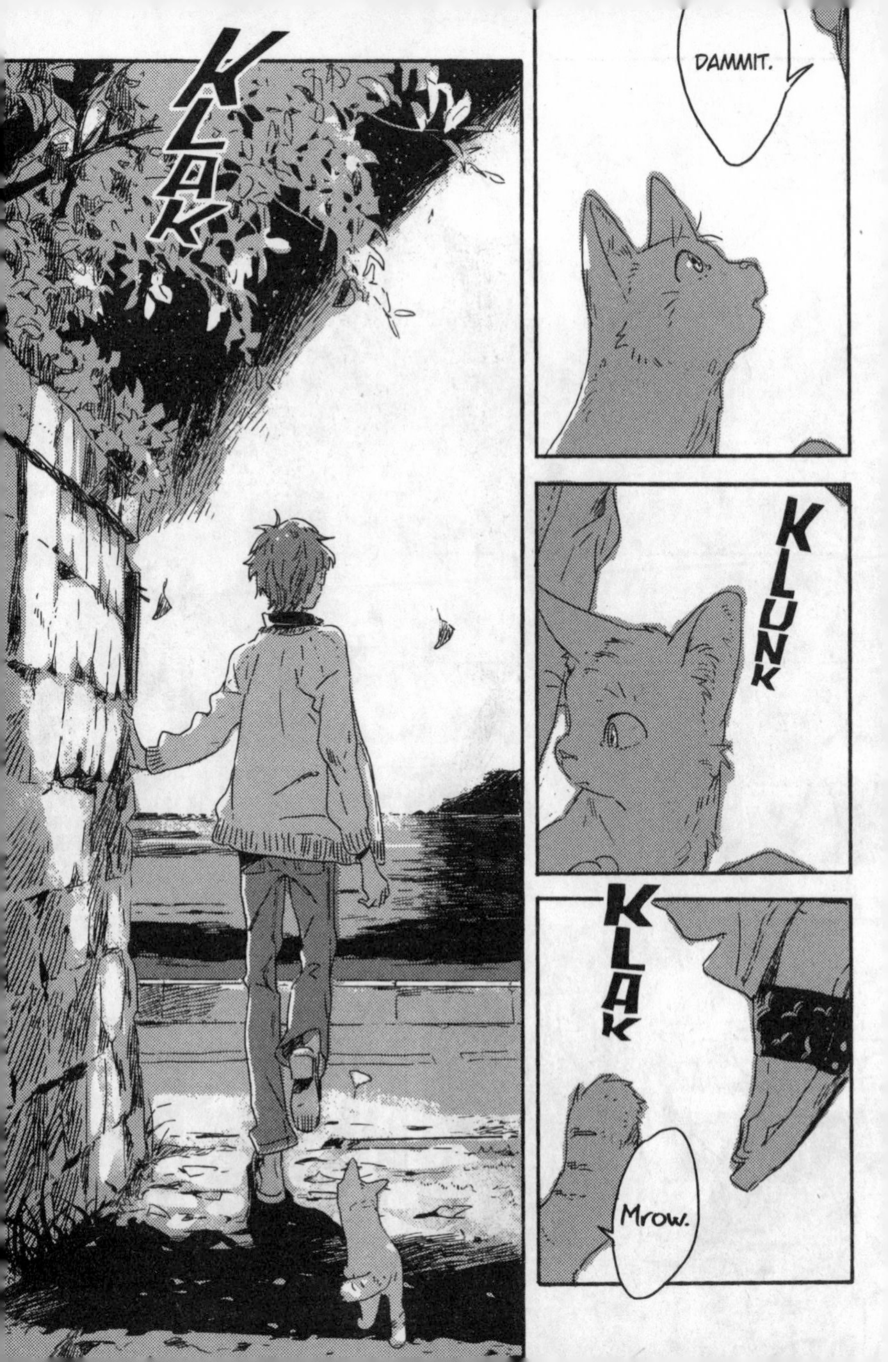
DAMMIT.
KLUNK
KLAK
Mrow.
KLAK

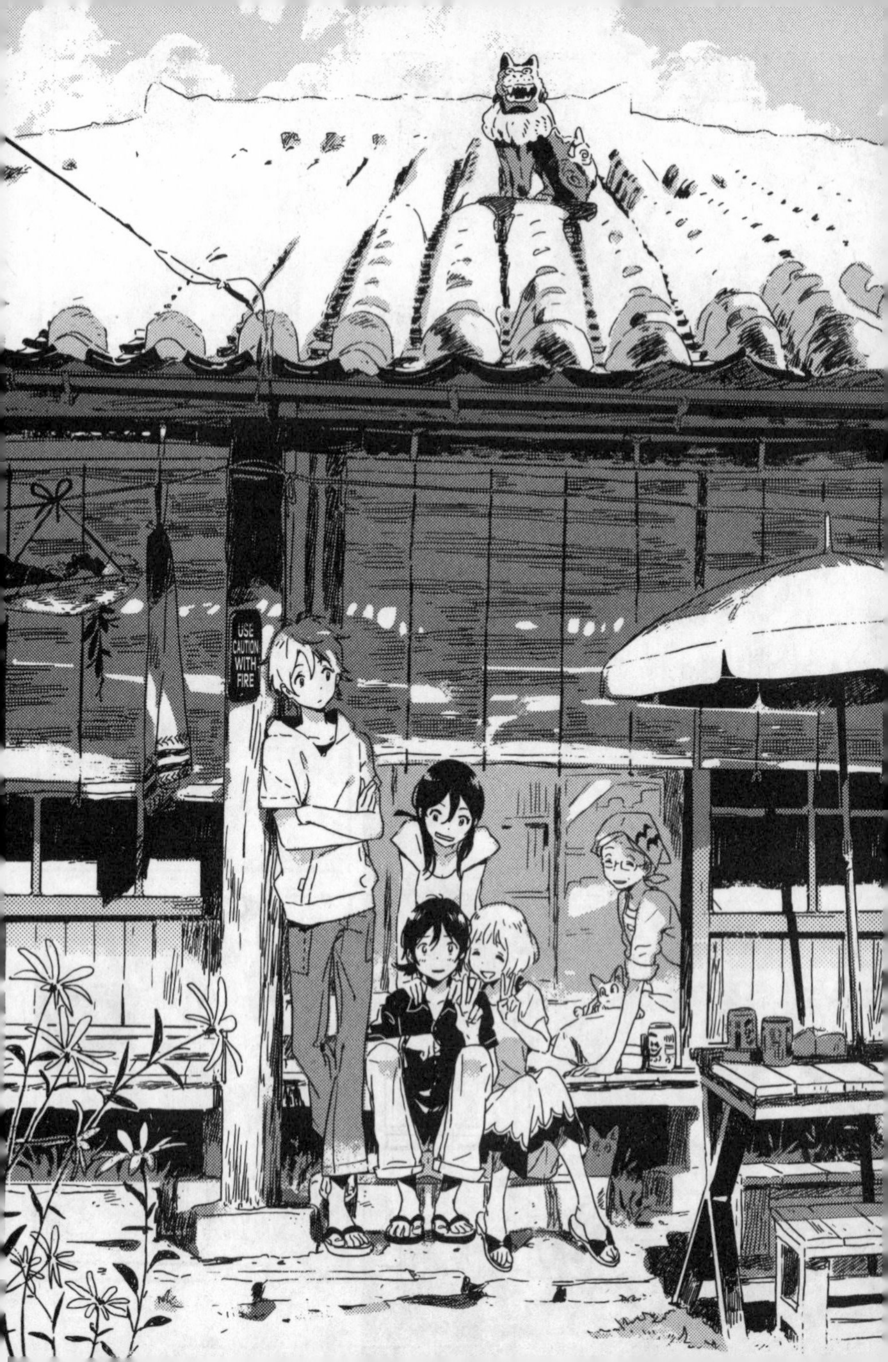
USE CAUTION WITH FIRE

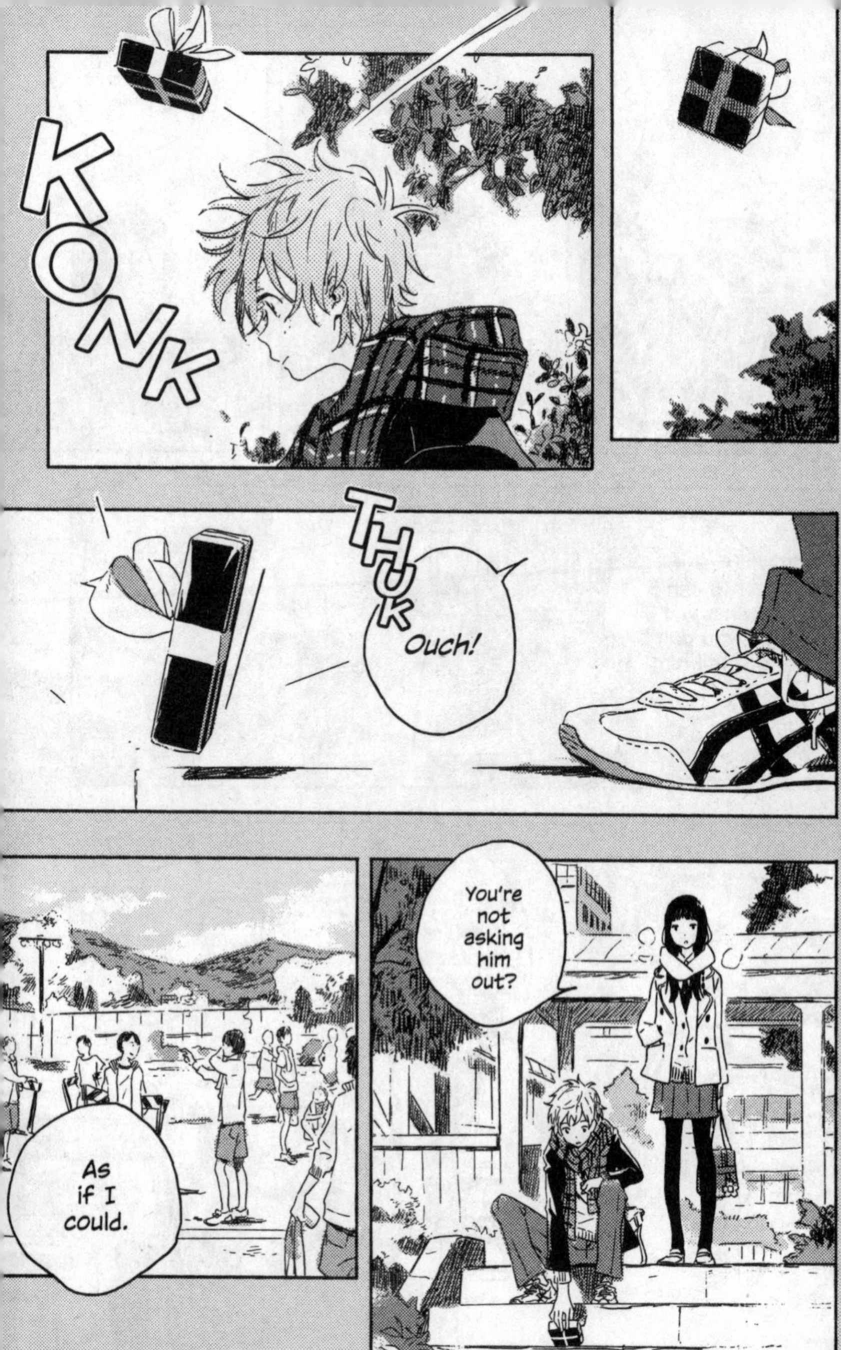
KONK
THUK
Ouch!
You're not asking him out?
As if I could.

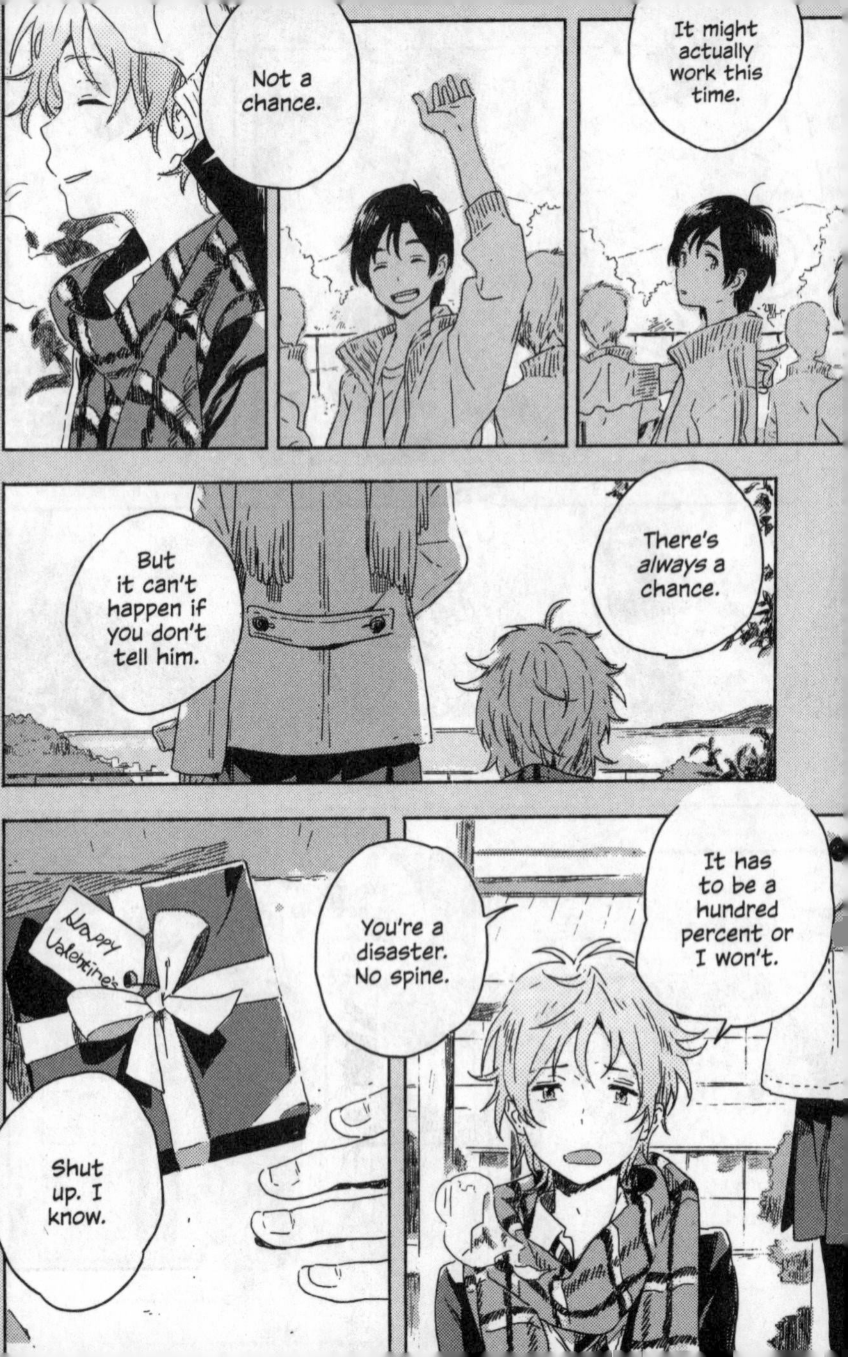
It might actually work this time.
Not a chance.
There's *always* a chance.
But it can't happen if you don't tell him.
It has to be a hundred percent or I won't.
You're a disaster. No spine.
Happy Valentine's
Shut up. I know.

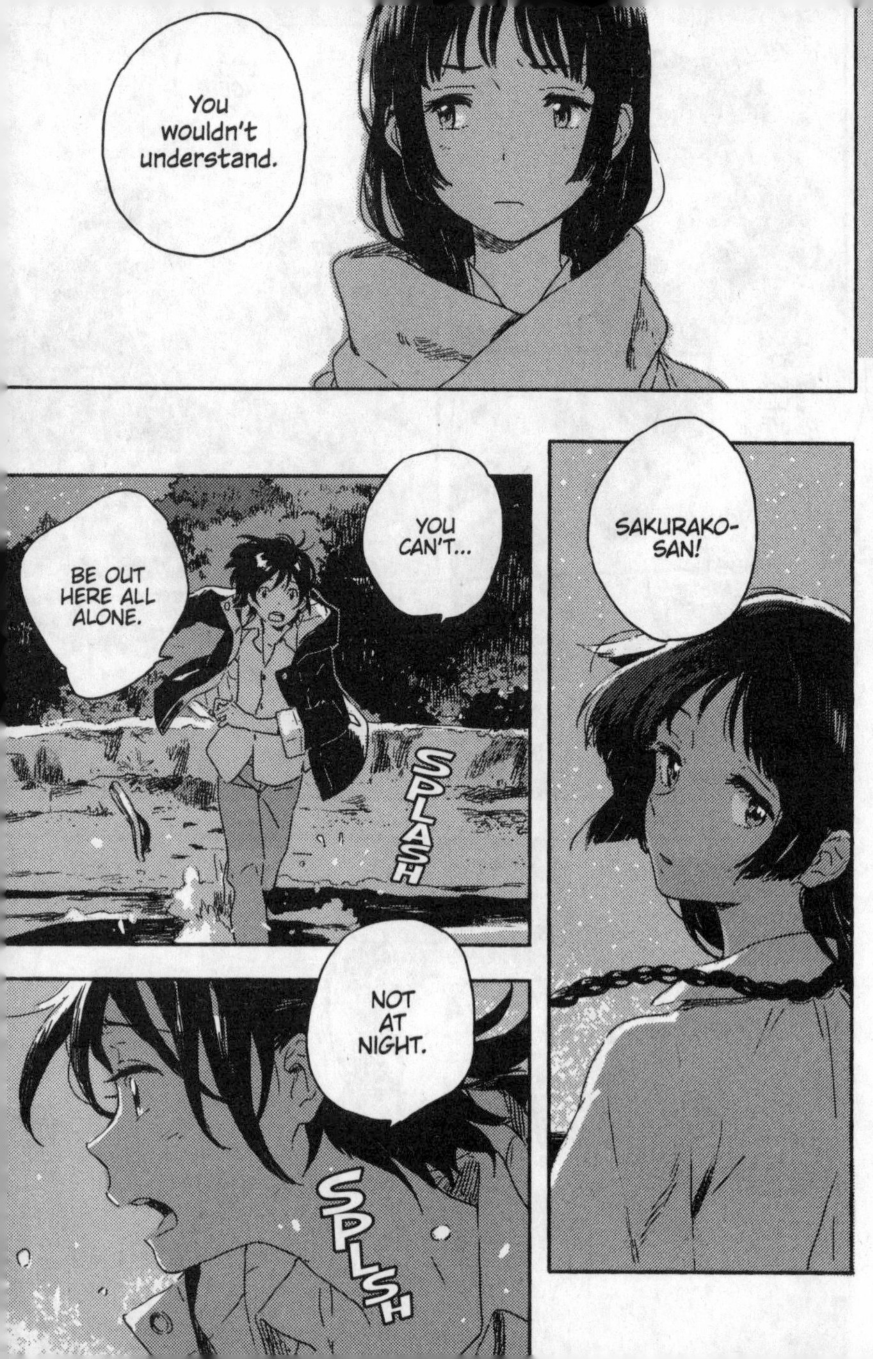
You wouldn't understand.
SAKURAKO-SAN!
YOU CAN'T...
BE OUT HERE ALL ALONE.
SPLASH
NOT AT NIGHT.
SPLSH

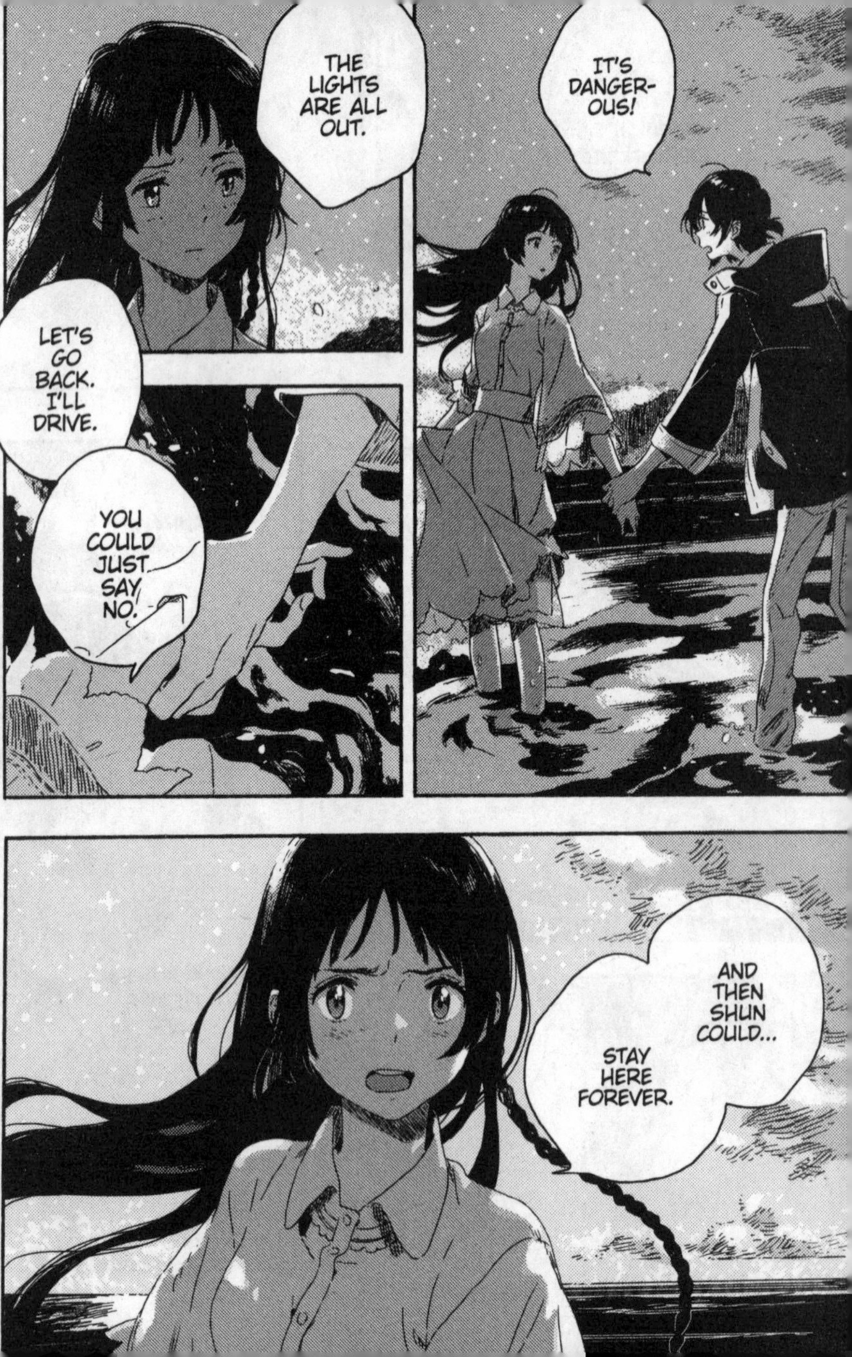
IT'S DANGER-OUS!
THE LIGHTS ARE ALL OUT.
LET'S GO BACK. I'LL DRIVE.
YOU COULD JUST SAY NO.
AND THEN SHUN COULD...
STAY HERE FOREVER.

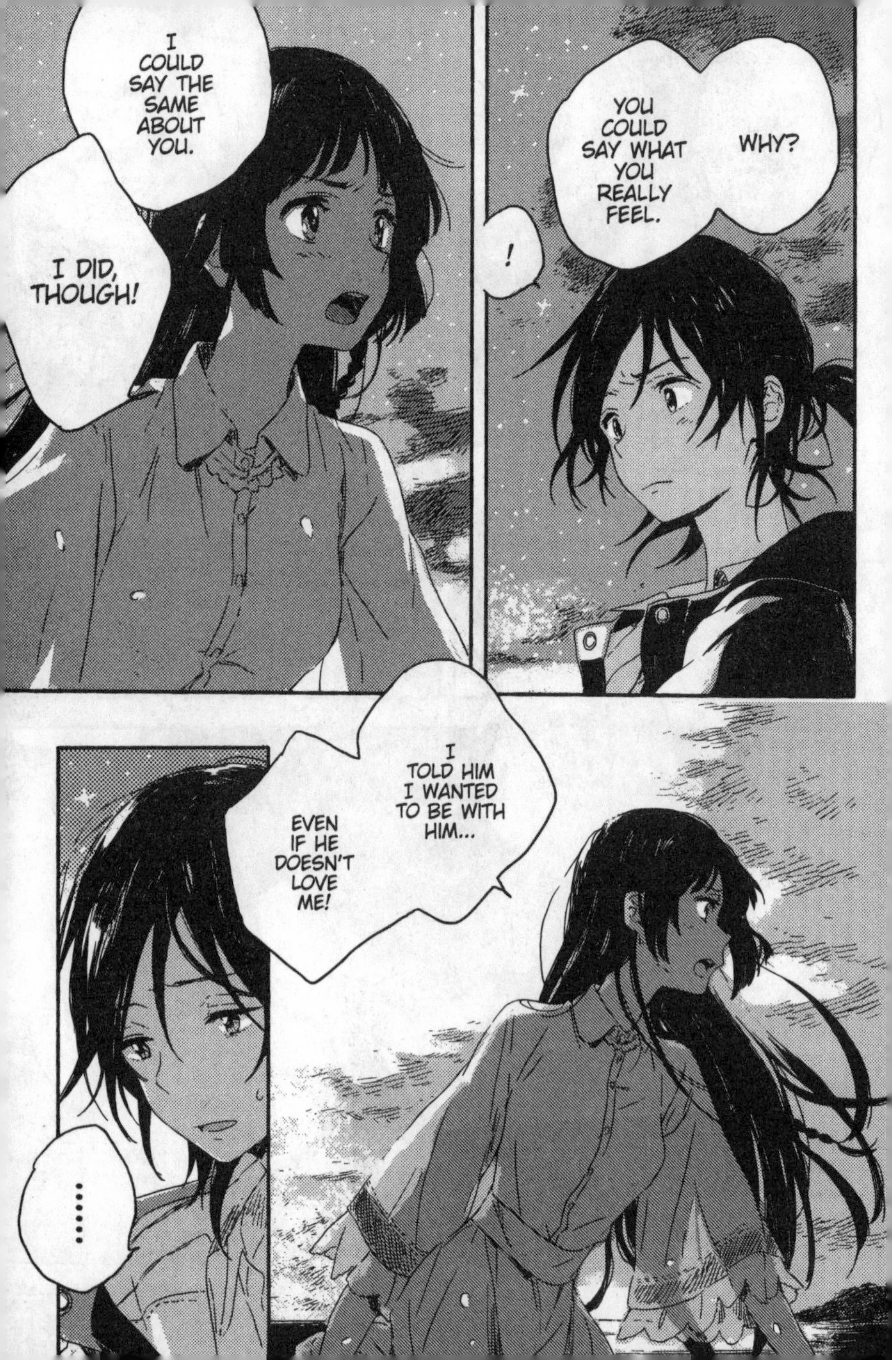
WHY?
YOU COULD SAY WHAT YOU REALLY FEEL.
!
I COULD SAY THE SAME ABOUT YOU.
I DID, THOUGH!
I TOLD HIM I WANTED TO BE WITH HIM...
EVEN IF HE DOESN'T LOVE ME!
......

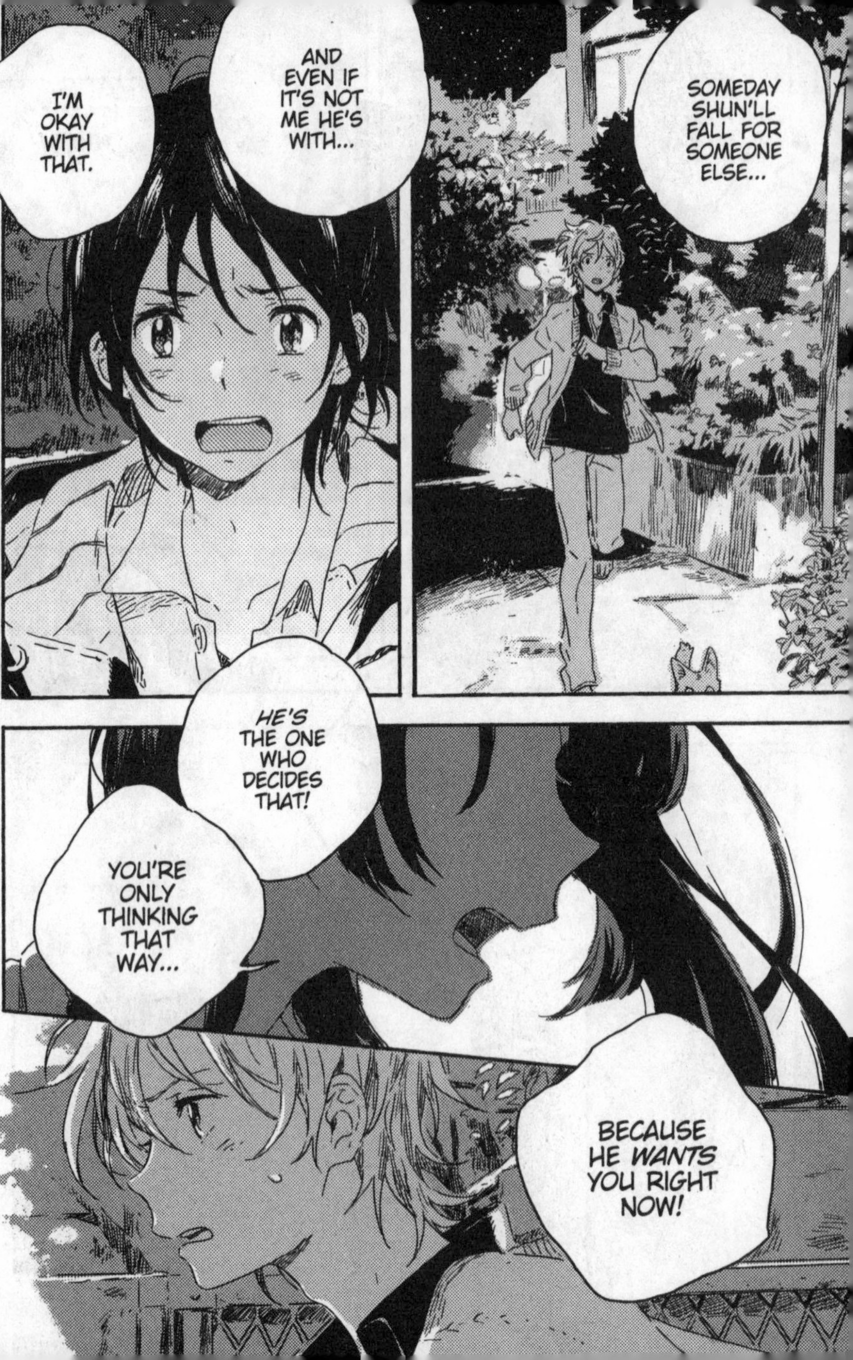
SOMEDAY SHUN'LL FALL FOR SOMEONE ELSE...
AND EVEN IF IT'S NOT ME HE'S WITH...
I'M OKAY WITH THAT.
HE'S THE ONE WHO DECIDES THAT!
YOU'RE ONLY THINKING THAT WAY...
BECAUSE HE *WANTS* YOU RIGHT NOW!

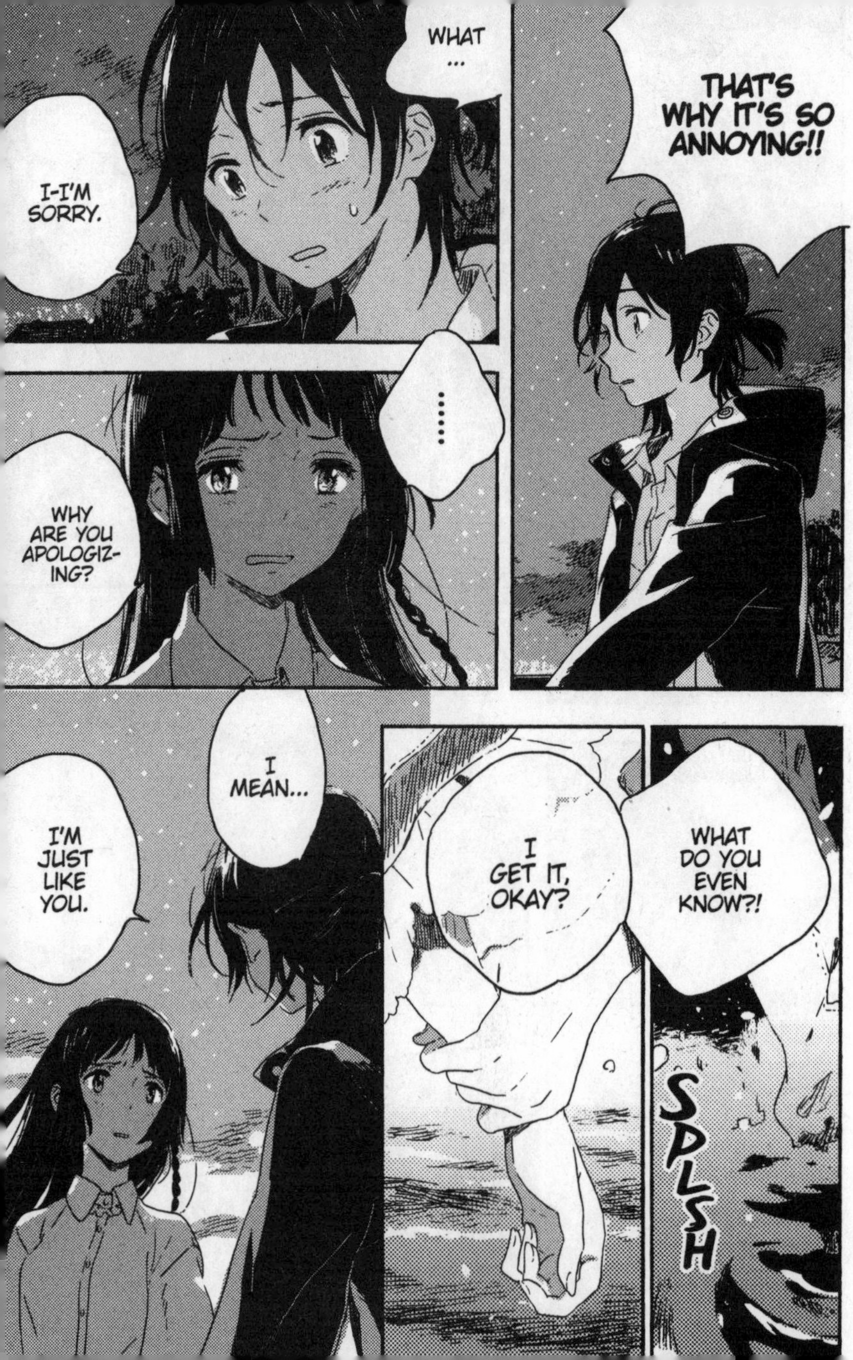
THAT'S WHY IT'S SO ANNOYING!!
WHAT ...
I-I'M SORRY.
......
WHY ARE YOU APOLOGIZ-ING?
WHAT DO YOU EVEN KNOW?!
SPLSH
I GET IT, OKAY?
I MEAN...
I'M JUST LIKE YOU.

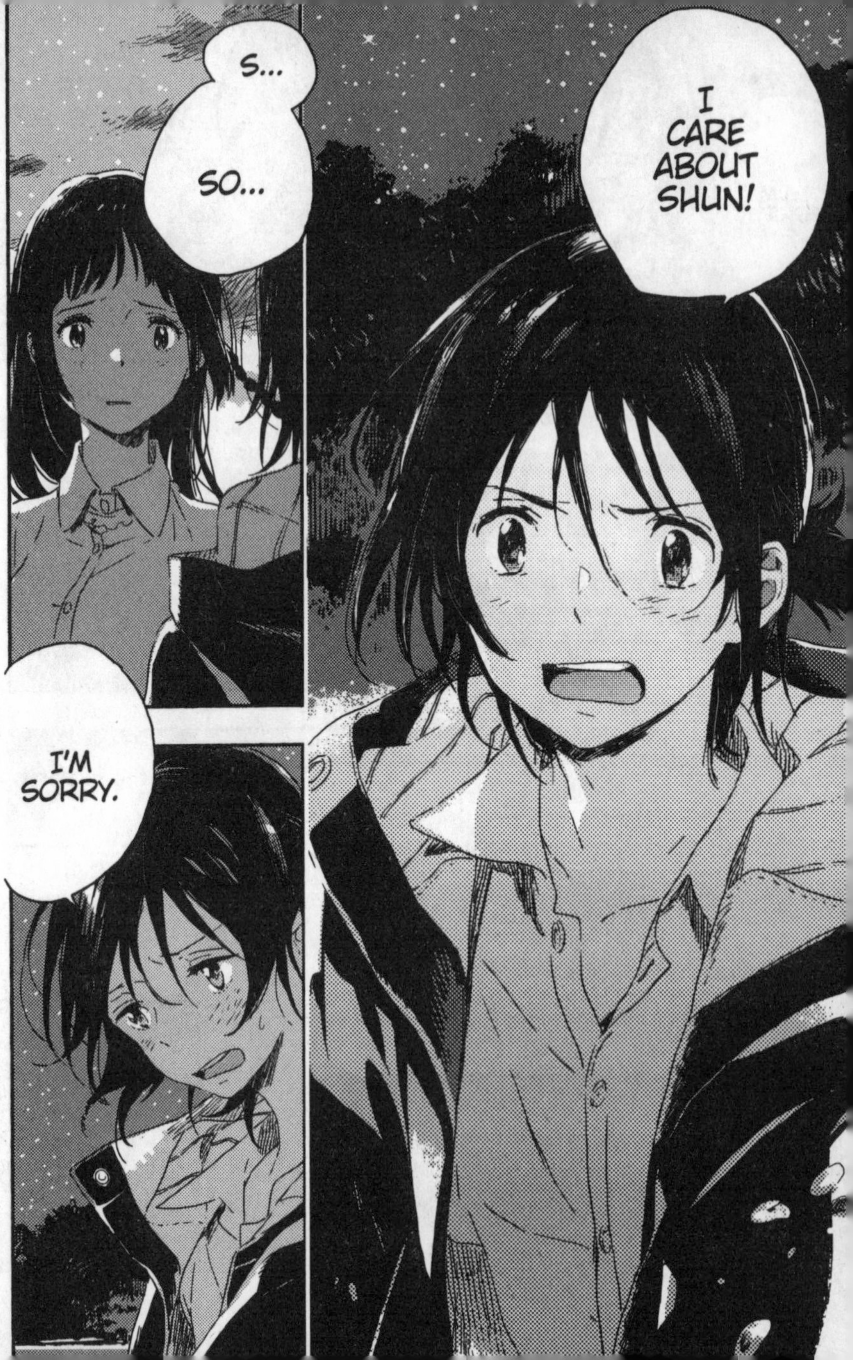
I CARE ABOUT SHUN!
S...
SO...
I'M SORRY.

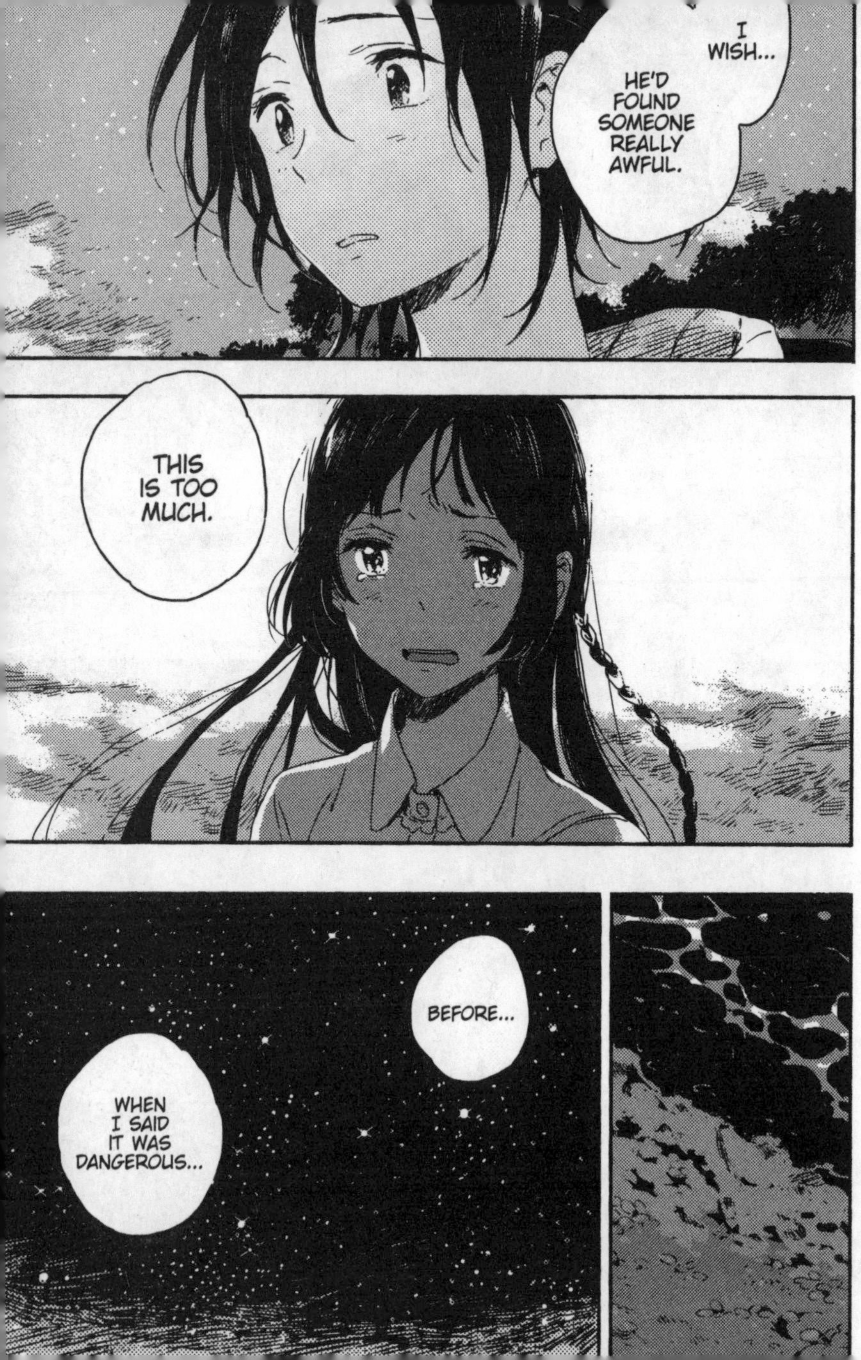
I WISH...
HE'D FOUND SOMEONE REALLY AWFUL.
THIS IS TOO MUCH.
BEFORE...
WHEN I SAID IT WAS DANGEROUS...

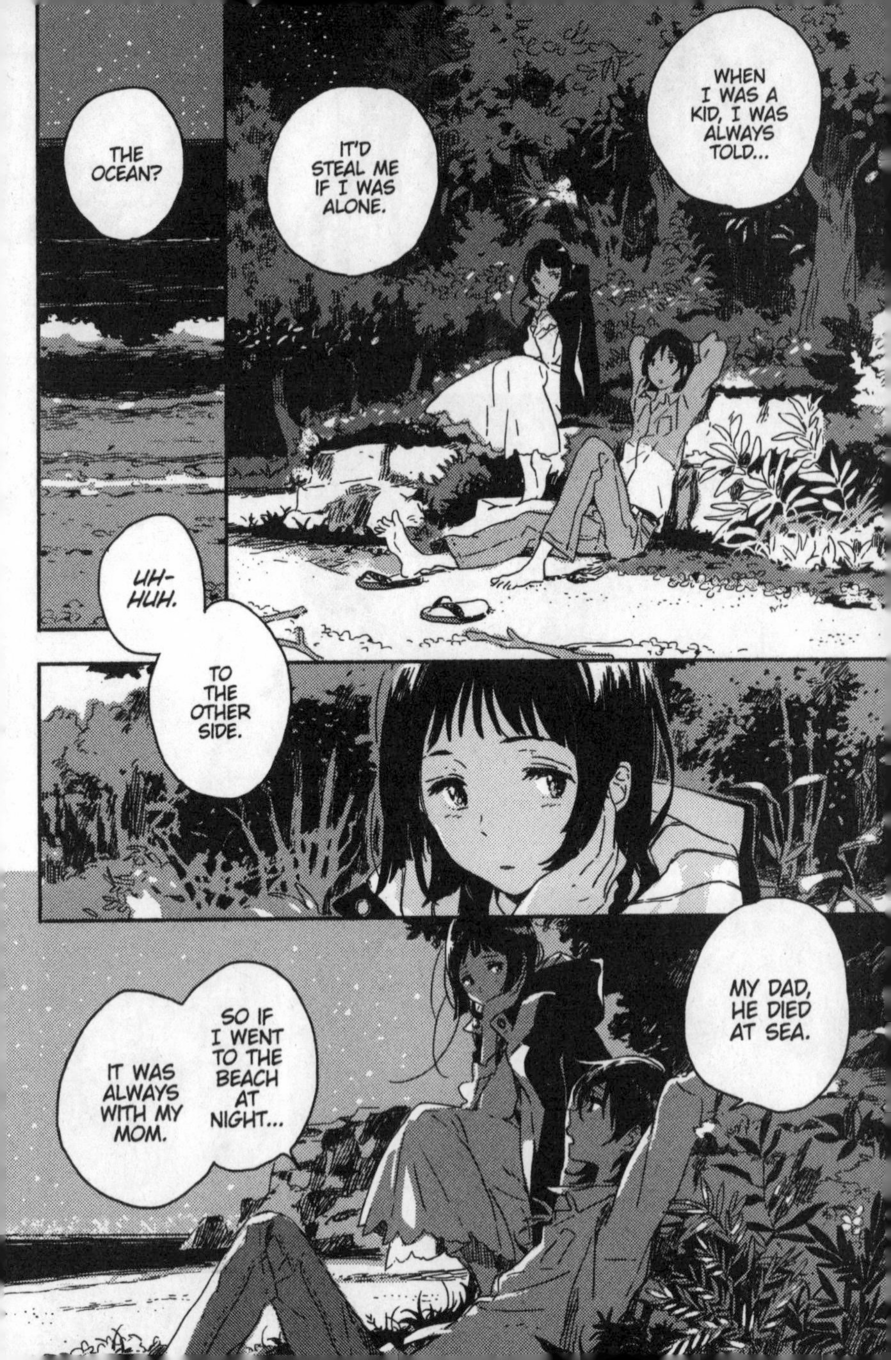
WHEN I WAS A KID, I WAS ALWAYS TOLD...
IT'D STEAL ME IF I WAS ALONE.
THE OCEAN?
UH-HUH.
TO THE OTHER SIDE.
MY DAD, HE DIED AT SEA.
SO IF I WENT TO THE BEACH AT NIGHT...
IT WAS ALWAYS WITH MY MOM.

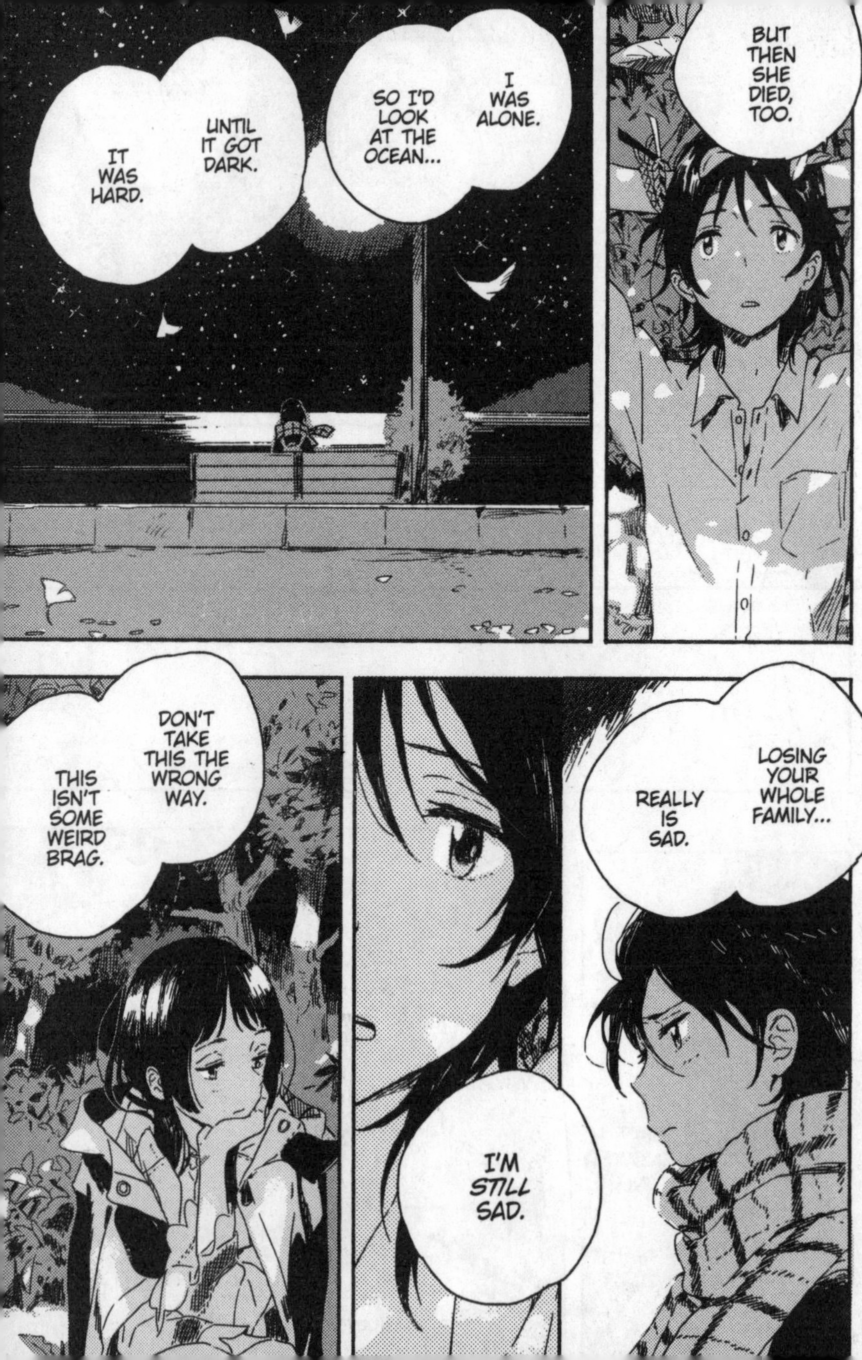
BUT THEN SHE DIED, TOO.
I WAS ALONE.
SO I'D LOOK AT THE OCEAN...
UNTIL IT GOT DARK.
IT WAS HARD.
LOSING YOUR WHOLE FAMILY...
REALLY IS SAD.
I'M STILL SAD.
DON'T TAKE THIS THE WRONG WAY.
THIS ISN'T SOME WEIRD BRAG.

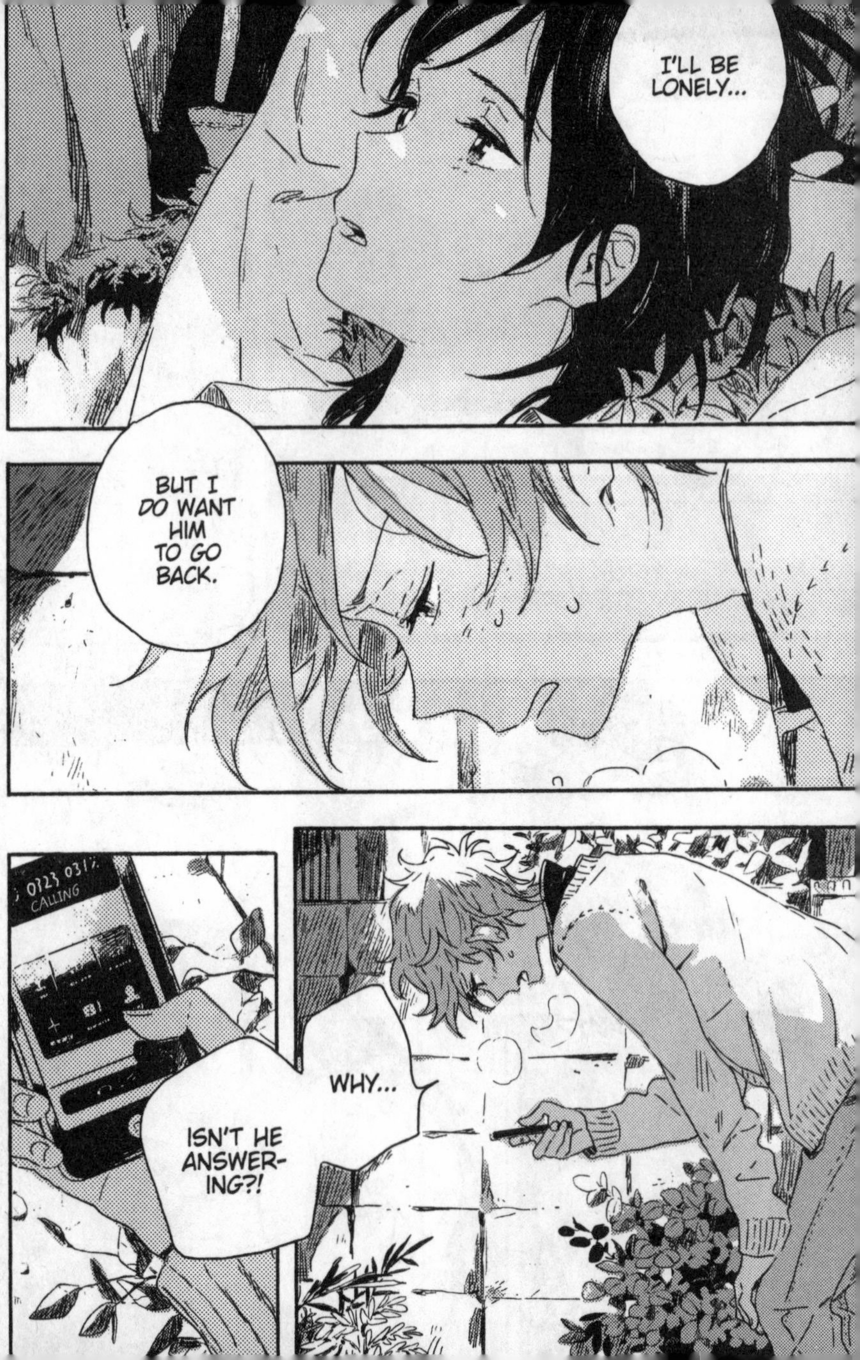
I'LL BE LONELY...
BUT I DO WANT HIM TO GO BACK.
WHY...
ISN'T HE ANSWER-ING?!
CALLING

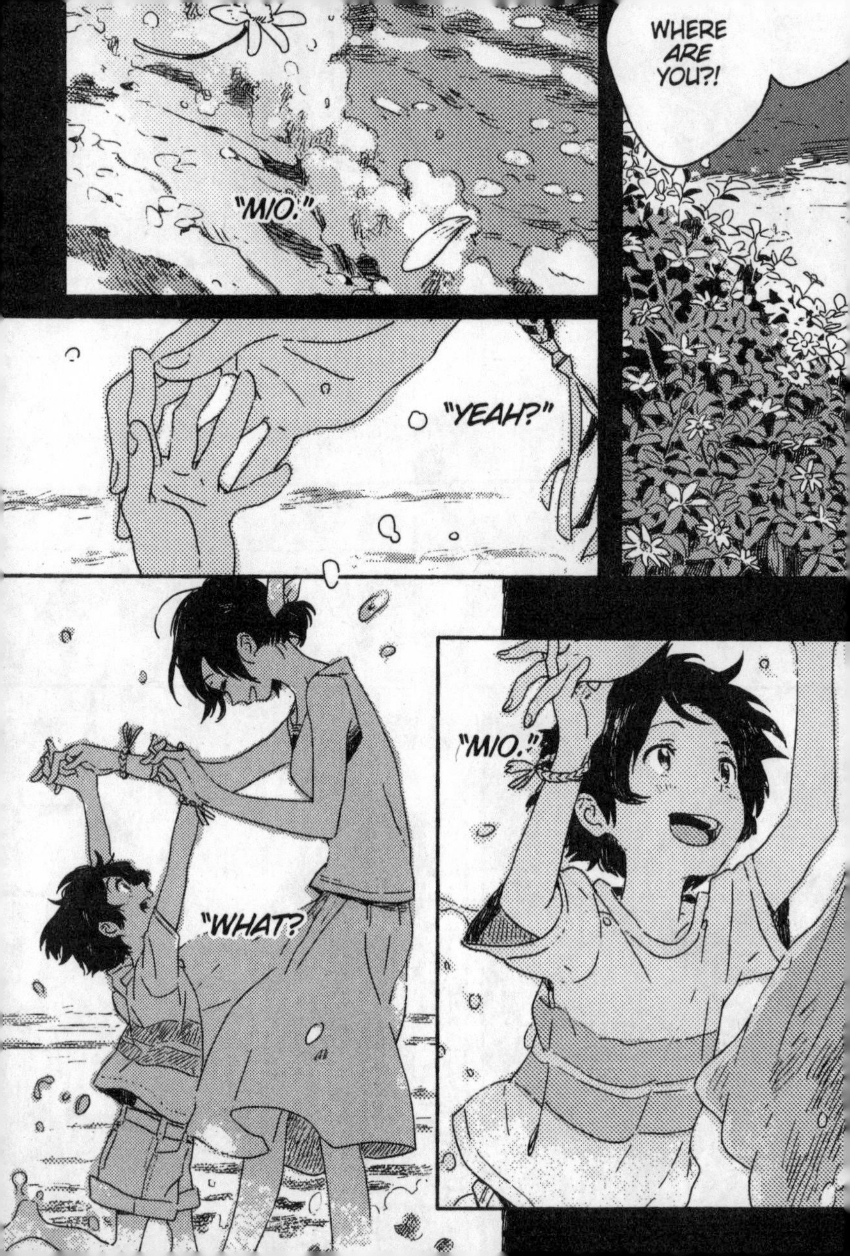
WHERE ARE YOU?!
"MIO."
"YEAH?"
"MIO."
"WHAT?

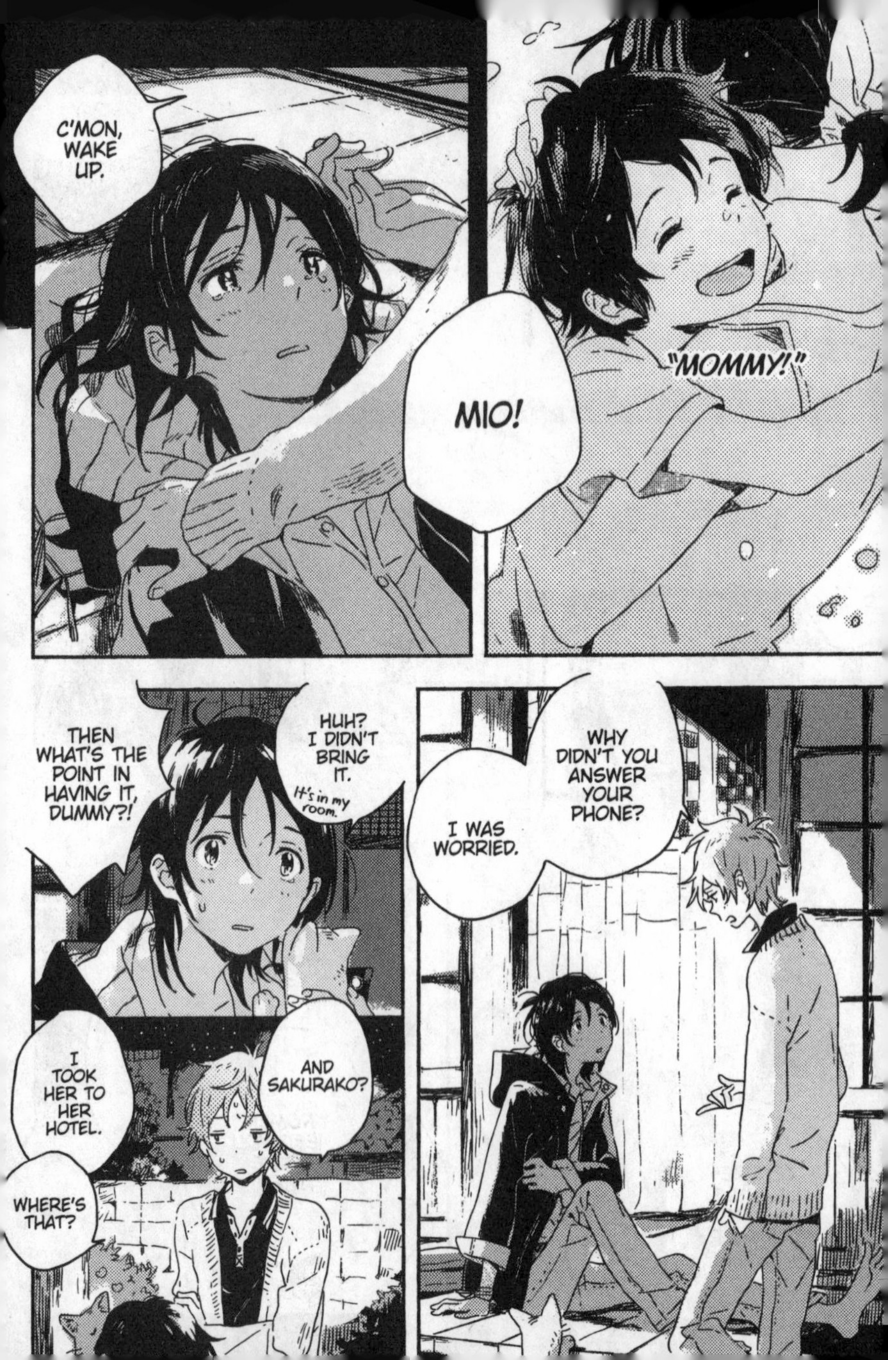
"MOMMY!"
MIO!
C'MON, WAKE UP.
WHY DIDN'T YOU ANSWER YOUR PHONE?
I WAS WORRIED.
HUH? I DIDN'T BRING IT.
It's in my room.
THEN WHAT'S THE POINT IN HAVING IT, DUMMY?!
AND SAKURAKO?
I TOOK HER TO HER HOTEL.
WHERE'S THAT?

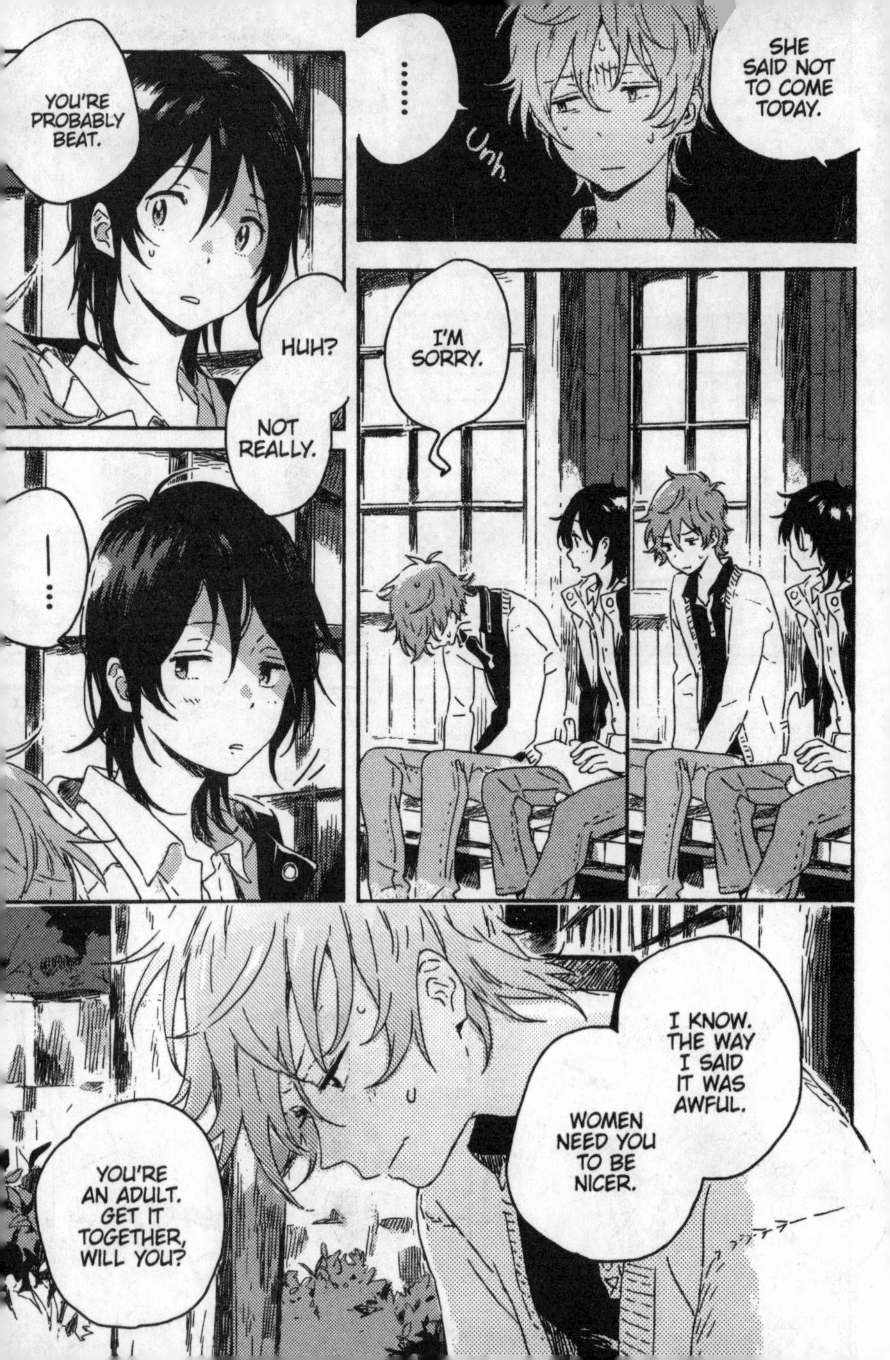
SHE SAID NOT TO COME TODAY.
......
Unh.
YOU'RE PROBABLY BEAT.
HUH?
I'M SORRY.
NOT REALLY.
......
I KNOW. THE WAY I SAID IT WAS AWFUL.
WOMEN NEED YOU TO BE NICER.
YOU'RE AN ADULT. GET IT TOGETHER, WILL YOU?

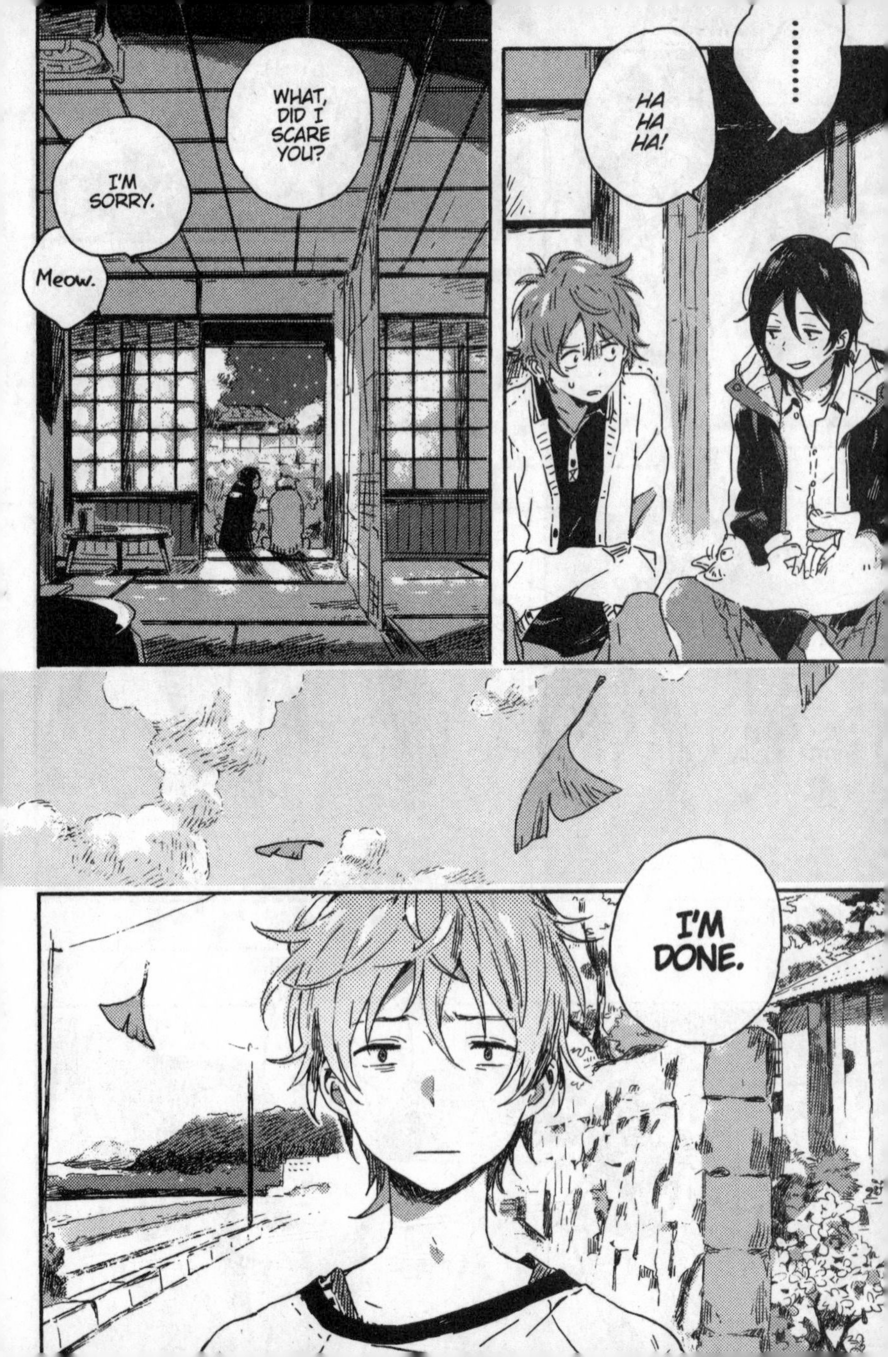
……
HA HA HA!
WHAT, DID I SCARE YOU?
I'M SORRY.
Meow.
I'M DONE.

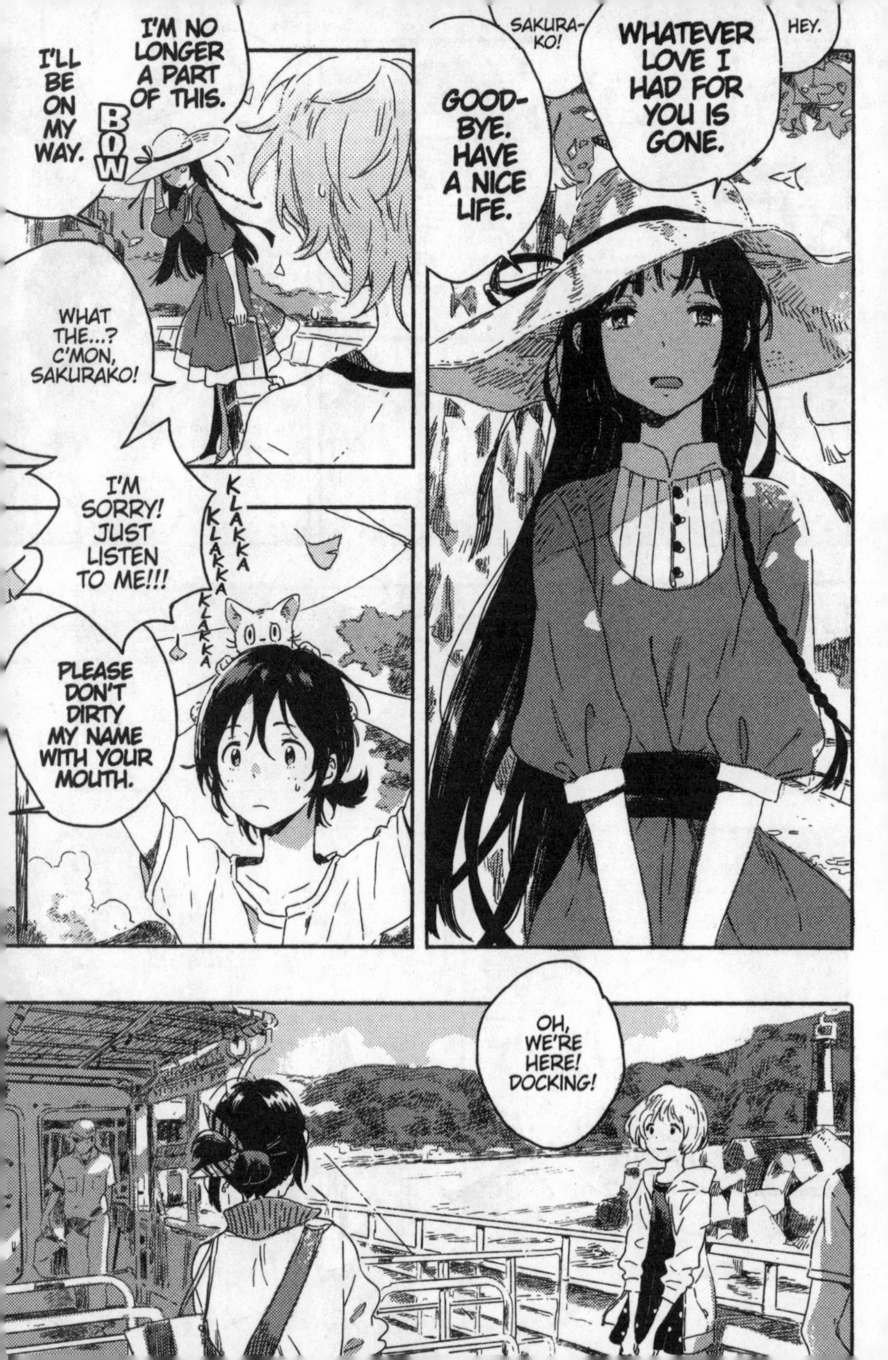
HEY.
WHATEVER LOVE I HAD FOR YOU IS GONE.
SAKURAKO!
GOOD-BYE. HAVE A NICE LIFE.
I'M NO LONGER A PART OF THIS.
I'LL BE ON MY WAY.
BOW
WHAT THE...? C'MON, SAKURAKO!
I'M SORRY! JUST LISTEN TO ME!!!
KLAKKA KLAKKA KLAKKA
PLEASE DON'T DIRTY MY NAME WITH YOUR MOUTH.
OH, WE'RE HERE! DOCKING!

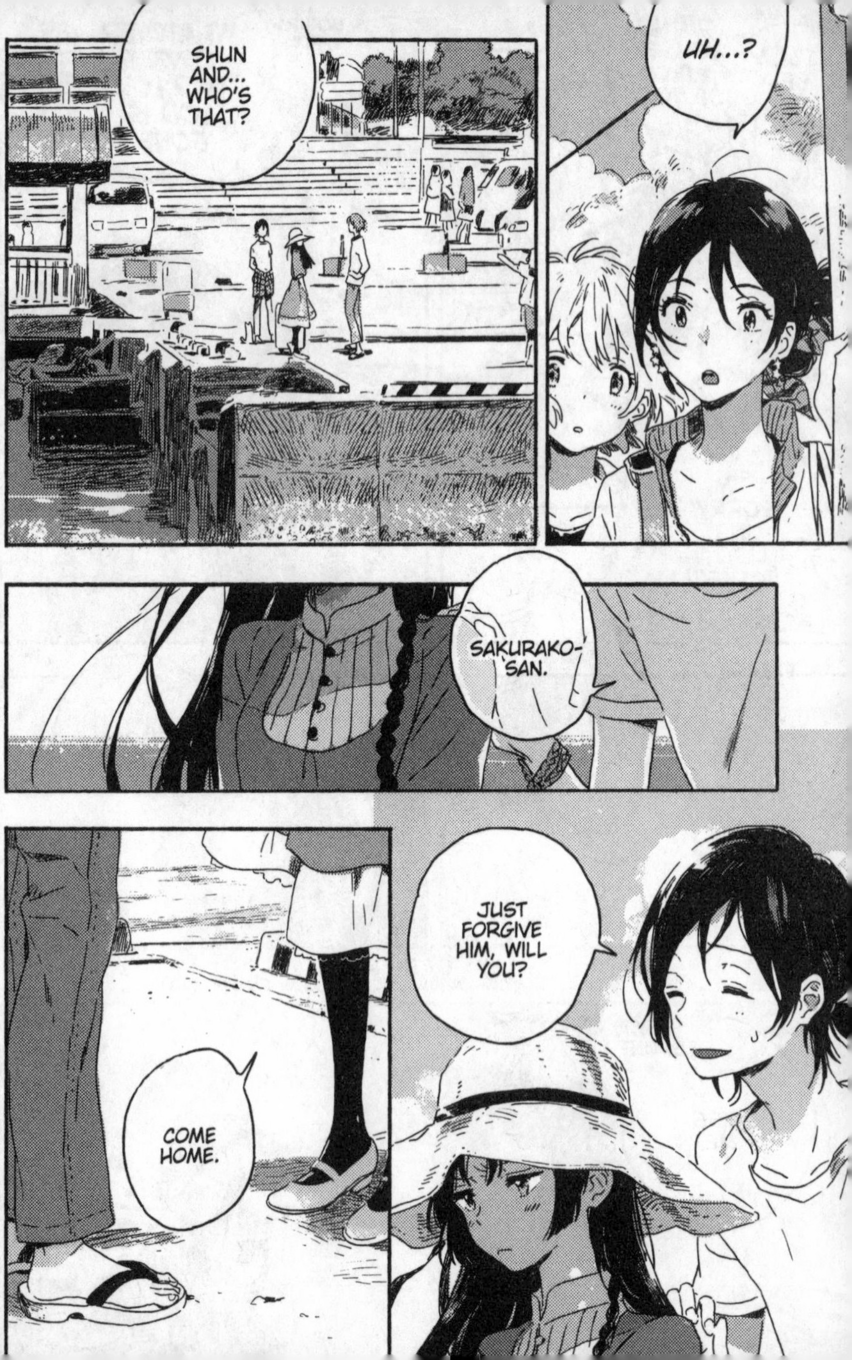
UH...?
SHUN AND... WHO'S THAT?
SAKURAKO-SAN.
JUST FORGIVE HIM, WILL YOU?
COME HOME.

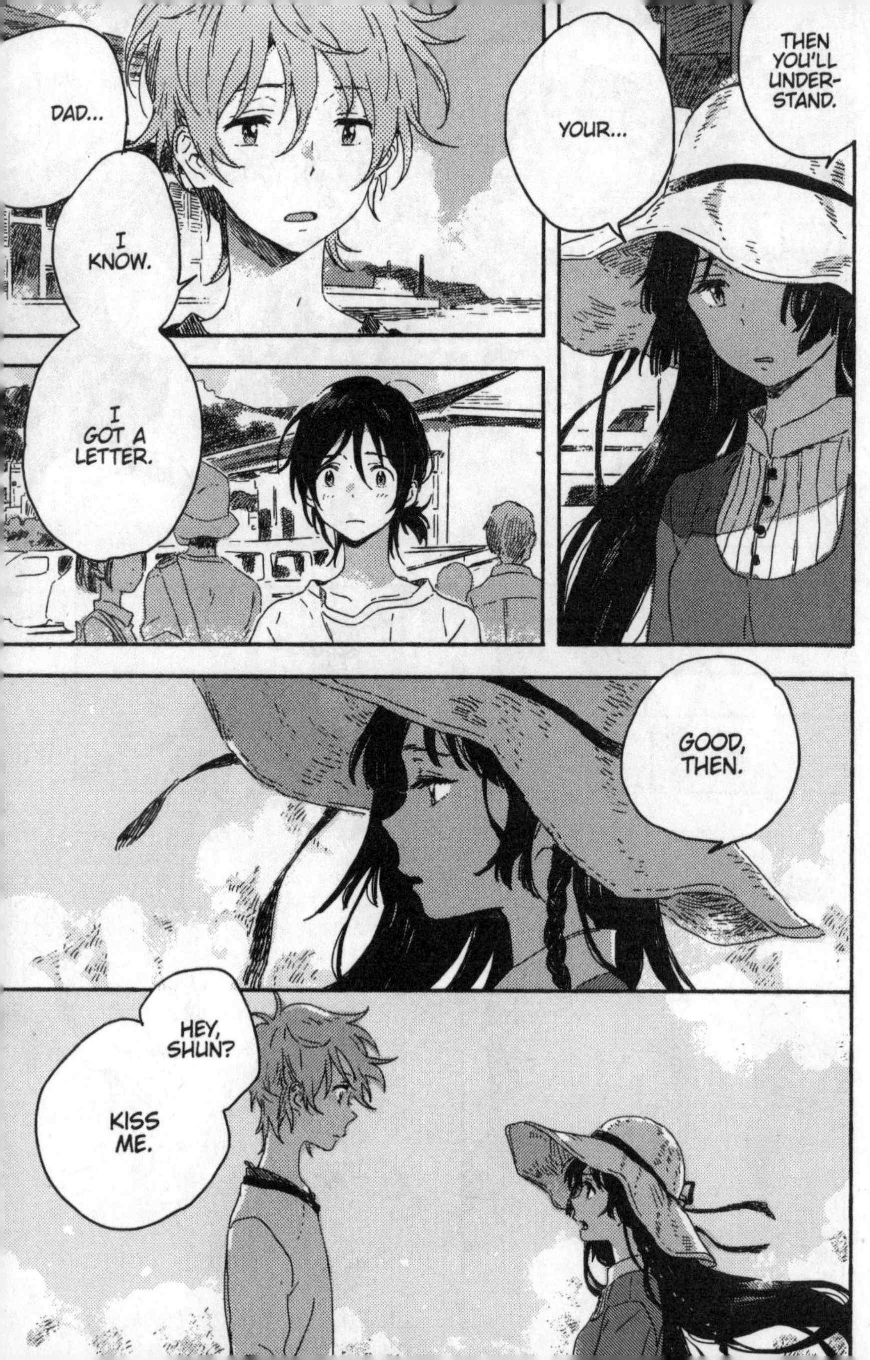
THEN YOU'LL UNDER-STAND.
YOUR...
DAD...
I KNOW.
I GOT A LETTER.
GOOD, THEN.
HEY, SHUN?
KISS ME.

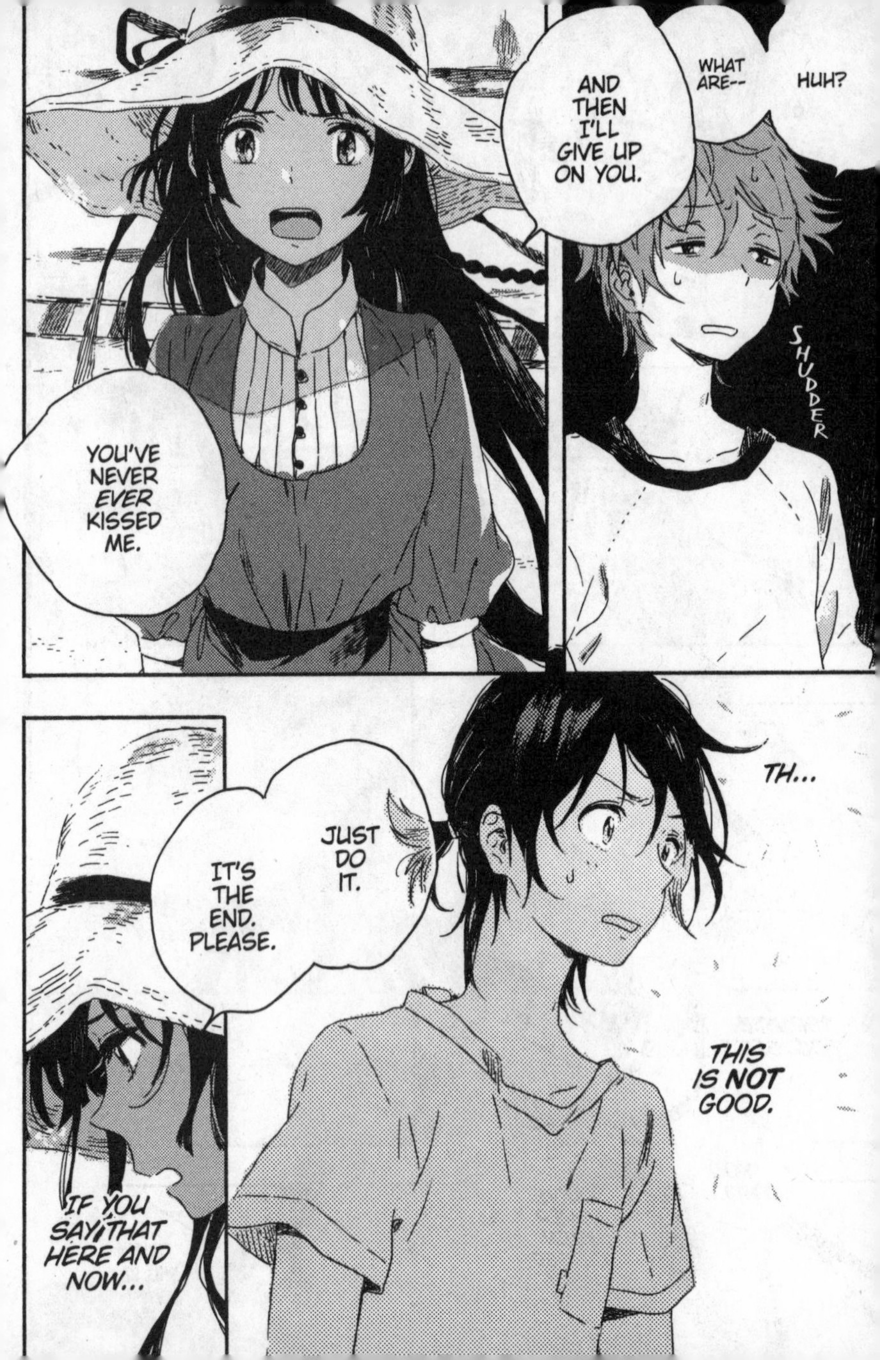
HUH?
WHAT ARE--
SHUDDER
AND THEN I'LL GIVE UP ON YOU.
YOU'VE NEVER *EVER* KISSED ME.
TH...
THIS IS NOT GOOD.
JUST DO IT.
IT'S THE END. PLEASE.
IF YOU SAY THAT HERE AND NOW...

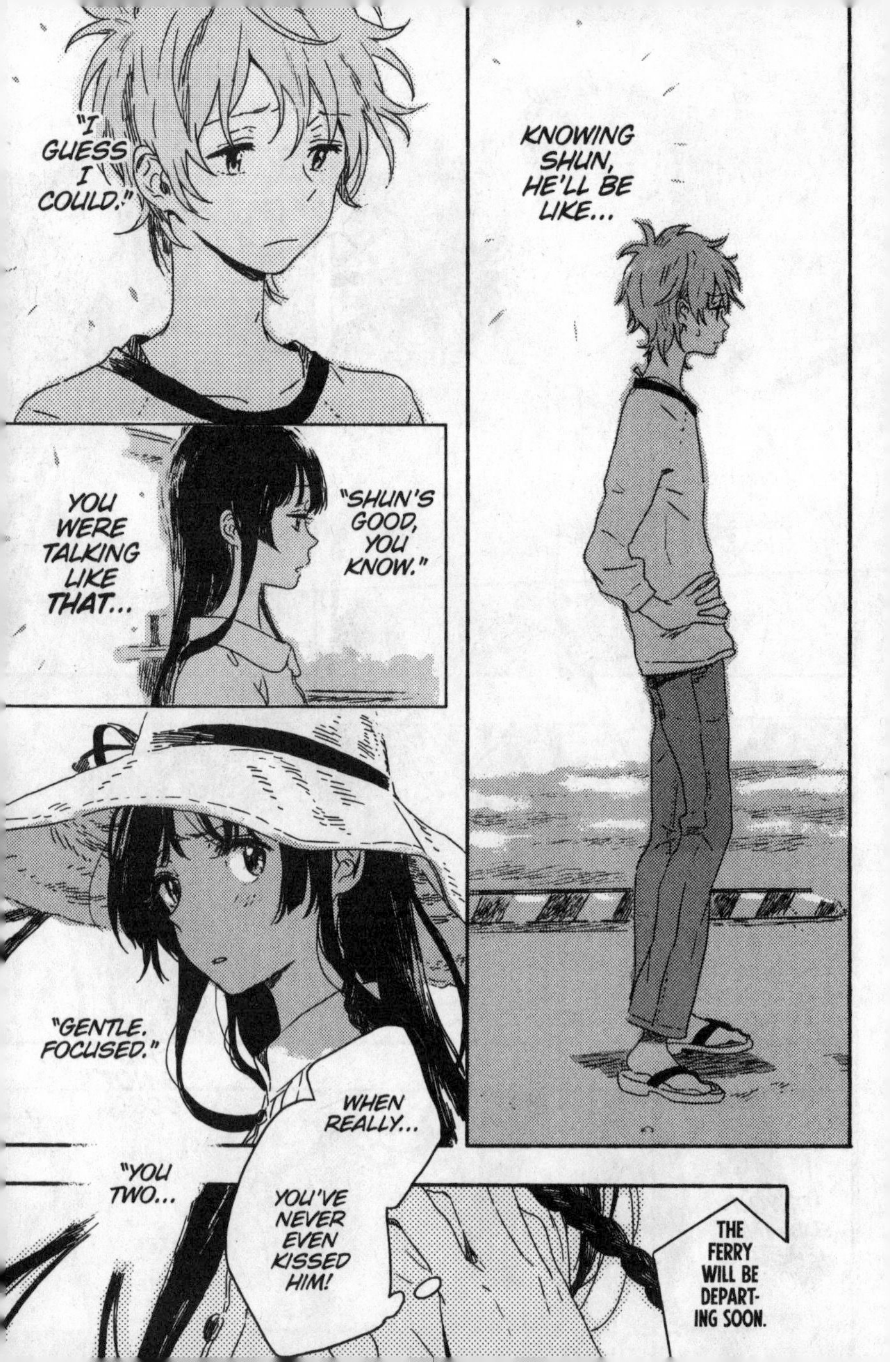
KNOWING SHUN, HE'LL BE LIKE...
"I GUESS I COULD."
"SHUN'S GOOD, YOU KNOW."
YOU WERE TALKING LIKE THAT...
"GENTLE. FOCUSED."
WHEN REALLY...
THE FERRY WILL BE DEPART-ING SOON.
"YOU TWO...
YOU'VE NEVER EVEN KISSED HIM!

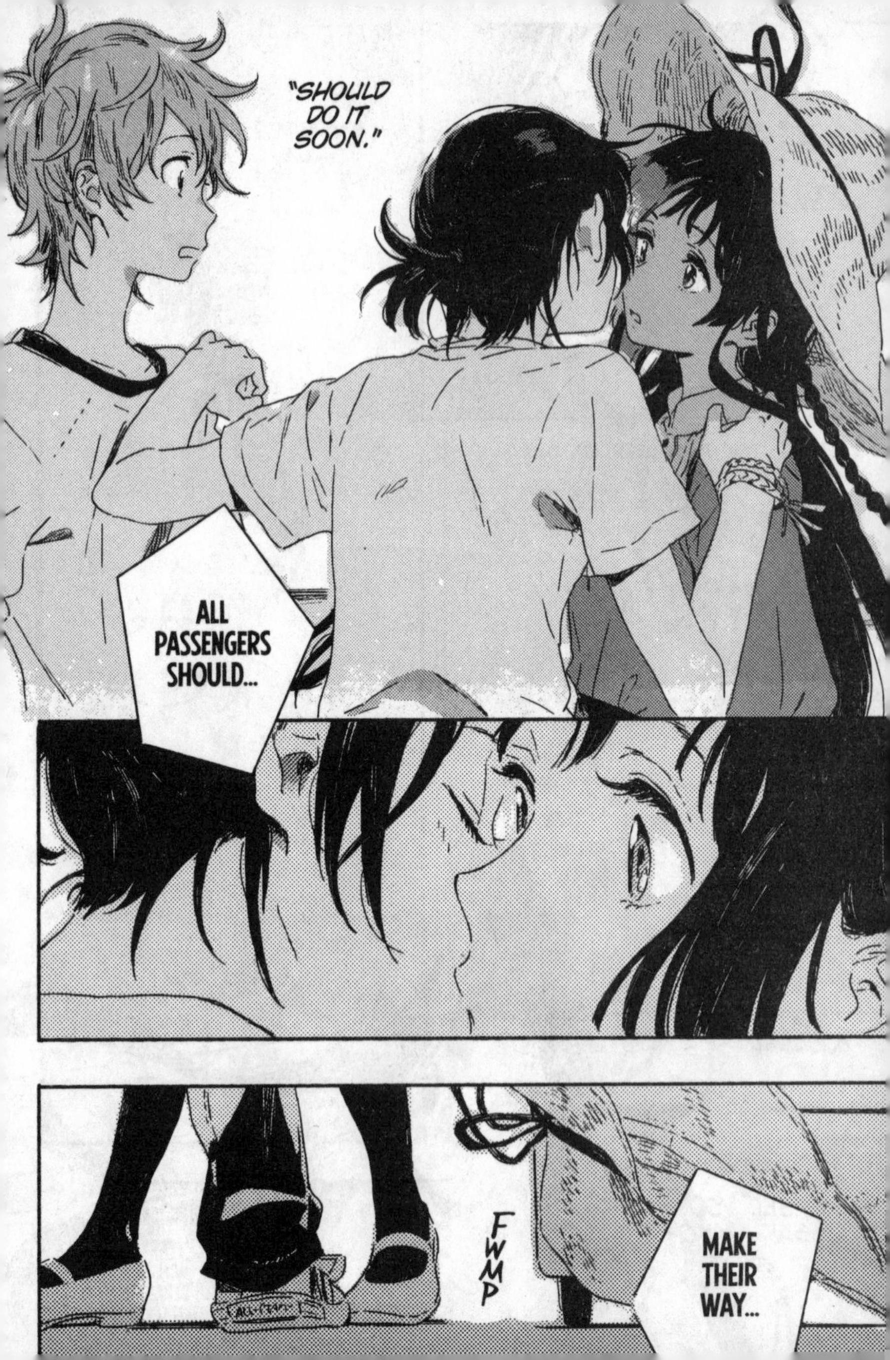
"SHOULD DO IT SOON."
ALL PASSENGERS SHOULD...
MAKE THEIR WAY...
FWMP

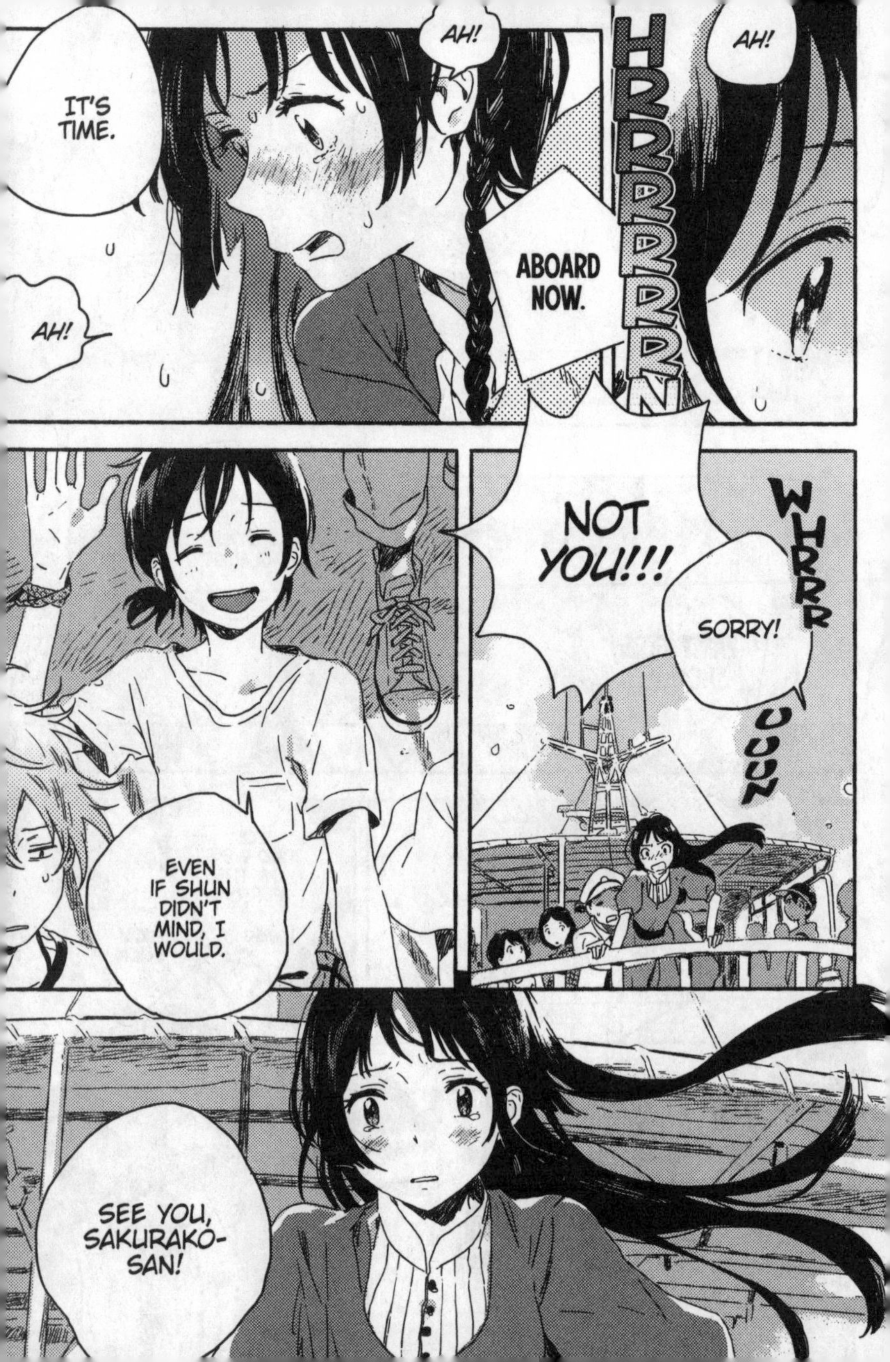
AH!
HRRRRRRN
AH!
IT'S TIME.
ABOARD NOW.
AH!
NOT YOU!!!
WHRRR
SORRY!
UUUN
EVEN IF SHUN DIDN'T MIND, I WOULD.
SEE YOU, SAKURAKO-SAN!

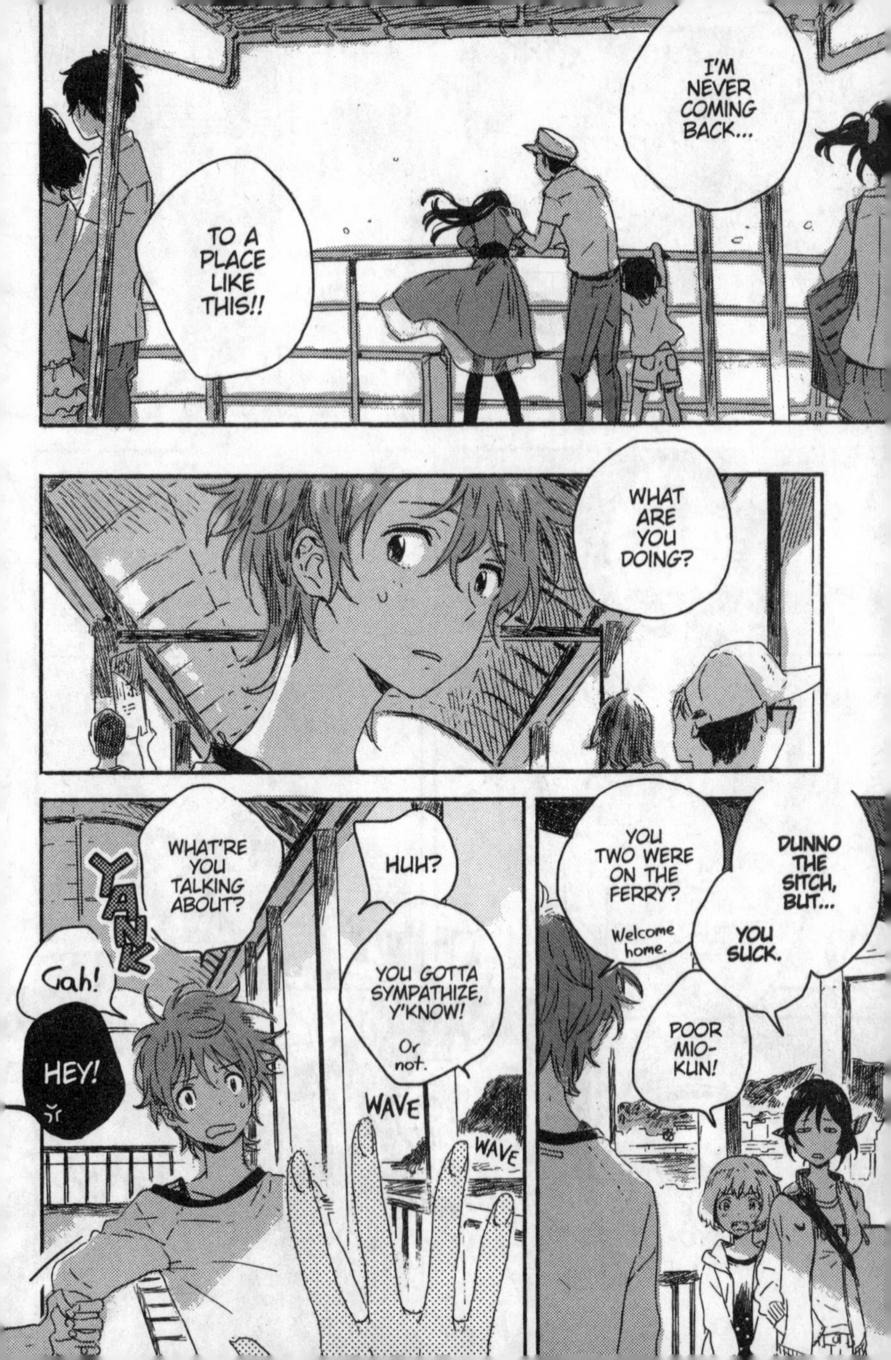
I'M NEVER COMING BACK...
TO A PLACE LIKE THIS!!
WHAT ARE YOU DOING?
DUNNO THE SITCH, BUT...
YOU SUCK.
YOU TWO WERE ON THE FERRY?
Welcome home.
POOR MIO-KUN!
HUH?
WHAT'RE YOU TALKING ABOUT?
YANK
Gah!
HEY!
YOU GOTTA SYMPATHIZE, Y'KNOW!
Or not.
WAVE
WAVE

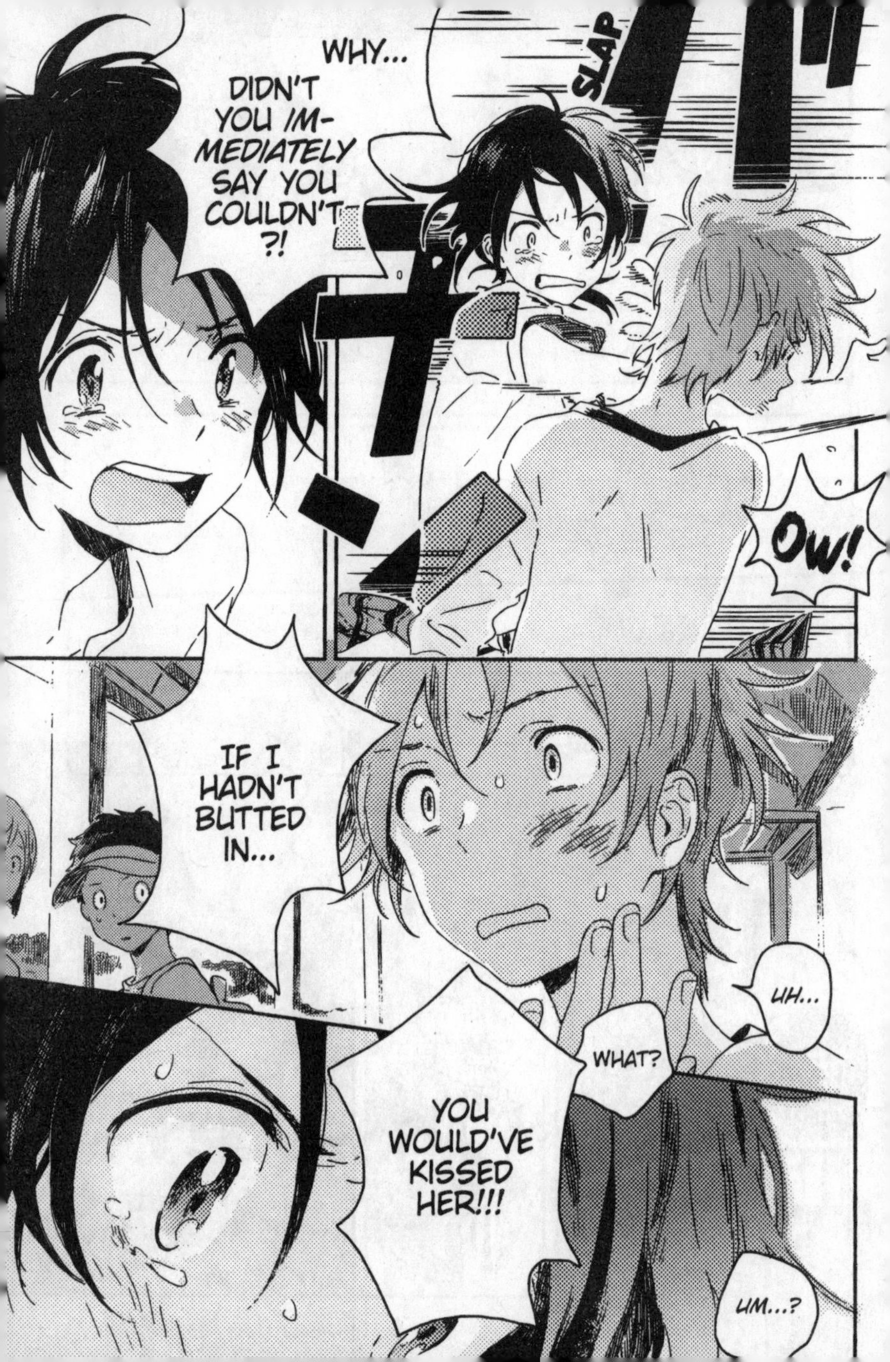

SLAP
WHY...
DIDN'T YOU IMMEDIATELY SAY YOU COULDN'T?!
Ow!
UH...
IF I HADN'T BUTTED IN...
WHAT?
YOU WOULD'VE KISSED HER!!!
UM...?

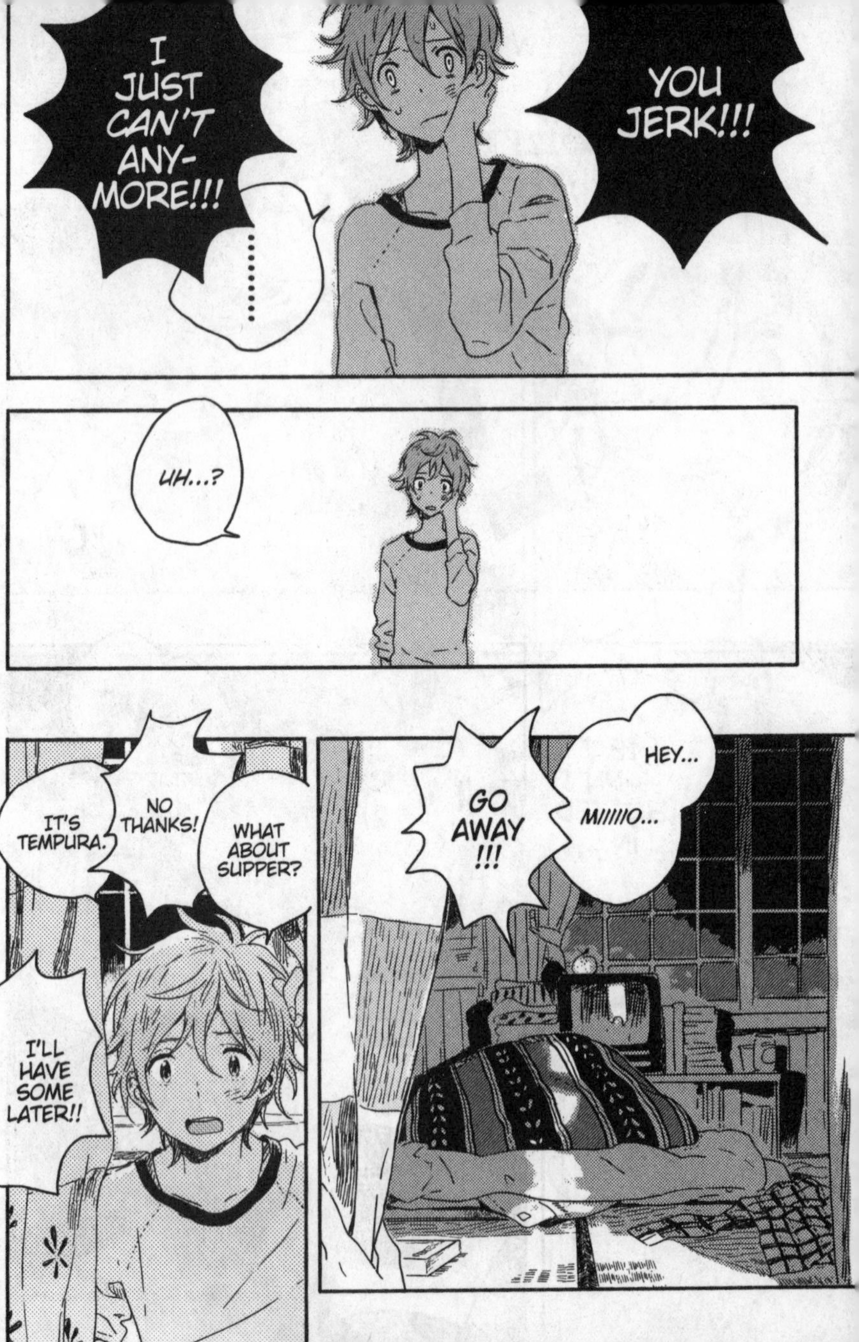
YOU JERK!!!
I JUST CAN'T ANYMORE!!!
......
UH...?
HEY... MIIIIIO...
GO AWAY !!!
WHAT ABOUT SUPPER?
NO THANKS!
IT'S TEMPURA.
I'LL HAVE SOME LATER!!

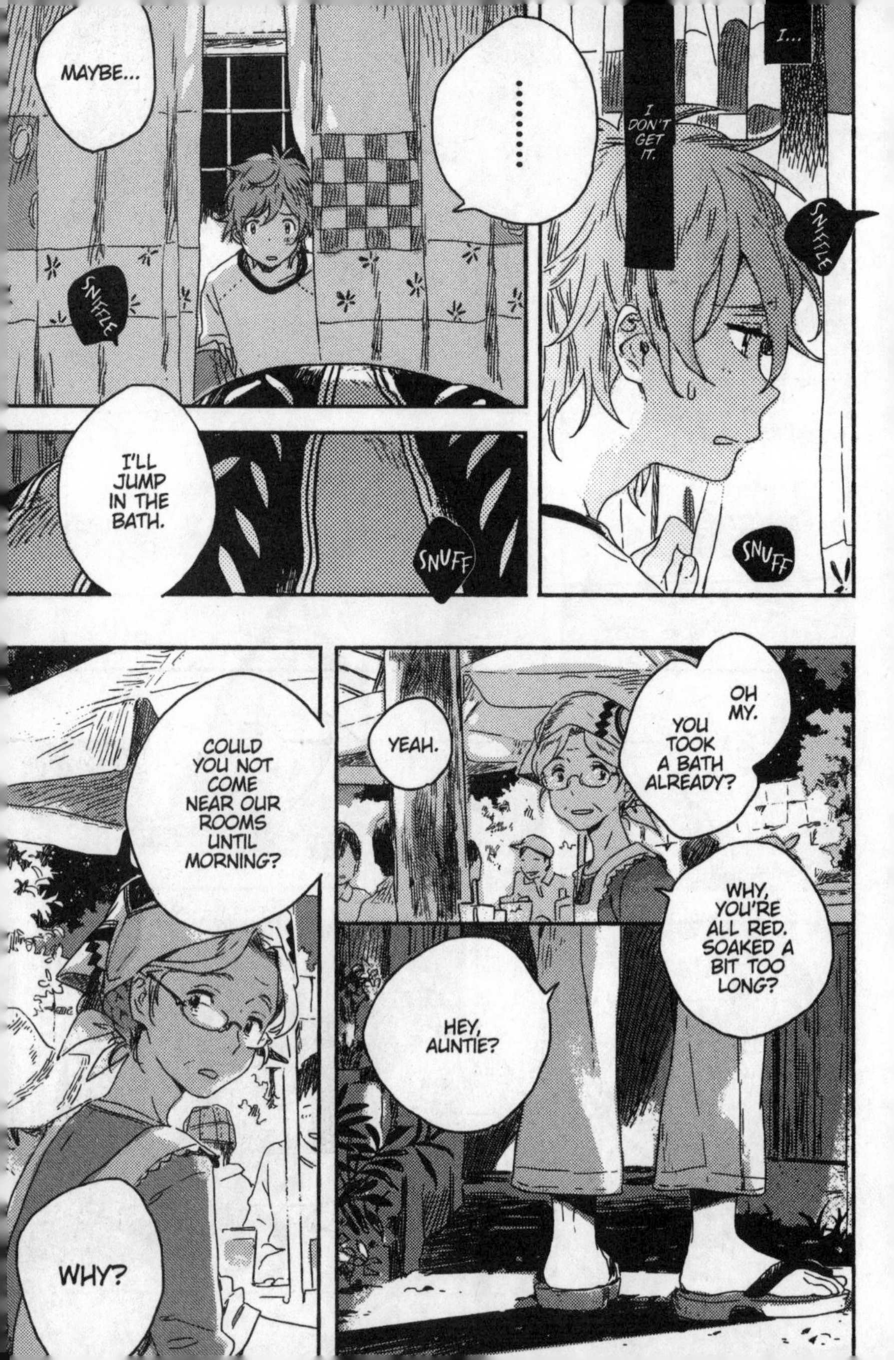

I...
I DON'T GET IT.
SNIFFLE
SNUFF
......
MAYBE...
SNIFFLE
I'LL JUMP IN THE BATH.
SNUFF
OH MY. YOU TOOK A BATH ALREADY?
YEAH.
WHY, YOU'RE ALL RED. SOAKED A BIT TOO LONG?
HEY, AUNTIE?
COULD YOU NOT COME NEAR OUR ROOMS UNTIL MORNING?
WHY?

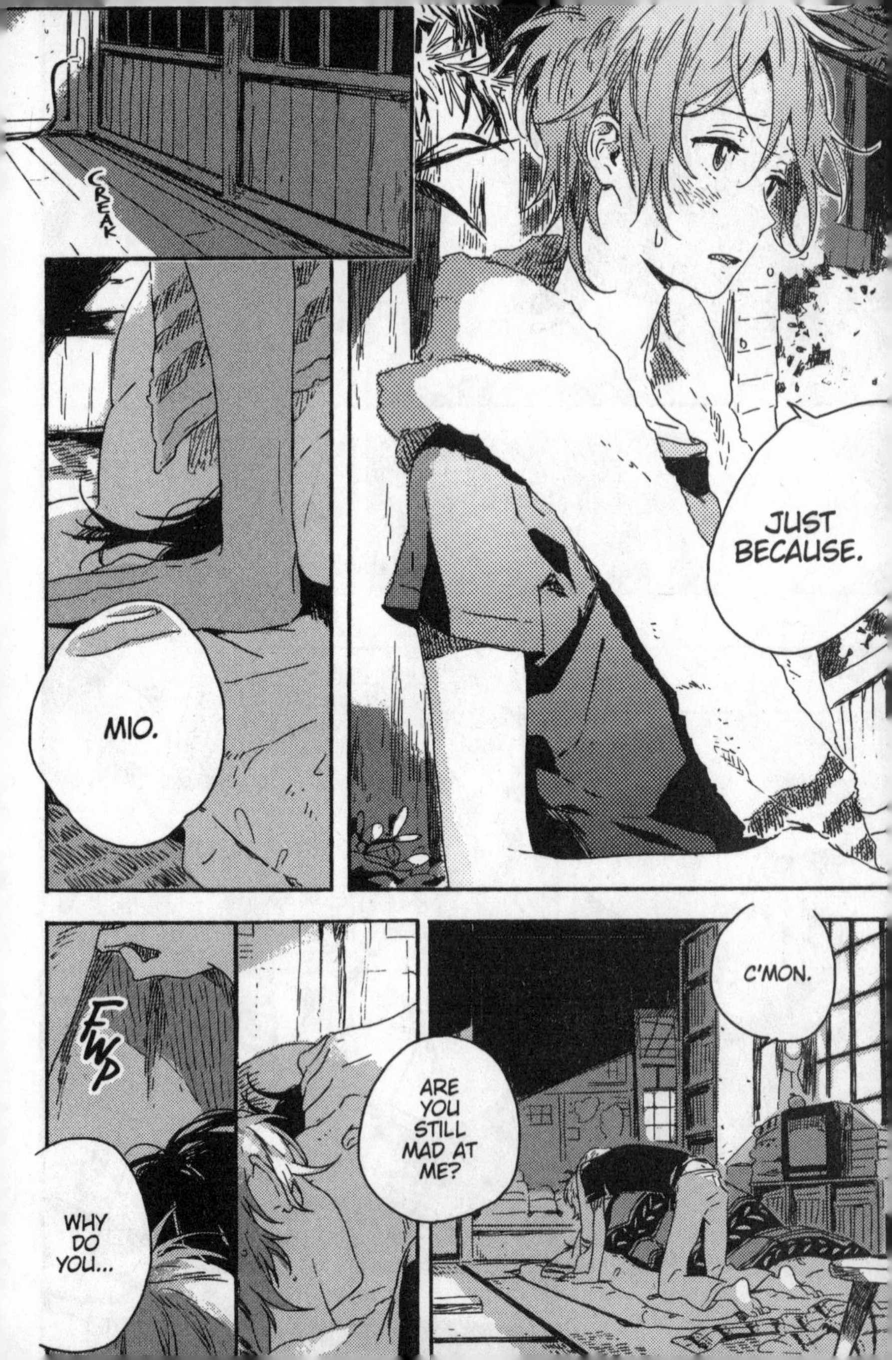
JUST BECAUSE.
CREAK
MIO.
C'MON.
ARE YOU STILL MAD AT ME?
FWP
WHY DO YOU...

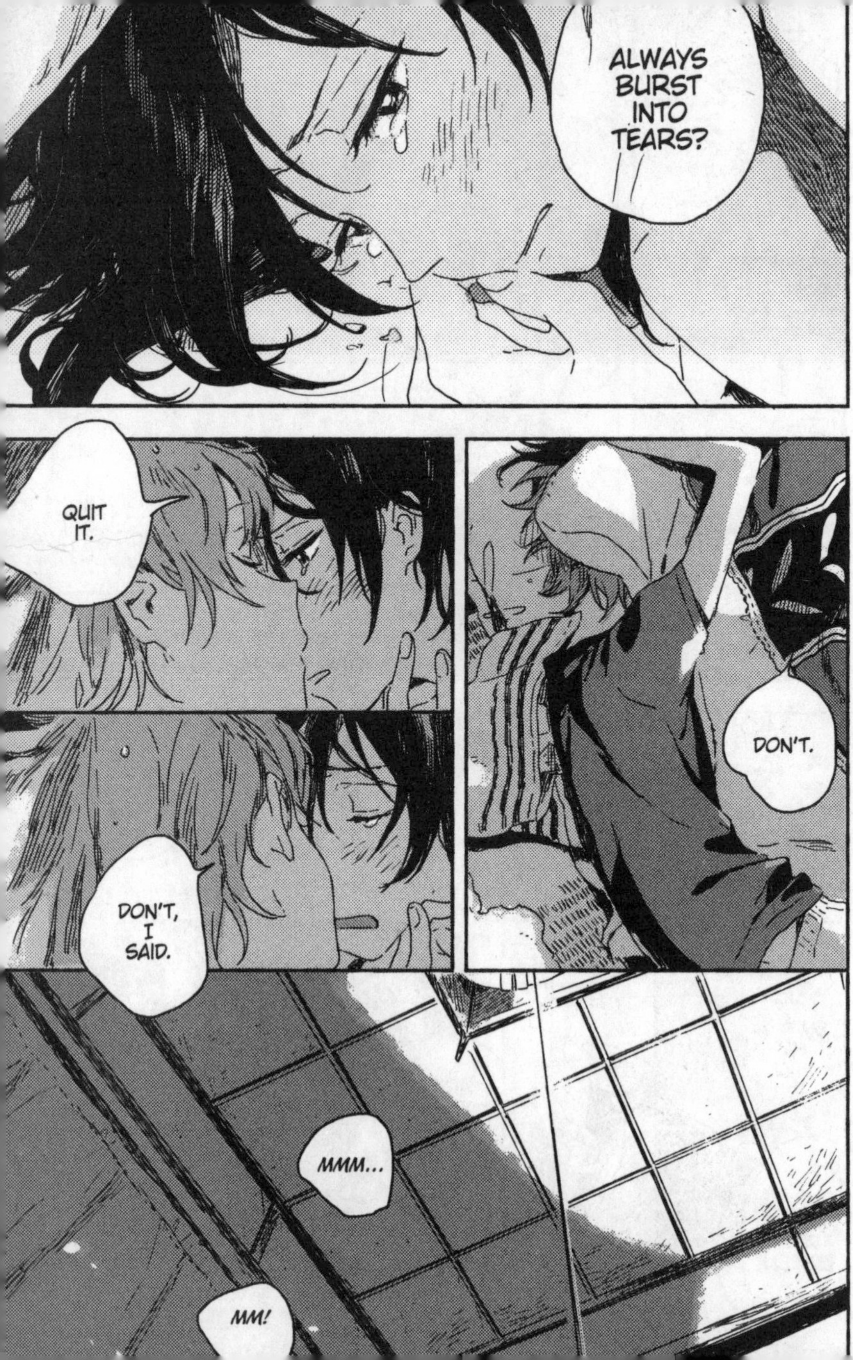
ALWAYS BURST INTO TEARS?
DON'T.
QUIT IT.
DON'T, I SAID.
MMM...
MM!

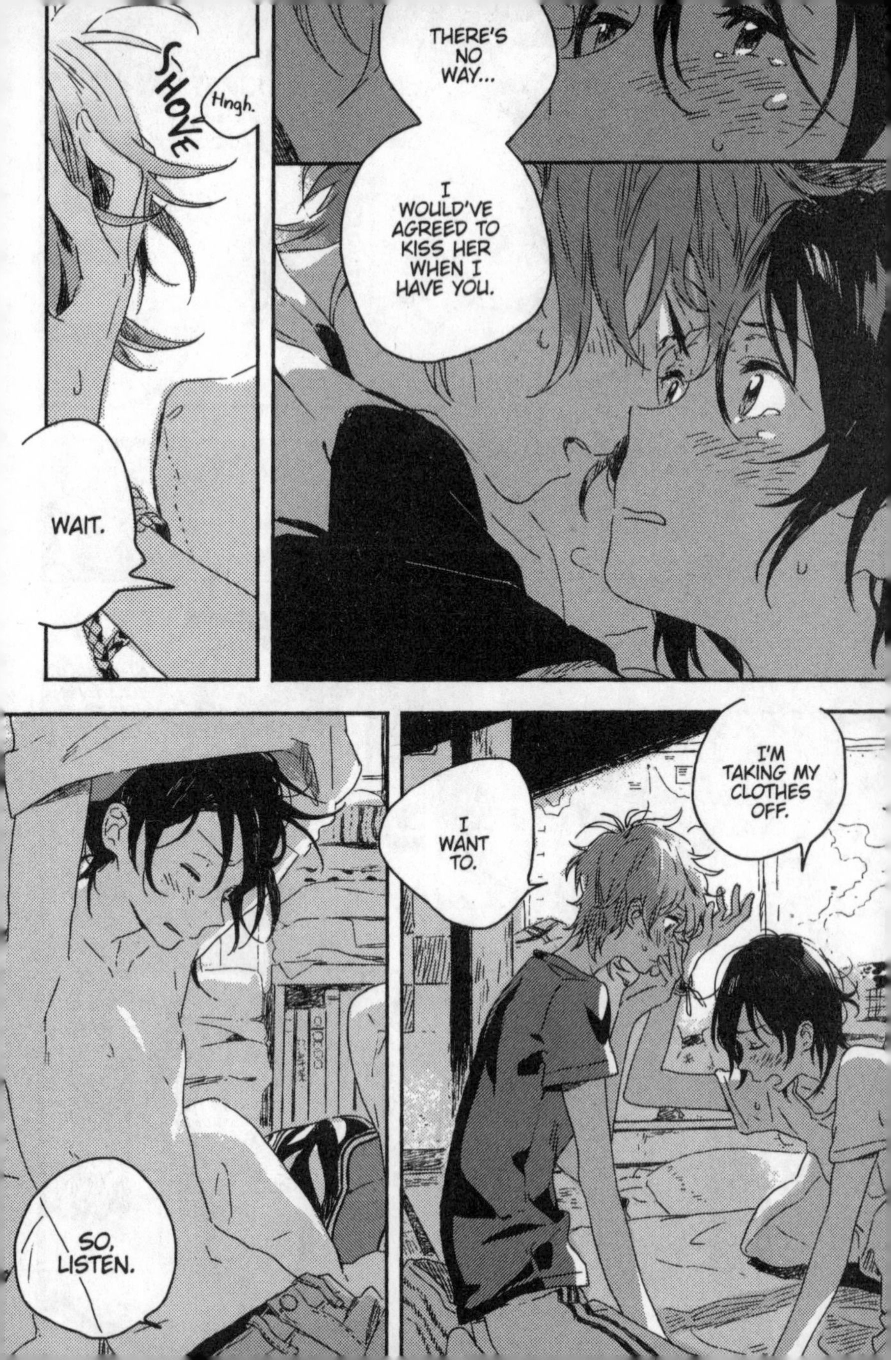
THERE'S NO WAY...
I WOULD'VE AGREED TO KISS HER WHEN I HAVE YOU.
SHOVE
Hngh.
WAIT.
I'M TAKING MY CLOTHES OFF.
I WANT TO.
SO, LISTEN.

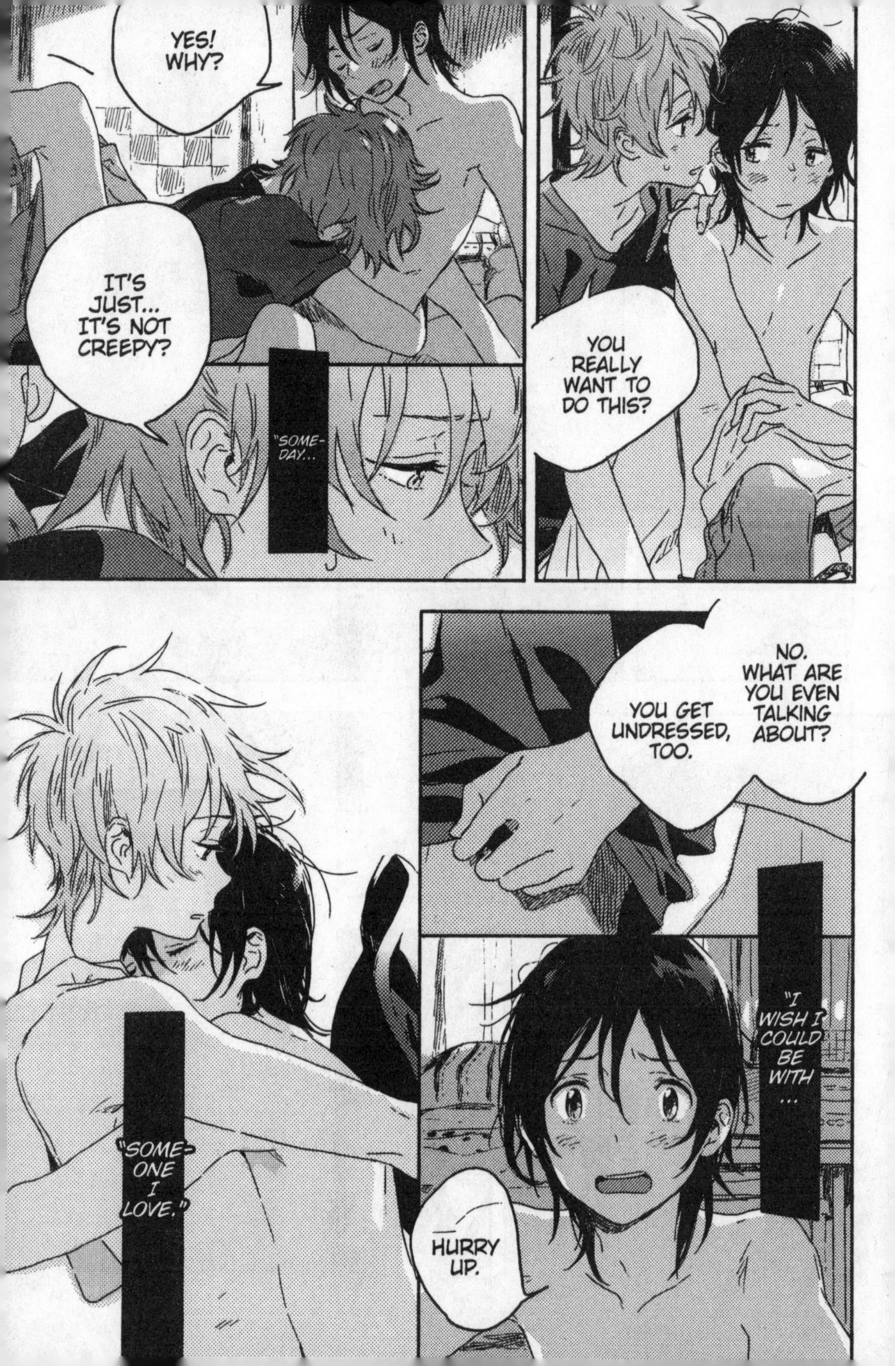
YOU REALLY WANT TO DO THIS?
YES! WHY?
IT'S JUST... IT'S NOT CREEPY?
"SOME-DAY...
NO. WHAT ARE YOU EVEN TALKING ABOUT?
YOU GET UNDRESSED, TOO.
"I WISH I COULD BE WITH ...
HURRY UP.
"SOME-ONE I LOVE."

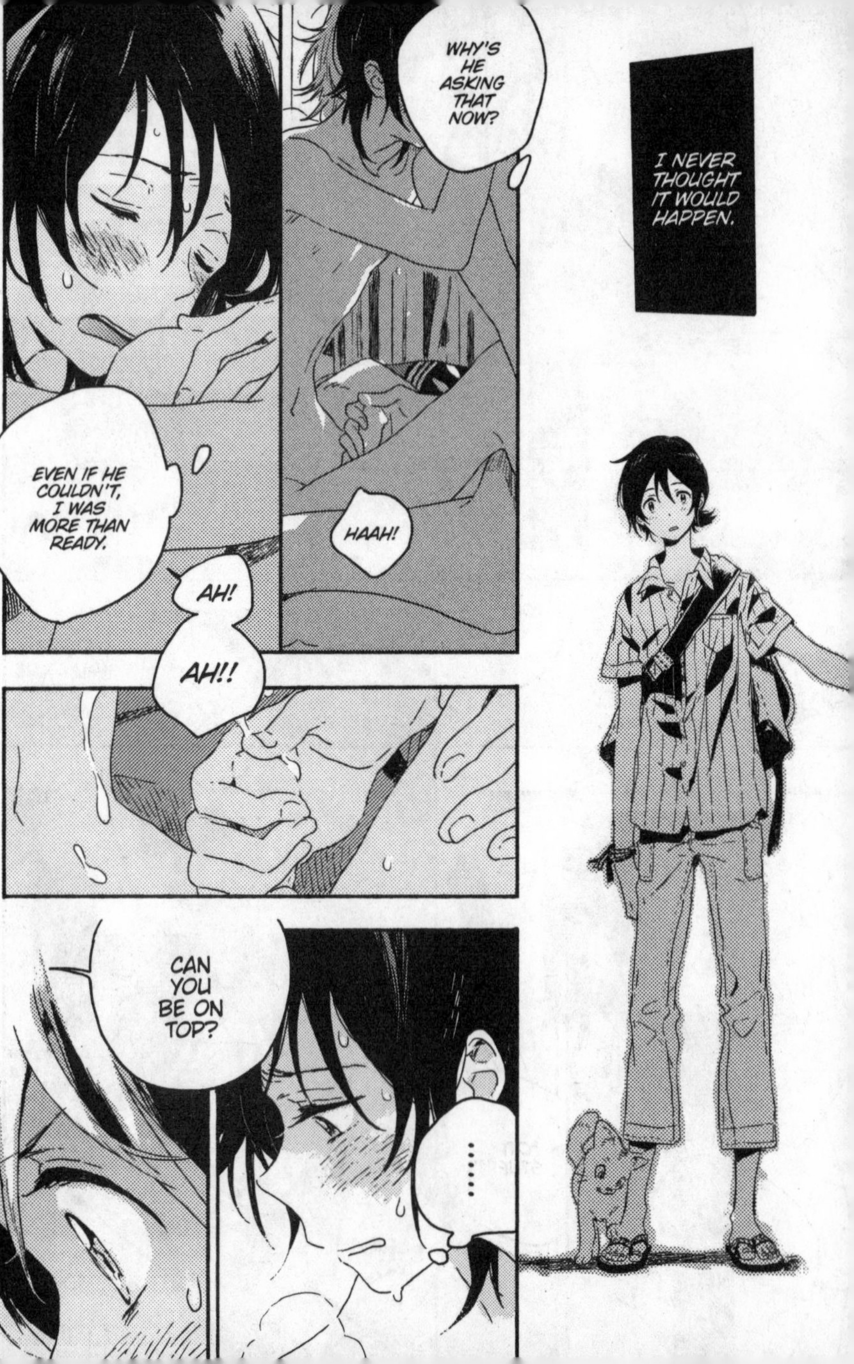
I NEVER THOUGHT IT WOULD HAPPEN.
WHY'S HE ASKING THAT NOW?
HAAH!
EVEN IF HE COULDN'T, I WAS MORE THAN READY.
AH!
AH!!
CAN YOU BE ON TOP?
......

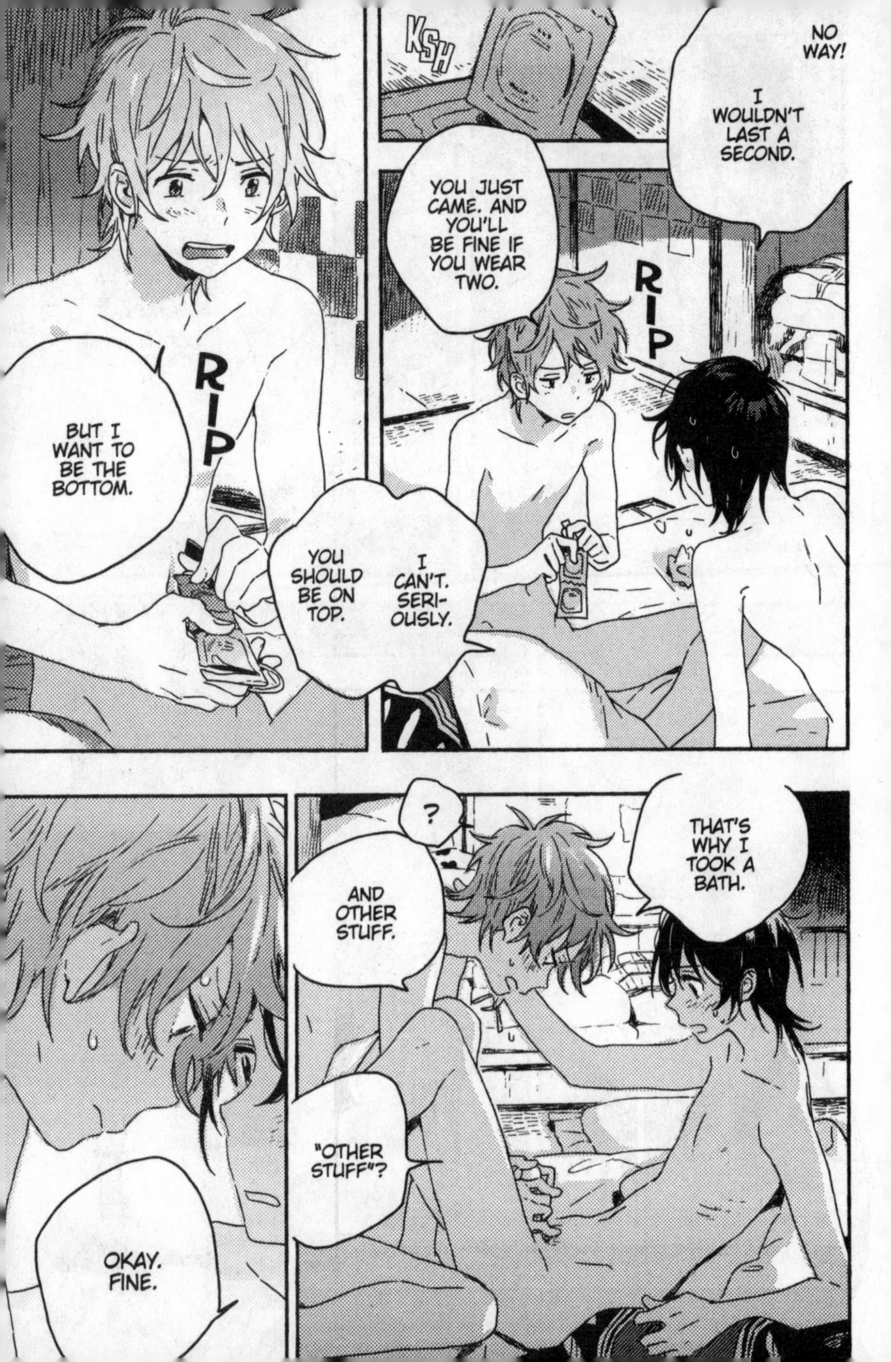

KSH
NO WAY!
I WOULDN'T LAST A SECOND.
YOU JUST CAME. AND YOU'LL BE FINE IF YOU WEAR TWO.
RIP
I CAN'T. SERIOUSLY.
YOU SHOULD BE ON TOP.
RIP
BUT I WANT TO BE THE BOTTOM.
?
THAT'S WHY I TOOK A BATH.
AND OTHER STUFF.
"OTHER STUFF"?
OKAY. FINE.

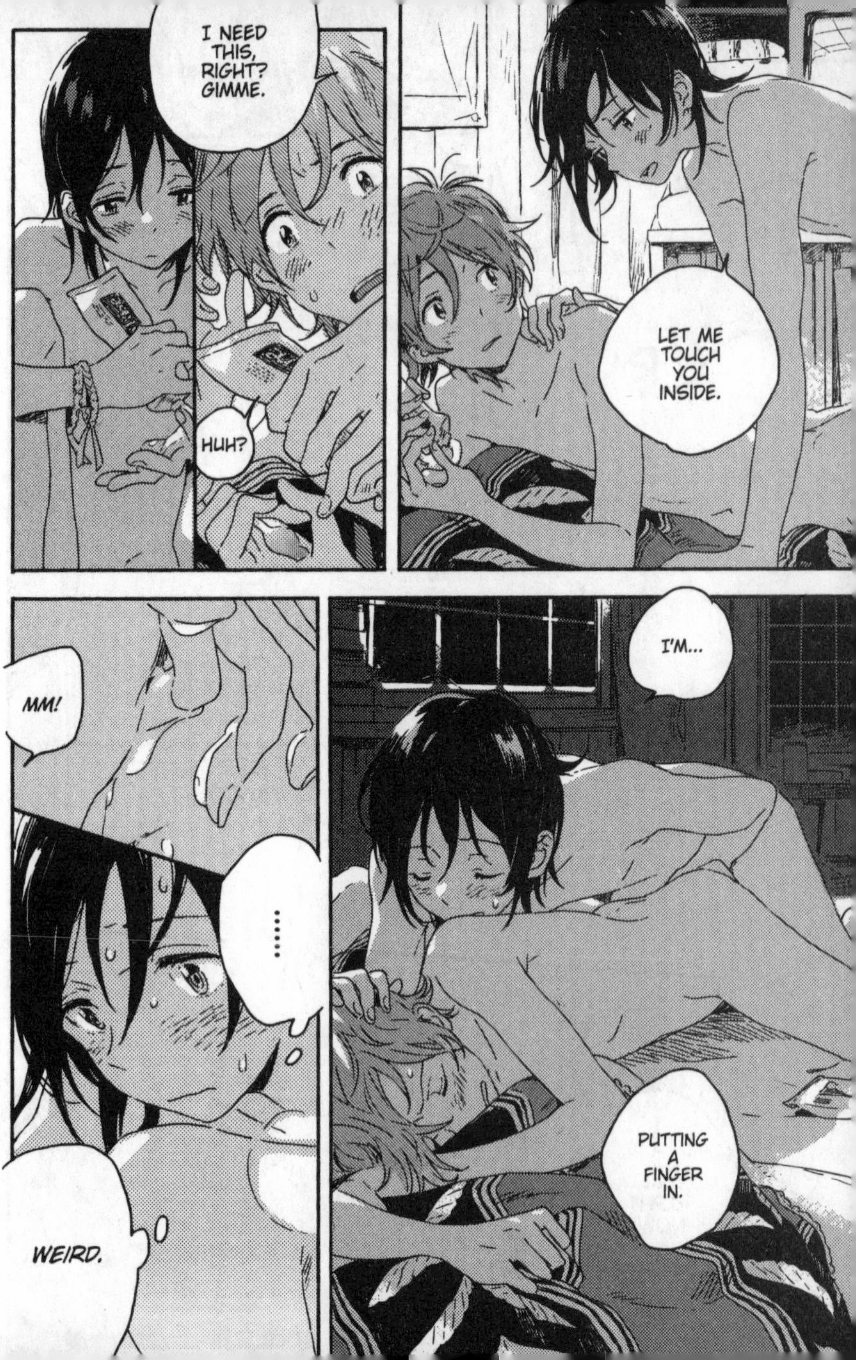
LET ME TOUCH YOU INSIDE.
I NEED THIS, RIGHT? GIMME.
HUH?
I'M...
PUTTING A FINGER IN.
MM!
......
WEIRD.

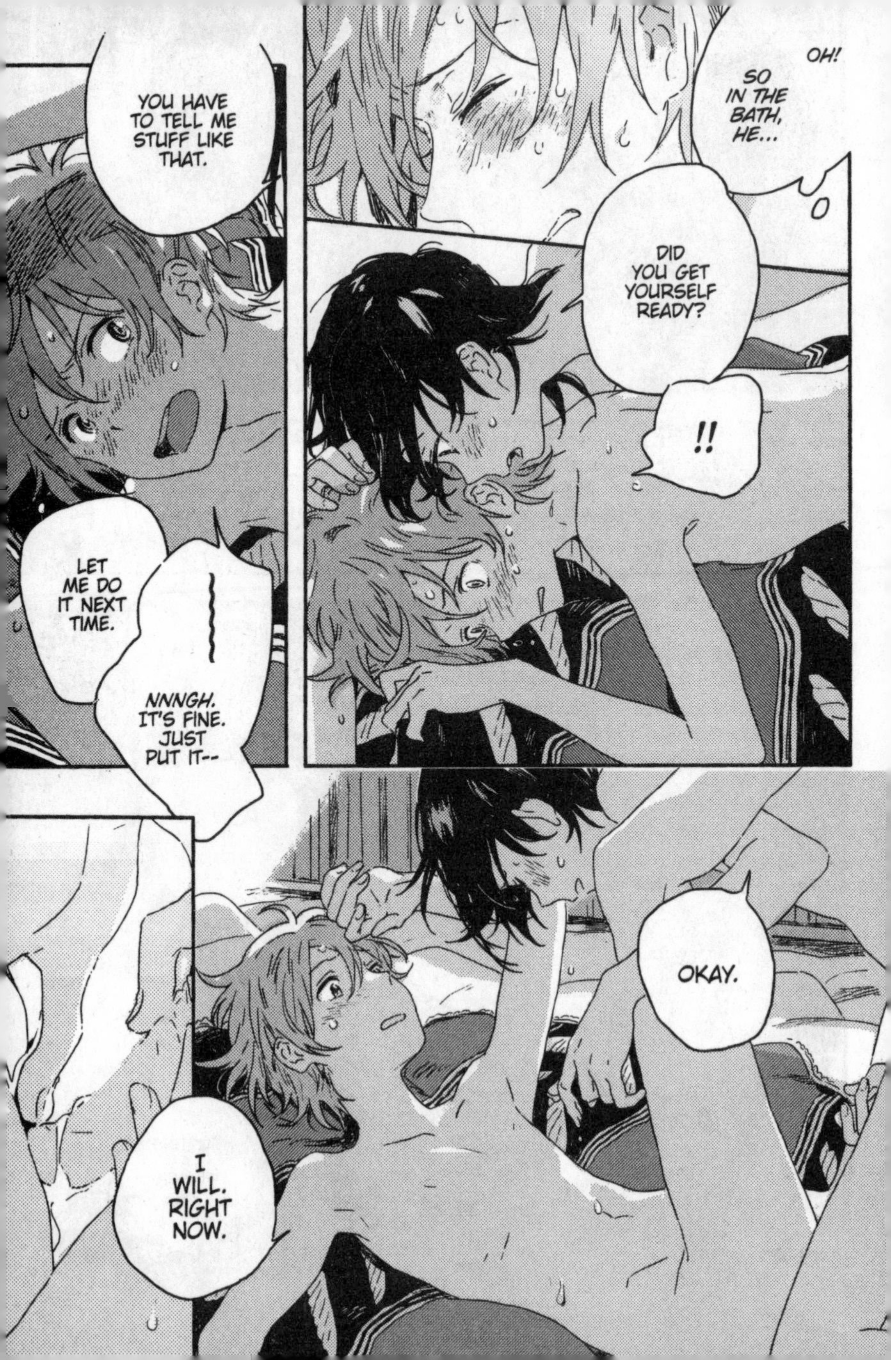
OH!
SO IN THE BATH, HE...
DID YOU GET YOURSELF READY?
!!
YOU HAVE TO TELL ME STUFF LIKE THAT.
LET ME DO IT NEXT TIME.
NNNGH. IT'S FINE. JUST PUT IT--
OKAY.
I WILL. RIGHT NOW.

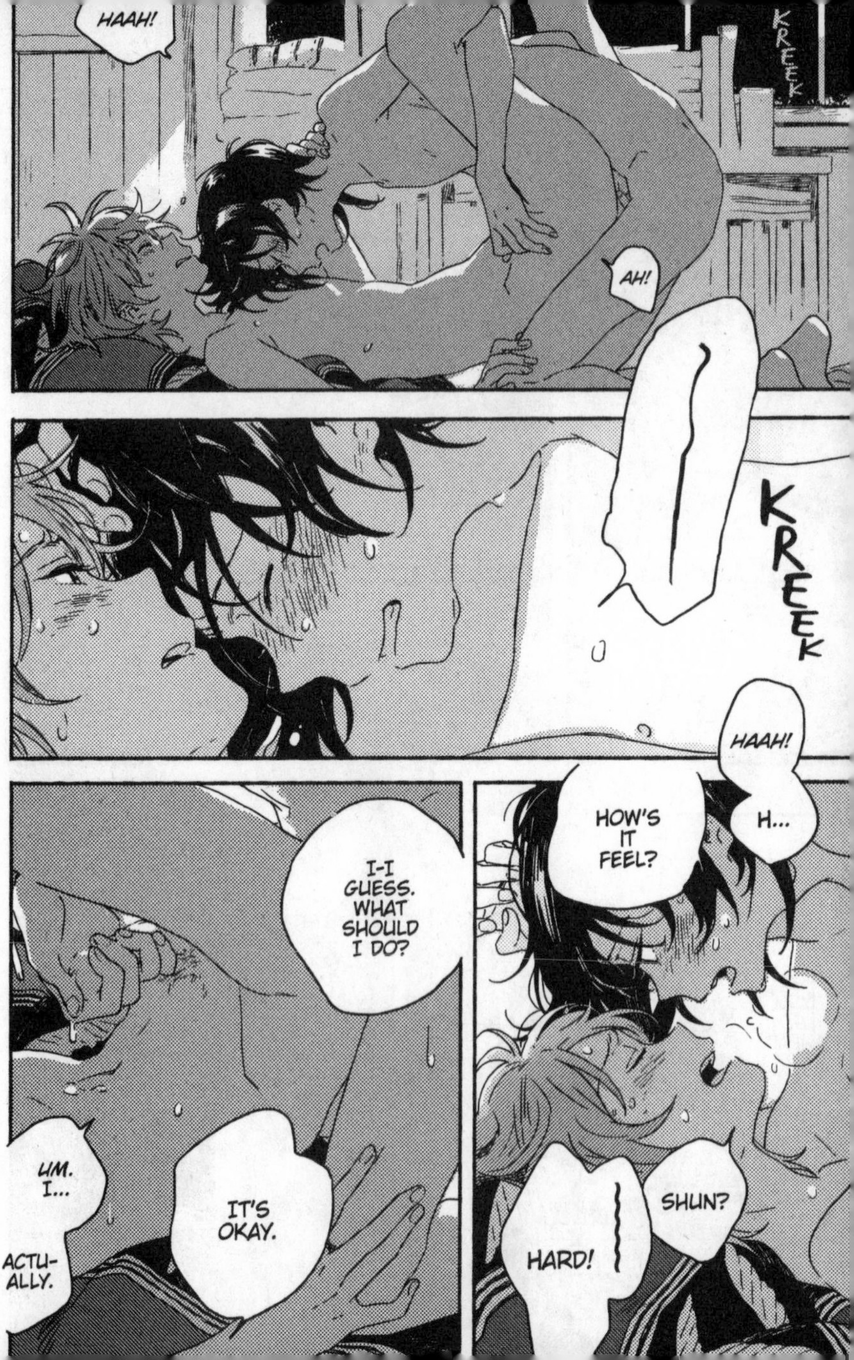
KREEK
AH!
HAAH!
—
KREEK
HAAH!
H...
HOW'S IT FEEL?
SHUN?
— HARD!
I-I GUESS. WHAT SHOULD I DO?
IT'S OKAY.
UM. I... ACTUALLY.

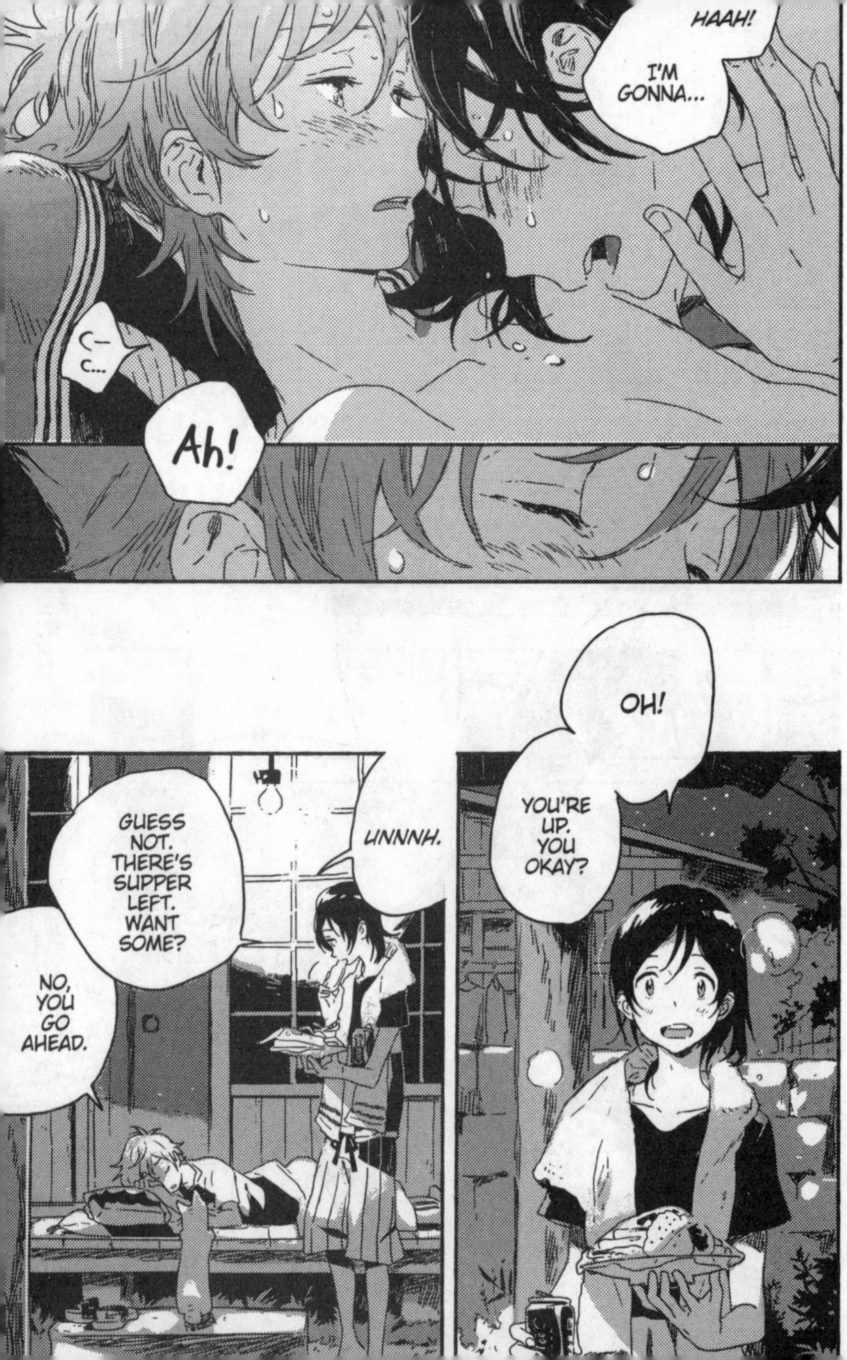
HAAH!
I'M GONNA...
C— C...
Ah!
OH!
YOU'RE UP. YOU OKAY?
UNNNH.
GUESS NOT. THERE'S SUPPER LEFT. WANT SOME?
NO, YOU GO AHEAD.

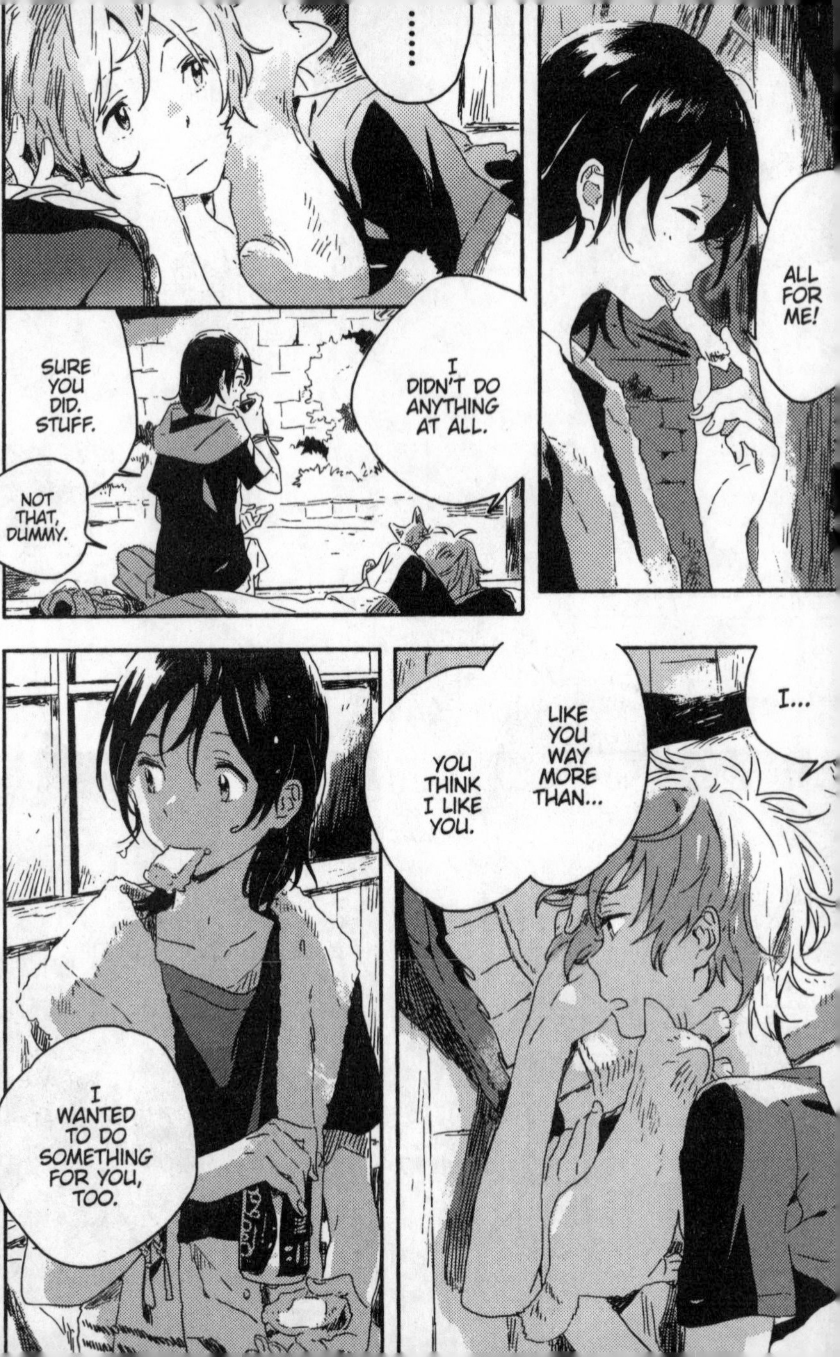
ALL FOR ME!
......
I DIDN'T DO ANYTHING AT ALL.
SURE YOU DID. STUFF.
NOT THAT, DUMMY.
I...
LIKE YOU WAY MORE THAN...
YOU THINK I LIKE YOU.
I WANTED TO DO SOMETHING FOR YOU, TOO.

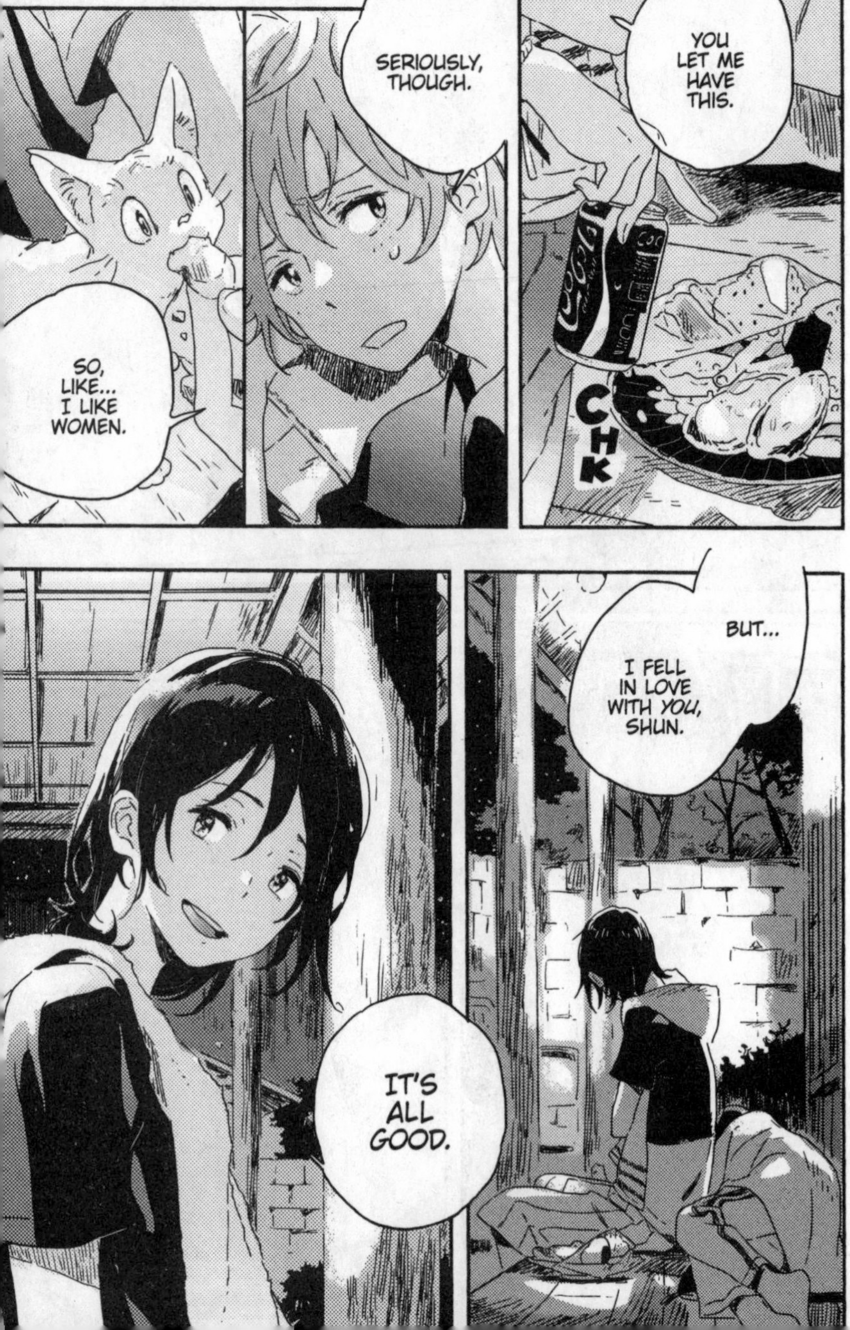
YOU LET ME HAVE THIS.
CHK
SERIOUSLY, THOUGH.
SO, LIKE... I LIKE WOMEN.
BUT...
I FELL IN LOVE WITH *YOU*, SHUN.
IT'S ALL GOOD.

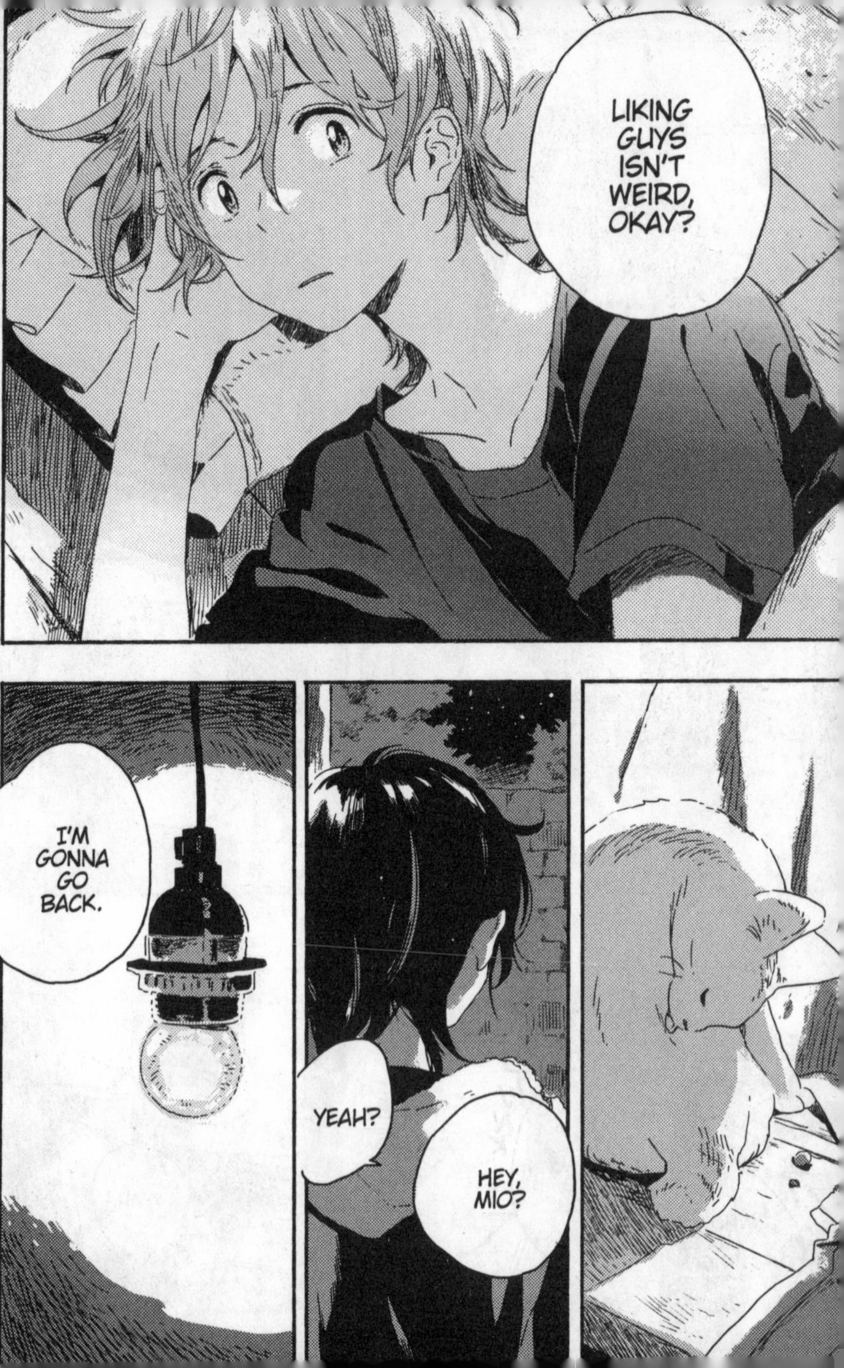
LIKING GUYS ISN'T WEIRD, OKAY?
HEY, MIO?
YEAH?
I'M GONNA GO BACK.

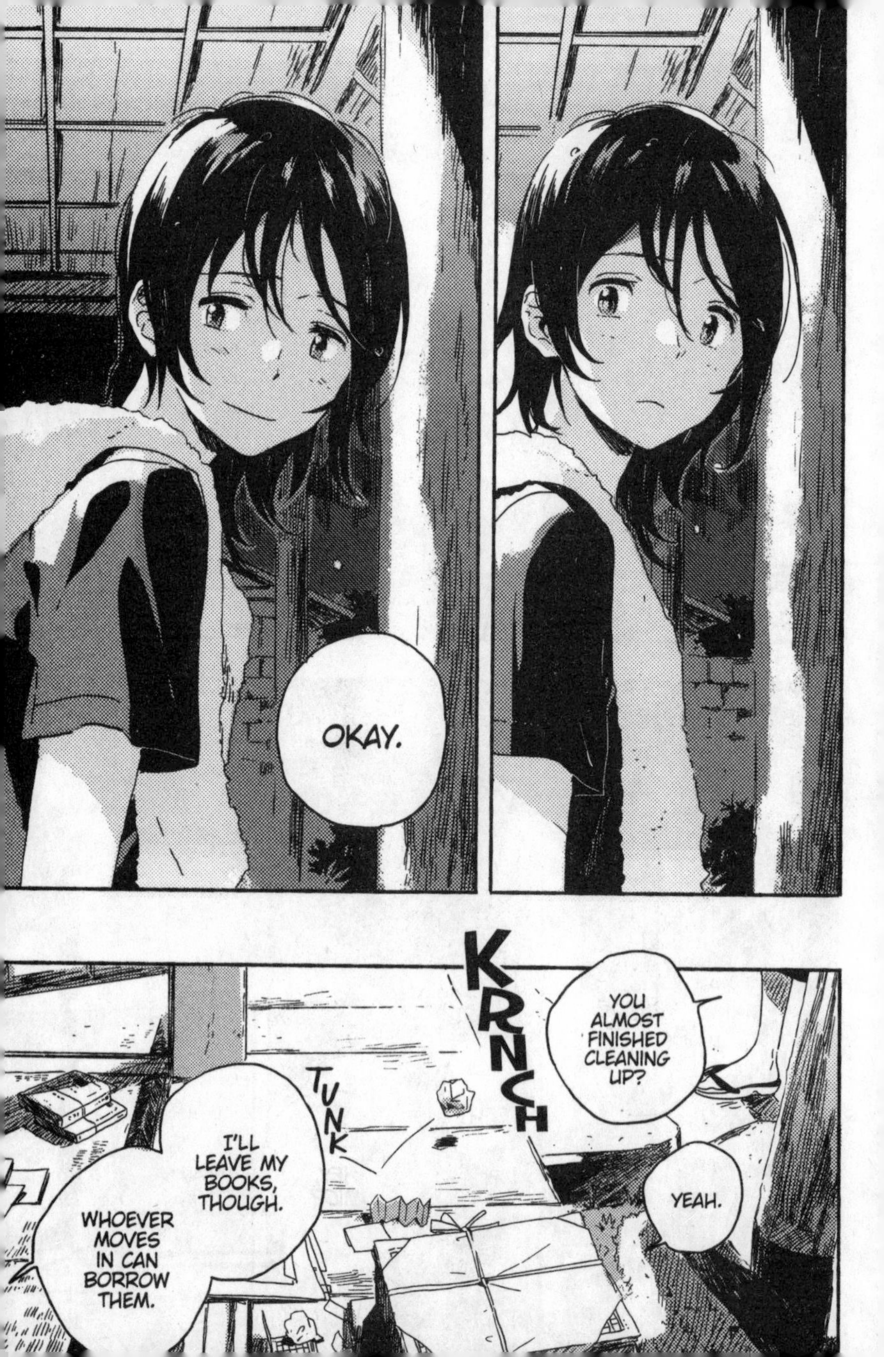
OKAY.
YOU ALMOST FINISHED CLEANING UP?
KRNCH
YEAH.
TUNK
I'LL LEAVE MY BOOKS, THOUGH.
WHOEVER MOVES IN CAN BORROW THEM.

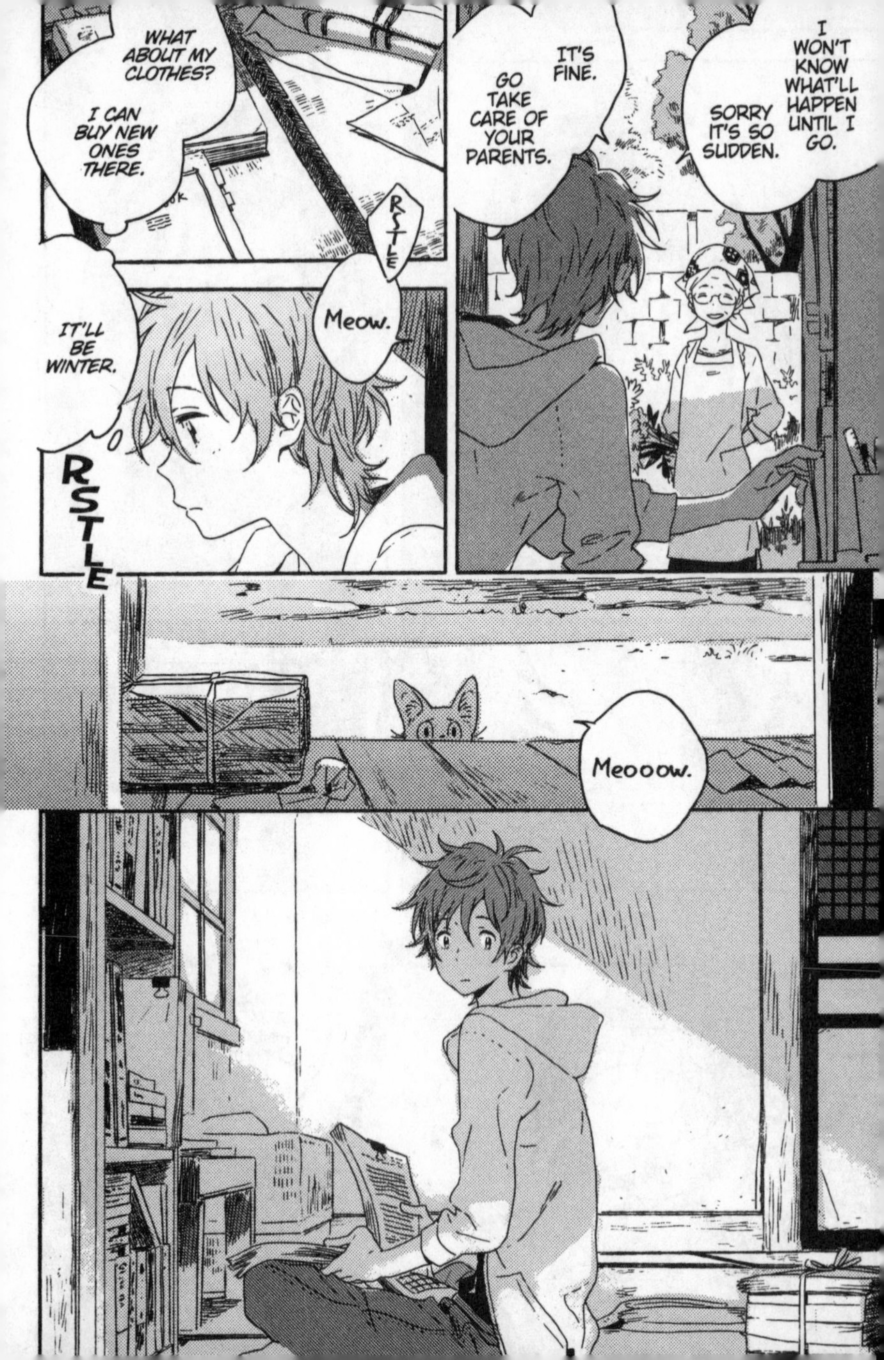
I WON'T KNOW WHAT'LL HAPPEN UNTIL I GO.
SORRY IT'S SO SUDDEN.
IT'S FINE.
GO TAKE CARE OF YOUR PARENTS.
WHAT ABOUT MY CLOTHES?
I CAN BUY NEW ONES THERE.
RSTLE
Meow.
IT'LL BE WINTER.
RSTLE
Meooow.

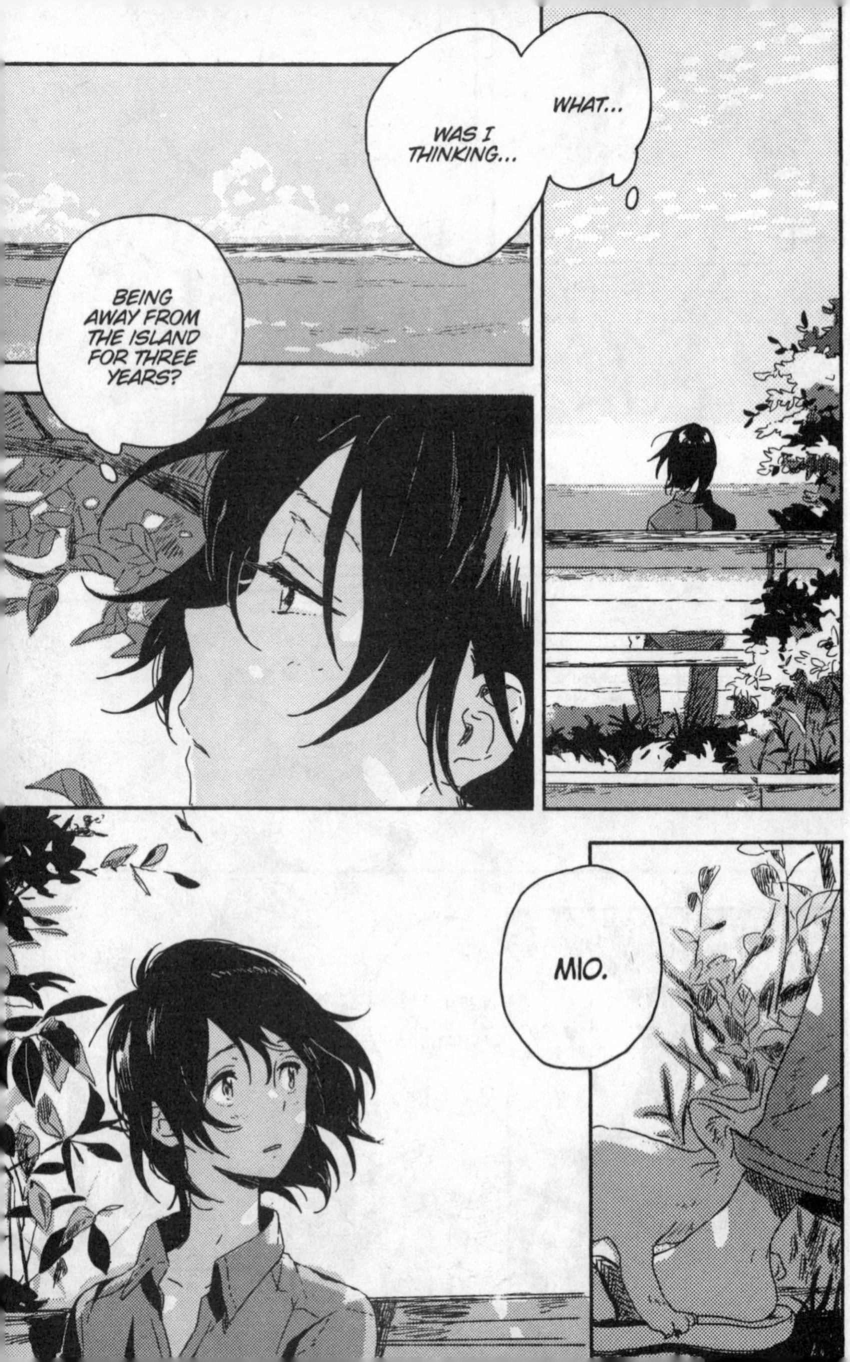
WHAT... WAS I THINKING...
BEING AWAY FROM THE ISLAND FOR THREE YEARS?
MIO.

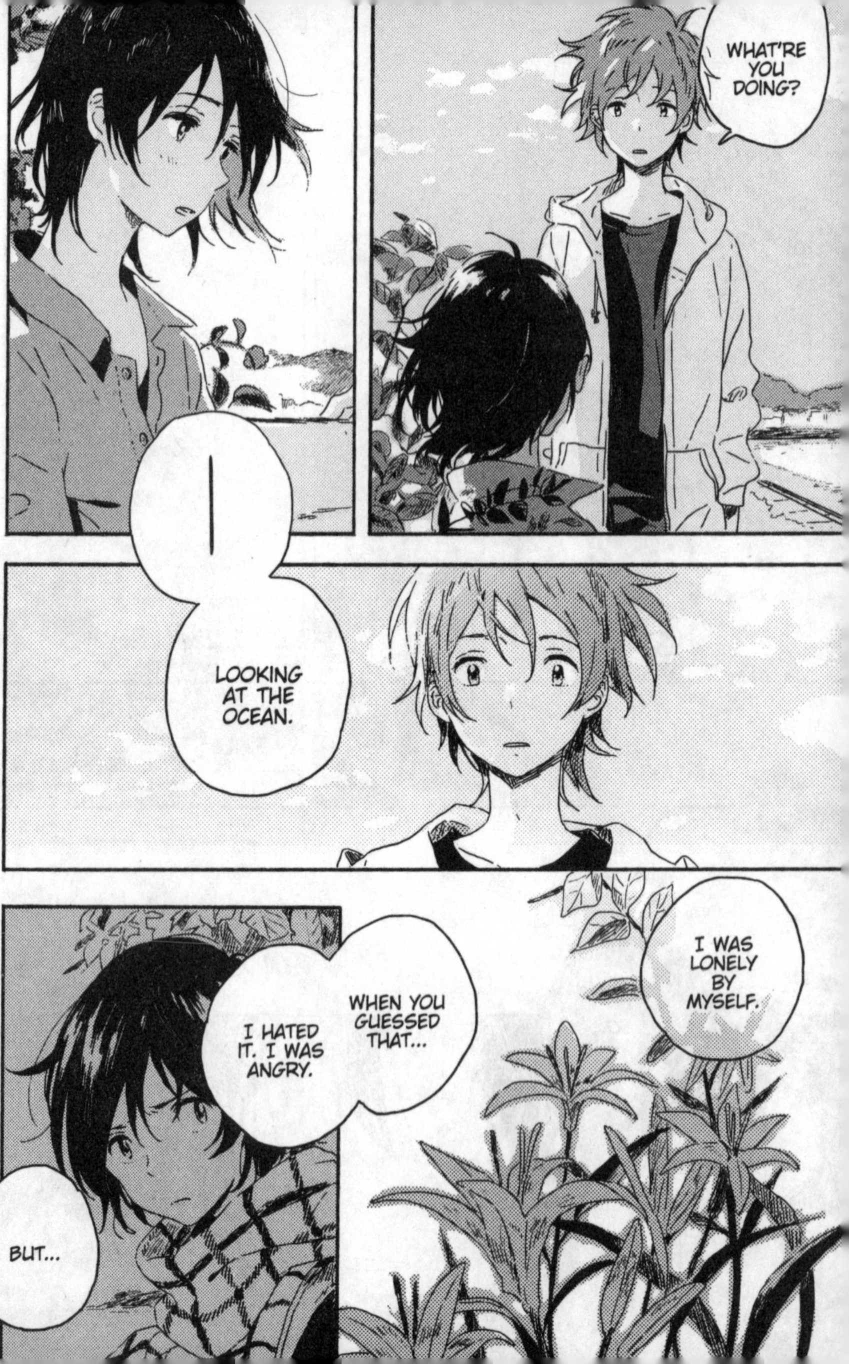
WHAT'RE YOU DOING?
LOOKING AT THE OCEAN.
I WAS LONELY BY MYSELF.
WHEN YOU GUESSED THAT...
I HATED IT. I WAS ANGRY.
BUT...

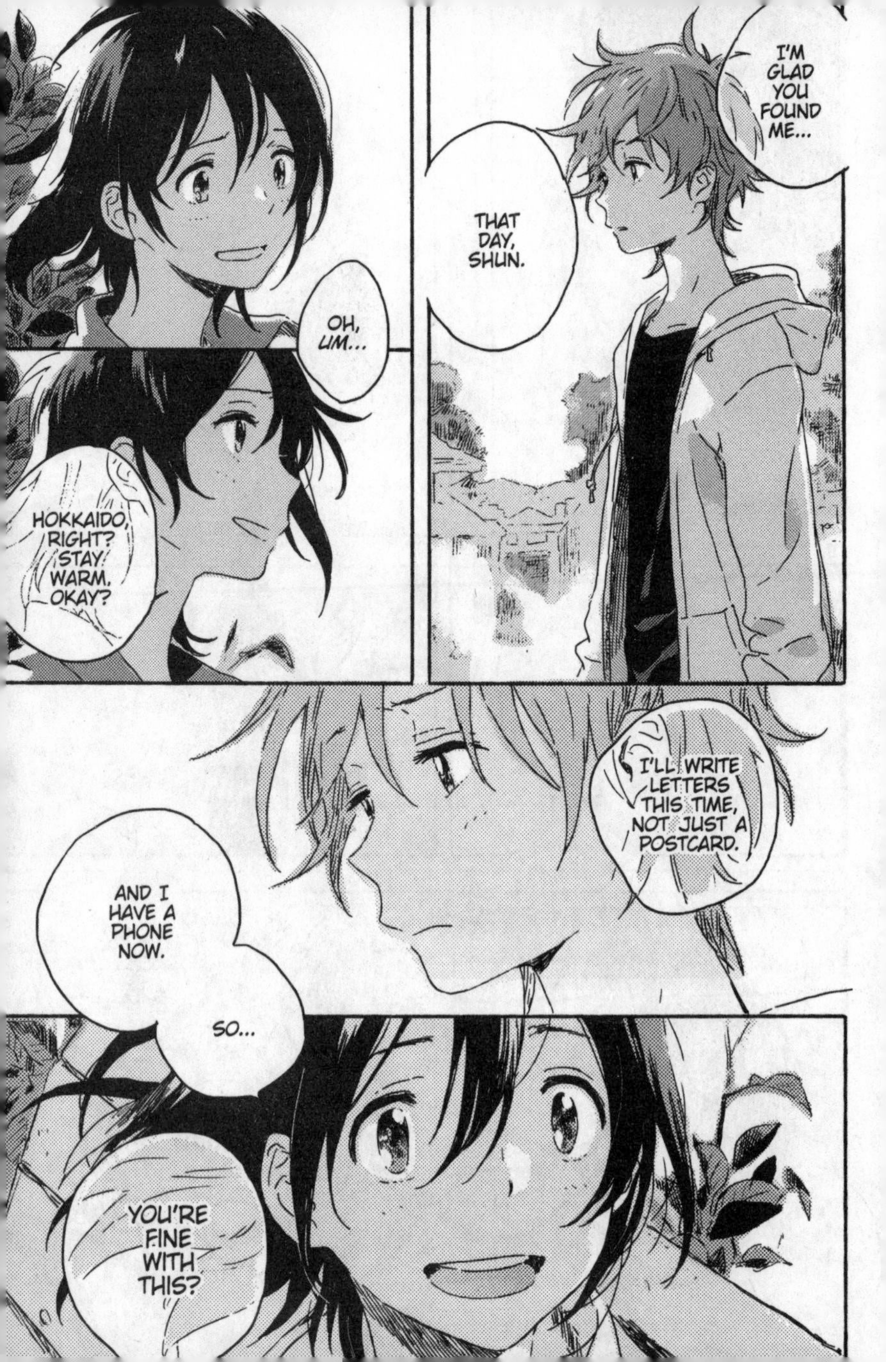
I'M GLAD YOU FOUND ME...
THAT DAY, SHUN.
OH, UM...
HOKKAIDO, RIGHT? STAY WARM. OKAY?
I'LL WRITE LETTERS THIS TIME, NOT JUST A POSTCARD.
AND I HAVE A PHONE NOW.
SO...
YOU'RE FINE WITH THIS?

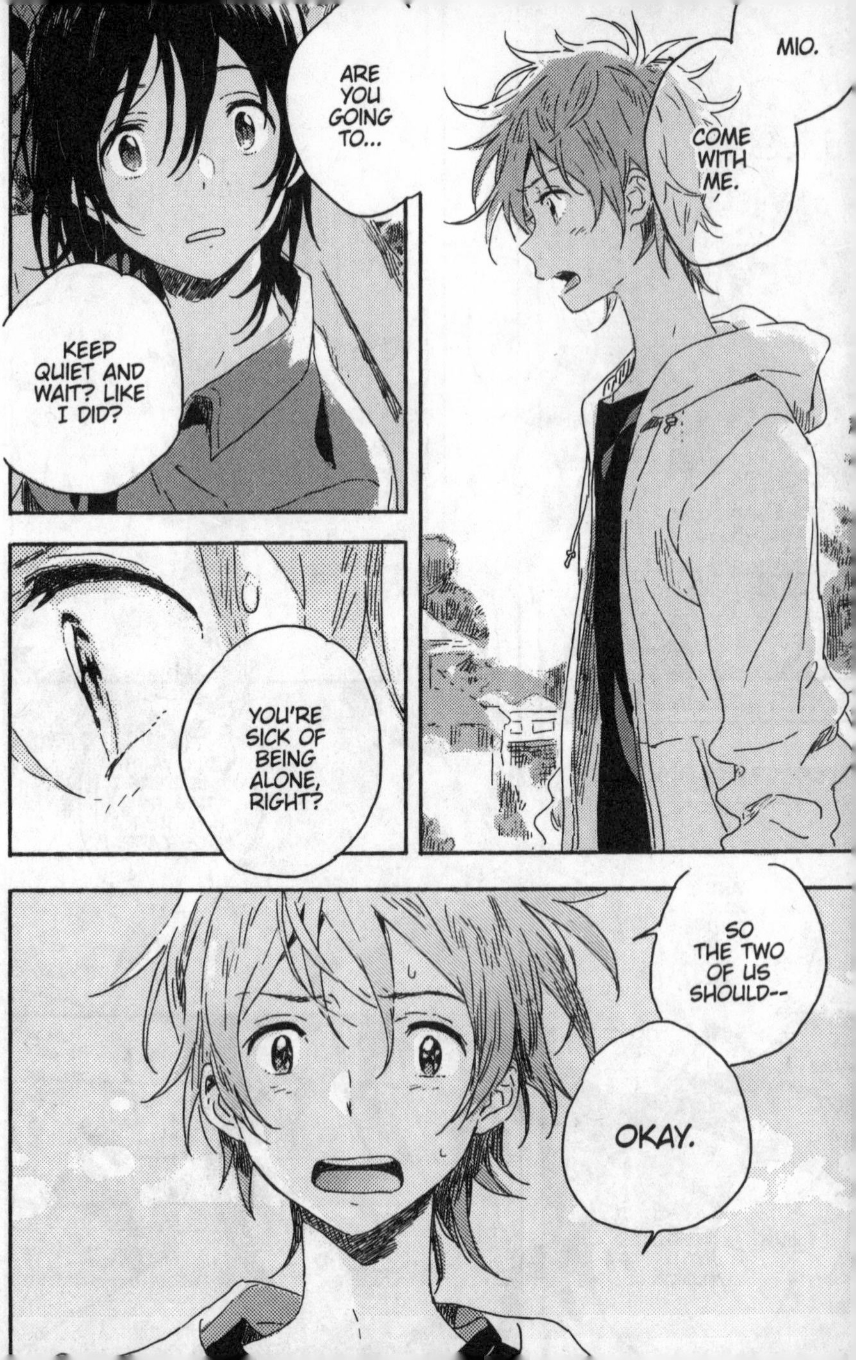
MIO.
COME WITH ME.
ARE YOU GOING TO...
KEEP QUIET AND WAIT? LIKE I DID?
YOU'RE SICK OF BEING ALONE, RIGHT?
SO THE TWO OF US SHOULD--
OKAY.

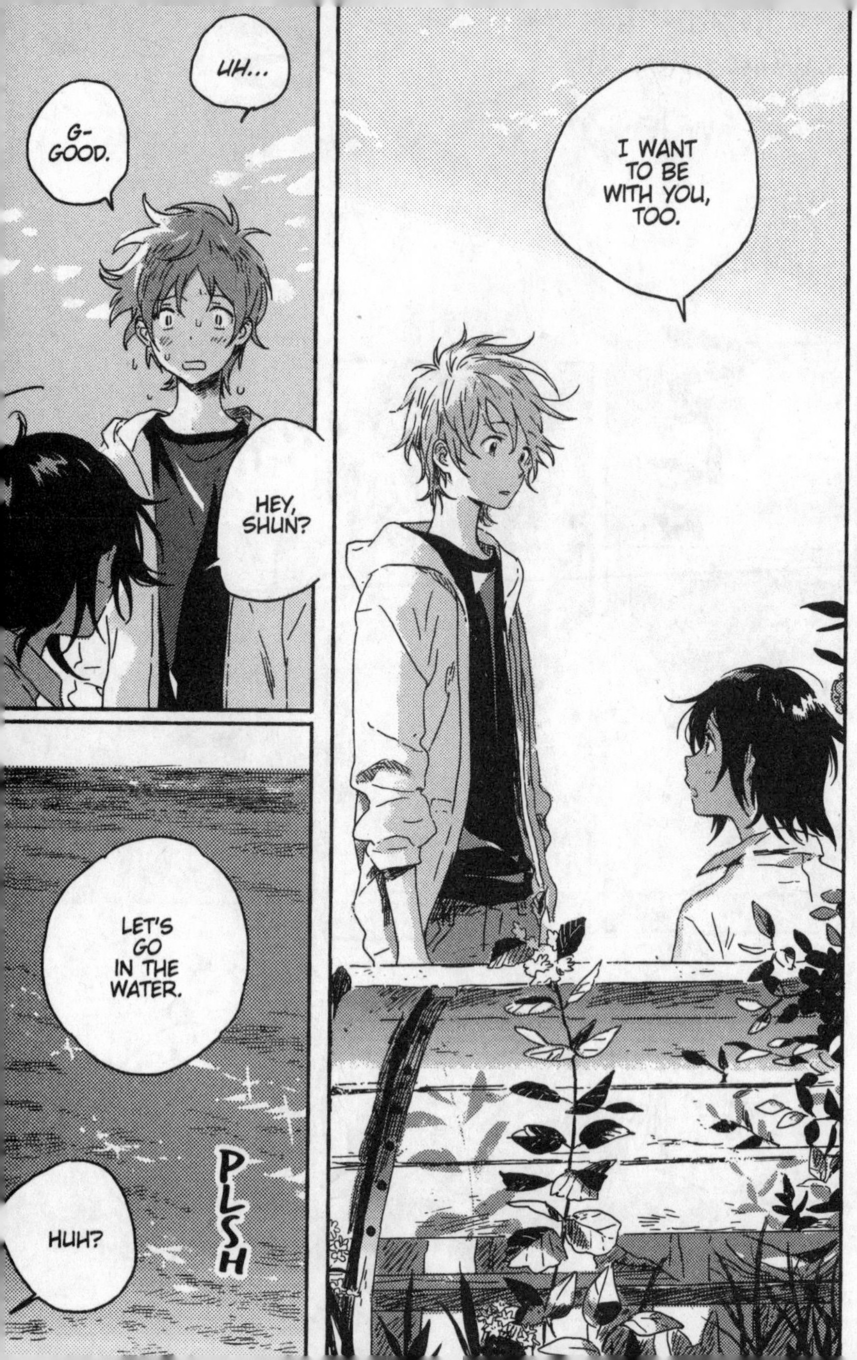
I WANT TO BE WITH YOU, TOO.
UH...
G-GOOD.
HEY, SHUN?
LET'S GO IN THE WATER.
PLSH
HUH?

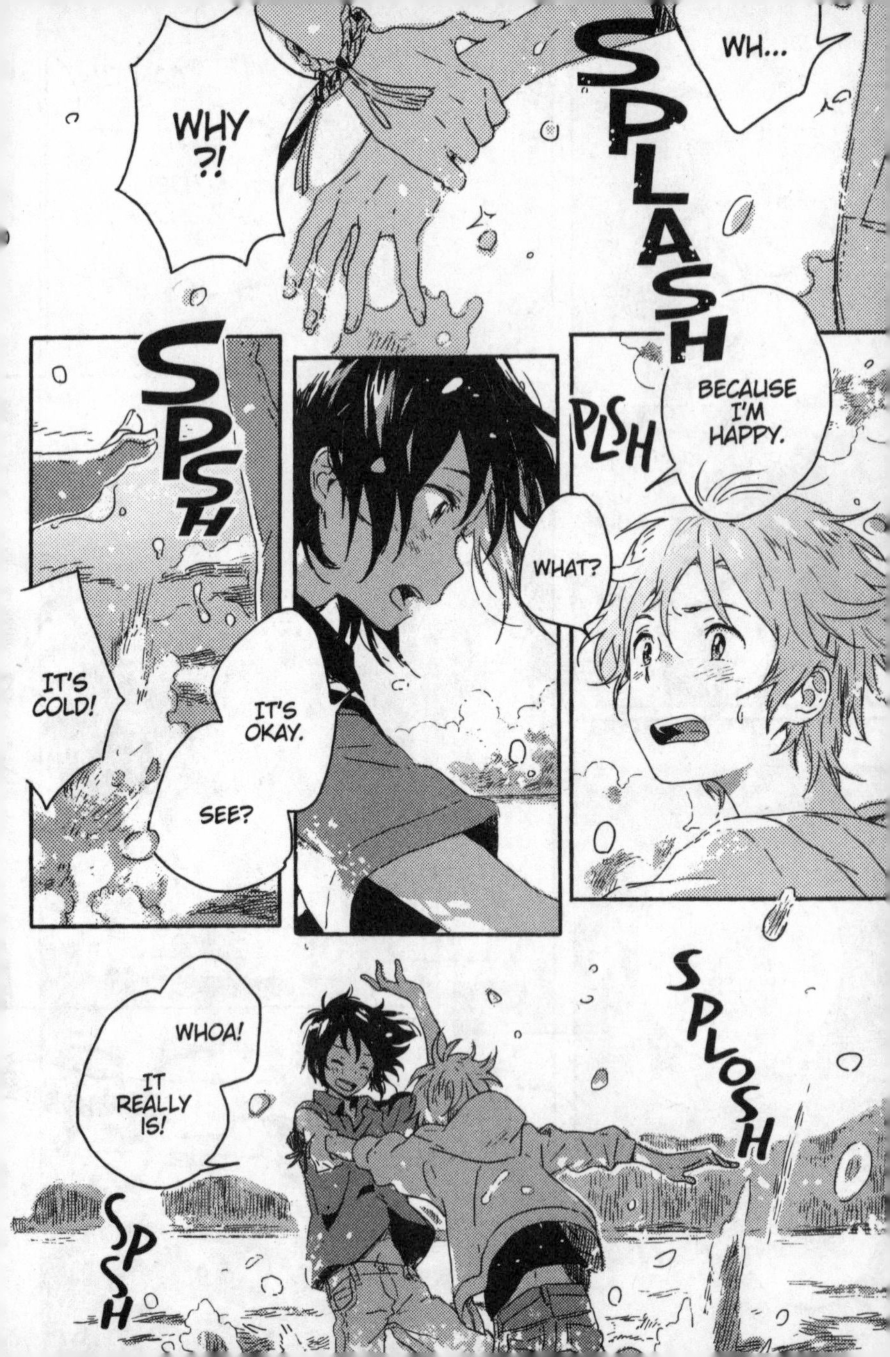

WH...
SPLASH
WHY ?!
BECAUSE I'M HAPPY.
PLSH
WHAT?
IT'S OKAY.
SEE?
SPSH
IT'S COLD!
SPLOSH
WHOA!
IT REALLY IS!
SPSH

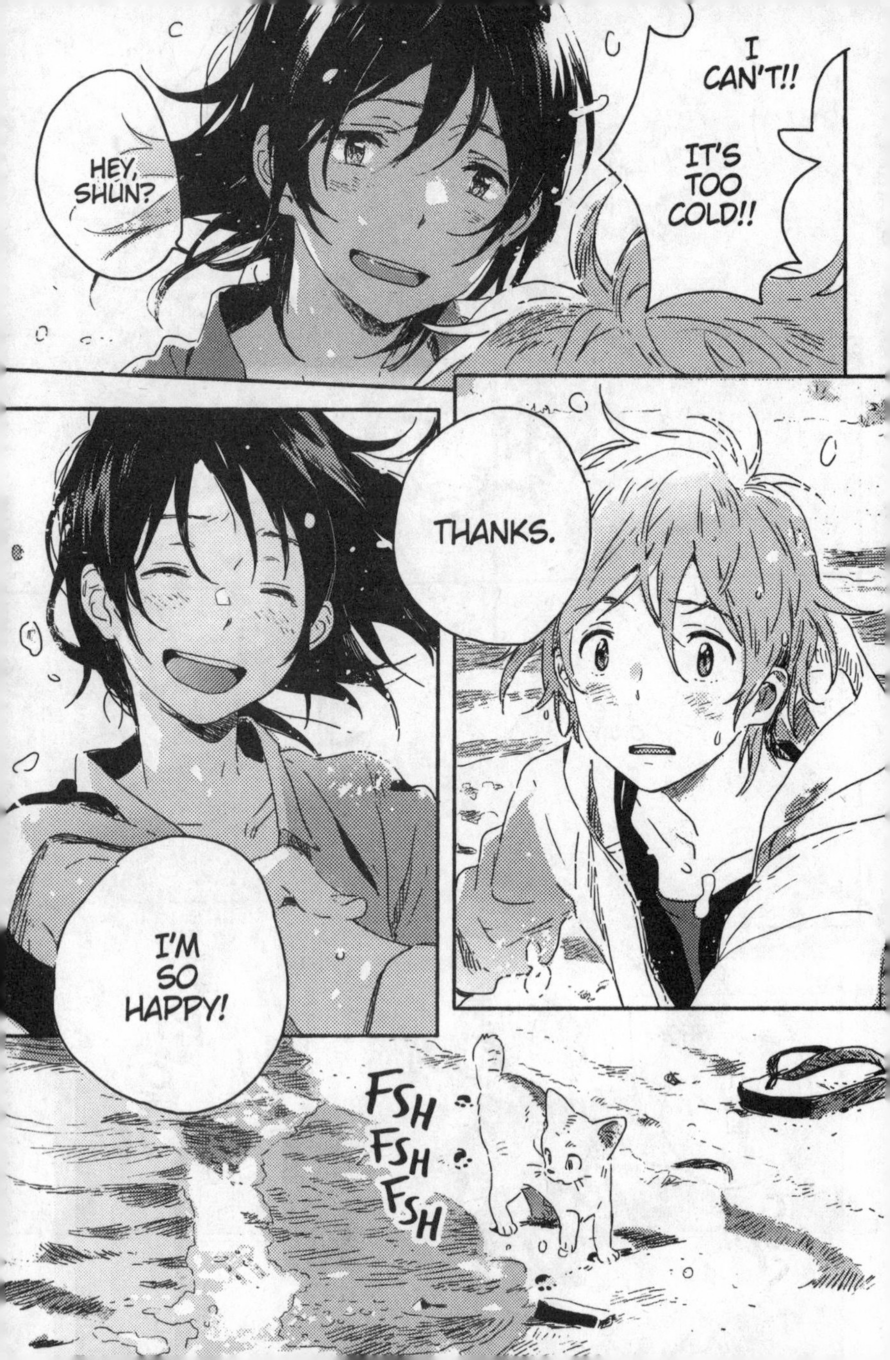
I CAN'T!!
IT'S TOO COLD!!
HEY, SHUN?
THANKS.
I'M SO HAPPY!
FSH FSH FSH

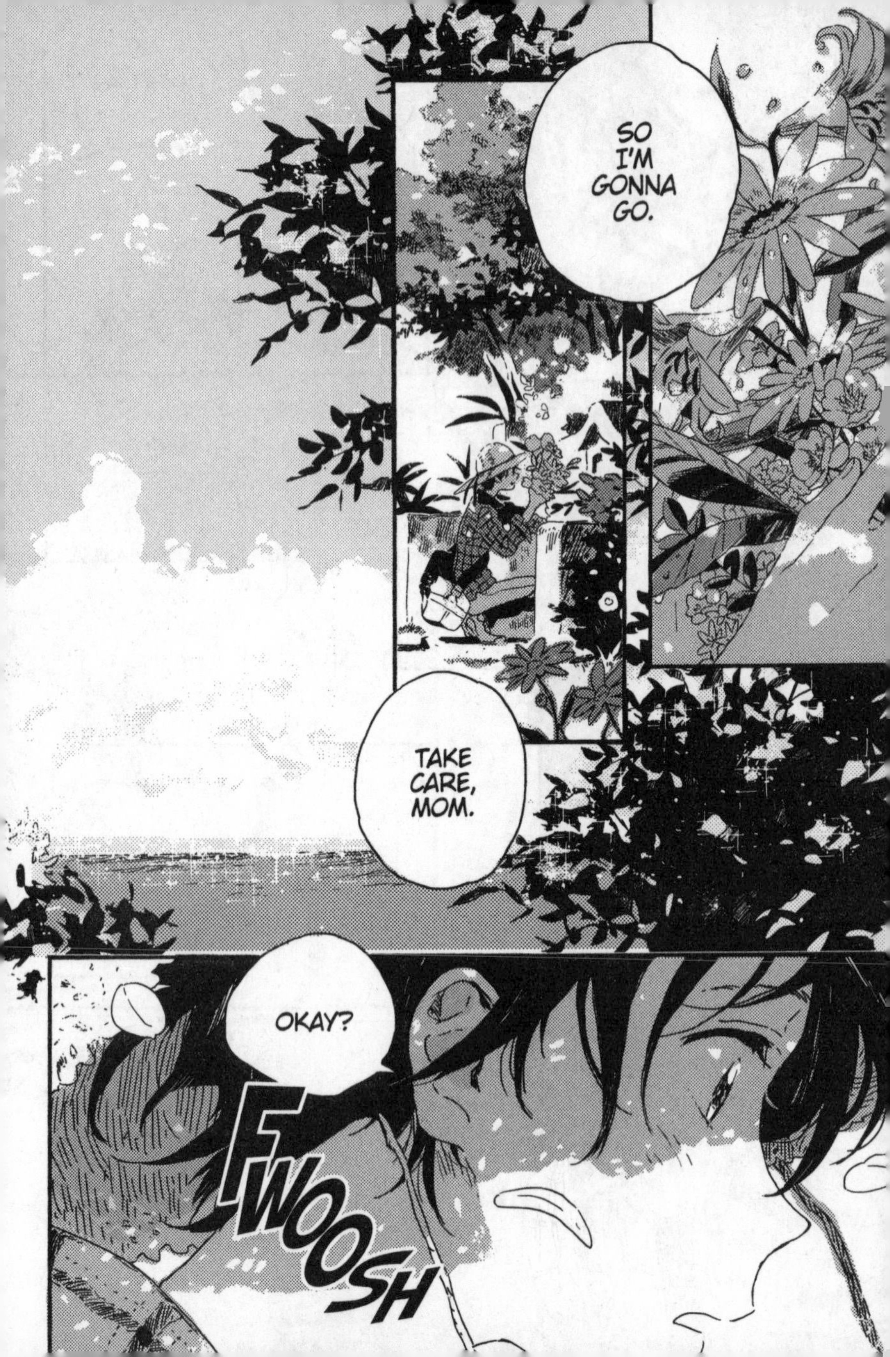
SO I'M GONNA GO.
TAKE CARE, MOM.
OKAY?
FWOOSH

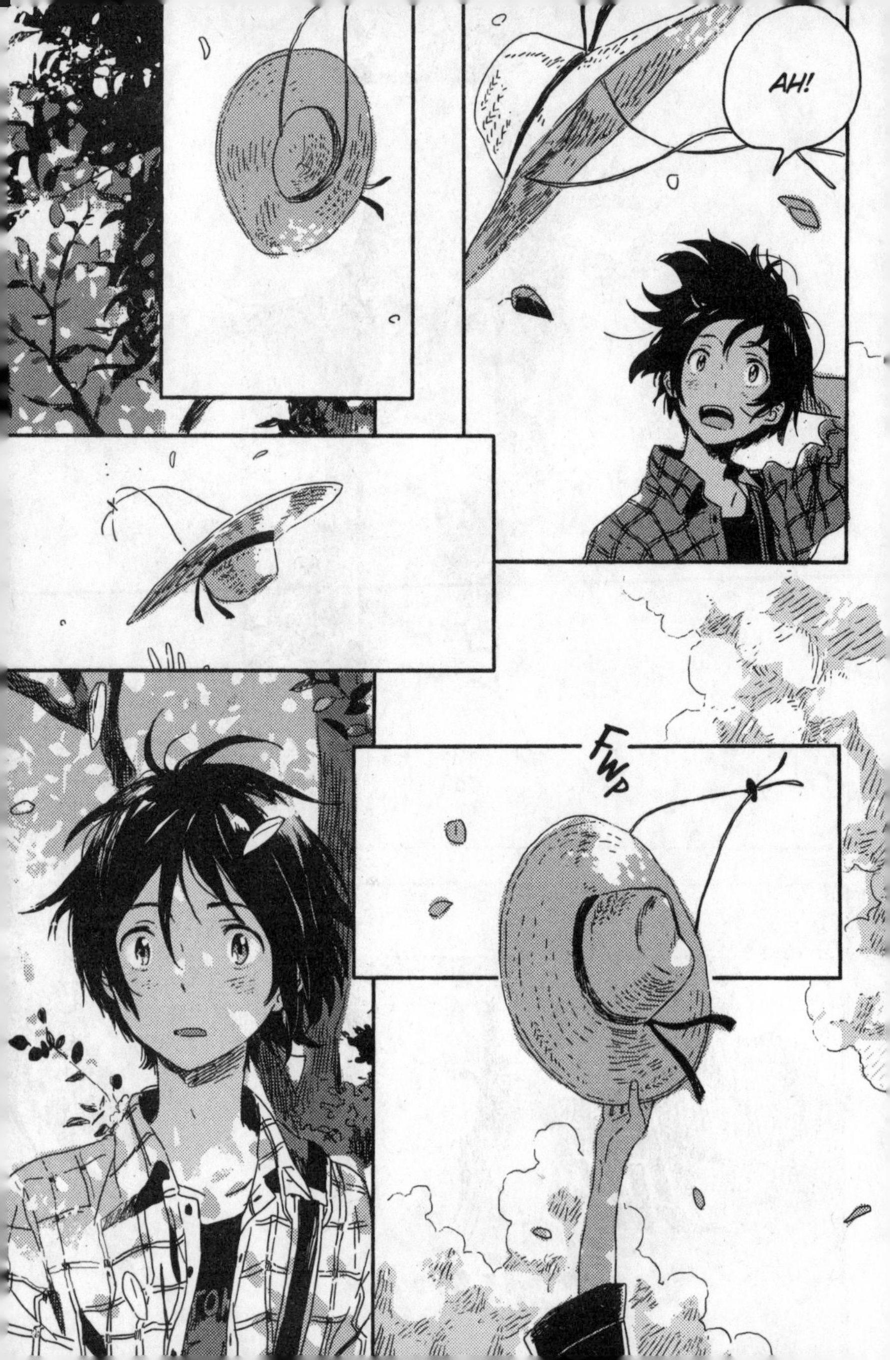
AH!
FWP

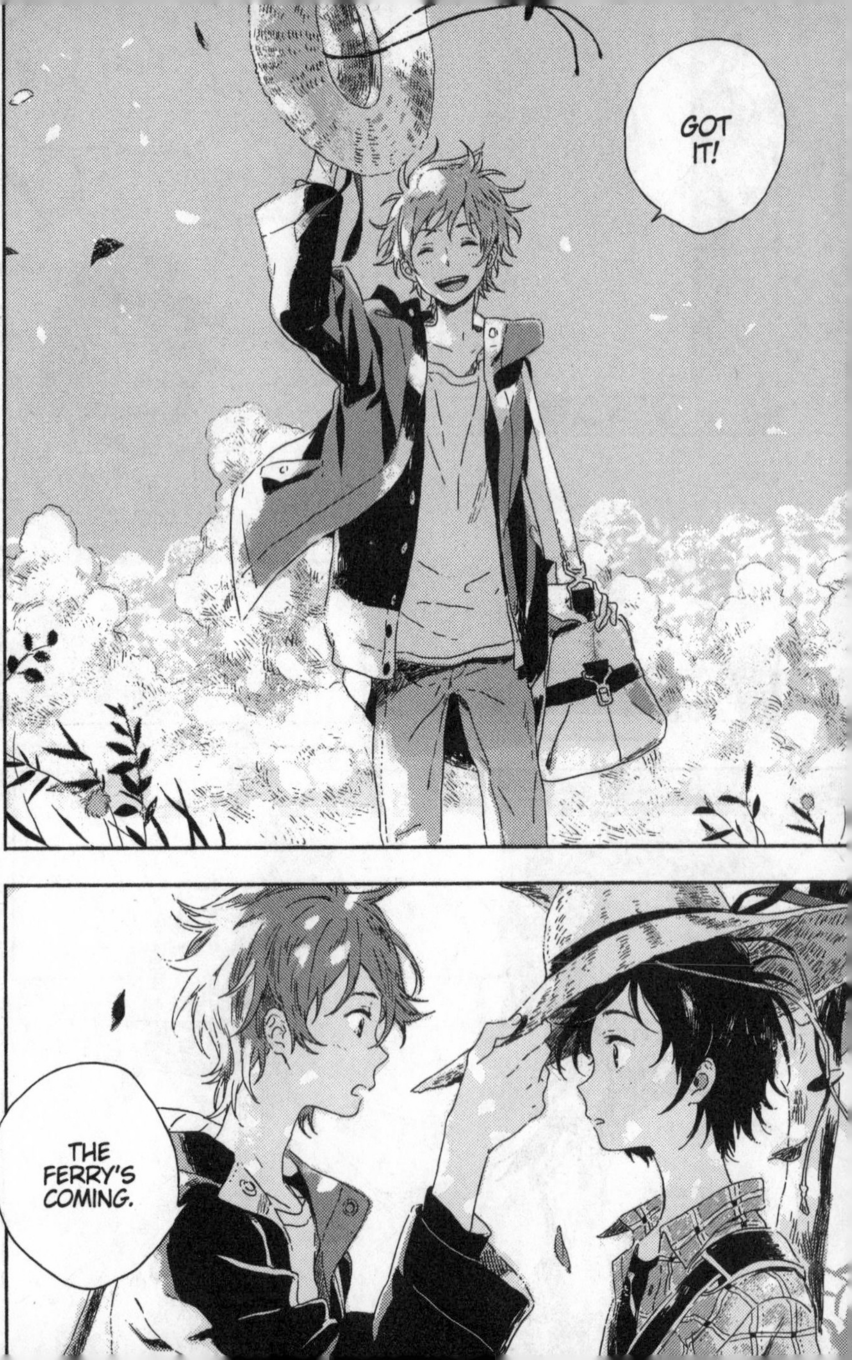
GOT IT!
THE FERRY'S COMING.

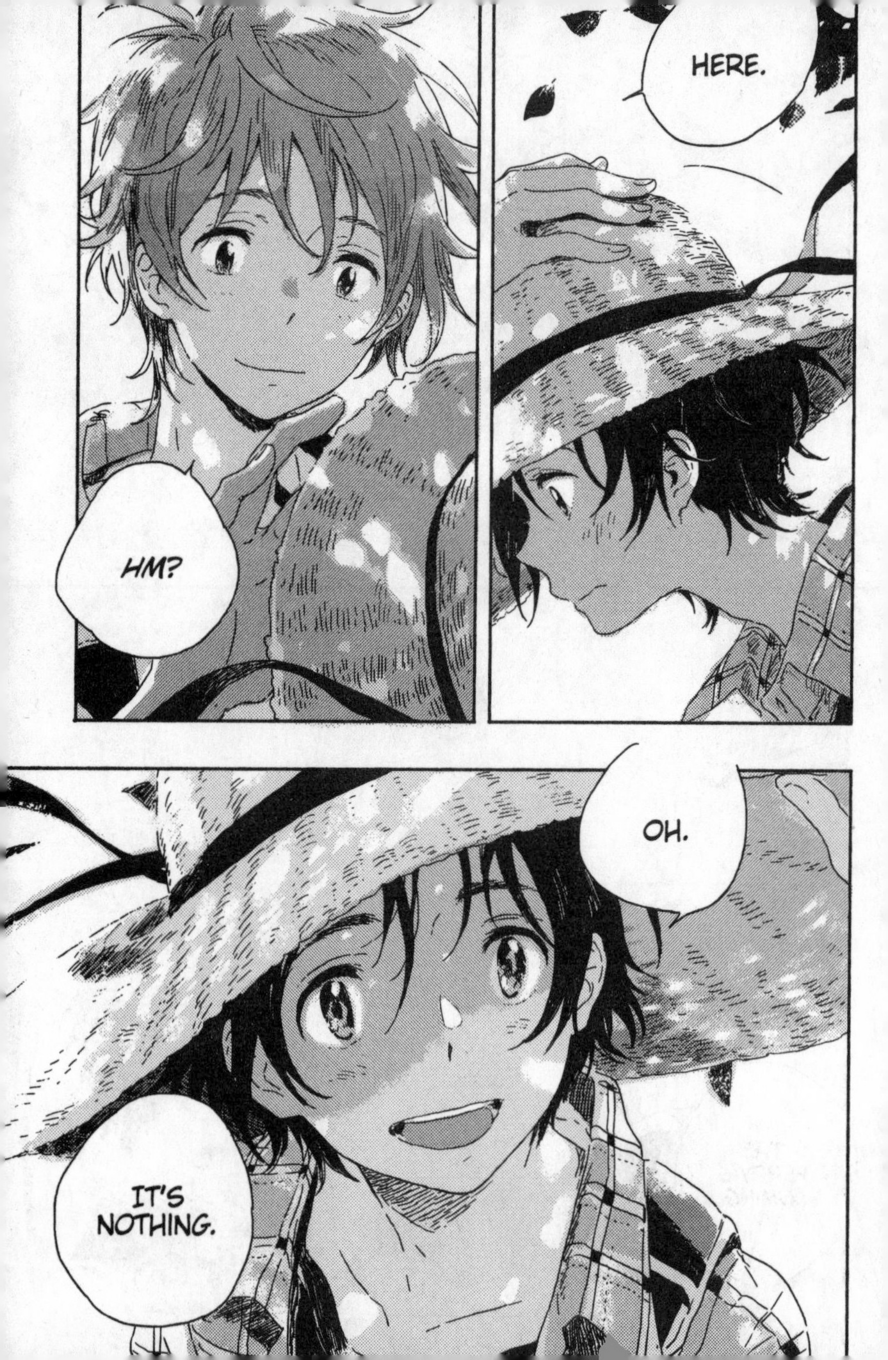
HERE.
HM?
OH.
IT'S NOTHING.

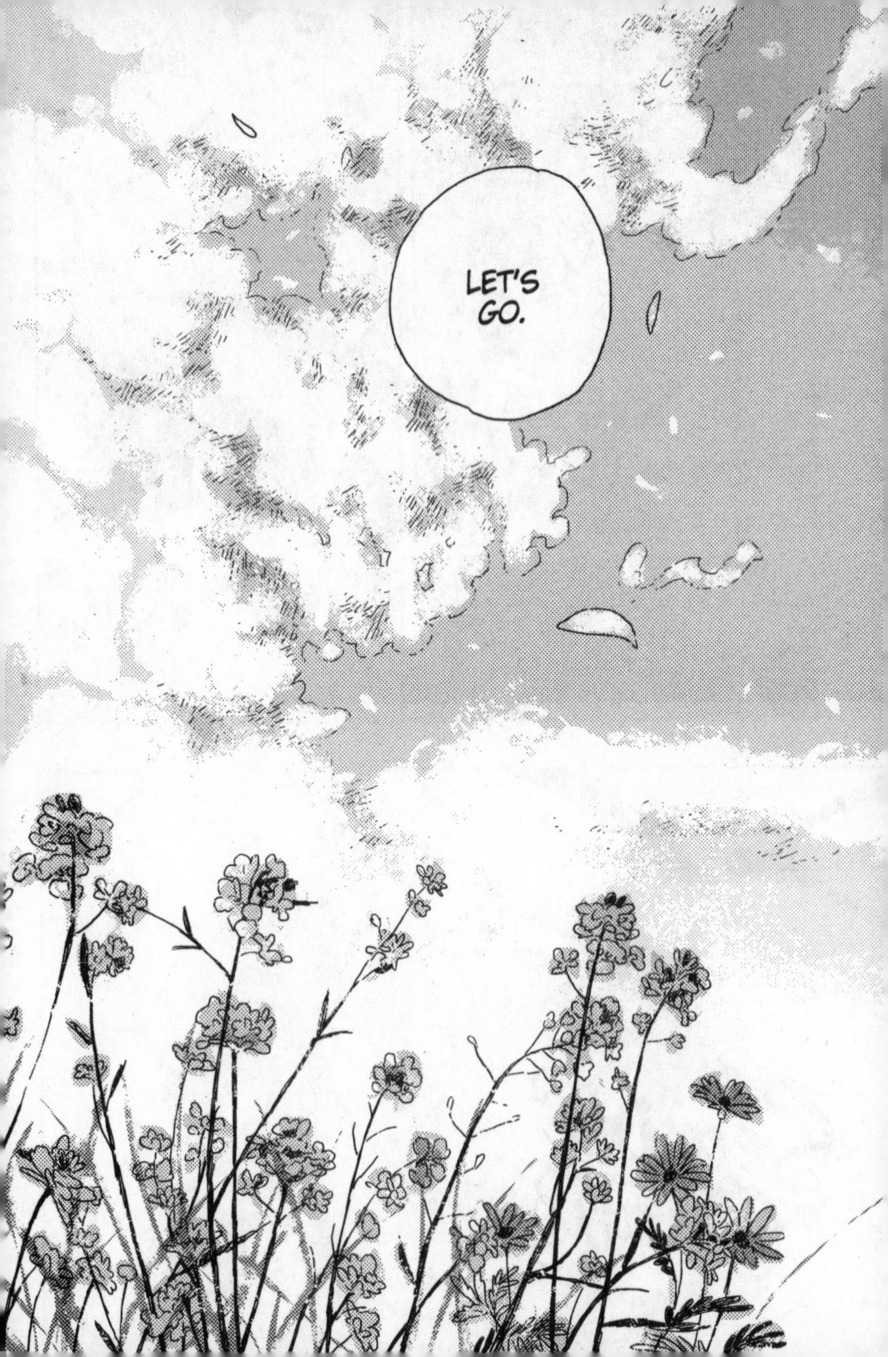
LET'S GO.

Seaside
Stranger

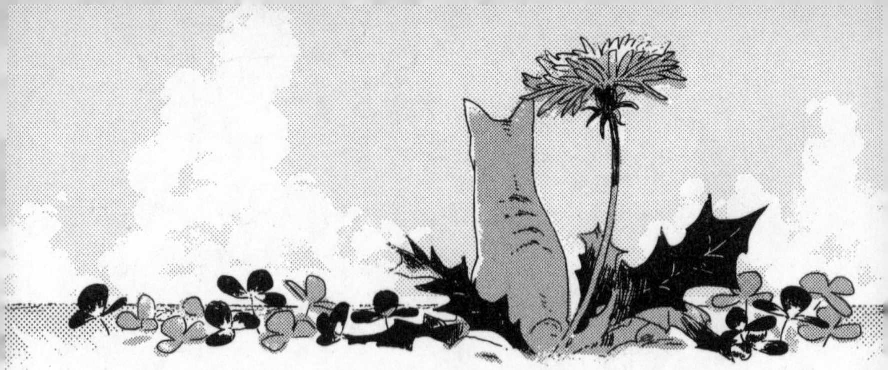

Seaside Stranger started out as a short story, but then it kept going, and then the book that was supposed to be "one and done" turned into a series. This story was blessed by the greatest good fortune.

My aim was to tell a straightforward tale about a cute couple that would make readers happy. While I was working on it, I really fell in love with Shun and Mio. I hope that all you readers also fall at least a little in love with them.

Likes Deer

Finally, a huge thank you to my editor, Horikawa-san, to the book designer, Kawana-san, and to you, for picking this book up!

Stylish

With the deepest gratitude,

Kii Kanna
Summer 2014

Afterword

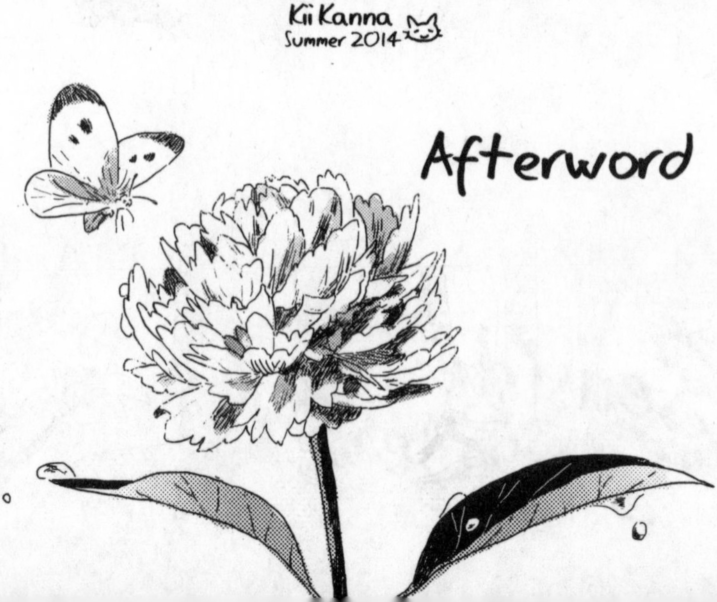

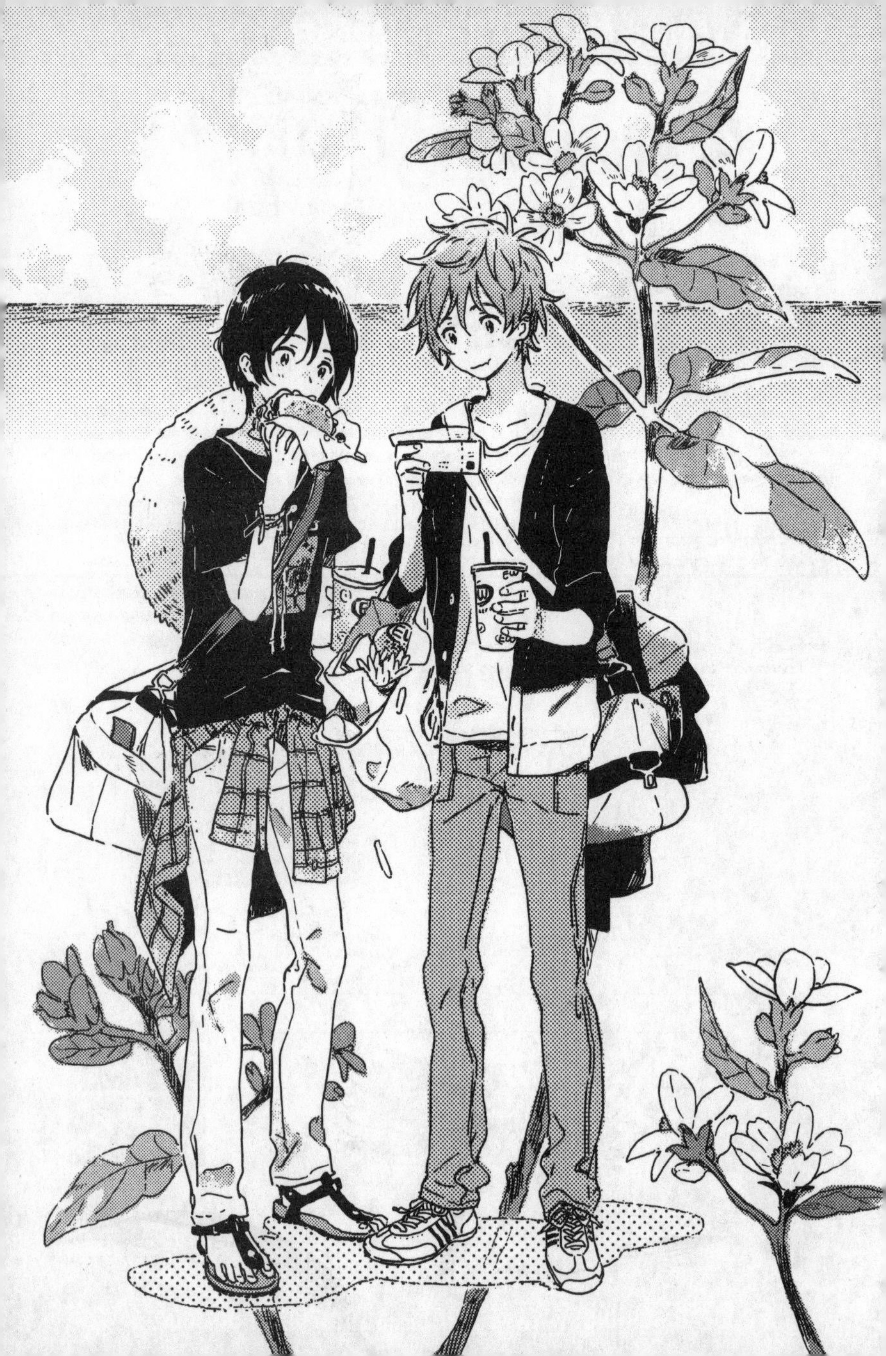

SEVEN SEAS ENTERTAINMENT PRESENTS

Seaside Stranger
Volume One:
Umibe no Étranger

story & art by KII KANNA

TRANSLATION
Jocelyne Allen

ADAPTATION
Ysabet Reinhardt MacFarlane

LETTERING
Annaliese "Ace" Christman

COVER DESIGN
Hanase Qi

PROOFREADER
Kurestin Armada

EDITOR
Peter Adrian Behravesh

PREPRESS TECHNICIAN
Rhiannon Rasmussen-Silverstein

PRODUCTION ASSOCIATE
Christa Miesner

PRODUCTION MANAGER
Lissa Pattillo

MANAGING EDITOR
Julie Davis

ASSOCIATE PUBLISHER
Adam Arnold

PUBLISHER
Jason DeAngelis

Seven Seas press and purchase enquiries can be sent to Marketing Manager Lianne Sentar at press@gomanga.com. Information regarding the distribution and purchase of digital editions is available from Digital Manager CK Russell at digital@gomanga.com.

Seven Seas and the Seven Seas logo are trademarks of Seven Seas Entertainment. All rights reserved.

ISBN: 978-1-64827-584-5
Printed in Canada
First Printing: July 2021
10 9 8 7 6 5 4 3 2 1

▨▨▨ READING DIRECTIONS ▨▨▨

This book reads from *right to left*, Japanese style. If this is your first time reading manga, you start reading from the top right panel on each page and take it from there. If you get lost, just follow the numbered diagram here. It may seem backwards at first, but you'll get the hang of it! Have fun!!

Follow us online: www.SevenSeasEntertainment.com